A CULTURAL HISTORY OF FURNITURE

FURNITURE

VOLUME 4

A Cultural History of Furniture
General Editor: Christina M. Anderson

A CULTURAL HISTORY OF FURNITURE

IN THE AGE OF ENLIGHTENMENT

*Edited by Sylvain Cordier,
Christina M. Anderson,
and Laura Houliston*

BLOOMSBURY ACADEMIC
LONDON • NEW YORK • OXFORD • NEW DELHI • SYDNEY

BLOOMSBURY ACADEMIC
Bloomsbury Publishing Plc
50 Bedford Square, London, WC1B 3DP, UK
1385 Broadway, New York, NY 10018, USA
29 Earlsfort Terrace, Dublin 2, Ireland

BLOOMSBURY, BLOOMSBURY ACADEMIC and the Diana logo are trademarks of
Bloomsbury Publishing Plc

First published in Great Britain 2022

A catalogue record for this book is available from the British Library.

A catalog record for this book is available from the Library of Congress.

ISBN: Pack: 978-1-4725-7789-4
         HB: 978-1-4725-7785-6

Series: The Cultural Histories Series

Typeset by Integra Software Services Pvt. Ltd.
Printed and bound in Great Britain

To find out more about our authors and books visit www.bloomsbury.com
and sign up for our newsletters.

CONTENTS

LIST OF ILLUSTRATIONS

PLATES

FIGURES

CONTRIBUTORS

Megan Aldrich is an independent scholar who lectures, writes, and teaches aspects of architectural and design history, including interiors and furniture, and consults in the heritage sector. Recent publications include *Antiquaries and Archaists* (2009); *Art and Authenticity* (2012); *Thomas Rickman and the Victorians* (Victorian Society, 2019); and articles in the journals of *Garden History* (2016) and *Furniture History* (2018). She is a Fellow of the Society of Antiquaries.

Antonia Brodie is a curator and historian of seventeenth- and eighteenth-century decorative arts. She has worked with country house collections, and in museums in Britain and the United States.

Yannick Chastang studied at the École Boulle in Paris and the Université Pierre et Marie Curie. Between 1995 and 1997, he was junior conservator at the Musée des Arts Décoratifs, Paris, and from 1997 to 2003 he was Conservator at the Wallace Collection, London. Since 2003, Yannick Chastang has run a conservation studio specializing in the conservation and making of decorative arts. His publications include the book *Paintings in Wood: French Marquetry Furniture* (2001), as well as many articles on conservation and history of marquetry furniture.

Jeffrey Collins is Professor of Art History and Material Culture at Bard Graduate Center, New York, where he specializes in seventeenth- and eighteenth-century Europe. A Fellow of the American Academy in Rome, he is the author of *Papacy and Politics in Eighteenth-Century Rome: Pius VI and the Arts* (2004) and a principal contributor to *Pedro Friedeberg* (2009) and *History of Design: Decorative Arts and Material Culture, 1400–2000* (2013).

Sylvain Cordier is the Paul Mellon Curator and Head of the Department of European Art at the Virginia Museum of Fine Arts in Richmond, Virginia. Prior to this, he was Curator of Early Decorative Arts at the Montreal Museum of Fine

Art. He completed his Ph.D. in Art History at the Paris Sorbonne University. He has published widely on the history of taste for furniture and the relation between decorative arts and the discourse of power in early nineteenth-century France.

Frédéric Dassas is Senior Curator in the Department of Decorative Arts at the Musée du Louvre, France.

Michaël Decrossas has been a *pensionnaire* of the Institut national d'histoire de l'art (INHA) since 2012 for the domain "decorative arts, design and material culture". He defended, in 2008 at the École pratique des hautes études under the supervision of Guy-Michel Leproux, a doctoral thesis titled "Le château de Saint-Cloud des Gondi aux Orléans: architecture et décors (1577–1785)".

Barbara Lasic is a Lecturer at Sotheby's Institute of Art, London. Prior to her academic career, she worked at the Victoria and Albert Museum as part of the curatorial team involved in the redevelopment of the Europe: 1600–1800 Galleries, and she held curatorial positions at the Wellcome Trust and the National Maritime Museum, Greenwich. She has published on the subject of architecture, decorative arts, the history of taste, and the history of collecting. Her current research interests include the collecting of French art, and the intersection of the art market and curatorial practice in the early twentieth century.

Peter N. Lindfield is Lecturer in History and the Country House at Manchester Metropolitan University, UK. His research centers upon Georgian design history—architecture, interiors, furniture—antiquarianism, and heraldry. His three-year project, "Antiquarian by Design: Fakery and the Material Object in Britain 1720–1824," examines the role of fakery and forgery across the arts in Georgian Britain.

Marie-Ève Marchand is Affiliate Assistant Professor of Art History at Concordia University, Canada. She teaches art history and museology as a sessional lecturer in the Province of Quebec. Her research focuses on the decorative arts, especially their materiality and the epistemological issues arising from their collecting and display in both museums and domestic interiors. She is the co-editor of *Design & Agency: Critical Perspective on Identities, Histories and Practices* (Bloomsbury, 2020).

Tessa Murdoch is Rosalinde and Arthur Gilbert Research Curator, Victoria and Albert Museum, 2019–21. She has forty years curatorial experience at the Museum of London from 1981 and at the V&A since 1990, where she has worked in the Furniture, Sculpture, Metalwork, and Ceramics Collections. Tessa is a fellow of the Society of Antiquaries, a trustee of the Huguenot Museum, Rochester, and of the Idlewild Trust. Her forthcoming book *Europe Divided: Huguenot Refugee Art and Culture* was the focus of her Getty Rothschild Fellowship in 2019 and will be published in November 2021.

SERIES PREFACE

A Cultural History of Furniture is a six-volume series examining the changing cultural framework within which furniture was designed, produced, and used, as well as the cultural construction of furniture itself, from antiquity through to the present day in the Western tradition. All the volumes follow the same structure: an editorial overview of the historical context of the period under consideration followed by chapters written by specialists that each correspond to one of the following themes: design and motifs; makers, making, and materials; types and uses; the domestic setting; the public setting; exhibition and display; furniture and architecture; visual representations; and verbal representations. The configuration of the series means that readers can use the material synchronically or diachronically: an individual volume provides a thorough grounding in the furniture of a particular period while following one distinct theme across all volumes presents the reader with the evolution of a specific aspect of furniture over time. The six volumes divide the history of furniture in this way:

Volume 1: A Cultural History of Furniture in Antiquity (From the beginnings to 500 CE)

Volume 2: A Cultural History of Furniture in the Middle Ages and Renaissance (500–1500)

Volume 3: A Cultural History of Furniture in the Age of Exploration (1500–1700)

Volume 4: A Cultural History of Furniture in the Age of Enlightenment (1700–1800)

Volume 5: A Cultural History of Furniture in the Age of Empire and Industry (1800–1900)

Volume 6: A Cultural History of Furniture in the Modern Age (1900–twenty-first century)

Christina M. Anderson
General Editor

Introduction

MEGAN ALDRICH WITH SYLVAIN CORDIER

The eighteenth century was, on the whole, a time of optimism when science and technology developed out of the foundations laid in the previous hundred years and began to accelerate as the century drew to its close. An interest in good government and in philosophy and literature became central to conversations in fashionable salons around Europe. The acquisition of knowledge was part of fashionable life, and intelligence and intellectual accomplishments were celebrated in women as well as men. It became important for the higher social classes to acquire at least the rudiments of "good taste" in the arts, which was dominated by the classical tradition in architecture and design. For a time, the naturalistic rococo style asserted itself during the first half of the century, while the stirrings of other styles of design such as chinoiserie and the Gothic began to emerge during this period. In many respects, the eighteenth century served as a transition between the older world order of received authority and strict social hierarchy and the world we recognize today.

During the eighteenth century furniture and furnishings evolved away from late baroque forms such as the state bed and the commode into a greater variety of shapes and designs, with different decoration, mechanisms, and functions. Private rooms began to multiply in residences, and to be nearly as richly furnished as those in public spaces. Marie Antoinette, for example, the ill-fated queen of Louis XVI of France, developed well-furnished, private spaces at Versailles where she could relax in more personal pursuits such as music and literature, away from the taxing demands and formal behavior of life at court (Plate 1). Early in the century, at the end of the reign of Louis XIV, the aristocrats formerly in attendance at Versailles had begun to spend more time in private townhouses in Paris, where salon culture was born. This is reflected in one of the most influential architectural publications of the first part of the century, Jacques-François Blondel's *De la distribution des maisons de plaisance* (1737–8), in which the private apartment for the first time became a focus for the designer's art, and the concept of comfort—or *commodité*—in the interior became key. Interiors became spaces for fashionable and comfortable living, not just spaces for performances of power and rank.

During the first half of the eighteenth century, the furnishing schemes of aristocratic salons and private rooms often placed armchairs and console tables side by side in asymmetrical arrangement, but always with concern for integrating them into a coherent visual language within the same space. In France, the understated way that asymmetrical design was used during the rococo period resulted in the ordered but subtle movement of forms. Outside France, particularly in the German states, this asymmetry of design was far more pronounced. For this reason, it is easy to misunderstand the rococo interior, with its integration of furniture and architecture. Pieces of furniture in the best interiors were no longer single elements but became parts of a greater design. A richly upholstered and gilded armchair, for example, when analyzed in isolation, will have inevitably lost part of its aesthetic discourse once detached from other components of the interior for which it was intended. Such aesthetic precepts were understood by educated men and women of the day but tended to become lost in later revivals of eighteenth-century styles during the nineteenth century.

If it is possible to identify two kinds of furniture that sum up the age of the Enlightenment, those might be the commode (or chest of drawers) and the side table, which also functioned as a pier table or console. In terms of grand interiors, French cabinetmakers led a typological revolution in the development of the commode, at once a functional piece of storage furniture, and yet one supremely glamorous. This type is showcased in the creation of the sumptuous and iconic gilt-bronze mounted, turtleshell and brass marquetry commode made by André-Charles Boulle (1642–1732) and supplied in 1708–9 to Louis XIV for the Grand Trianon at Versailles. Not long afterward a companion piece of equal quality was produced by Boulle; it is now in the Metropolitan Museum of Art in New York (Plate 2). These were not the first examples of the commode to emerge from a cabinetmaker's workshop, but they gave this type of eighteenth-century furniture status and glamour. Boulle's commodes, still squarely in the late baroque style, were copied during the eighteenth, nineteenth, and twentieth centuries, such was the enduring interest in the commodes he made for the Sun King. Moreover, the fame of these commodes led the way later in the century for this useful form of storage furniture to become widely available for a much less elevated clientèle.

By the middle of the eighteenth century in London, designers such as Thomas Chippendale (1718–79), who came from a modest family background in Yorkshire, took the French form of the commode and adapted it to English taste and smaller pocket books. His famous pattern book of designs for furniture, *The Gentleman and Cabinet Maker's Director*, published in three editions (1754, 1755, and 1762), illustrated a simplified commode design for an English audience that pays homage to the famous design of Boulle for Versailles (Figure 0.1). Chippendale probably had access to the designs of Boulle that were published in Paris during the second quarter of the eighteenth century. The early designs he created during the 1750s illustrate a familiarity with French designs, combined with chinoiserie and the occasional Gothic design. By the final edition of the *Director* in 1762, there is evidence of a shift toward the newer, fashionable style of neoclassicism that was beginning to take London by storm, thanks in part to the return of architect-designers such as James Stuart and Robert Adam, both of whom had conducted lengthy Grand Tours investigating classical remains in Italy and—in Stuart's case—Greece. The winds of design were changing, and Chippendale felt the shift in direction keenly. Working in particular with the Scottish neoclassical architect Robert Adam during the 1760s and 1770s, he produced highly accomplished examples of neoclassical furniture for country house owners, as at Harewood House in Yorkshire, featuring light, giltwood frames and delicate marquetry designs in light-colored woods.

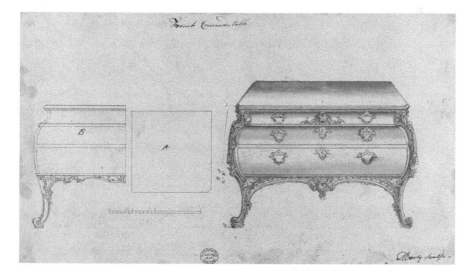

FIGURE 0.1 Thomas Chippendale, drawing for a "French commode table", *c.* 1754. Rogers Fund, 1920/The Metropolitan Museum of Art. Photograph courtesy of the Metropolitan Museum of Art.

In addition to the commode, perhaps equally important to the eighteenth-century interior was the pier table, or side table, an essential element of grand apartments in the baroque era. During the first part of the eighteenth century it continued as a focal point for furnishing a room that could especially showcase a carver's mastery of the rococo style. Chippendale included such designs in the *Director*, and every region of Europe produced its own version of the side table, or rococo console table, which continued to evolve. By the neoclassical era during the second half of the century, tables had developed into a family of different types to suit the many functions of private living spaces. Both these types of furniture—the commode and the pier table—had moved from being "parade" furniture in the apartments of princes at the beginning of the century to being fashionable but ultimately functional furniture for prosperous, middle-class houses by the close of the eighteenth century.

During the 1750s in France, some arbiters of taste began to criticize the rococo style, judging it improbable and extravagant and paving the way for the early phase of neoclassicism known as the *goût grec*, or Greek taste. The first manifestations of *goût grec* in the late 1750s is widely considered to be a set of writing furniture for the government minister La Live de Jully by Joseph Baumhauer. Of ebony veneer with prominent gilt-bronze mounts, this furniture looks back to the classicism of the baroque furniture produced by André Charles Boulle, whose designs were also a source of inspiration for Thomas Chippendale in London. From the 1770s onward, a new idea of stricter morality began to redefine perceptions of beauty and nobility in interior decoration. A new taste for what was understood as "Greek" brought back a regard for simplicity of outline, offering a structure for a refined and delicate ornamental repertoire of carved forms. If the rococo was about integrating the rule of nature into aesthetics, it is tempting to interpret the development of neoclassicism as an assertion of the place of mankind, and humanism, within European cultural values. Rather than playing at imitating the creators of the world by surrounding oneself with plant and natural forms, memories of ancient civilizations reminded eighteenth-century man of the nobility and power of his ancestors of bygone days, and their taste for sobriety.

In keeping with the age of the Enlightenment and the burgeoning interest in science, there was an interest in technology in furniture. One technological masterpiece produced in the middle of the century was the cylinder desk (or *bureau*) of 1760–9 by Jean-François Oeben and Jean Henri Riesener, ordered by Louis XV toward the end of his reign and now known as the *bureau du roi*; it is displayed in the Palace of Versailles (Plate 3). The enduring fascination with this piece of furniture is demonstrated by the fact that, as with the Boulle commodes cited above, the *bureau* was copied on a number of occasions. A simplified version of it was made in the eighteenth century and is now in the Wallace Collection in London. During the nineteenth and early twentieth centuries multiple copies of the *bureau* were made. The *bureau du roi* fascinated cabinetmakers not only because of its royal associations and the skill displayed in its marquetry decoration, but also for its mechanical devices such as the roll-top form of the upper stage, which made the desk seem to transform into a different shape. This was a piece of furniture that was actively used by Louis XV and Louis XVI during their reigns, so there was a sophisticated locking mechanism for the safe storage of confidential papers of state. While this object was originally made for a powerful king, other cabinetmakers in places such as London and Berlin took the idea and simplified it for a more middle-class audience. By the end of the eighteenth century, Thomas Sheraton (1751–1806), a Baptist preacher who trained as a cabinetmaker in the North of England, published four volumes of furniture designs entitled *The Cabinet Maker and Upholsterer's Drawing Book* of 1791–4 (Figure 0.2). In the *Drawing Book* was a "cylinder bureau" derived from the French royal tradition but scaled down and with details of construction noted, so that even a prosperous merchant in a regional town could afford to have a version of one. Letter writing became

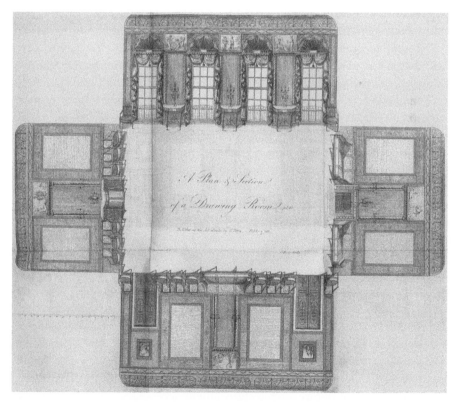

FIGURE 0.2 A Plan and Section of a Drawing Room, Thomas Sheraton, 1802. Rogers Fund, 1952/The Metropolitan Museum of Art. Photograph courtesy of the Metropolitan Museum of Art.

an important activity amongst educated people, especially those of the upper classes and the ambitious individuals who wished to emulate them.

It may be a useful observation, therefore, to say that in eighteenth-century Europe, cabinetmakers at the French court created furniture of the highest quality with new forms, decoration, and technology, while the more modest furniture that typified output and designs in London by the middle of the century took these high-end ideas and simplified them, making them available to a wider range of clients who wanted well-made, stylish furniture that also served the needs of modern life. If one looks at the furniture produced in Paris and London during the eighteenth century, one can understand a great deal. The ideas emanating from these two capital cities spread across different European centers and to colonies around the globe, from Mauritius to Philadelphia. French ideas and designs had a profound impact on British cabinetmakers during the first sixty years of the eighteenth century, at which point British ideas and styles—especially neoclassical furniture made of plain mahogany— began to cross-pollinate French furniture across the Channel, resulting in the so-called *goût anglais*, or English taste. Even Thomas Chippendale's *Director* had a French-language edition in 1762–3. The French-English dialogue was a continuous one in furniture design during the eighteenth century.

Eighteenth-century culture occupies a place all of its own within the broader, collective culture of Europe and the European colonies. In the nineteenth century, it was viewed nostalgically as a "Golden Age" of civilization, when good manners were emphasized and *politesse* came to govern the way men and women treated one another. Good taste was meant to be cultivated by every educated person, and it was a century of great literary achievements. The disciplines of sociology and anthropology were in their infancy—that is, the study of man and nature— and it was fashionable to debate political questions and to study philosophy. Principles and ideas that had originated in previous centuries came to maturity, including scientific and medicinal discoveries, reflections on the relationship between man and religion, and geographical exploration. It was, on the whole, a period marked by optimism and enthusiasm for the future, although it was also a century marred by warfare and, at its close, the French Revolution (1789) and the subsequent instability caused by the period of the Terror (1792–4). At the end of the century and into the early nineteenth century, the rise of Napoleon Bonaparte led to great upheaval and the Napoleonic Wars across Europe. The aftermath of the Congress of Vienna and final defeat of Napoleon at the Battle of Waterloo in 1815 marked the end of the "long eighteenth century" and, at the same time, sparked a tremendous nostalgia for the lost *ancien régime* that gave rise to a revival of eighteenth-century styles in the nineteenth century. Thereafter, eighteenth-century furniture, architecture, and design—especially that of France and England—became accepted as the model for "good taste," just as classical design had defined good taste in earlier periods.

Above all, the eighteenth century was a literary century, and the multiplication of forms of furniture for writing, reading, and other activities in private apartments was a defining feature of the age. Eighteenth-century developments in philosophy, literature, and the nascent social sciences are reflected in part in the development of a wide range of furniture for use in writing, such as the *bureau*, as well as bookcases and library furniture. Boulle's designs for *bibliotèques*, or highly refined bookcases for use in high-status apartments, were published in Paris by Jean Mariette, the influential Parisian print seller and publisher. Public libraries were in their infancy, but private libraries were not only status symbols for aristocratic house owners but also were increasingly open to those with a letter of recommendation who were seen as worthy of consulting the expensive volumes, maps, and atlases contained in them. Robert Adam, the architect who led the development of the British neoclassical country house interior during the second half of the eighteenth century, designed mahogany bookcases at Croome Court, Worcestershire (*c.* 1763) in the form of a temple to knowledge, such was the importance of the private library.

In keeping with its literary culture, the eighteenth century was an era when rational systems to organize knowledge and information were highly valued and laid the foundations of many institutions still in existence today. The great Swedish naturalist Carl Linnaeus (1707–78) developed the binomial system of classifying all life, giving rise to Linnaean method, which is still in use. Ten years after his death, the Linnean Society was founded in London, and today it is the oldest society still actively pursuing knowledge in the area of the biological sciences. Even more comprehensive, and based upon an earlier English publication, the *Encyclopédie ou Dictionnaire Raisonné des Sciences, des Art et des Métiers* by Denis Diderot and Jean Le Rond d'Alembert (first published in 1751) was an attempt to rationalize and bring together in an orderly fashion all factual knowledge of the world, thereby democratizing knowledge by making it accessible across class boundaries (Figure 0.3). The printed encyclopedias of the twentieth century and online resources such as Wikipedia in our own era are direct descendants of this Enlightenment idea that knowledge should be accessible to all and organized in a rational way.

The eighteenth century was also an era when the principles of politics and government were examined like no other century before it. During the age of the Enlightenment, it was thought that reason and wisdom should be brought to the aid of politics, and that leaders might be held to account. After winning a war for independence against Britain with the help of the French, the young Republic of the United States of America was born amidst these principles and the idea of a achieving a new, rational form of governance without an inherited monarchy in which "all men are created equal." The eagle became the symbol of the new Republic, and furniture with carved eagles that had previously signified Jupiter in earlier classical styles such as Palladianism became fashionable again,

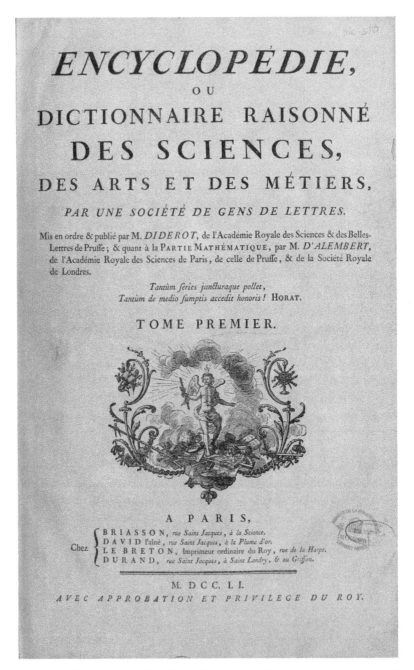

FIGURE 0.3 Title page, *Encyclopédie ou Dictionnaire Raisonné des Science, des Arts et des Métiers* by Denis Diderot and Jean Le Rond d'Alembert, 1751. Photograph courtesy of Jaybear/Wikimedia Commons.

only with a new Republican meaning. In Britain, much of political life during the eighteenth century was dominated by the aristocratic Whig Party, with its liberal values and dislike of autocratic leaders. One admirer of perceived English political liberty was François-Marie Arouet (1694–1778), better known by the pen name of Voltaire, whose ideas of free speech and freedom of religion resonated across Europe. When Admiral John Byng of the British navy was unfairly court-martialed and shot on the deck of his ship in 1757 for insufficient success against the French in the Balearic islands, Voltaire made no secret of his shock and disgust at the irrational execution of the Admiral in order that the British government might make an example of him. His outrage was shared by many.

The loosening of formal and geometrical baroque garden designs into more natural curves and the introduction of "wilderness" plantings in British landscape gardens was understood by some contemporary observers as a commentary on political structures, as well. Lord Temple, one of the Duke of Marlborough's generals in the wars against Louis XIV, developed the celebrated landscape gardens at Stowe in Buckinghamshire during the first half of the eighteenth century partly to reflect his lack of sympathy for autocratic government. Out went formal, French-style gardens such as those Temple had visited at Versailles, and in came less geometrical and more varied kinds of gardens that were developed over the course of the eighteenth century at Stowe and other sites. The Temple to the Liberty of our Ancestors (also known informally as the Gothic Temple) at Stowe was built during the 1740s by a young gardener named Lancelot Brown under the direction of the architect James Gibbs (Figure 0.4). It was constructed in a curious version of the Gothic style that had come to signify the Anglo-Saxons and their wise leader King Alfred of Wessex, who was also known as the king of the West Saxons. This association with historic "Germanic liberty" was not lost on enlightened German rulers like Leopold III, Duke of Anhalt-Dessau, known as Prince Franz, who was an Anglophile and supporter of the Enlightenment. Prince Franz traveled with his architect, Friedrich Wilhelm von Erdmannsdorff, in England to learn the latest political and landscape ideas and bring them back home, creating his own impressive landscape garden at Wörlitz in Saxony, designed in 1769–73, based on his visits to Stowe, Claremont, and other British gardens. It was the first English-style landscape garden in Continental Europe. He incorporated Picturesque garden structures of widely varied styles, shapes, and materials. The earliest Gothic Revival building in any German landscape garden was the Gotische Haus begun in 1774 for Prince Franz at Wörlitz. It was partly based on Strawberry Hill in Twickenham, the Gothic villa of another great eighteenth-century man of letters, Horace Walpole.

Walpole broke new ground in a number of ways. A prolific writer of letters, he can be regarded as an early art historical writer through publications on

FIGURE 0.4 Temple to the Liberty of our Ancestors [aka Gothic Temple], Stowe, Buckinghamshire, England; built by Lancelot Brown under the direction of James Gibbs, with additions by Sanderson Miller, 1741–9. Photograph courtesy of Daderot/ Wikimedia Commons.

Italian and Dutch painters as well as a volume on the landscape garden. Walpole is also credited with inventing the genre of the Gothic horror novel in *The Castle of Otranto* (1764). The son of the most powerful British Prime Minister of the eighteenth century, just before the middle of the eighteenth century he purchased a small working man's cottage as a country retreat in the summer months and set about refashioning it and substantially enlarging it to be the first major house of the Gothic revival. Strawberry Hill in Twickenham was radically asymmetrical in its architecture, and was furnished with a mixture of antique and modern furniture, paintings, and *objets d'art* in a kind of "free style" that was neither rococo nor neoclassical, nor fully Gothic. Walpole formed a Committee of Taste consisting of himself and a few trusted friends to design interior fittings and furniture based on the antiquarian books he had in his library. In creating Strawberry Hill, Walpole transferred the British aesthetic concept of the Picturesque from the landscape garden, bringing it inside the house in a highly original way. The accessibility of Strawberry Hill to visitors even during Walpole's own lifetime helped to spread the idea of the Gothic as a suitable, alternative style to classicism for country house building and furnishing during the second half of the eighteenth century. The Gothic style in this context represented an owner who was bookish, with antiquarian leanings, and interested in the history of northern Europe. Classicism was increasingly being viewed as the style of southern Europe, and therefore a "foreign" imported style in the north. This attitude gained greater traction during the Romantic movement toward the end of the eighteenth century.

The German states—one could not yet speak of a nation—had adopted the French rococo style early in the eighteenth century perhaps because of its emphasis on nature as the basis of ornament. It was developed to great heights at the courts of Saxony in Dresden, Bavaria in Munich, and Prussia in Potsdam. In Munich, the extraordinarily talented Walloon designer François Cuvilliés, who began his career as a dwarf at the Bavarian court of the Wittelsbachers, created a groundbreaking rococo interior as an "ancestor gallery" in the Munich Residenz by 1730; he then went on to create a rococo masterpiece, the Amalienburg Pavilion in the grounds of the Nymphenberg Palace, during the 1730s. It featured a rethinking of the Hall of Mirrors at Versailles, with silvered decoration laden with naturalistic ornament overtaking the wall and ceiling, complemented by large mirrored surfaces, thereby bringing the gardens of the pavilion inside and making light bounce over every surface. It was as fluent and graceful as Louis XIV's Hall was static and magnificent. The complexity of the age, however, is demonstrated by the fact that the autocratic ruler Frederick the Great of Prussia (1712–86), an ardent Francophile and builder of lavishly furnished rococo palaces, was also a great admirer of the philosopher Voltaire. Frederick was the prolific builder of a number of elaborate palaces scattered around Potsdam, yet his grave is extraordinary for its simplicity. In accordance with his wishes, he was buried "as a philosopher" amongst his pet dogs, with a simple stone marker at his country retreat of Sans Souci, a single-storey rococo villa set into a landscape of terraced gardens. To this day, fresh potatoes are left on Frederick's grave stone to honor his introduction of this new food, which helped to avert cyclical periods of starvation among the Prussian peasantry (Figure 0.5). He was an autocratic ruler, but one who felt his obligations to his subjects.

By the end of the eighteenth century in Britain, the Industrial Revolution had begun, and a permanent transformation of society was underway. Wealth was no longer a matter purely of inheritance or rank. For these creators of new money, new and less traditional types of furniture and interiors were developed using new, less expensive materials like silver plate and *carton pierre*, a form of ornament made from "composition" with molds rather than the traditional and laborious technique of carving details from wood and gesso by hand. The repetitious small-scale ornament used particularly in neoclassical designs during the final quarter of the eighteenth century readily lent itself to such techniques, which anticipated the full-scale industrial production of the nineteenth century. Coade stone, an artificial stone that could be molded rather than chiseled by hand, was perfected by Eleanor Coade (1733–1821), an independent female

FIGURE 0.5 The grave stone of Frederick the Great. Photograph courtesy of Hannes Grobe/Wikimedia Commons.

manufacturer who operated in South London. Born into a mercantile family, Eleanor Coade became highly successful and supplied members of the aristocracy and the court with ornaments for the exteriors of buildings. Her own small country house in the quaint town of Lyme Regis in Dorset survives today and still displays the kinds of neoclassical ornaments of artificial stone that she perfected and which found their way onto grand country house exteriors as well as more modest structures (Figure 0.6).

Toward the end of the eighteenth century, women emerged as more independent members of society, and a surprising number ran businesses, including silversmithing and furniture-making workshops, or designed textiles. Often this was in the context of a broader family involvement. The widow of Jean-François Oeben, for example, the maker of the *bureau du roi*, continued his workshop after his death in 1763 through marrying his journeyman assistant, Jean Henri Riesener. Mme Oeben was, herself, the daughter of a famous Parisian cabinetmaker of Flemish heritage, François Vandercruse, and her sister married the younger brother of her husband. Moreover, Jean-François Oeben had trained with Charles-Joseph Boulle, a son of the famous maker of the Grand Trianon commode for Louis XIV. Oeben's sister married another famous French neoclassical furniture maker of Germanic origin, Martin Carlin.

FIGURE 0.6 Belmont House, Lyme Regis, Dorset, England; once the home of Eleanor Coade, it displays late eighteenth-century Coade stone ornaments on the exterior. Photograph courtesy of Ballista/Wikimedia Commons.

These family relationships were often key to maintaining continuity in the production of luxury goods by highly skilled workshops. Numerous different craftsmen, of course, collaborated in making the same piece of furniture, and this collaboration encouraged dialogue, renewal, and innovation. The evolution of techniques often intruded into traditional crafts, and the guilds that represented and controlled craftsmen. Information was circulated thanks to publications such as Diderot's *Encyclopédie*, and spread through practice on the workshop bench, but these family relationships were also vital.

The production of furniture was to a considerable extent conditioned by the rules of different markets in different regions. It was subject to the demand of clients, of course, and to the availability of raw materials. In the case of the most luxurious French furniture, the value of the materials required to make these pieces meant that the furniture makers were subject to the requirements of the *marchands-merciers*, the highly influential merchant-dealers who directed the production of the highest quality furniture in Paris. They had the means to furnish the *ébénistes* with lacquer panels, porcelain, or hardstone plaques needed to carry out the commissions that were increasingly received during the neoclassical period, when demand for exotic and unusual materials was at its height. Such furniture was made via a highly "vertical" process, whereby the aristocratic client decided on the type of object he desired, on the advice of the *marchand-mercier*. It was, however, the hands of the craftsmen that could realize the design and develop the methods and manual skills that enabled the bending of lacquer panels, the matching of gilt bronzes to the marquetry design, or the accurate cutting out of the carcase to create a thoroughly graceful form. The luxury goods trade often involved international networks for circulating merchandise that conditioned and formed fashions and the history of taste. This phenomenon had been well established by the seventeenth century, of course, and continued through the eighteenth.

The culture of artisanal life was often a migratory one. It was characteristic of furniture production to bring together a large number of itinerant workers who circulated from one region to another. The Flemish and German-speaking communities occupied a dominant position among Parisian *ébénistes*: Boulle, Oppenord, the van Risenburghs Latz, Oeben, Riesener, and Carlin each forged an identity within the world of French furniture, despite their Netherlandish or German origins. France herself exported artisans and ornament specialists to other regions, beginning with the Protestant diaspora in the 1680s after the Revocation of the Edict of Nantes. Meissonnier established himself in the Germanic world, Petitot produced his designs for the princely interiors of Parma, and Bélanger and the *marchand-mercier* Daguerre traveled to London, to name a few. These travels and exchanges raise question marks concerning the idea of "national identity" in expressing a culture that could, in fact, be quite international—the commode delivered by the Netherlandish BVRB (Bernard II van Risenburgh) to the *mobilier de la Couronne* (Royal Furniture Depot) for the Polish Queen of France at Fontainebleau, fitted with Japanese lacquer panels, provides us with an instructive example of this phenomenon.

The American colonies provided fresh opportunities for furniture makers and craftsmen in the eighteenth century, especially those from the British Isles, whereas during the nineteenth century there was a strong Germanic influx and influence in towns on the Eastern Seaboard. Philadelphia was one of the largest and most important towns in the English-speaking world after London and Dublin in the eighteenth century, and styles traveled between the three cities. Thomas Johnson, a highly talented carver in mid-eighteenth-century London, has left us an autobiographical account entitled *The Life of the Author* (1778) in which he describes his training with Matthias Lock, an outstanding carver in London. Then, after getting a servant pregnant but not wanting to marry her, Johnson left London, initially for Liverpool, where he taught ships' carvers and left samples of his work. Next he decided to board a ship to Dublin, where he taught the leading Irish carver, Hercules Courtenay, who in turn emigrated to Philadelphia and established a school of Philadelphian rococo carving that is sometimes referred to today as "Philadelphia Chippendale" (Simon 2003: 3–4). Chippendale's *Director* was well known in Philadelphia and available in the public library in the final quarter of the eighteenth century. In such ways were styles and techniques transferred from place to place.

Inevitably, the bulk of surviving eighteenth-century objects come from the interiors of the most leisured and prosperous classes of European society— normally, the aristocratic and land-owning classes. However, the furnishing of not only royal palaces but also country houses or *châteaux*, *palazzi*, and private *hôtels*, or town houses (in cities), as well as the affluent households of prosperous financiers and successful merchants in the large towns of Europe and on the East Coast of the United States, all provided opportunities for talented cabinetmakers to develop their production and to innovate in creating new types of furniture for interiors and activities. It could be argued that, during the eighteenth century, society was more concerned with the appreciation of life as it should be lived than the assertion of one's rank in the social order via furnishings, which had characterized the seventeenth century. The new kind of citizen of the Enlightenment is portrayed in the portrait of the chemist and aristocrat Antoine Lavoisier, depicted in an informal pose with his remarkable wife by Jacques-Louis David (1788) (Plate 4). The Lavoisiers are depicted with their scientific instruments and apparatus, rather than in a setting with rich furnishings. Mme Lavoisier was not an aristocrat, but the daughter of a wealthy financier and French parliamentarian. She was an accomplished scientist in her own right and helped to establish the protocols for scientific methods of investigation that we still use today. Unfortunately, because of his birth, her husband, himself a respected and accomplished chemist, was executed in 1794 during the period of the Terror in France, demonstrating the darker side of the so-called age of reason.

In the field of eighteenth-century furniture, France unquestionably occupied an outstanding position due in part to its centralized system of patronage, whereby luxury goods were created to serve the monarch and the court. This, in turn, has affected the historiography of furniture especially during the nineteenth and twentieth centuries, when French furniture and *objets d'art* were sought after by collectors. Such collecting began in the post-Revolutionary period when British collectors, led by George IV, acquired large numbers of French objects that remain in country house collections and have since gone into public collections, as with the Wallace Collection in London. Later in the nineteenth century, British owners and dealers began to sell their collections in large numbers to American institutions and individuals like Jean Paul Getty, whose mother was French, thus reinforcing the importance of French furniture and *objets* to the history of the eighteenth century. Even collectors in places such as Buenos Aires in Argentina, which retained close cultural ties with Europe, acquired French and British eighteenth-century furniture and decorative art. The design books of figures such as Chippendale and Sheraton were reprinted and collected in the United States as part of a perceived common cultural heritage during the nineteenth century. While wealthy society figures like Alva Vanderbilt styled herself on occasion as Marie Antoinette, and collected French royal furniture by Jean Henri Riesener, other collectors such as the author and arbiter of taste Edith Wharton preferred a quieter mixing of styles of different periods and centers in which the eighteenth century remained dominant. The decorating guide she wrote with the society architect Ogden Codman, *The Decoration of Houses* (first published in 1897), demonstrates this quiet, refined approach to using European decorative art and furniture of the eighteenth century—particularly of the neoclassical period—as an antidote to what she saw as the heavy and oppressive furniture commonly used in American houses of the nineteenth century. The decorative art of the eighteenth century, therefore, became enshrined as an important, shared cultural heritage between Europe and the Americas, and one that provided enduring access to "good taste" across time.

CHAPTER ONE

Design and Motifs

BARBARA LASIC

France's production of luxury furniture in the eighteenth century was celebrated throughout Europe. Renowned for their technical skill, makers were supplying their elite clientele with pieces that could be both functional and exquisitely designed, and which boasted precious exotic veneers or expensive hardstones. The motifs that adorned furniture drew on a large palette of sources, ranging from classical ornament to botanical treatises, and echoed contemporary interests such as, for instance, Europe's fascination for the Orient. Inscribed within the broader stylistic frameworks that inflected domestic architecture and its furnishings, the decorative motifs found on eighteenth-century French furniture could also sometimes be arranged into complex iconographic compositions derived from the realm of painting or sculpture, thereby blurring the boundaries between the fine and the decorative arts.

Acquisitions of furniture were the subject of public discussion in eighteenth-century France. Commenting on the virtuosity of the marquetry adorning the mineralogical cabinet offered by the King of Sweden Gustav III (1746–92) to the Prince de Condé (1736–1818) for his residence in Chantilly in 1772, the botanist and naturalist Valmont de Bomare (1731–1807), director of the natural history displays at the Château of Chantilly, wrote emphatically on the quality of the central marquetry panel depicting garlands and mining tools "si artistement travaillés qu'on le prendroit pour l'ouvrage du plus habile pinceau" (so artistically worked that it would be taken for the work of the most skillful brush) (Rozier 1774: 376). Presented to the Prince de Condé for his celebrated collection of mineralogical specimens, the cabinet was the result of the combined efforts of three Swedish men, the royal furniture maker Georg Haupt

(1741–84) and the bronze maker Jean-Baptiste Masreliez (1753–1801) after a design by the architect Jean-Eric Rehn (1717–93) (Forray-Carlier 2010: 67–8). A well-traveled craftsman, Haupt is thought to have trained in France under Simon Oeben (1722–86) and appears to have later joined Linnell's workshop in London. By his return to Sweden in 1769, Haupt had fully mastered the art of pictorial marquetry in the neoclassical style, incorporating swags, husks, ribbons, and antique vases (Wood 2014: 238–75).

If, by the end of the eighteenth century, European furniture makers thus evidently excelled at pictorial and figurative marquetry, their skill can be traced back to the Grand Siècle and the reign of King Louis XIV. Inheriting a northern tradition that arguably found its apogee in the work of Jan van Mekeren (c. 1658–1733) through the influx of Dutch furniture makers settled in France, the country witnessed the emergence of a rich and naturalistic palette of patterns on furniture, cabinets in particular (Baarsen 2006: 32–3).

FLORAL MARQUETRY

The Dutch-born Pierre Gole (1620–84) can be rightly regarded as the most prominent maker of the early reign of Louis XIV. He started his career making elaborate ebony cabinets before specializing in the 1650s in the crafting of pieces with intricate and highly naturalistic marquetry panels not unlike those of contemporary Dutch flower painters such as Ambrosius Bosschaert the Elder (1573–1621), Balthasar van der Ast (1593–1657), Roelandt Savery (1576–1639), and Jacob Vosmaer (1574–1641). Patronized by the king and the court as well as by a glittering Parisian clientele, Gole had a large workshop near the Louvre while also being employed by the Royal Manufacture of the Gobelins, which produced objects exclusively for royal palaces or to be used as royal gifts. A small coffer (or chest) on stand attributed to Gole that may have belonged to Cardinal Mazarin (1602–61) boasts a ravishing marquetry decoration of birds and flowers on a turtleshell and ivory ground. All individually identifiable, the flowers would have been originally stained, but today only their ivory leaves have retained some of their green coloring, a subtle reminder of the coffer's original polychromatic scheme (Lunsingh-Scheurleer 2005: 88–9). The bouquet of flowers tied by a ribbon was a recurrent motif in seventeenth-century marquetry, and one in fact that would also be employed in many marquetry panels during the following century. Also seen on a table attributed to Gole, now in the Metropolitan Museum of Art, the pattern echoes the numerous prints of small bouquets after the Franco-Flemish painter Jean-Baptiste Monnoyer (1636–99) published in Paris in the second half of the seventeenth century.[1]

The widespread popularity of painted floral still lives did not just derive from their aesthetic and decorative appeal. By bringing the marvels of the garden inside the home, they echoed contemporary botanical and scientific interests, while simultaneously evoking the flora of distant and exotic lands. Often containing complex symbolism and invested with the function of a *vanitas* and *memento mori* that are reminders of death and the transience of life, their compositions could also be enhanced by objects made of precious materials such as porcelain and silver. While floral marquetry rarely contained the same degree of complex allegorical iconography that could characterize some of its painted counterparts, the technical skill required to create such panels combined with their erudite botanical associations made them prized possessions for a cultivated and wealthy urban clientele.

BOULLE MARQUETRY (METAL MARQUETRY)

Gole's treatment of naturalistic marquetry, however, represented the first stage of its development and, as the author and furniture historian Pradère rightly noted, it lacked the depth and realism characterizing the production of some of the next generation craftsmen (Pradère 1989: 49). André-Charles Boulle (1642–1732), one of the most prominent *ébénistes* (cabinetmakers) of the reign of Louis XIV, who rose to the position of cabinetmaker to the king in 1672, is arguably better known for the technique of metal marquetry, which he perfected (Pradère 1989: 67–108). Yet during the early part of his career his workshop was known for its production of imposing cabinets incorporating intricate panels of wooden floral marquetry. Such pieces present a great stylistic unity and exhibit recurrent features and elements in their compositions such as elaborate vases of flowers in full bloom that could be enlivened by the presence of insects and birds, as seen in an armoire at the Louvre with central door panels depicting vases of blooming flowers on pedestals with birds and butterflies (Durand 2014: 138). A panel *c.* 1690, now in the Bowes Museum, testifies to the exceptional vitality and minutious naturalism of Boulle's output. While the composition owes much to Monnoyer's paintings, archival sources suggest that Boulle worked from a number of precise other sources: he had indeed in his workshop over 220 studies of flowers and birds drawn from life by Patel fils (1646–1707), and archival records inform us that he also owned floral still lives by Nicolas Baudesson (1611–80) (Pradère 1989: 94). His cabinet on stand of *c.* 1675–80 celebrating the Treaty of Nijmegen that sealed France's victory over the Spanish, Dutch, and Imperial armies exhibits a complex allegorical program. Probably a royal gift, it boasts two medallic portraits of Louis XIV, while the figures of Hercules and Hippolita on the supporting stand, allegories of strength and bravery, allude to the virtues required in battle. The central panel of the cabinet is dominated by a rich and intricate marquetry composition of flowers entwined in acanthus scrolls, with a French cockerel triumphantly dominating over the Spanish lion and the Habsburg eagle (Figure 1.1) (Sassoon and Wilson 1986: 2–3). The rich polychromy of the ensemble is now sadly lost but Boulle's virtuoso naturalistic and dramatic treatment of the marquetry is still very much evident.

FIGURE 1.1 André-Charles Boulle, Cabinet on Stand, *c.* 1675–80. Gift of J. Paul Getty Museum. Photograph courtesy of J. Paul Getty Museum.

PIETRA DURA

Pictorial naturalism was not confined to wood marquetry. Perfected in the sixteenth century in the Gallerie dei Lavori, the Florentine workshops founded by Ferdinando I de' Medici (1549–1609) in 1588, the technique known as *pietra dura*, namely the carving and inlay of hardstones, was appropriated by French craftsmen in the second half of the seventeenth century and flourished at the Gobelins workshops under the direction of Ferdinando Migliorini (d.1683), Filipi Branchi (d.1699), and Domenico Cucci (1635–1704). The costly pieces produced in the royal manufactory displayed a very high level of virtuosity, and their complex compositions, usually integrating fauna and flora, were remarkable for their high degree of pictorial realism, as seen in a tabletop made at the Gobelins at the end of the seventeenth century and now in the Louvre (Tabletop, Manufacture Royale des Gobelins, 1680–90; Musée du Louvre, MR406). The thick and colorful parrot feathers, the delicacy and organic movement of the flowers, and the fleshy texture of the fruits with seeds bursting from ripe and open pomegranates, are all a triumph over the harsh materiality of the colored stones that make the scene (Durand 2014: 136). The importance and intrinsic value of rare marbles and precious and semiprecious stones meant that seventeenth-century *pietra dura* furniture never completely went out of fashion in the eighteenth century, as evidenced by the presence of two royal Cucci cabinets in the celebrated collection of the Duc d'Aumont that was sold at auction in 1782. The furniture did not always survive intact, however, and *pietra dura* panels were often remounted on furniture whose forms followed the latest fashions. A cabinet of *c.* 1785 by the royal cabinetmaker Adam Weisweiler (1746–1820) combines an austere and chaste neoclassical shape with lavish and colorful seventeenth-century Florentine hardstone panels depicting birds, baskets of flowers, and fruits (Cabinet, Adam Weisweiler, 1785–90; Royal Collection Trust, RCIN 2593). Their presence on a fashionable piece of furniture is both a testament to the remarkable durability of the *pietre dure* plaques, but also the enduring appeal of the lustrous precision of their iconography.

REVIVAL OF FLORAL MARQUETRY: NATURALISM

The Regence saw the disappearance of naturalistic marquetry in favor of geometrically shaped veneers, but the advent of the rococo style witnessed a revival in the use of floral marquetry, first in a stylized form before evolving into a highly naturalistic manner in the neoclassical period at the end of the eighteenth century. The *ébéniste* Bernard II van Risenburgh (1700–60), generally known under the acronym BVRB, is widely credited with having revived the use of floral marquetry. Patronized by the Garde-Meuble, the French royal furniture depository, as well as the leading *marchands-merciers* (dealers in *objets d'art*) of the capital, he supplied furniture to the court and the wealthy urban elites, occasionally sending goods beyond France's frontiers. The double desk in the Getty Museum (Plate 5), thought to have been made by BVRB for the tax collector François-Balthazar Dangé (1696–1777), exemplifies his restrained yet fluid use of formalized flowers. The flowers and tendrils work in harmony with the shape of the desk, echoing its sinuous and gently curving lines. Often made out of kingwood, such flowers were commonly positioned against a background of reddish tulipwood, thereby creating a strong and appealing contrast between the two elements (Chastang 2008: 57).

If BVRB was arguably a key figure in the rediscovery of floral marquetry, he was quickly emulated by most Parisian *ébénistes*, for instance, Pierre Migeon (1696–1758) or Jean-Pierre Latz (1691–1754). The latter's botanical renditions became more realistic as his career progressed, fully echoing the general trend toward a more naturalistic treatment of floral ornament (Pradère 1989: 158). Latz's later production in turn begs the question of his potential collaboration with the celebrated maker and royal furniture maker Jean-François Oeben (1721–63), who raised marquetry's realism to new heights (158–9). No longer satisfied with approximative and simplified blooms, Oeben's marquetry work was characterized by a superb accuracy and adherence to nature. Appointed *ébéniste du roi* in 1754, he enjoyed the privilege of a workshop at the Gobelins and, later, in the enclave of the Arsenal that was above guild regulations. Oeben worked for three years in the workshop of Charles-Joseph Boulle (1688–1754), the son of the celebrated Grand Siècle furniture maker, where he may have perfected his marquetry technique. The realism, depth, botanical accuracy and precision of Oeben's marquetry recall indeed that of André-Charles Boulle himself, as demonstrated by the top panel on a mechanical table executed for the royal mistress Madame de Pompadour in 1761 at the Metropolitan Museum of Art (Plate 6). The elaborate vase arrangement surrounded by gardening tools and the attributes of arts and sciences echoes the complexity and refinement of Boulle's early productions, albeit in a less monumental format better suited to the more intimate scale of rococo interiors. Like those of his predecessor, Oeben's floral compositions owe much to the paintings of Jean Baptiste Monnoyer, but the craftsman was also very much indebted to the floral designs published in printed form by the flower painter Louis Tessier (1719–81) under the title of *Le Livre de Principe des Fleurs* (Chastang 2007: 115–26). Also listed as a flower painter to the Royal Manufacture of the Gobelins, Tessier provided a ready-made repertoire of motifs for artisans and designers that could easily be applied to furniture.

The art of floral marquetry did not cease at Oeben's death, and, as furniture conservator Chastang has noted, "by the time of [his] death, floral marquetry had attained an unrivalled sophistication" (Chastang 2008: 70). The cyclical taste for naturalistic floral marquetry in the long eighteenth century reached an apex of sophistication and realism in the 1780s before being superseded by the fashion for plain mahogany or burr veneers. Arguably one of the most gifted *marqueteurs* of his age, the German-born Jean Henri Riesener (1734–1806) had in fact trained in Oeben's workshop, eventually marrying his widow and taking over the running of the business before being appointed *ébéniste du roi* in 1774. The minutiae and skill of Riesener's work is fully visible in the *bureau du roi*, the desk started by Oeben and finished by Riesener that was ordered by the Garde Meuble for the King's interior cabinet at Versailles. The latter is thought to have executed the marquetry panels and the floral compositions. Derived from Tessier's designs, the bouquets are tied with ribbons and contain readily identifiable blooms, very much reflecting a rococo aesthetic that was soon going to become obsolete. The delicacy and precision of Riesener's marquetry reached new heights with a small table he supplied to Marie Antoinette in the 1780s, possibly for the Petit Trianon and now at Waddesdon Manor. Here the complexity and virtuosity of the marquetry evoke that of painted canvas, and this naturalism was matched by the jewel-like gilt-brass mounts executed by the virtuoso Parisian gilder François Rémond (1747–1812).

THREE-DIMENSIONAL CARVINGS

The quality and sophistication of Oeben and Riesener's two-dimensional naturalism found its match in three-dimensional form in the delicate carvings of the seat furniture and beds produced by the workshop of the joiner George Jacob (1739–1814). Having become a master joiner in 1765, Jacob quickly became a regular supplier to the French Crown, and he also enjoyed the patronage of a distinguished foreign clientele that included the future George IV of England. Jacob mostly worked in the neoclassical idiom and his large workshop employed a team of skilled craftsmen such as the carver Jean-Baptiste-Simon Rode (1735–99), who is documented to have worked on a number of royal pieces (Leben 2007: 127–41). Jacob's furniture was at the height of fashion and the carvings found on the furniture made in the Jacob workshop show strong similarities with the designs published by contemporary ornamental artists such as Richard Lalonde (dates unknown) or Jules-François Boucher le Fils (1736–82). For example, a canopied bed attributed to George Jacob in the Victoria and Albert Museum with stiles in the form of tapering quivers and a carved decoration on the theme of love consisting of Hymen's torch, Cupid's bows and arrows, and elegant bouquets of flowers, echoes the decorative repertoire seen on the bed designs published by Lalonde in his *Cahiers d'Ameublements* in the late 1770s (Figure 1.2) (Victoria and Albert Museum [hereafter V&A], 29364:17).

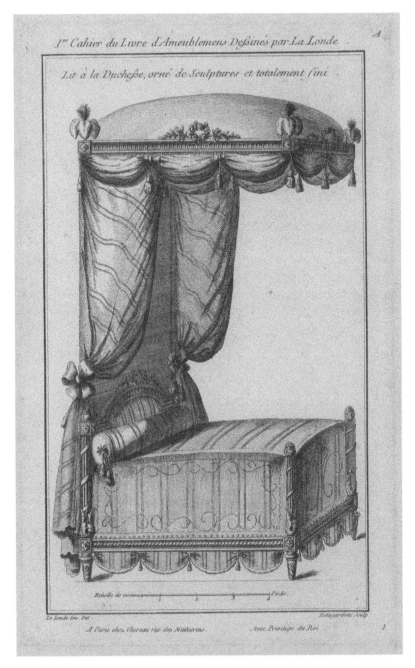

FIGURE 1.2 Richard de Lalonde, Design for a Bed, late eighteenth century. Harris Brisbane Dick Fund, 1933/The Metropolitan Museum of Art. Photograph courtesy of the Metropolitan Museum of Art.

CLASSICAL INFLUENCES

If nature was an important source of inspiration in eighteenth-century French furniture, the classical world and its architectural language were equally significant and pervasive features, encompassing both the treatment of the structural elements of pieces of furniture and their veneers as well as their gilt-bronze mounts. For instance, Pierre Gole's stands were often in the shape of fluted Doric columns, as seen on an ivory cabinet thought to have been made for the Palais Royal in the early 1660s, or the table discussed above (Cabinet on Stand, attributed to Pierre Gole, 1661–5; V&A, W.38-1983). Stands were of course ideally suited to the employment of Vitruvian orders, and such obvious aesthetic and architectural synergies were sustained throughout the eighteenth century, as evidenced by the spectacular lacquer cabinet by Adam Weisweiler made in 1792 for the collector William Beckford (1760–1844). Here the mounts evoke Ionic capitals hybridized by the inclusion of elephant heads, exotic features presumably deemed appropriate complements to the lacquer panels (Pradère 1989: 399). A less obvious and more playful and irreverent reference to Vitruvian principles can be seen in Rene Dubois's green *vernis Martin* desk possibly designed by the architect Charles de Wailly (1730–98) for Catherine the Great of Russia in 1765 (Wallace Collection, F330; Jacobsen 2017: 14). Here the thick tasseled cushions assisting the elegant caryatid sirens positioned at each corner with the task of supporting the tabletop may be a direct reference to the downward-sloping volutes of the Ionic order. A decorative motif frequently employed by Weisweiler was the use of slender caryatids supporting woven baskets of flowers, more precisely known as canephorae (basket-bearers), as seen on this cabinet on stand at the Getty Museum (Figure 1.3), or on the table supplied to Marie Antoinette for her *cabinet doré* at Versailles in 1784 and now in the Louvre (Plommer 1979: 97–102; Durand 2014: 418). One could argue that such basket-bearing caryatids could also be interpreted as a reference to the creation of the Corinthian order, as narrated by Vitrivius, who explained that the Corinthian sculptor Callimachus designed the order after seeing acanthus leaves emerging from a votive basket on a young girl's tomb (Vitruvius rep. 1914: 104, 106). The neoclassical period and its rediscovery and reinterpretation of the classical idiom saw a plethora of pieces of furniture ornamented with motifs taken from antiquity. The simplicity of Vitruvian scrolls and Greek keys combined with their visual impact made them particularly ubiquitous features on late eighteenth-century furniture. For instance, Joseph Baumauer's desk made in the late 1750s for Ange-Laurent La Live de Jully (1725–79) in the bold and pioneering *goût grec* style after designs by the architect Louis-Joseph Le Lorrain (1715–59) incorporates a vigorous frieze of Vitruvian scrolls below its tabletop, while the upper part of the filing cabinet is framed by a Greek key (Château de Chantilly, OA357; Forray-Carlier 2010: 57–8; Alcouffe

FIGURE 1.3 Adam Weisweiler (attrib.), Secretaire, 1780–3. Gift of J. Paul Getty/
J. Paul Getty Museum. Photograph courtesy of the J. Paul Getty Museum.

et al. 2015: 178–9). Harking back to the aesthetics of the Grand Siècle, the desk is a powerful affirmation of the growing obsolescence of the rococo style.

GROTESQUES ON FURNITURE

The grotesque was another pervasive motif. Originally emanating from Emperor Nero's Domus Aurea in Rome (68 CE), the grotesque was rediscovered at the end of the fifteenth century and widely employed by artists and architects thereafter. Grotesques consisted of verticalized and playful compositions mixing human figures, animals, and fantastical creatures, entwined with plants and flowers. Such compositions found their way into André-Charles Boulle's furniture, via the inventive mediation of his colleague Jean Berain (1640–1711) who held the post of chief designer at the office of the Menus Plaisirs, the department in charge of designing temporary festivities at court. One of Boulle's most fluent treatments of the grotesque is arguably found on a toilette mirror supplied in 1713 to the Duchesse de Berry (1695–1719), daughter of the future Regent of France, and now in the Wallace Collection (Mirror, attributed to André-Charles Boulle, 1713; Wallace Collection, F50). Boulle was evidently inspired by one of Bérain's designs but allowed himself to depart slightly from the original. For instance, the central figure of Bacchus is no longer adorned by satyrs but accompanied by musicians, and he is standing on an imposing shell-like motif adorned with imbricated circles. The central theme of the composition, however, remains intact: a playful and festive bacchanal, it is a celebration of the pleasure of the senses, a very appropriate subject for the ritual of the toilette. It could, however, also be interpreted as a potent reminder of the fugitive nature of such pleasures, and the transience of beauty and life. This idea is reinforced by the presence of extinguished candles next to the musicians, candles being recurrent features of *vanitas* paintings.

Such elaborate and extensive grotesques were, however, rare on pieces of furniture. Usually, only elements of grotesque compositions were extracted and applied to pieces. This is visible on the gilt-bronze friezes with scrolling acanthus and ivy leaves, goats, playful infant fauns, or sphynxes adorning a number of Weisweiler's cabinets, as seen, for instance, on the *commode à vantaux* (with hinged panels rather than drawers) sold in 1790 by the *marchand-mercier* Dominique Daguerre (fl.1772–93) and his associate Martin-Eloi Lignereux (1751–1809) to the King of Naples Leopold IV (1790–1851) (Plate 7). The jewel-like quality and the richness of such friezes has been associated with the hand of the bronzier François Rémond (1747–1812) who, like Weisweiler, worked regularly for Daguerre. The latter may in fact have been responsible for the design of the frieze and could have been inspired by the ornamental sculptor and cabinetmaker Gilles-Paul Cauvet's *Frises et ornements à l'usage des sculpteurs* published in 1777.

TROPHY DESIGNS

Classical vases and trophies were frequently employed as motifs on eighteenth-century furniture. The book of designs produced in 1768 by the French designer and self-styled architect Jean-Charles Delafosse in his *Nouvelle Iconologie Historique* provided a rich source of inspiration for furniture makers (Perrot 2017: 173–83). The publication underwent three re-editions and contained designs for furniture, vases, and various classical trophies. These were not intended to be followed *à la lettre* and the painter, gilder, and japanner Jean-Félix Watin (1728–?) warned of the prohibitive cost of precisely following and executing Delafosse's creations: "if one should seek to follow his [Delafosse's] designs in all their intricate detail, the cost of doing so would surely be too high for even the most wealthy private person" (Eriksen 1974: 171). Only specific elements of his designs were therefore meant to be abstracted and employed by craftsmen. For instance, the marquetry vases and pedestals adorning the commode delivered by Pierre-Antoine Foullet in 1768 for the apartment of the King's daughter Madame Victoire at Versailles are very much in the vein of those produced by Delafosse (Château de Versailles, OA10586; Verlet [1955] 1992: 58–9).

THE INFLUENCE OF ILLUSTRATIONS

Delafosse did not just produce a rich repertoire of classical ornament, he also provided his own personal interpretation of Cesare Ripa's influential illustrated edition of the *Iconologia* of 1603, testifying to the ongoing popularity of the early seventeenth-century publication. Containing a visual conspectus of allegories and emblems, Ripa's *Iconologia* quickly became an essential resource for both visual artists and writers. The physical and moral allegories it contained were frequently represented on eighteenth-century furniture. The celebrated *bureau du roi*, a desk made by Oeben and Riesener and delivered to King Louis XV for his Cabinet Interieur at Versailles in 1769, boasts indeed on a gilt-bronze plaque on the back of the desk a charming allegory of prudence whereby Ripa's grown woman holding a mirror with a snake entwined on her arm has been replaced by a chubby-cheeked putto distractedly looking into a mirror, a small lizard-like snake playfully wrapped around its handle (Château de Versailles, OA5444). This was part of a broader allegorical composition and complemented the rest of the iconographic program that included the attributes of royalty, the cardinal virtues, allegories of eloquence and the liberal arts, as well as the emblems of the Army and the Navy, and the riches of the sea and the earth (Meyer 2002: 122–30). In short, the decoration of the secretaire was fully intended to be read as appropriate pictorial representations of the qualities and virtues required of a powerful head of state. This is not to say that all allegorical depictions on furniture were as complex and extensive as those found on the *bureau du roi*. Furniture makers would often simply include just a single allegorical program to ornament their pieces, the theme of the seasons being a common and easily legible one, as shown on the mounts of a cabinet attributed to André-Charles Boulle, which shows the old figure of Winter warming his hands by a fire being faced by the triumphant figure of Ceres as Summer (Pradère 1989: 75). The dialogue between form and function was also not always as clearly and extensively articulated as on the *bureau du roi*. The *bureau plat* attributed to Boulle in the Wallace Collection boasts an harmonious balance between three-dimensional gilded mounts and metal marquetry characteristic of the output of the furniture maker (Wallace Collection, F427). Here the bacchic masks and satyrs' heads do not evoke erudite pursuits, but the inclusion of mounts representing the faces of Democritus and Heraclitus, the laughing and weeping philosophers, are evidently appropriate ornaments for a piece of furniture, which would have most likely belonged to an educated patron.

MYTHOLOGICAL SOURCES

Stories and characters from Greek and Roman mythology were another important source of inspiration for craftsmen. For instance, a cabinet richly decorated with metal marquetry attributed to Pierre Gole, thought to have been gifted by King Louis XIV to his mistress Madame de Fontanges, is supported by four pairs of vigorously carved gilded figures representing Hercules and Omphale. With their classical education and knowledge of classical myths, there is little doubt that the seventeenth-century viewers of this cabinet would have fully understood the iconographic meaning of the stand and recognized the characters' attributes: the powerful Queen of Lydia, having conquered Hercules, is triumphantly holding his club, while the now-defeated hero is reduced to holding the spindle with which he is spinning wool. The reversal of these gendered roles would have also been evident to educated seventeenth-century eyes who would have also understood it as a reference to Louis XIV's professed humble love for and devotion to his *favorite* Madame de Fontanges (Lunsingh-Scheurleer 2005: 91).

CLASSICAL NARRATIVES

The dramatic stories found in Ovid's *Metamorphoses* also provided artists and craftsmen with a rich repertoire from which to develop their iconographic narratives. André-Charles Boulle famously depicted on some of his gilt-bronze mounts episodes from the story of Apollo, namely, his unsuccessful pursuit of the nymph Daphne, and the Slaying of the unfortunate satyr Marsyas. Thought to have been inspired by drawings by the Italian Renaissance artist Raphael (1483–1520) in Boulle's collection (more of which later) such mounts were found on a number of his armoires, perhaps because such pieces of furniture were then thought to be adequate repositories for collections of prints and drawings. Boulle's three-dimensional interpretation of the Ovidian story of Apollo could however take a more restrained form and in some instances he merely employed small-scale masks representing the faces of the Olympian god and the nymph (Pradère 1989: 89). Used on a number of his *coffres de toilette*, coffers on stand intended as repositories for the personal items associated with the daily ritual of the toilette, the metamorphosis they allude to may have been perceived as eminently suitable motifs for a piece of furniture intended as part of a beautifying ritual (86).

The inclusion of themes and iconographic elements found in the grand genre of history painting evidently shows that the boundaries between fine and decorative arts were permeable in the eighteenth century. This fluidity was, once again, evident in the work of Boulle. As previously mentioned, he is thought to have modeled his gilt-bronze group of Apollo and Daphne after a drawing by Raphael. He appears to have employed his collection of prints and drawings as a regular source of inspiration, as demonstrated by the figure of Saturn on a number of his clocks that is modeled on a print by Ugo da Carpi (1480–1523) after a design by Parmigianino (1503–40) (Lunsingh-Scheurleer 1936: 286–8). Boulle's sources of inspiration also included decorative painting and the gilt-bronze mounts depicting the Greek philosopher Socrates and the cultured teacher Aspasia engaged in an animated debate found on a number of his armoires and cabinets taken from a painting by Michelle Corneille (1642–1708) in one of the arches of the Salle de Garde in the Queen's State Apartment at Versailles (Durand 2014: 140).

FÊTES GALANTES

This borrowing from the realm of fine and decorative painting was not limited to Boulle and, during the years of the French Régence after the death of Louis XIV, one saw the ethereal world of *fêtes galantes* permeating that of furniture. Coined to mark the creation of a new official category of painting for the acceptance of the painter Antoine Watteau (1684–1721) at the French Royal Academy of Painting and Sculpture in 1717, the term *fête galante* refers to generally small-scale paintings with unidentifiable and elegantly dressed men and women in idealized garden settings engaged in polite and amorous pursuits. The scenes derived from medieval representations of the Garden of Love, and were inspired by the coloring of sixteenth-century Venetian paintings and the festive scenes of seventeenth-century Dutch and Flemish genre paintings. Highly popular in the opening decades of the eighteenth century for their wistful eroticism and psychological tension, they were avidly collected by the urban elites for their elegant townhouses.

The aesthetics of the *fêtes galantes* permeated the field of domestic furnishings and, for instance, its characters formed part of the painted decoration of the fashionable *boiseries*, or carved wood paneling produced by the workshop of Claude Audran in the early part of the eighteenth century.[2] Charles Cressent (1685–1768), who was appointed *ébéniste* to the Duc d'Orléans, Régent of France, also borrowed from the world of Watteau for his furniture: the corner mounts in the shape of smiling female heads positioned at the top of the cabriole legs of some of his desks are called espagnolettes, and their delicate headdresses are directly taken from the pictorial world of Watteau and his followers (Watson 1966: 2:540).

THE USE OF PORCELAIN IN FURNITURE

The boundaries between fine and decorative arts were thus often permeable and, when it came to furniture motifs, craftsmen often drew their inspiration from the pictorial creations of their fellow artists. The fashion for inlaying furniture with plaques of soft-paste Sèvres porcelain multiplied the possibilities offered by such dialogues. The decorative practice of mounting porcelain on to furniture was pioneered by the *marchand-mercier* Simon-Philippe Poirier (1720–85) and is thought to have been inspired by the Oriental practice of ornamenting furniture with Cantonese enamel (Watson 1966: 1:LVI). It was envisaged as an expedient and visually appealing means of sustaining the polychromy on furniture since, unlike marquetry panels that faded over time, Sèvres plaques never lost their vibrant colors to the damaging effect of light. While most porcelain plaques intended for furniture were adorned with charming floral compositions echoing their marquetry counterparts, some pieces of furniture fully exploited the pictorial potential offered by the medium of porcelain.

The royal mistress Madame du Barry (1743–93) was particularly fond of Sèvres-mounted furniture and owned a number of spectacular pieces such as the commode by Martin Carlin (1730–85) delivered in 1772 by the *marchand-mercier* Poirier for her bedchamber at Versailles and now in the Louvre (Durand 2014: 406). Veneered in pearwood and ornamented with opulent neoclassical gilt bronzes, the commode is, however, dominated by large plaques of soft-paste porcelain decorating its front and sides. The three frontal plaques were based on paintings by Watteau's followers, Jean-Baptiste Pater (1695–1736) and Nicolas Lancret (1690–1743), thereby testifying to the ongoing popularity of the iconography of *fêtes galantes* well into the neoclassical era. The central, larger panel is framed by a neoclassical gilt-bronze mount with an elaborate tripartite molding evidently intended to evoke the framing and display of easel paintings. As for the side panels on the commode, they were referred to as "paintings" in the Sèvres registers. Executed by the foremost painter at Sèvres, Nicolas Dodin (1734–1803), they represent allegories of Comedy and Tragedy after two overdoors executed by Carle van Loo (1705–65) for Madame de Pompadour at her Château de Bellevue. It is unclear why du Barry decided to appropriate the iconography of her predecessor, and whether she had any part to play in their inclusion on the commode. The side plaques were in fact not made specifically for the commode and had to be extended at the top and bottom to fit their allocated space so it is possible that they were simply recycled on the piece without du Barry's knowledge of their iconographic provenance.

TRANSFERRAL OF EASEL SCENES

Scenes inspired by easel or decorative paintings could also be found directly painted on furniture. For instance, George Brookshaw's's demi-lune console table was decorated using the encaustic method of painting with scenes taken from Angelica Kauffman's engravings *Abra* and *Innocence* published in 1782 and 1783, respectively (Jones 2012: 240). A similar bowfront console table, designed by William Chamber's talented pupil John Yenn (1750–1821) and probably executed in the 1780s for the future George IV at Carlton House, depicts *The meeting of Bacchus and Ariadne on the Island of Naxos* (Figure 1.4). Adapted from a painting by Guido Reni (1575–1642) for the bedroom ceiling of the Queen's House in Greenwich, the scene was skillfully painted, most likely by Giovanni Baptista Cipriani (1727–85) (Kisluk-Grosheide et al. 2006: 184–6). Reni's mythological composition is here rendered in a delicate grisaille. The monochrome treatment of the decoration reminds us that Cipriani would have probably worked from Jakob Frey's print of the 1720s. Yet this treatment also skillfully departs from the original medium to evoke the sculpted forms of classical bas-relief to harmonize with the overall classical idiom of the table reflected through an abundance of laurel leaves, paterae, acanthus, bucrania, and urns.

Contemporary painting could also provide furniture makers and designers with sources of inspiration. In France, Claude Joseph Vernet's series of the Ports de France executed between 1754 and 1765 is arguably one of the country's most spectacular royal commissions. It was fully intended to magnify France's naval and commercial might while simultaneously meticulously recording and aestheticizing contemporary social customs. The king's patronage secured Vernet's career and his picturesque classicizing seascapes soon found a ready clientele among France's urban elite. A small bow-front commode executed about 1770 and attributed to René Dubois (1737–99) fully encapsulates this taste for idealized port scenes. Painted across its front drawers and side panels

FIGURE 1.4 Side Table, *c.* 1780, probably after a design by John Yenn. Fletcher Fund, 1929/The Metropolitan Museum of Art. Photograph courtesy of the Metropolitan Museum of Art.

with *vernis Martin*, the European imitation of lacquerware, the piece was once sold by the Parisian luxury good dealer Charles-Raymond Granchez (dates unknown) in his aptly named shop *Au Petit Dunkerque* (Sargentson 1996: 121–2). Although not a faithful reproduction of one of Vernet's scenes, there is little doubt that the commode would have been inspired by Vernet's royal commission, which was regularly presented to public scrutiny at the highly popular biannual Salon that was held at the Louvre.

A reference to the fine arts is perhaps made physically more explicit in the cylinder desk produced in the late 1770s for the author and polymath Pierre-Augustin Caron de Beaumarchais (1732–99), possibly by the furniture maker Jean-François Leleu (1729–1807). Much of the elaborate marquetry decoration makes specific references to the owner's writings, such as, for instance, the inclusion on the writing surface of a trompe l'œil title page of his pamphlet *Observations sur le Mémoire justificatif de la cour de Londres* published in 1779, or a similarly illusionistic sheet entitled "Considérations sur L'Indépendance de L'Amérique," the latter reflecting Beaumarchais's support for the American insurgents. The desk, however, also alludes to the author's aesthetic pursuits and the contents of his own art collection: the three marquetry panels on the upper section of the desk represent classical capricci after prints by Giovanni Paulo Panini (1691–1765) and are all hinged and fitted with an in-built stand to facilitate their upright viewing (de Bellaigue and Blunt 1974: 308–26). No longer mere static "paintings on woods," the flexibility of the marquetry panels further blurs the boundaries between them and their two-dimensional sources.

GLOBAL ECONOMY

Material culture in the early modern period cannot be understood outside of global commercial networks of exchange between Europe and the rest of the world. Europe's reliance on imported luxury goods, ranging from porcelain and silk to coffee, has been the subject of extensive scholarly scrutiny. As Berg has shown, "in the eighteenth century a global trade in luxuries and manufactured consumer goods provided not just the labour and the materials that went into making of new goods, but the designs, fashions, and sophisticated marketing that shaped the product development of the period. Consumer products, if not consumption more broadly, were forged then in a global economy" (Berg 2005: 331). Foreign and colonial commodities were integrated into European furniture via the extensive use of wood veneers, and it is well known that eighteenth-century French furniture heavily relied on the colorful and lustrous materiality of exotic woods such as mahogany, kingwood, and ebony to name just a few. The repertoire of ornament and motifs in furniture was in turn equally inflected and enriched by those foreign imports (Dobie 2006: 13–37).

The vibrant chintzes known as *Indiennes*, which were imported from India, were "one of the most revolutionary commodities to appear in western markets" (Lemire and Riello 2008: 887). Their exquisite and colorful patterns were widely employed in the domestic interior and for clothing, despite consistent and unsuccessful import bans throughout the seventeenth and eighteenth centuries. A very rare example of the direct influence of printed cottons on furniture is found on a little table attributed to Oeben and now in the Cognacq-Jay museum in Paris. Intended to be used as a writing and toilette table, the piece is ornamented with a marquetry pattern imitating the flowers found on Indian chintzes. Set within a narrow undulating frame, the marquetry pattern is stretched over the tabletop, its sides and legs. Oeben deliberately cut some of the flowers on the top instead of centering them to enhance the illusion of a tucked-in fabric (Alcouffe et al. 2015: 164).

The appeal of Oriental ceramics and their importation to the West has a long tradition, and Chinese porcelain was avidly collected by European elites and ubiquitous in wealthy domestic interiors. Unable to emulate its physical properties, Western potters nevertheless easily succeeded in copying its blue and white aesthetics. A small pavilion designed by Louis Le Vau was built on the grounds of Versailles in 1670. Intended to house the king's collection of Oriental ceramics, it was dubbed the *Trianon de Porcelaine* as its roof and external walls were lined with blue and white earthenware tiles mostly produced in Rouen and Nevers. Pierre Gole was commissioned to produce some of its furniture, an example of which survives today in the collection of the Getty Museum (Table, Pierre Gole, 1670–5; J. Paul Getty Museum, 83.DA.21). The shape of the small table is in itself unremarkable for its day, its design corresponding to contemporary fashions. Gole, however, incorporated white ivory and blue horn adorned with foliate marquetry to match the porcelain displayed in the Trianon's interiors (Sassoon and Wilson 1986: 25; Pradère 1989: 46–7).

LACQUER AND JAPANNING

Prized by European elites since the sixteenth century, the arrival of stocks of Oriental lacquer to the West increased in the seventeenth century with the creation of the English, Dutch, and French East India Companies. As the East Asian resin necessary to produce the precious lacquerwork could not be transported, only finished products, sometimes specifically made for export, were shipped to Europe. They came in a plethora of forms, ranging from small document boxes to rice bowls, large folding screens, or imposing coffers. The desirability of lacquerwork, Japanese in particular, meant that such objects rarely survived intact and that they regularly, though not systematically, underwent processes of dismemberment and recycling onto new pieces throughout the years. These processes severely affected their original shapes and function, but also guaranteed an ongoing supply to an urban clientele yearning for fanciful effect and exotic novelty. Due to their large sizes, lacquer screens and cabinets were more likely to be dismantled to be fitted onto European-made pieces of furniture. The practice originated in the seventeenth century and gained momentum in the eighteenth under the aegis of the *marchands-merciers* who bought from wholesalers or trading companies. In short, French luxury good dealers fueled the development and expansion of costly cabinetmaking using precious and exotic materials such as porcelain, *pietra dura*, or lacquer (Durand 2014: 66).

The Paris-based dealer Thomas-Joachim Hebert (1687–1773) delivered such a piece to Queen Marie Leszczyńska (1703–68) in 1737 for her private study at the Château de Fontainebleau. Stamped by cabinetmaker Bernard II van Risenburgh, the commode is recorded in the inventory of the *Garde-Meuble*, the royal furniture repository, and recycled a large panel taken from the inside of a Japanese coffer for the decoration of its frontal medallion depicting elegant dwellings in a luxuriant landscape. The lateral panels showing vases of flowers also recycled Japanese lacquerwork but the overall black veneer and floral decoration were the work of European japanners, possibly the Martin brothers whose productions were famously extolled by Voltaire (Durand 2014: 248). Not all inclusions of Oriental lacquerwork were as carefully considered as BVRB's commode: a small chest of drawers made by Nicolas-Jean Marchand (1697– after 1755) also delivered to Queen Marie Leszczyńska but this time for her bedroom at Fontainebleau in 1755, exhibits a considerably more arbitrary and illegible iconography in its central medallion. Unlike the carefully composed self-contained scene of BVRB's 1737 commode, Marchand's counterpart included a haphazardly cut and subsequently assembled panel of Chinese lacquer depicting what appears to be the roof of a pavilion (The Wallace Collection, F88). This seeming desultory iconographic treatment on a royal piece fully testifies to the high value ascribed to original Oriental lacquer. Evidently, its motifs and iconography did not need to be intact and legible to be prized.

The desirability of Oriental lacquer encouraged the widespread production of European imitations. Applied to small objects such as toilette boxes and larger pieces like cabinets or even coaches, japanning came in a variety of vibrant hues. The harpsichord made in 1681 by Jean-Antoine Vaudry is thought to be the earliest French object decorated with chinoiserie ornament (Schott 1985: 63; Miller and Young 2015: 121). The case was japanned in black and gold in 1681, while the underside of the lid was painted in red at a later date and by a far less competent hand. The Oriental iconography of the seventeenth-century lacquering is conveyed by the presence of a landscape with pagodas and characters wearing pseudo-Oriental costume. Yet the decoration is based on pastoral scenes by the seventeenth-century French artist Jacques Stella (1596– 1657), testifying to the degree of licence with which the Orient was constructed and interpreted in the early modern period.

A commode executed by Mathieu Criaerdt (1689–1776) via the agency of the luxury goods dealer Thomas-Joachin Hebert was offered to the King's mistress Madame de Mailly in 1742 to furnish her bedroom at the Château de Choisy. While its tripartite division was inspired by the 1737 commode made by BVRB for the Queen, Criaerdt's piece is noteworthy for its exquisite monochrome japanned blue decoration framed by elaborate rococo silvered mounts. The color scheme of Criaerdt's commode evidently echoed Oriental porcelain (and its European imitations). Depicting flowers and birds against a white background, the painted scenes however owe more to Indian printed cottons than to the Chinese or Japanese repertoire of ornament (Durand 2014: 256–7).

The taste for Oriental motifs in furniture outlived the rococo period, and both real lacquer and European japanning continued to be employed on furniture until the end of the eighteenth century, as shown by the extensive output of the *ébéniste* René Dubois whose clientele, as previously seen, included

Catherine the Great of Russia (1729–96). The Orient could also be evoked without the use of lacquer or varnish, and a trope occasionally used by the furniture maker was the inclusion of marquetry panels featuring chinoiseries. The German cabinetmaker David Roentgen (1743–1807), who inherited his father's workshop in Nieuwied, was famed for his mechanically ingenious furniture adorned with superb marquetry and mounts. A small cylinder desk based on a model by the English cabinetmaker Thomas Chippendale (1718–79) has on its front a panel of pictorial chinoiserie marquetry after drawings by the German painter Januarius Zick (1730–97), who regularly collaborated with Roentgen's workshop. The panel would have been originally highly colored, thus creating a striking visual effect. Set on a small stage in a shallow three-dimensional outdoor space, the figures in Oriental costume, reused by the workshop on a number of pieces, are rooted in rococo aesthetics and mark a departure from the chaste neoclassical shape of the desk (Kisluk-Groscheide et al. 2006: 172–6).

Panels of Oriental lacquer were often contained within stylized geometric borders or against the background of geometric patterns. The latter were appropriated by French furniture makers as early as the seventeenth century. André-Charles Boulle repeatedly used the motif of a quatrefoil inserted in interlaced circles on his metal marquetry, the gold and black coloring of the brass and turtleshell further emphasizing the Oriental effect of the veneers (Chastang 2008: 96–7). A century later, the royal cabinetmaker Jean-François Oeben similarly attempted to imitate Japanese motifs, this time through the medium of wood marquetry. For instance, a small mechanical writing and toilette table made *c.* 1764 and exhibiting both rococo and neoclassical stylistic features, is decorated on its front and sides with intersecting circles and cubes, both features deriving from Oriental patterns, as seen on a small late seventeenth-century lacquer box in the collections of the Metropolitan Museum of Art (91.1.672; Wallace Collection, F110). Oeben was in fact particularly fond of cube veneering (known in French as *placage à dés*), employing it extensively on his secretaires and commodes with straight shapes "à la Grecque," the simplicity of the cubic pattern perhaps deemed eminently compatible with the Greek keys and entwined circles generally found on such pieces. A few years later, in the inside of the cylinder desk made for the Comte d'Orsay in 1769, Riesener employed the repetitive quatrefoil in circle pattern discussed above, which he referred to as being in the taste of Boulle, thereby bypassing the Oriental origins of the decoration (Chastang 2008: 99).

TURQUERIES

Exoticism in eighteenth-century French furniture also found its expression through the use of Turqueries, the fashion for imitating aspects of Turkish art and culture. Like Chinoiseries, Turqueries were the products of designers' fertile imaginations. They happily mixed real and imagined exotic features and aesthetic effect was the primary goal. This taste for Turkish ornament needs to be envisaged within a wider cultural framework. The publication of Antoine Galland's *Thousand and One Nights* in several volumes between 1704 and 1717, and the 1721 visit of Turkish ambassadors to Paris had widely contributed to the popularization of an idealized Middle Eastern culture. Permeating all aspects of French art, Turqueries were very much in demand, as evidenced by the publication of Le Hay's *Recueil de Cent Estampes Representant Differentes Nations du Levant* (1714), or by the erotic novel written by Claude-Prosper Jolyot de Crébillon entitled *Le Sopha: Conte Moral*, officially published in 1742. A witty encounter between the world of furniture, Turqueries, and libertinism, the tale is narrated by an Indian Brahmin who finds himself transformed into a sofa against his will until the unfortunate spell is broken by two young lovers losing their virginity on the aforementioned piece of furniture, thereby delivering the narrator's soul. The inclusion of India into the realm of Turqueries is unsurprising as geographical accuracy was of negligible importance. The term sofa, however, was in itself a Turkish word and the first edition of the *Dictionaire de l'Académie Francaise* tells us that "that term came from Turkey, being a sort of day bed [...] being used since recently in France" (*Le Dictionnaire de l'Académie Françoise, dédié au Roy* [Académie Française 1694]: 483). The fashion for Turqueries prompted the creation of a number of Turkish boudoirs in the 1770s, those of the Comte d'Artois and his sister-in-law Queen Marie Antoinette being among the most celebrated and best preserved (albeit in fragmentary and incomplete states). The Turkish Boudoir of the Comte d'Artois at the Palais du Temple in Paris was created in 1777 and overseen by the architects Etienne-Louis Boullée and Pierre Jubault. Its walls were hung with bright yellow silk in an imitation of a Turkish tent, a remnant of which is found today in the upholstery of the seat furniture made for the room, a modern reproduction of the original fabric. Delivered by the joiner George Jacob, the two armchairs and four chairs are his first dated commission to a member of the royal family. The bold saber legs of the seats echo the blades of Ottoman swords, and the cornucopia armrests are filled with luscious exotic fruits. The carved decoration executed by Jean-Baptiste-Simon Rode was originally painted white and incorporates pearl beading and crescent moons, further allusions to the pseudo-Turkish identity of the furnishings (Durand 2014: 435).

Today, a voyeuse, a chair specifically designed to be knelt on to facilitate the viewing of table games, survives in the collections of the Nissim de Camondo Museum in Paris, and testifies to the enduring popularity of Turqueries well into the neoclassical period. It was delivered by George Jacob to Madame Elisabeth's Turkish Boudoir at her country retreat of Montreuil near the Château de Versailles twelve years after that commissioned by the Comte d'Artois for the Temple. Jacob used similar saber legs and the same motifs of crescent moons and pearls on a set of chairs, albeit combined with scallop shells, and an upholstery of blue pastoral Toile de Jouy. Evidently rustic aesthetics were not seen as mutually exclusive to Middle Eastern imagery.

AFTER THE REVOLUTION

The French Revolution of 1789 abolished the guild system in France and severely disrupted the furniture trade. Royal emblems were subjected to quasi-systematic removal. For instance, Riesener was employed by the revolutionary government to replace royal motifs on some of his furniture: substituting the front panel of the commode delivered to Louis XVI's private bedroom at Versailles bearing the King and Queen's monogram with a neutral composition of flowers and a vase (Forray-Carlier 2010: 75–7). Revolutionary fervor also encouraged the use of new motifs glorifying the republican values of equality and duty such as stonemason's levels, Phrygian caps, and *tricolor* flags. A wardrobe in the Carnavalet Museum was aptly "revolutionized" by the inclusion of mottos extolling the values of liberty and fraternity, and by the motif of the eye of providence on its pediment echoing that depicted at the top of the Declaration of the Rights of Man. This decorative political propaganda was, however, happily juxtaposed with the simple prerevolutionary motifs of antique pedestals, vases, and flowers.

In the closing decade of the eighteenth century, obvious and direct political motifs and mottos rarely affected furniture to such an extreme level. Craftsmen instead continued to employ the more traditional and long-standing symbols that had been found in the furniture made pre-1789, such as the laurel of victory, the oak of longevity, or the Roman fasces of the power of jurisdiction and strength in unity, as seen, for instance, on a secretaire by Bernard Molitor (Cleveland Museum of Art, 1979.36). The use of such motifs was in turn sustained by the second wave of neoclassicism known as the empire style that bridged the nineteenth century. Subsequent stylistic revivalisms throughout the nineteenth century ensured that, while techniques in furniture making changed as a result of industrialization, many of the motifs discussed in this chapter did not become obsolete.

CHAPTER TWO

Makers, Making, and Materials

YANNICK CHASTANG

INTRODUCTION

With no abrupt political changes to mark the turn of the eighteenth century, or to derail the social and economic progress made during the seventeenth, eighteenth-century furniture makers continued to be inspired by the new materials and techniques they had discovered in the preceding century. The luxury furniture market was one of the greatest beneficiaries of the technical progress of the seventeenth century and the relatively stable political climate. While regional furniture continued to be traditional in both style and construction, furniture produced for the royal courts and the social elite saw great changes in style and techniques. Provincial furniture, even that made for the aristocracy, was years behind and the changes had very little impact on the type of furniture produced for those of the working class lucky enough to own furniture. The luxury furniture trade represented only a fraction of a furniture industry that was itself relatively small as owning furniture was very much reserved for the wealthier members of society. Because of their exclusivity, retained value, and housed conditions, a very large amount of luxury furniture produced during the eighteenth century has survived. Compare this to regional furniture that was often destroyed by neglect or the damp environment associated with the living conditions of the poorer classes. The study of luxury furniture is therefore made easier by the surviving examples and by the archival sources and documents related to them and, while not necessarily representative of the entire furniture industry, the luxury furniture industry spearheaded changes in design and technique that would eventually be adopted by a wider range of makers.

The seventeenth century introduced European cabinetmakers at the forefront of the industry to a wealth of imported materials, including exotic timbers, tortoiseshell,[1] and mother-of-pearl. European technological developments, furthermore, opened their eyes to the opportunities inherent in the incorporation of known materials in novel ways. Foremost among these was metal. Although wrought iron fittings had been a common feature during the medieval period, in the seventeenth century designers and makers were instead able to use brass. As a result, during the eighteenth century almost every piece of furniture produced with metal fixtures featured brass in the form of gilt-bronze decoration, fittings, and mechanical devices or as brass sheets that could be worked in a technique known as Boulle marquetry.[2] The importance of brass cannot be underestimated. Brass opened the way for new designs and new possibilities but it was also the catalyst that changed working practices. In the large furniture production centers, particularly Paris, the principal European city for the decorative luxury trades, the eighteenth century saw the beginning of collaborative work between specialized workshops and highly specialized craftsmen. While provincial practises generally remained unchanged from the beginning of the century to the end, the proximity of forward-thinking craftsmen of diverse *métiers* in the cities gave rise to great advances in ideas and techniques, many of which would be incorporated into highly ingenious, expertly fabricated pieces of furniture.

The detailed accounts and memoirs of the French royal cabinetmaker Jean-Henri Riesener (1734–1806) allow historians to estimate the cost and time spent on each aspect of a piece of furniture. The pieces of extravagant furniture he made for the French royal court and aristocracy each integrated many different materials and techniques, with gilt bronze being by far the most desirable and expensive form of decoration. The total cost of the roll-top desk made for Louis XV, and delivered in 1769, for example was 62,985 livres (Château de Versailles, accession no. Vmb14454). The cost was divided as follows: one-sixth for the marquetry; one-sixth for the mechanism; slightly less than one-sixth for the design, prototype, bronze models, and woodwork construction; and almost half the total value for the gilt bronze (of which one-third of this, or one-sixth of the total value, was just for gilding). Gilt bronze, sometimes called ormolu, is often used to describe any metallic decorative fittings on furniture. Furniture mounts were, however, most likely made of brass, an alloy of copper and zinc, rather than bronze, which is an alloy of copper and tin. Despite the name, mounts were not always gilded. Lower priced furniture mounts were often made of lacquered brass, imitating the finish of real gilding at a lower cost. High-end furniture would be gilded using the expensive and poisonous technique known as "fire gilding" or "mercury gilding."[3] The study of furniture manufacture in the eighteenth century, however, should not be confined only to the study of cabinetmaking practices, marquetry, or bronzes but extended to a very large array of trades and techniques where innovation and tradition, two opposite mindsets and ideologies, were together the key to a successful furniture industry.

COLLABORATION, TRADITION, AND INVENTION

A seventeenth-century marquetry cabinet would commonly be made entirely in one workshop. However, no less than nine highly skilled workshops were recorded as being involved in the making of a desk for Louis XVI in 1786 (De Bellaigue 1974: 458–65). Besides these nine workshops, a small army of unlisted suppliers and makers of minor parts must also have been involved. The furniture industry of the eighteenth century was thus one of collaboration. There was a constant search for new ideas and designs so that collaboration became the norm; indeed, the only way to produce the masterpieces that the rich aristocracy demanded. This resulted in remarkable and imaginative inventions and innovations that raised furniture from the functional to the highly artistic. Few could have predicted, for instance, that furniture would be decorated with Sèvres porcelain plaques that would be more valuable than the furniture into which they were mounted or that clock mechanisms would evolve into mechanical devices that were then incorporated into the multifunctional furniture of the 1760s Parisian maker Jean-François Oeben (1721–63).

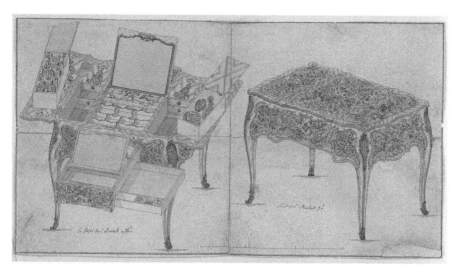

FIGURE 2.1 Design for a toilet-table, mid-eighteenth century. Photograph courtesy of Jérôme Letellier. © The National Trust, Waddesdon Manor.

Furniture made by David Roentgen (1743–1807) in Neuwied, Germany, required the expert input of Johann Christian Krause (1748–92), known for the development of wood polishes and varnishes, to devise a finish that would not spoil Roentgen's colorful marquetry. The list goes on. With *haute societé* desiring novelty and excellence in craftsmanship, and prepared to pay thousands of livres for each hand-worked masterpiece, furniture makers inspired by the scientific advances of the Enlightenment reached fantastical heights of design, innovation, value, and workmanship. While innovation was key to the success of the French eighteenth-century furniture industry, the freedom required to experiment and innovate was difficult to achieve. All work was controlled by traditional guilds whose charters and modes of operation dated back to the Middle Ages (de Lespinasse and Bonnardot 1879: 574). Guild membership was almost unavoidable, training was regimented and secrets protected. Each guild, whether it was woodworking or metalworking, whilst there to look after members in bad times also regulated its members with quality control and a strict tax collection system that would be regarded as unfair today. There was no authorized crossover of activity, resulting in bitter disputes with particular tensions arising between cabinetmakers and bronze makers (Pradere 2003). For example, on three occasions in 1722, 1735, and 1743, the Parisian Corporation of Bronze makers sued cabinetmaker Charles Cressent (1685–1768) for making bronzes in his cabinetmaking workshop. The court case resulted in Cressent having to pay damages to the Corporation for the offense and an interdiction against employing his own bronze makers.

Progress in acquiring the necessary freedom, though slow, was inevitable. The benefits of new machinery, new ideas, and alternative methods eventually outweighed guild disapproval and repression. The publication of minutely detailed encyclopedias and technical treatises, some written by the makers themselves, exposed many of the trades' most closely guarded secrets. The most detailed treatise on the art of carpentry, furniture making, coach making, and even garden trellis making, was published between 1769 and 1782 by the son of a carpenter, André-Jacob Roubo (1731–91). With more than 1,300 pages of text and 389 detailed plates of engravings, the Roubo treatise is still regarded as the most comprehensive encyclopedia about eighteenth-century woodworking. Writing this treatise must have presented significant challenges to the son of a carpenter and there was no one better positioned than Roubo himself to describe the effort of discovering the many secret methods and writing about them. In the chapter on wood dyes, Roubo wrote:

> La teinture des bois eft d'une très-grande importance pour les ébéniftes [...] Cependant les ébéniftes ont toujours fait un très-grand fecret de la compofition de leurs teintures, afin de s'en conferver la jouiffance exclufive, et de ne pas trop augmenter le nombre des ouvriers: de-là vient que la plupart des compofitions

dont les anciens ébéniftes fe fervoient, ou ne sont pas venues jufqu'à nous, ou bien ont été mal imitées; et que celles dont on fe fert a prefent, ou font defectueufes, ou font défectueufes, ou bien, fi elles font bonnes, ne peuvent fe perfectionner, vu que ceux qui les poffedent en cachent les procédés, non-feulement a leurs confreres, mais même a ceux dont la théorie pourroit leur être utile pour perfectionner la compofition de leurs teintures.

(Dying wood is very important to the cabinetmaker [...] however, cabinetmakers have always made great secrets of the dye recipes in order to preserve exclusivity and to stop the increase of new makers. Because of that, the majority of the recipes used by old cabinet makers have not been passed to us, or are not good, or if they are good, they cannot be improved because the people who know the recipes hide the process not only to their colleagues but also to knowledgeable people who know the theory of dying and could help them improve the composition of their dye recipe.)

(Roubo 1772: s. III, p. 792, my translation)

With dissemination of information by many authors such as Jean Felix Wattin (1772), Duhamel du Monceau (1757), and of course the great *Encyclopédie* by Diderot and d'Alembert (1751–72), to name just a few in the French language that were widely distributed and translated, came inevitable experimentation and, with an ever-growing demand for luxury interiors from the nobility and the emerging bourgeoisie, the eighteenth century was a buoyant and dynamic century for furniture. The furniture trade flourished and enough objects survive today to show the scope and brilliance of these makers' works.

ARTISTS AND MAKERS

During the eighteenth century, furniture making was recognized as an art form to a greater extent than ever before. The most elaborate pieces of furniture were celebrated for their triumph of craftsmanship, elegance of form, marquetry, *pietra dura*, and extravagant metalwork. As furniture making was accepted as an art form, so the very best of those craftsmen who produced it became elevated to the status of artists. Jean-Henri Riesener promoted himself to the Parisian market as an artist, choosing to be shown in the act of designing a piece of furniture (Antoine Vestier [1740–1824], Portrait of Jean Henri Riesener, 1786, Musée de Versailles, accession no. MV8136). Yet his daily activity would, to our minds, be more that of a businessman directing a workforce, dealing with clients and coordinating suppliers. Charles Cressent (1684–1768), Thomas Chippendale (1718–79), Bernard (active c. 1730 to c. 1767) (standing for Bernard II van Risenburgh) but above all André-Charles Boulle (1642–1732), Riesener, Jacques Caffiéri (1678–1755), and Pierre Gouthière (1732–1813) were rare in

FIGURE 2.2 André-Charles Boulle, *Nouveaux Deisseins*. One of eight plates drawn and engraved by Boulle and published by Pierre-Jean Mariette, first quarter of the eighteenth century. Photograph courtesy of Yannick Chastang.

that they were famous in their own time: they are the very few makers named in eighteenth-century auction sale catalogs (Verlet 1958: 28). While the legends of these makers as masters par excellence survived well into this century, the study and understanding of eighteenth-century workshops is skewed by a lack of breadth in surviving documentation. Chippendale, Boulle, and Riesener all left behind an abundance of written documentation upon which nineteenth-century furniture historians could embellish their legends. However, there were plenty of workshops whose demise was met with obscurity. Recent archival research has added many previously unknown names to the list of master cabinetmakers compiled by these early historians. For example, despite its large and unmistakable maker's stamp "Leleu" (Jean-François Leleu [1729–1807]), and the very obvious similarities with known work by Oeben by whom Leleu had been trained, a small worktable (F110, Wallace Collection; Hughes 1996: 1068, cat. no. 210) bought at Christie's in June 1864 by the 4th Marquess of Hertford and now in the Wallace Collection in London was ascribed in the auction catalog to "David de Luneville" (David Roentgen). Leleu was not a well-known French cabinetmaker in the nineteenth century but twentieth-century research has conclusively disproved this attribution, demonstrating that this table is unlike anything in Roentgen's oeuvre. In fact, Comte François de Salverte compiled the first dictionary of eighteenth-century cabinetmakers *c.* 1923. It contained long entries for hundreds of makers who were previously unheard of, including Leleu, Jean-Pierre Latz (*c.* 1691–1754), and the three generations all named Pierre Migeon (active *c.* 1637–1775), among others. Today, researchers continue to unearth new names in an effort to attribute works more correctly; research that, given what is now known of eighteenth-century working collaborations, may prove fruitless. Recent work by the Bayerisches Nationalmuseum in Munich has shed light on a large production of Boulle marquetry furniture that, until only a few years ago was commonly attributed to French workshops (*Magnificent Furniture at the Munich Court—A Close Look at Baroque Décor* 2011). Equally interesting was the rediscovery in 1991 of the work of Bernard I van Risenburgh, a Dutch cabinetmaker working in Paris (d.1738) (Augarde and Ronfort 1991).

Parisian workshops were relatively small. The workshop inventory of Joseph Baumhauer (1747–72), for instance, compiled after his death, listed only eight benches while that of Jean Pierre Latz, who died in 1754, had nine. These were both very successful workshops and we can suppose from these and other inventories that a typical workshop would comprise about eight makers and a couple of apprentices working under one roof and under the name of the master (Verlet 1968: 74). Small workshops were the norm and larger workshops could only flourish in premises that were under the protection of the king of France or, to be precise, in any special circumstances where makers would benefit from freedom from restrictive guild regulations. Boulle had a large workshop outside the strict French guild regulations at the Louvre, comprising nearly one thousand square meters and employing at least fifteen cabinetmakers as well as many bronze workers and apprentices during the first quarter of the eighteenth century (Ronfort 2009: 45). Riesener's workshop in the 1770s at the Royal Arsenal of Paris, based simply on its output, was certainly larger than was usual for the period even if no accurate number of craftsmen can be estimated. Outside the strict French guild regulations and outside France itself, cabinetmakers with an entrepreneurial drive developed even larger workshops but these larger workshops were still rare. David Roentgen, for example, employed around eighty craftsmen in his Neuwied workshop in the 1780s (Voskuhl 2015: 109) and, during the third quarter of the eighteenth century, Thomas Chippendale's workshop in London employed an estimated fifty craftsmen. When Sophie von La Roche visited the workshop of George Seddon (1727–1801) in 1786, at that time considered to be one of the most successful furniture makers in London, she wrote about the unusual size and set up of this workshop with an incredible four hundred workers laboring on all aspects of furniture making (Beard and Gilbert 1978: 793–8; Gilbert 1997b: 1–29).

Despite the generally small size of workshops, however, furniture production during the eighteenth century was prodigious. In Paris, the numerous workshops supported one another, often subcontracting different aspects of their work to others deemed more qualified, cheaper, or simply more available to carry out the task. This supply of luxury furniture was motivated by unprecedented demand that was in turn driven by a new breed of merchants of *objets d'art*, or *marchands-merciers*, who were at the forefront of interior design and fashion. They were shopkeepers, interior decorators, and general contractors and were the designers and commissioners of many pieces of furniture and other decorative art. The *marchands-merciers* worked inside their own guild system and allowed for a crossover between trades, mounting brass onto porcelain or combining furniture with Japanese lacquer or porcelain plaques. This system of communication and collaboration between makers would have been difficult without the directorship and financial investment of the *marchands-merciers*. Few cabinetmakers could have afforded *pietra dura* panels or porcelain plaques and the furniture trade relied on the *marchands-merciers* to fund and supply expensive parts. Their involvement stimulated trade by exciting customer demand and empowering the makers to greater heights of achievement. The stamping of furniture was mandatory by the guild of Paris during the second half of the eighteenth century but was not necessarily done, especially if a piece was to go straight to a buyer or to a *marchand-mercier*. Many cabinetmakers became *fournisseurs*, or purveyors of furniture, rather than operating in isolation. Buyers would still go directly to the cabinetmaker and there were many comfortably established makers who would subcontract most of their pieces and sell them under their own name, Léonard Boudin (1735–1807) being one example. The practice of attaching a name to a piece of furniture became established less as a measure of quality control, as originated by the Guild, and more as a sales ploy, with the name of the dealer taking precedence over that of the maker. There is evidence of some maker's stamps being coarsely removed by the dealer who then applied his own stamps on top, obscuring as much as possible the identity of the true maker (Augarde 1985: 52–7).

The recent understanding of subcontracting has opened many new avenues in the study of eighteenth-century furniture. Furniture scholars for the majority of the twentieth century concentrated on attributing furniture to one specific workshop or maker; today, the approach is more cautious. For example, Gilles Joubert (1689–1785) was historically considered to be a major cabinetmaker. He was appointed *ébéniste ordinaire du Garde-Meuble* in 1758 and succeeded Oeben as *Ébéniste du Roi* upon the latter's death in 1763. In the subsequent decade he is known to have supplied over two thousand pieces to the royal household. Modern research and, in particular, the publication of his post-death inventory show that most of his production was supplied by other cabinetmakers, including Macret, Boudin, and Delorme, all respected makers in their time who have stamps of their own and were listed in Salverte. The majority of the pieces delivered by Joubert to the king in the 1770s seems to have been made by Roger Vandercruse Lacroix (1728–99). In 1773 Riesener succeeded Joubert in his royal appointment and subsequently took over what remained of the Joubert workshop. Despite the large body of work stamped by Joubert, Pradère argues that a mere half a dozen pieces of those delivered to the royal household after 1751 can be attributed to Joubert himself. Modern attempts to identify the real makers of pieces can prove challenging given the collaborative practices of the time.

GUILDS, MASTERS, AND WORKERS

Daily life for the average furniture maker, like that of many tradespeople in the eighteenth century, was arduous. Since medieval times, the guild had imposed strict rules, at every level, governing all aspects of the cabinetmaking industry. Many of these rules were there to protect the interest of the makers and help them during difficult times. Working at night, on Sundays, or during public holidays was not allowed by the guild system, and widows of masters and invalid craftsmen would receive financial help and even lodgings (Verlet 1968). Poor-quality work was not permitted, establishing a minimum standard of manufacture that would guarantee fair competition. Training, however, was long and expensive and the road to success uncertain. Starting out as an apprentice at twelve or fourteen years of age, only a few, from the thousands of furniture makers who worked at the bench, could hope to become masters themselves and set up their own workshop one day. They stipulated the number of years of apprenticeship, the complexity of an aspiring master's "masterpiece" and controlled the number of masters allowed in Paris. No more than 895 masters were allowed at one time by the Paris guild of Furniture Makers and Carpenters during the second half of the eighteenth century. This guild included all cabinetmakers, carpenters, coach makers, billiard makers, and musical instrument makers. It is estimated that of this 895, 280 were furniture makers. Progressing from simple bench worker to master was governed by regulation, personal challenges, and above all, expense. In the 1744 guild regulations a son of one of the six masters in charge of the guild's office in Paris could apply to become a master at the reduced cost of 121 livres, while the son of a simple master would have to pay 180 livres; but if this son was born before his father became a master, then the cost would increase to 292.10 livres. The cost for a simple apprentice with no family in the profession was an astronomical 386 livres. Foreigners installed in Paris had to pay the hugely inflated sum of 536 livres and the complexity of the masterpiece they were required to produce was twice as difficult as a masterpiece for a French maker. With a daily salary of between 1 and 2 livres for a *compagnon* (a qualified maker) during the second half of the eighteenth century, and with the price of 500 grams of bread at about 3 to 4 sous (20 sous to 1 livre), or the price of 500 grams of butter at nearly 1 livre 3 sous, the guild system certainly did not facilitate upward occupational mobility. A conservative estimate is that there were ten bench workers for every master, which means there were about 2,800 cabinetmakers active in Paris under the control of the guild, all with very little hope of progressing further in the profession.

Not surprisingly, many eighteenth-century master cabinetmakers came from dynasties of furniture makers or from other artisanal backgrounds. Being born into a family of cabinetmakers would guarantee an apprenticeship as well as access to the position of master quickly and relatively cheaply. Another route would be marriage, either to the daughter of a cabinetmaking family or, most fortuitously, marrying the widow of a master. Widows were allowed to continue running the workshop of their deceased husband and there is no doubt that Jean-Henri Riesener's marriage to Oeben's widow helped him obtain his mastership very quickly.

There were, however, some alternatives to the strict guild system. A few Parisian makers, specially recognized for their talents or helped by royal patronage, could receive lodgings in workshops and studios protected from the guild regulations such as the Louvre, the Arsenal, or the Gobelins. Additionally, there were areas in Paris, such as the Faubourg Saint Antoine and the Enclos du Temple, to name only two, that were outside the fortified walls of the old city and whose residents had for centuries been granted freedom from guild regulation. This was a delicate situation and cabinetmakers located there were engaged in constant battles as the guild continually tried to overturn this old privilege. There was also a large, unrecorded number of unlicensed craftsmen known as *faux ouvriers* (Thillay 2002) who worked outside the guild regulations. This was a risky way to operate, as being caught would result in the confiscation of all tools and stock.

Despite these vigorous restrictions, many successful makers, thought in 1789 to be about one-third of the Parisian master cabinetmakers, were foreigners. Most came from the areas that now form modern Germany, Belgium, and Holland. Dutch and German craftsmen had a strong tradition in the making of fine furniture, but shifts in economy, political climate, and fortune led to the emigration of many of them. France had become the center of luxury manufacture and the ready market and the considerable patronage available in Paris attracted many newcomers. As the eighteenth century progressed and the size of the foreign communities increased, a support network was established between those originating from the same region. Language barriers were eased and there was the comfort of similar forms of religious worship. The story of Jean-François Oeben illustrates the possibilities for foreign workers with ambition, talent, and presumably contacts. Born in 1721 in Aachen (now in modern Germany on the western border with Belgium), Oeben is known to have been established in Paris by the 1740s (Stratman Döhler 2002). Little is known about Oeben's earlier years and there is no evidence that he trained in Aachen as a cabinetmaker and no evidence of connections with cabinetmakers. His father, a coach driver or *voiturier*, would certainly not have been able to advance Oeben's career. No apprenticeship contract for Oeben has yet been found, but his legacy is that of an exceptionally talented and ingenious craftsman. His furniture would come to combine some of the most refined mechanisms ever seen, suggesting that he may not even have been an apprentice cabinetmaker but could have trained in metal working or clock making. While little is known of his earliest time in Paris, his marriage in 1749 to the daughter of François Vandercruse, an immigrant cabinetmaker from the Low Countries, is documented. In the early 1750s, he is known to have been subcontracted for marquetry works for furniture by the cabinetmaker Jean-Pierre Latz, who was from Cologne, a neighboring city of Aachen. Oeben even managed to secure some of the best available lodgings, first renting a workshop in the Louvre from Charles-Joseph Boulle, before his talents secured him the royal workshop at the Gobelins factory on the death of Charles-Joseph. Bigger and better premises followed on his move to the Royal Arsenal of Paris where space and freedom for a large set-up enabled him to explore in-house all aspects of luxury cabinetmaking, including making gilt bronzes and, more importantly, forging his own metal mechanisms. At the time of his death in 1763, aged only forty-one, Oeben was a celebrated artist-maker, master, and owner of a large workshop with royal patronage, and was delivering some of the most expensive furniture ever made. This was a significant rise for an unconnected immigrant and his success must have resonated all over the Lowlands and German states. His younger brother Simon-François Oeben, who also became a cabinetmaker, soon followed Jean-François to Paris and his sister married the German cabinetmaker Martin Carlin. Not surprisingly, Oeben's successor, Jean-Henri Riesener, who started as an apprentice in Oeben's workshop, came from the neighboring city of Gladbeck and there are many workers listed among Oeben's records with typically German or Flemish names, such as the marqueteur Wynant Stylen. Oeben achieved immense professional success yet his inventory after his death shows that this did not lead to financial reward. The investment in making luxury furniture, the cost of materials and supplies, the lack of payment from an aristocracy that made it a habit not to pay on time, if at all, made it difficult for any cabinetmaker to succeed. Many workshops went bankrupt and Oeben's own, once taken over by Riesener, quickly ran into financial difficulties. What truly attracted these young immigrants to Paris remains a mystery and, given the harsh and obstructive guild conditions, these foreigners must have been extremely talented and unusual in achieving some degree of financial or professional success. In view of the numerous immigrants working abroad during the eighteenth century, it is now common for furniture scholars to question the true Frenchness of French furniture, given that it was made by a majority of German craftsmen, and equally the Englishness of English furniture that was largely made by Huguenot immigrants at the end of the seventeenth century. There is no doubt that immigration and geographical mobility played an important and valuable role in the dissemination of taste and techniques.

In 1791 the *Le Chapelier* law dismantled the power of the guilds in Paris, paving the way for more freedom in creativity and development. There was an entrepreneurial drive among nineteenth-century furniture makers who took full advantage of the lack of regulation to produce works of immense scope and craftsmanship. On the down side, the *Le Chapelier* law also resulted in the loss of protection for workers and this led to poverty and poor working conditions for many nineteenth-century furniture makers. It also resulted in substantially cheaper and poorer quality pieces.

The furniture industry was supported by innumerable other trades, supplying an immense range of goods and products that had a vital part to play in the history of furniture. The best Paris makers had access to exotic materials from all over the world and were prepared to go to considerable lengths in their search for the best-quality products. Despite the repeated hostilities and wars between England and France, Parisian makers relied on English translucent horn for Boulle marquetry and iron key blanks because of their superlative quality. There are no famous names associated with these supportive industries but their contribution was invaluable as was that of the hundreds of women and children employed in various cottage industries producing, among other things, screws. Blacksmiths would forge wrought iron bars and cut them into small pieces, more or less in the shape of a nail. During the eighteenth century millions of small nails were threaded by hand into screws using a hand file. Little is known about the industry of one of the most important elements in furniture making: the glue. Animal glue, essentially gelatine obtained from boiling the bones, tissues, and carcasses of many animals, came from many countries and provinces. Contemporary publications praise English glue as the best (*la colle d'Angleterre*), but also describe glues coming from the tanneries in Paris, or the Auvergne in central France, that were of inferior quality and smelly. Luxury furniture was not simply the output of one talented designer-maker; each piece was the fruit of the inventiveness and hard work of thousands of people and small industries.

FURNITURE MAKING: MATERIALS AND TECHNIQUES

In pre-Industrial Revolution Europe, forward-thinking furniture manufacturers waged a constant battle between the desire to innovate in terms of both design and manufacturing techniques and the limitations of tradition and expectations that restricted advancement. Research and development had no place in the seventeenth-century workshop; experimentation would have been hampered by time constraints, commercial practicalities of demand and supply, and lack of information sharing among makers.

Great changes in Europe's knowledge of science and how things worked paved the way for the eighteenth-century Industrial Revolution but these changes were only made possible by new intellectual movements and changes in economic models, most of which originated at the end of the previous century. The Royal Society of London for the Improvement of Natural Knowledge founded in England in 1660 and the *Académie des Sciences* founded in Paris in 1666 are two of numerous societies and groups of intellectuals and scientists that encouraged and protected research and helped achieve progress in science and technology. The eighteenth century became known in France as "le siècle des lumières" and in England as "the Age of Enlightenment." As a result, all industries, including the furniture industry, and more importantly its supportive industries, experienced great changes during the eighteenth century. What had been almost insurmountable technical challenges, like casting clean and precise brass components or making clean, quality steel, would become common practice thanks to the dissemination of knowledge through numerous encyclopedias and scientific publications that helped with the general understanding of materials. The thirty-five volume *Encyclopédies* by Denis Diderot and Jean le Rond d'Alembert with a print run of 4,255 copies was an unprecedented success and its completion in 1772 overcame much controversy. The king's council, supported by opposition from the Catholic Church, tried to suppress its publication on numerous occasions. The information contained in the *Encyclopédie* was not new and most of its content about trade practises was heavily derived from the *Descriptions des Arts et Métiers* published by the Académie Royale between 1761 and 1788. The less famous *Descriptions des Arts et Métiers* was the result of a project originating as far back as 1675 at the request of the French finance minister Jean-Baptiste Colbert. Colbert and the Colbertist economic model, which encouraged foreign workers to bring their skills to France, were at the source of many developments in France, as was the more widely disseminated Mercantilism model that encouraged tradesmen to relocate throughout Europe during the seventeenth and eighteenth centuries. Greater religious tolerance also promoted geographical mobility. However, while knowledge and innovation spread, the converse result was the formal implementation of protectionist rules and regulations and the application of strict import and export policies. These trade protections reinforced the feudal guild systems, tempering the technological developments promised by intellectuals and scientists.

The "Age of Enlightenment" may have offered many new solutions and opportunities, but for makers themselves, implementing them was inherently challenging. Either the technology described in the *Encyclopédies* was not available to them or they were limited by old-fashioned working practices that could or would not adapt. The transformation of the raw log into planks of woods or veneer sheets, ready to be used by the cabinetmaker, illustrates certain difficulties encountered during the eighteenth century. For centuries, round trees were either split (cleaved) or sawn. Splitting timber, almost certainly the earliest technique used for the preparation of timber for carcass construction and solid wood furniture, worked well for straight-grained oak producing a stable material resistant to shrinkage and warping. However, splitting round logs into planks produced planks that were thicker on one length than the other so needed additional transformation work before they could be useful.

Cleaving timber was extensively used up to the nineteenth century with evidence of its use found on surviving royal as well as provincial furniture. Sawing, however, was the only way to produce veneers and sawing timber by hand, a time-consuming and complicated process, was in use for centuries. Early designs of mechanical sawmills, powered by wind or water, exist from as early as c. 1250, the first of these was a design by Villard de Honnecourt (Boithias and Brignon 1985). Mechanical sawmills were set up all over Europe, often installed near the forests that supplied the raw timber or in boat yards to meet the ever-increasing demands of a growing population for wood in naval construction, buildings, and furniture making. However, this mechanical revolution was not well received by the long established hand-sawyer community. The mill erected in London by Charles Dingley in 1767–8 was burnt down by the pit-sawyers who were worried about losing their livelihoods. Today, studies of historical furniture have failed to produce evidence of mechanical sawmills being used in the preparation of timber for furniture and it appears that mechanical sawmills were not the primary source for furniture timber before the nineteenth century. This is an extremely interesting observation considering that both the working designs and technology to build sawmills existed well before the eighteenth century, but it illustrates how guilds and tradition can restrain development. In *L'Art du Menuisier* by Jacques-André Roubo, published in 1771–4, plate 278 illustrates two sawyers cutting a log into thin sheets of veneer entirely by hand and guided only by their experienced eyes. Roubo claims that ten to eleven sheets of veneer could be obtained for every inch of wood (Figure 2.3). This is an amazing accomplishment considering the thickness of the saw blade, which would have allowed no room for mistakes when cutting expensive exotic timbers. Years of training must have been necessary to achieve this level of precision by hand, but this work was almost certainly exhausting and not very well paid. The resistance to using modern machinery in the preparation of veneer must be attributed to human preference, habit, or guild control. The end of the guild regulations in France in 1791 coincided with the introduction of patent legislation in France and the result is an almost immediate explosion of new techniques and tools that had been previously restrained in their development. In 1814,[4] Maurice Cochot, a cabinetmaker in Auxerre, France, invented and patented a veneer sawmill made, apart from the blade, almost entirely of wood. The simplicity of its design means that it could well have been invented a hundred years earlier but, to date, no evidence of mechanical saw marks on veneer have ever been found on furniture produced before the nineteenth century.

In many cases, the old ways were quite satisfactory and there was no need for change. Abrasive paper, rarely the subject of academic or even trade publications, offers a representative insight into the eighteenth-century workshop. All furniture, from the simplest solid piece to the finest marquetry tour de force will, during their creation, need the rough wooden edges to be smoothed away. Sandpaper, nowadays cheap, disposable, and a staple of any DIY tool kit, was not widely available until the mid-nineteenth century. Securing abrasive dust onto a cloth or backing paper to make what is today known as sandpaper (Edwards 2000: 1) was impossible with the glues available at the time and makers looked to nature to resolve their problems. Some reeds were known to have abrasive properties (such as the common *prêle*, known as horsetail or in Latin *equisetum*) but the most widely used abrasive product was fish skin, particularly that of the dogfish. Dried, and known as shagreen,[5] the dermal dentils, effectively the small sharp projections on the surface of the fish skin, provided an abrasive surface that could be rubbed over the wood. Nearly all grades of abrasion could be obtained from one fish, the main body producing a coarse abrasive with the tail of the fish producing a much finer abrasive. It served its purpose well and its use was still being recommended to cabinetmakers in Holtzapffel's publication of 1846 (Holzapffel 1846).

Throughout the centuries, furniture makers have desired strong, glossy, almost transparent, and easy to apply long-lasting varnishes, polishes, and protective finishes. To this day, even with the range of modern synthetic resins available, the perfect finish is yet to be developed, and woodworkers and scientists still regularly address themselves to the challenge. Prior to the twentieth century only natural products were available including tree sap resins or animal by-products. Shellac, an important lacquer resin, was not as widely used in the eighteenth century as first thought. Shellac is obtained from the cocoon of an Indian tree insect but was only available in a dark reddish brown color. Shellac was certainly favored for dark mahogany or rosewood furniture but it was too dark for colorful marquetry or light colored woods. Clarifying shellac by removing the wax content is thought to be a nineteenth-century invention and prior to clear, dewaxed shellac, only a handful of pine resins (including sandarac, one of the main components in historical recipes) were translucent and almost colorless. Tolbecque (1903) produced an extensive list of historical transparent finishes, supposedly for musical instruments, but many of his recipes also appear in more general cabinetmaking encyclopedias and treatises. One fascinating aspect of these recipes is their complexity. Modern reconstructions and our better understanding of the properties of certain materials have demonstrated that many of the ingredients added to eighteenth-century polishes increase the complexity of the recipe without necessarily adding any advantages. Overcomplication appears to be a general trend of the enlightened age, the joy of writing things down leading to a tendency to overformulate and overexplain.

Paintings and contemporary representations of furniture certainly show a high level of gloss on furniture finishes. Paintings by the American artist John Singleton Copley (1738–1815) often depict his English and American sitters next to pieces of very glossy furniture in which the sitters' reflections can clearly be seen (Portrait of Paul Revere, *c*. 1768–70, accession no. 30.781 and portrait of Mrs Ezekiel Goldthwait, accession no. 41.84, both by J.S. Copley, Museum of Fine Arts, Boston). These paintings, together with the multitude of published recipes for glossy varnish, would suggest that furniture at the time was generally finished with thick, shiny polishes. However, this is contradictory to common belief that glossy "French polish" was invented at the beginning of the nineteenth century. The level of gloss and thickness of contemporary finishes is still open to discussion (Bowett 2002: 167–8; Stichting Ebenist 2014) and while it was possible to achieve a glossy and transparent polish during the eighteenth century, there are doubts about its practicality. The "best white Polish" by Stalker and Parker, published in 1688 and reviewed, translated, and republished by many authors after that date, including Jean Felix Wattin during the second half of the eighteenth century, is a very successful recipe, as proven by modern attempts to replicate it. However, although successful, modern reproductions have demonstrated that it is an extremely slow-drying varnish and questions must be asked about whether commercial makers would truly have used it. Unfortunately, our study and understanding of furniture is limited by the lack of original surviving examples to study: varnish was commonly removed and reapplied during regular restoration. However, the study of memoirs and bills can offer an insight into the true practice of the makers in their workshop. It is easy to work out how long Jean-Henri Riesener and his colleagues took to repair on site Louis XV's roll-top desk, and the memoir makes it clear that Riesener did not have the physical time to use any of the slow-drying varnishes proposed in the treatises. In fact, a few years later in 1786, Riesener was billing the Crown for simple wax polishes. One must therefore be extremely cautious in creating a picture based only on treatises and published encyclopedias. These books were not necessarily written by craftsmen or written with the productivity of a commercial workshop in mind.

While many technological challenges were met by readily available natural resources or clever inventions, some technological challenges could not easily be overcome during the eighteenth century. Screws, as mentioned above, were made by hand and there was no easy alternative until the invention of a metal lathe with thread-cutting facilities opened the door for mass-produced screws, (Rybczynski 2001) but commercial success was attained only during

FIGURE 2.3 André-Jacob Roubo, L'art du Menuisier Ebéniste (1772), section III, plate 2P78. Two sawyers cutting a log into thin sheets of veneer, entirely by eye without any mechanical guides. Photograph courtesy of Yannick Chastang.

the following century. Technical advances in furniture making were dictated by need, inventiveness, and technical limitations and controlled by commercial reality and guild regulation. The Age of Enlightenment was a pivotal point in the history of manufacturing techniques and, while it may not be obvious at first sight, it was only thanks to the numerous advances in technology that furniture of the quality associated with the eighteenth century could be produced. At their height these pieces integrated some of the finest and most complex manufacturing processes developed at the time, comprising porcelain, bronze casting, gilding, glassmaking, metallurgy, and so on.

Despite these constant tensions between people and technology, the day-to-day manufacture of furniture saw many interesting changes during the eighteenth century. Some of these developments are so significant that they are still in use today. The construction of a simple drawer exemplifies this point with its construction slowly evolving to become, by the end of the century, a model that is still in use today. Early eighteenth-century drawers were constructed on the principle of a box, with two sides, a back and a front assembled with traditional dovetails and with the bottom panels glued and nailed in position. The bottom panels of most drawers were large and suffered from natural shrinkage and expansion. In a dry season the drawer would run loose and in wet conditions the drawer would remain stuck inside the piece of furniture. The movement of the wood would also result in cracking. Toward the 1760s, the construction of the drawer was completely redesigned to our present form. By 1760 the best and most innovative Parisian workshops would be making bottom panels that were not glued or nailed in position. The thickness of the two sides, back and front panels was slightly increased to allow for a groove to be cut into them, into which the bottom panel would freely sit so that it could expand or shrink without causing damage or inconvenience. It was a simple solution, but one that had taken centuries to develop.

While cabinetmakers continued to operate along traditional lines, adopting new practises at a generally slow pace, drastic changes were taking place in the metalworking workshops. New metallurgical processes, invented mainly in England, included the puddling furnace, which was used to create much-improved quality iron, and in turn better steel. This technology kept the impurities of the fuel powering the blast furnace separate from the iron, resulting in a cleaner product. This cleaner, less brittle iron could be rolled and reworked, another eighteenth-century development. Brass, used for ormolu and, in sheet form for Boulle marquetry, is an alloy of copper and zinc. For centuries, metallic zinc was extracted from calamine ore in Europe, but, not on a commercial scale. The production of brass using calamine ore instead of metallic zinc resulted in low zinc brass of average quality. With the development of new smelting techniques patented by William Champion in 1738, metallic zinc became more widely available during the second half of the eighteenth century and the quality of castings increased dramatically. Recent scientific analyses clearly demonstrate a slow increase in the amount of zinc in the brass alloy, enabling better casting but, above all, better soldering with the higher zinc content. With the improvements in quality of the raw materials and alloys, bronziers were able to push the boundaries of bronze making. At the apex of bronze making the name of Pierre Gouthière is synonymous with work of the highest quality. Even today, the quality of Gouthière's mounts and mounted vases has arguably never been matched, with many technical aspects of his production still cloaked in mystery. While very traditional in his hand chasing, the jewel-like quality of his casts exemplifies the progress made during the eighteenth century. Gouthière is credited with the baffling "dorure au mat," a matt fire-gilding process that has proved impossible to explain. Fire gilding, or mercury gilding, an ancient gilding technique used on what was called during the eighteenth century "ormolu," produced the best gilding, with differentiation of matt and burnished that no other technique has ever matched. During the middle of the eighteenth century, the matt gilding process was developed using chemicals and etching agents yet, despite being described in *L'Art de Dorer le Bronze* by Jean-Pierre-Joseph d'Arcet in 1818, the process of matt gilding is now lost and the handful of modern mercury gilders around cannot replicate the finish successfully. These difficulties in replicating the quality of the work and gilding associated with Gouthière certainly augmented the reputation of Gouthière but also demonstrate that, by the end of the eighteenth century, Parisian bronze making had reached a level of unmatched quality.

FURNITURE DESIGN, CREATION, AND INNOVATION

Makers supplying the top end, aristocratic market were those most likely to look to take advantage of the new technological advances. Some designs and construction models are so complex that even today we struggle to comprehend the level of resourcefulness involved, and the wide range of technologies and contrivances they entailed. The historian is continually faced with evidence of unusual finishes or techniques that further challenge our understanding of eighteenth-century manufacture. For example, the presence of mercury on some Boulle marquetry made of pewter and tin is a recent discovery. The author has speculated that an application of mercury would give a desirable mirror-like finish to the Boulle marquetry but no contemporary documentary sources have been found to date (Chastang forthcoming). For those cabinetmakers working at the high end of the market, surface appearance was everything and they looked to the new technologies to inspire their innovation and novelty. But beneath the extravagant surfaces, construction was often basic and, in a large majority of cases, decidedly inferior. A scholar who has the privilege to study the carcase construction of an extravagant piece will be surprised by the basic and poor quality of some pieces. Unfortunately rarely illustrated (for illustrations of furniture construction, see Wilson, Bremer-David, and Weaver 2008), pieces by makers such as Jean-Pierre Latz, Léonard Boudin, or even André-Charles Boulle, to name only three, could have crudely constructed undersides and poorly finished insides. This remains difficult to explain considering the quality control measures of the guild system. It is perhaps best explained as cost saving rather than as an inability to produce better.

For those makers responding to a demand for originality and extravagance, durability was not necessarily an issue. Marquetry has never been resilient to changing climatic conditions and it was usual for a maker, sometimes the original, sometimes a restorer, to attend to the piece by regularly regluing the elements and reapplying a finish. On numerous occasions, Riesener was called to Versailles to restore the furniture. Riesener's memoirs of 1774 show him restoring a Boulle wardrobe, now at the Louvre, that was apparently in a very dilapidated state. Similarly, Gerrit Jensen, in the spring of 1699, billed Kensington Palace for "mending ye Varnish and Polishing ye Marquettree Tables and Stands and Bookcase and varnishing the clockcase in the Gallery" (Fryman 1689–1714). These makers were not looking to conserve the past; their brief would have been to make the pieces appear as good as new. Regilding furniture was common in an age when smoking fires, candles, and general pollution would have resulted in grimy gilding. Marquetry color was fugitive and, while Roubo believed that his best white varnish would perfectly "seal" the color of the marquetry and stop it from changing, the truth is that no varnish could prevent natural discoloration when exposed to sunlight. Riesener certainly knew the truth and regularly scraped and polished his marquetry to revive the colors. This worked for a while but marquetry tends to be less than a millimeter thick, therefore only a couple of scrapings and sandings were possible before holes appeared in the thinned surface.

Once the owner no longer admired the piece, it was entirely normal for elements to be reworked and reincorporated into more fashionable furniture. There are few surviving seventeenth-century *pietra dura* cabinets as many of these pieces were broken up and reused in the eighteenth and nineteenth centuries in more fashionable furniture. The *marchands-merciers* Claude-François Julliot (d. 1794) and Dominique Daguerre (*c.* 1740–96) specialized in acquiring old cabinets and commissioning makers such as Adam Weisweiler (*c.* 1750–*c.* 1810) to incorporate the precious elements into some of the finest pieces of neoclassical style.

Unsurprisingly, the most detailed manufacturing accounts are for the most extravagant pieces ever produced. These accounts are a testament to the difficulties faced by any maker pushing the boundaries of fine furniture making. When Jean-François Oeben started making the famous roll-top desk for King Louis XV, no doubt the king did not expect it to take nine years to complete, or that it would cost an outrageous 62,985 livres, almost 150 times the average annual salary of a qualified maker. The desk is the most expensive piece ever made for Louis XV, and the second most expensive piece acquired during the *ancien régime*.[6] The death of Oeben in 1763 jeopardized the project but his successor Jean-Henri Riesener gave a clear account of its completion in his memoirs. The documentary evidence related to this desk was published by Verlet in 1955 (Verlet [1955] 1992: 65) and forms a fascinating description of the manufacturing process of one of the most extravagant pieces ever made.

The creative side of the desk's manufacture has historically been romanticized. However, makers were not necessarily artists or even the designers of the pieces. The idea of portraying a maker as an artist was one Riesener and Roentgen were quite happy to promote and nineteenth-century historians, in a desire to elevate furniture to a recognized art form, continued the trend and invented romantic biographies to support their theories. Riesener's writing, as well as his choice of portrait, shows his desire to elevate his status beyond that of a craftsman. His memoirs' account of the roll-top desk certainly distorts the truth regarding the design of the marquetry and was another way to justify the extravagant cost and to take personal credit for some of the design aspects. Riesener claims that the marquetry designs were specifically drawn and painted for the desk.

However, it was recently discovered that the floral marquetry was heavily based on Louis Tessier's published flower studies (Chastang 2007: 115–26). The memoirs provide an important insight into the making of a piece but should be treated with caution as the design of this roll-top desk undoubtedly owed a considerable debt to various makers, artists, and above all, contemporary and available published materials. Riesener was a master at appropriating external sources and coordinating contributions from a variety of sources to produce the masterpieces for which he is famed, but his career, according to our modern definition, is more recognizable as that of a shrewd entrepreneurial businessman rather than an artist.

The best makers were not necessarily the best designers. Marquetry would have required specialist draftsman skills and those that could design marquetry were unlikely to be those who could design a prototype piece of furniture. Sharing of designs and use of common sources was the norm. For example, flower shapes based on Tessier designs are found not only on pieces by Oeben and Riesener but also on marquetry by Roger Vandercruse Lacroix and David Roentgen, with each maker treating and interpreting the original Tessier designs in their own personal way, often related to their technical ability. Very few designs for furniture from this period exist today (Alcouffe 2015: 48–52) and those that do are mainly small-scale chalk drawings. Occasionally these drawings approximate to finished items, with some dimensions and maker's instructions, but most of them differ substantially from any finished piece to the point that they appear more as speculative designs offered to potential clients. The Bibliothèque of the Musée des Arts Decoratifs in Paris has a collection of drawings of furniture designs by André-Charles Boulle. Some of these drawings are finished to a high degree, while some are only sketched ideas. However, Boulle's drawings are almost unique in one respect: they were almost certainly drawn by Boulle himself and not by an architect or a *marchand-mercier*. Very few makers had any drawing ability and, recognizing this, a free drawing school was opened in Paris in 1767 by the painter J.-J. Bachelier to address this deficiency. The school, however, achieved very little success and was not well received by the cabinetmakers (Leben 2004).

Today, cabinetmakers require a detailed set of full-scale construction drawings before they start work. However, there are no surviving full-scale designs that predate the nineteenth century. The closest thing to a full-scale design that has ever been found is a drawing on the underside of a drawer in a Pierre Langlois commode at Woburn Abbey, in the collection of the Duke of Bedford. This part construction drawing, sketchily drawn in pencil on a piece of wood, is indicative of the little time spent making full-scale drawings.

We know from Riesener's memoirs and other sources that the first stage of design came in the form of a small wax model. Very few of these wax models have survived (Pallot 1987: 41) though we do have a 1780 small wax model of a chair, previously in the collection of Hector Lefuel, made under the direction of Jacques Gondoin, and which was executed at one-seventh of the finished dimensions of the chair. It also shows various options of legs and arms for the same chair. These wax models, as for most of the drawings that have survived, must have been working models, and not finished versions (Plate 8). The next stage was the making of full-scale models in soft wood. These full-scale models not only gave a better representation of the finished object but also clay models of the gilt bronzes could be fitted directly onto them. Boulle's workshop inventory of 1715 lists many "modeles en bois blanc," namely, plain wooden models that must have been used for this purpose. François Linke, active in Paris during the early twentieth century, was still making furniture in exactly the same way and the study of Linke's archive does in fact offer a fairly good insight into working practises that had remained unchanged since the eighteenth century (Payne 2003). Today, of course, 3D computer modeling allows furniture designers a quick way to achieve the same result. Even toward the end of the twentieth century, it was still common practice to create a succinct "plan sur planche," or a drawing on a wood board giving essential information including proportion and dimensions. This would have been a perfectly logical approach during the eighteenth century when paper was an expensive commodity. Studies of eighteenth-century furniture often reveal that many changes of direction were taken during the construction of the piece. There are many unpublished examples of mistakes, badly placed joints or moved panels synonymous with a change of mind during early construction. The first known *bureau plats* or writing tables were made by Boulle *c*. 1700 and show interesting examples of modification in the course of construction. The large *premiere partie* and *contre partie* pair, one previously in the Wildenstein collection (Christie's London 2005) and its counterpart now at Uppark House, property of the National Trust, both show evidence that the recessed back panel had to be removed after it had been fixed in place. This removal was necessary to allow access for clamping and engraving. Later desks securely attributed to Boulle all have back panels that can be taken off with the removal of screws. Another example of modification during construction is the pair of *c*. 1770 cabinets stamped by Dubois now at Stratfield Saye House, in the collection of the Duke of Wellington. One of the two cabinets' carcases had blocks and wood added in an unorthodox manner, clearly with the intention of reworking the shape until the desirable form was achieved. The second cabinet has none of this awkward construction and clearly benefited from the experimental work done on the design of the first that should be regarded as the prototype for this model of cabinet. This desire to experiment with and play with the proportions and shape of a cabinet show the maker's desire to move his furniture toward art, introducing a sculptural aspect and taking furniture beyond function. Rarely, even when of identical design and originating from the same workshop, are two pieces of furniture constructed in exactly the same manner. Each piece reflects the individuality of the maker responsible for it and there are often small degrees of variation, dependent on the craftsman's personal abilities and limitations.

Attributing an object on the basis of its execution, in an age of habitual subcontracting and absence of technical blueprints, is dangerous. However, there are examples of workshops that were known to produce better quality work. The extensive study of Roentgen furniture, compared to pieces by his contemporaries, demonstrates that, while the design of the furniture is almost identical and, on this basis, could easily be misattributed, Roentgen's pieces are of markedly superior construction. Whether this was simply the maker's higher level of ability, or whether it indicates that the workshop could charge higher prices and therefore could afford more investment in manufacture costs, it is true that pieces by Roentgen are better made and better resolved than other pieces of the same date. Comparison of the marquetry produced by Oeben, Roentgen, and Lacroix, that use exactly the same engraved sources, also demonstrate that some workshops were better than others, or had access to better standards of craftsmanship from their workers.

Riesener's memoirs provide great detail about the manufacture of the *bureau du roi* and illustrate how the desk's creation combined innovative construction with traditional techniques. The most impressive aspect is the complex mechanism of the locking device. The entire desk, including the tambour and all the front drawers, are locked by only one key. Originally, with a quarter turn of the elaborate key, the tambour would automatically rise to its full extent. A self-rising tambour was a novelty at the time and its invention, an arrangement of numerous metal springs and invisible mechanisms, is credited to Oeben in the mid-1750s. Roubo on Plate 263 of his 1772 *L'Art du Menuisier* encyclopedia publishes drawings of how the spring mechanism works. Riesener decided to go one better than his predecessor and spend one-sixth of the total cost of the desk, just over 10,000 livres, on devising a new spring mechanism that would close the same tambour automatically with a simple turn of the same key. This mechanism contradicts all laws of physics; how can one spring be strong enough to raise the tambour and then a second set of springs be strong enough to lower the tambour against the first set of springs? It was more usual to close mechanical furniture by hand or with a cranking device. However, with innovation came complication. The king's roll-top desk was fragile and was repaired on numerous occasions by Riesener himself until the complex mechanism was finally removed and replaced with a more simple mechanism during the nineteenth century. The exact design of Riesener's ambitious mechanism will remain a mystery forever. Mechanical furniture is perhaps the best example of the use of new technologies. However, the expense in creating them made such pieces a rarity. Other than Oeben and Riesener, the production of such pieces was almost entirely confined to the German father and son workshops of Abraham and David Roentgen, who employed similarly complicated mechanisms.

While Riesener's roll-top desk is innovative in many respects, it also pays tribute to a long tradition of manufacturing techniques. This is exemplified by the making of the marquetry decoration. Until recently, most modern literature assumed that the invention of Boulle marquetry during the seventeenth century had resulted in the demise of the inlaid technique. Boulle marquetry, essentially made entirely using a fine piercing saw, takes the form of a "jigsaw" of veneered elements assembled in a pattern and then stuck onto a backing board. Inlay is when all small pieces are "inlaid" or dug into the solid piece of furniture or plain veneer with a knife. Inlaid decoration is the most ancient form of "marquetry" decoration but cutting hard Boulle brass or turtleshell was not possible with an inlay knife. During the last quarter of the twentieth century restoration of furniture revealed many tool marks and evidence that suggested that a large majority, if not all, furniture decorated with floral marquetry during the eighteenth century was made using the primitive technique of inlay. This is true not only of coarse marquetry decoration but also for the finest marquetry decorations produced all over Europe, including pieces by Chippendale in England and Roentgen in Germany. By contrast, parquetry, a marquetry of geometrical designs, would have been cut using a technique similar to the newer Boulle technique. This coexistence of two techniques shows that makers would happily use ancient techniques if those were either tried or tested or if they answered specific needs. The difficulties of veneering the complex, curved and bombé shapes of the rococo period primarily dictated the return to the inlaid marquetry technique during the eighteenth century. Likewise, joint and carcass construction remained almost unchanged for centuries, drawing on a long tradition of cabinetmaking and carpentry. Dovetail joints, panel construction, frame construction, mortise-and-tenon joints all have their origins in the Middle Ages. However the eighteenth-century fashion for complex marquetry furniture highlighted a particular problem: the marquetry was glued on unstable solid wood carcasses. Solid wood, regardless of its quality, is unavoidably sensitive to climatic changes that all too often cause shrinkage and, ultimately, cracking and lifting of the marquetry. David Roentgen in the 1780s attempted to resolve this difficulty by creating some of the earliest composite panel constructions using narrow cross-grained planks to guarantee a flat and stable surface for his marquetry. Modern plywood or composite panels have since resolved this issue but it is fascinating that, despite the technical limitations of the time, Roentgen was already on the right track.

CONCLUSION

Alongside age-old traditions and a clearly defined guild system, the Age of Enlightenment offered cabinetmakers new opportunities. Information was shared across continents, there were possibilities to work abroad and knowledge of technical developments and refinements was made public. The turmoil of the French Revolution, and the wars that followed as the eighteenth century turned into the nineteenth, certainly slowed down these developments but they also opened new doors and new prospects. As Europe settled into the nineteenth century, furniture manufacture saw the real benefit of the endeavors of the previous generation.

But what is the most important cabinetmaking legacy of the eighteenth century? Which eighteenth-century invention or innovation had the greatest impact for our modern world? Among many, whether drawer construction, the screw, or indeed trade encyclopedias, a convincing argument can be made for another invention of David Roentgen. The mind that devised prototype laminate came up with many a creative solution including that of how to transport his pieces. Eager to sell his furniture throughout Europe, Roentgen developed the "flat-packed" luxury piece. Never before had furniture traveled abroad in such large quantities and never before had furniture needed to be easily dismantled for transport and easily reassembled. Foldable campaign furniture was not new in Roentgen's time but, by 1780, legs on Roentgen pieces of furniture could easily be unscrewed prior to travel. Advances in the quality of mechanical parts and improved, precisely manufactured woodwork meant that the flat-pack was invented to answer the growing demand of a global market. Roentgen's story alone embodies the spirit of the eighteenth century: a maker who challenged every aspect of furniture making while embracing the strong traditions bequeathed to him by his father. Roentgen traveled extensively, operating mainly in Germany but selling all over Europe, and his furniture was recognized in its day for its superiority and originality. David Roentgen's pieces, more than that of any other cabinetmaker, combine the heights of innovation with the quality of centuries of tradition (Koeppe 2012).

CHAPTER THREE

Types and Uses

MARIE-ÈVE MARCHAND

The eighteenth century was a bountiful period with regard to the creation of new types of furniture. A growing concern for comfort, cabinetmakers' increasingly expert skills, and the lure of fashion and novelties were among the factors that contributed to the production of objects that were in keeping with both the new emphasis given to the domestic interior and the decorum of social relationships. For eighteenth-century high society, to dress, write a letter, read, do needlework, play games, drink tea and eat, or even sit on a newly designed daybed were significant means of self-definition that were all, in one way or another, related to the use of furniture. What pieces of furniture were most in favor? How were new types of furniture and social practices articulated? By combining typological and thematic approaches, this chapter will provide an overview of the main innovations of the century. Through an examination of some of the daily activities performed within the domestic interior, it will also offer insights into how the uses of furniture contributed to self-definition and sociability.

The focus will be on furniture intended for bourgeois and high society. This bias is due in large part to the meagre variety of furniture used by the lower classes throughout this period: their possessions were typically limited to multipurpose traditional pieces such as benches and chests that were both less expensive and better suited to their, usually cramped, dwellings.[1]

Priority will also be given to French, in most cases Parisian, and British creations, with, when relevant, excursions to other European countries as well as the United States, which gained its independence from England in 1776. French and British forms often prevailed during this period, thanks in part to the dissemination of pattern books and engravings.[2] For instance, German furniture offered various interpretations of French prototypes; French designs were amongst Spain's principal sources of inspiration during the first half of the century; English furniture was significant to early eighteenth-century Portuguese designers; while Italian furniture was influenced by French, English, as well as German productions.[3] Cabinetmakers established in prominent cities of the East Coast of the United States followed and adapted English designs in ways that recalled goods produced in the settlers' various countries of origin. Similarly, pieces produced in New France shadowed, though with a significant time lag, French types, notably Norman and Breton, to which English features were integrated after the 1760 Conquest.[4] Furthermore, it is notable that French expertise in cabinetmaking was largely due to the work of foreign-born artists and that, as the country's political and economic power declined in favor of England following the Seven Years War (1756–63), France lost its ascendency as Europe's "taste maker" a role assumed during the reign of Louis XIV.

READING FURNITURE: HOW TO DECIPHER THE EIGHTEENTH-CENTURY DOMESTIC SPACE

Pierre Verlet has suggested that French eighteenth-century furniture can be grouped into two categories with regard to their function within the domestic interior: "architectural furniture" and "furniture of comfort and elegance" (1966: 117).[5] This division is sometimes ambiguous for, as Verlet has clearly shown, some pieces—such as certain types of seats—can be classified into both categories (1972: 1:233).[6] Generally speaking, "architectural furniture" refers to pieces of often large dimensions that were meant to stay in place within a room. Considered by Verlet as the "true foundation" of eighteenth-century furniture (1966: 177), they include cupboards and corner cupboards, bookcases, cabinets, desks, commodes, beds and daybeds, as well as various seats aligned against the walls and described by Verlet as *sièges meublants* (seat-furniture). Many of these pieces were included in architectural plans, sometimes even designed by architects, and thus contributed to consolidating a room's symmetry and decorative scheme. This was especially true of console tables, introduced in the seventeenth century, and of pier glasses, which were frequently combined with pier tables or integrated into the paneling.

One of the distinctive characteristics of architectural pieces of furniture was their coordination into ensembles that created unity within a room. The importance attached to the unified décor could be seen throughout Europe. Even before the eighteenth century, chairs and sets of stools were produced *en suite*, although fine upholstery was somewhat sparse in middle- and lower-class homes due to the high price of textiles. However, the coordination of furniture was raised to an unprecedented level of sophistication in Parisian townhouses thanks to the *meuble*.[7] The *meuble* consisted of a set of several pieces that, besides being upholstered with the same fabric and sharing the same colors, carving details, and profiles, was designed to fit perfectly into the room's paneling and décor (Verlet 1966: 127). This can be seen, for instance, in the *Grand Salon* of the Castle of Abondant (1747–50), today exhibited at the Louvre (accession no. OA 11234). In addition to the various seats, daybeds, and bed (when in a bedroom), the *meuble* also included screens, curtains, and wall hangings. Such extensive sets are depicted on the so-called "Choiseul Box" (1770–1), today in a private collection, a snuffbox adorned with miniatures representing rooms from the duc de Choiseul's (1719–85) townhouse (two illustrations can be seen in Praz [1964] 2008: 152–3). What is more, the *meuble*'s fabric could even be changed seasonally thanks to the creation, from the first decades of the century, of removable "drop-in" backs and seats (*sièges à chassis*).

Beyond its visually striking effect and its contribution to the formal articulation of the interior, the *meuble* also informed social practices. Mimi Hellman has argued that while the *meuble*'s components and ornamentation would vary from one house to another—thus partaking in both the expression of taste and the construction of social status—the "formulaic and predictable" quality of the ensemble made it easily legible to high society's insiders (2011: 131, 144–7). Indeed, by looking at the extent and arrangement of the *meuble* within a room, a guest would have been able to gauge the situation's degree of (in)formality and properly adjust their behavior to ensure the success of their social performance (144–7).

While architectural furniture dominated a house's most public spaces, "furniture of comfort and elegance," as termed by Verlet, was to be found in the more private rooms. These lighter pieces, which tended to follow the latest fashion, were moved around the house according to need. Rather than being designed by architects, pieces such as seats were supplied by upholsterers or dealers in luxury items for the aristocracy. *Sièges courants* (or "circulating chairs," in opposition to "seat-furniture"), small tables designed for specific or multiple uses, clocks, lighting appliances, as well as numerous trifles and trinkets—perfume burners, vases, and dog kennels, among others—are all included in this category, which will be further discussed in the course of this chapter.

GETTING THINGS IN ORDER

Due to their function, weight, and dimensions, storage pieces were not meant to be moved around and were thus part of the architectural furniture of a room. Traditional pieces such as cupboards and sideboards were still in use during the eighteenth century, especially outside major urban centers and in the colonies. A new type of cabinet for displaying precious objects—rather than concealing them in tiny drawers—was designed: the glass showcase or *vitrine*. It was probably created by wealthy Dutch merchants who added glass doors to the upper part of their writing cabinets to place imported porcelain on view while keeping them dust-free (Bouzin 2000). Also known as China cases, *vitrines* were part of a broader, long-lasting craze for *chinoiserie* and exoticism. In some instances, the furniture's shape even echoed its content: various models, crowned with pagoda-shaped canopies and resting on intricately carved feet that partook of a Eurocentric understanding of Asian design, were reproduced in Thomas Chippendale's (1718–79) third edition of *The Gentleman and Cabinet-Maker's Director* (1762: plate CXXXV).

One of the most, if not the most, favored storage pieces of the century was the chest of drawers or, in French, *commode*. A convenient—the literal translation of the adjective *commode*—way to replace a simple chest, a cabinet, or a cupboard, it became indispensable in aristocratic and bourgeois houses. Sometimes produced in pairs, it could be placed between windows, facing the chimneypiece, or underneath a pier glass, and its uses were not limited to the storage of clothes as it is often the case today.

The chest of drawers was not, in itself, a new piece of furniture. Chests with large and shallow drawers were used to store liturgical vestments (as in the case of a fifteenth-century example, today in the New York Metropolitan Museum of Art, accession no. 47.101.66) and various chests, as well as other pieces of furniture, had been fitted with drawers throughout Europe at least from the sixteenth century. In America, one of the earliest known dated examples, today at the Winterthur Museum, was made in 1678 and is attributed to the joiner Thomas Dennis (1638–1706) (accession no. 1957.0541). However, by modifying its profile and structure, turn-of-the-century French cabinetmakers transformed the chest of drawers into a luxurious and fashionable object, hence the designation of the *commode* as an eighteenth-century French innovation.

Commodes produced during this period were extremely varied. An illustrious sarcophagus-shaped pair, fitted with two tiers of drawers and standing on an unusual total of eight feet, was among the first French *commodes* designed by André-Charles Boulle (1642–1732), cabinetmaker to Louis XIV. Delivered in 1708, they were intended for the king's bedroom at the Grand Trianon, his intimate retreat (Hughes 2007). Similar models, called either *en tombeau* or *à la Régence*, had curved outlines and three tiers of drawers, the upper one being sometimes divided into two half-drawers for a total of four. The less common *commode en arbalète* had three or four large drawers and a crossbow front. Although these types, popularized during the Regency (1715–23), were produced throughout the first half of the century, a new lighter profile (sometimes called the "Louis XV commode") soon came into favor. Credited to Charles Cressent (1685–1768), it stood on higher cabriole legs, had a shaped apron, and was fitted with two tiers of drawers separated by a narrow horizontal rail. A similar one-drawer *commode* supported by only two front legs and known as *commode en console* was designed to stand underneath a pier glass. The rail separating the drawers disappeared around 1740, thus offering an ideal surface for intricate marquetry motifs or lacquered panels removed from pieces of furniture imported from Asia (Plate 11). The use of doors to conceal the drawers (*commode à vantaux*) also offered a surface ideally suited for ornamentation.

New shapes multiplied from mid-century. For instance, rectilinear *commodes* often had a projecting breakfront central section that gave the illusion of a tripartite vertical division of the two tiers of drawers. Others had a trapezoidal body with inward curved ends. Others still were semicircular or semioval in shape. This latter type, today known as the *commode en demi-lune*, had two tiers of drawers in the center and corner cupboards enclosing shelves on each side. The same profile was given to the *commode à l'anglaise*, except that the side shelves were apparent rather than concealed behind curved doors. *Commodes* were sometimes produced with a pair of matching corner cupboards, or *encoignures*, placed in the corners of a room. Instead of drawers, they had a single *bombé* door enclosing shelves. Corner cupboards were usually surmounted by a shelving unit (*gradin*) used to display porcelains or other precious objects. Finally, a variant of the *commode* was the *chiffonnier*, a tall and narrow piece of furniture introduced around 1750 and usually comprising five tiers of drawers.

English commodes often adopted, with some restraint, French profiles. This was especially true of Chippendale's "French commode tables" with luxurious examples designed in this taste being used to furnish drawing rooms (1762: plate LXV). However, English commodes were more commonly fitted with three tiers of drawers instead of two, as in the type designed by Cressent. The semicircular commode, whose sober lines were suited to the development of neoclassical forms, was very fashionable during the last quarter of the century, due in part to its use by the architects Robert (1728–92) and James (1732–94) Adam. Two decorative pilasters sometimes visually delineated the central space fitted with one or two doors. A shallow drawer could be located in the frieze underneath the top, a feature that was to be found on French examples as well. Chests of drawers based on English designs were produced in the United States, as well as "block-front" types, which were popular during the second half of the century. Also used for other pieces of architectural furniture, the block-front façade, which can be found in Dutch work, is recognizable by its tripartite vertical division with a slightly sunken central part. The innovative "block-and-shell" models, thus named due to the shells that were carved (or carved and applied) on the drawers' block-front façade, are emblematic of the best work produced by prominent Newport, Rhode Island, cabinetmakers such as John Townsend and John Goddard (Heckscher 2005: 104).

Two other showpieces of furniture were used throughout most of the century in England and the United States: the high chest and the chest-on-chest. Commonly found in bedrooms, both pieces were made of two usually independent sections, the upper one being traditionally narrower and shallower than the lower one. Introduced in the late seventeenth century, the high chest, also called chest on stand, was a chest of drawers resting on a table fitted with shallow drawers, an arched or carved apron, and tall legs (Plate 12). This lower section, also called lowboy, could be made as a separate piece of furniture, *en suite* with the high chest, and used as a dressing table (discussed below). Around mid-century, the chest-on-chest or tallboy (also known as highboy in the United States) tended to replace the high chest. Visually more massive, it was made of two superimposed chests of drawers.

THE TOILETTE

The morning *toilette* was a semipublic ritual performed in high society by women and men alike. Widespread in France, this custom was not unknown in Britain: the second scene of William Hogarth's *A Rake's Progress* (1733), entitled "The Levée," satirizes precisely this ritual. The performance in itself finds its origins in the *lever* (rising) of the king, a ceremonial codified by Louis XIV, during which he would get dressed in front of the courtiers who were privileged enough to be invited into the state bedchamber. As for the word "toilette," it comes from the small piece of cloth (*petite toile*) adorning the table used to display the mirror, combs, brushes, cosmetics boxes, perfume flasks, and other beauty implements. Indeed, at first the toilette table was merely a wooden frame covered with fabric and stored while not in use.[8]

Around 1730 cabinetmakers introduced purpose-built toilet or dressing tables equipped with side drawers and, hidden in the central part, an adjustable mirror as well as small compartments to store toilet articles. These tables would have been used with a *fauteuil à coiffer*, an armchair whose curved low back or heart-shaped back was designed to free the neck and shoulders, thus making the hairdressing process easier. Dressing tables varied in their shapes—even heart-shaped tables were created—and in the ways in which they opened. From mid-century, men too had their own dressing tables: larger than women's, they were used to store wigs and powder, and were thus sometimes called *poudreuses*. The *barbière*, or shaving table, used by men for shaving their beard, comprised storage compartments, a tilting mirror, and a basin, such as the one shown in Chippendale's third edition of the *Director* (1762: plate LIV). More generally, English dressing tables, also named bureau tables, looked like chests of drawers with a central kneehole cupboard potentially used to store a wig stand. A folding mirror and compartments could be concealed inside the upper drawer.

The most sophisticated dressing tables, often lavishly ornamented with intricate marquetry patterns, especially in France, were equipped with complex mechanisms. Hepplewhite's Rudd's table, for instance, was fitted with three retractable mirrors that enabled the sitter to see themselves from various angles simultaneously (Hepplewhite & Co. 1788: plate 79). According to Verlet, such ingenious pieces of furniture owed much to the inventiveness of German cabinetmakers such as David Roentgen (1743–1807) (Verlet 1972: 2:87). Furthermore, many of these tables concealed implements dedicated to other daily activities such as eating, drinking coffee, tea, or chocolate, writing, reading, or handwork. Some could even be transformed into bed tables by removing the legs.

While this versatility might have been useful while traveling, such combination tables were most likely meant to be used at home. This multifunctional dimension indicates that the toilette was not merely a vain and frivolous ritual,[9] but also what Kimberly Chrisman-Campbell has termed a "vital exercise in taste and sociability" (2011: 53). Indeed, a woman's toilette could be both the occasion to compose herself by staging her grace and taste, and an opportunity to exert her political influence by meeting with prominent guests with whom she could conduct business in an environment that was not regulated by the inflexible laws of court etiquette (71). Furthermore, as Chrisman-Campbell has argued, "a lengthy toilette did not necessarily imply a self-indulgent waste of the morning hours," for "it was during their toilettes that women read books, wrote letters, breakfasted, shopped, entertained, and studied music or languages" (71).

WORKING AND LETTER WRITING

The desk and the writing desk, or secretary, were the two main types of furniture used for writing. While the first was associated with business, as well as political, economic, and state affairs (Sargentson 2008: 33–50), the second was related to personal correspondence, an activity that acquired a new importance notably as a means of self-empowerment for women (Goodman 2009). This distinction, which was visible in the structure of each type—the writing surface of the desk was visible, whereas that of the secretary was usually smaller and could be concealed from view—also entailed a gender division. Women and men both used a secretary for their personal matters, but the desk was deemed a masculine type not suited for women because, as Dena Goodman has pointed out, the latter "were not admitted into the ranks of professionals, and ladies were not expected to engage in work" (2011: 186–7).

In France, one of the most popular types of *bureau* or desk, used throughout the century, was a large flat writing table named the *bureau plat*. In its most typical form, this more or less rectangular-shaped desk introduced as early as 1672 stood on four elegant legs and was fitted with three drawers underneath its leathered top. Toward mid-century, it was sometimes equipped with what might be described as a "filing-cabinet" (*cartonnier* or *serre-papiers*), a shallow box comprised of drawers and pigeonholes that was either mobile or joined to one end of the table's top. Found notably in libraries and cabinets, the *bureau plat* was used with a new type of seat, the desk chair (*fauteuil de cabinet*). Usually cane or leather upholstered, it had arms, a low curved back, and a deep prominent seat sometimes supported by a front leg. This unusual and innovative shape, which somehow recalls the bidet introduced during the first decade of the century, was specifically designed to support the thighs while leaning forward to write (Roubo 1772: 643). Desk chairs with a circular revolving seat were also created.

The library table, or pedestal desk, of which Chippendale offered various designs (1762: plates LXXVII–LXXXV), usually stood in the center of British libraries, as can be seen on the cover of this volume. With its wide rectangular or square top, this desk provided a large central space for the sitter's legs, flanked on each side by two pedestal feet (four when it had a square top) fitted with drawers or doors. Such a desk offered enough space to accommodate two to four persons.

The English writing desk, or bureau, was a case piece standing on short bracket feet and fitted with drawers and a slant hinged front that, once opened, revealed pigeonholes and rested on retractable supports to form the writing surface. This type, which combined the convenience of the commode and the privacy of a lockable writing surface, was adopted throughout Europe and in the United States. Among the numerous variations based on the English bureau were the bureau-cabinet and the bureau-bookcase, surmounted by a tall cabinet and a bookcase, respectively. Both were introduced during the first half of the century and recalled late seventeenth-century writing cabinets made in the Netherlands. Similarly, the German *Schreibschränke* were heavy pieces of furniture with bulbous shapes fitted with a variable number of drawers and doors (Plate 13).

Different types of writing desks, or *secrétaires*, were developed by French cabinetmakers. Inherited from the Spanish sixteenth-century *escritorio*, a form itself related to the cabinet, the French fall-front secretary (*secrétaire à abattant*) was usually placed against a wall. First created by Bernard II van Risenburgh (*c.* 1696–1766) as a small piece of furniture, its height rose to 1.5 meters during the second half of the century (Bedel 1996: 83). With its straight lines and its lower part sometimes comprised of drawers (*secrétaire en commode*) or doors (*secrétaire en armoire*), its profile evoked the cupboard and it was sometimes matched with a *chiffonnier*. Around 1730, the *secrétaire en pente* (later called *en dos d'âne*) was introduced in France. As with the English bureau, it had a sloping front that opened to form the writing surface. However, it had slender legs and was fitted with fewer shallower drawers thus making it a more elegant and easily movable piece of furniture.

This latter type led to the invention of the roll-top desk (*secrétaire à cyclindre*, sometimes called *bureau à cylindre*). The first example, begun in 1760 by the German-born cabinetmaker Jean-François Oeben (1721–63) and completed in 1769 by his pupil and successor Jean-Henri Riesener (1734–1806), was executed for Louis XV at Versailles (accession no. OA 5444). Often as large as the writing table, the roll-top desk had a semicylindrical front, either rigid or made of articulated wood slats, which rolled into the desk structure to reveal the writing surface and storage compartments. Numerous variations of this type were created by modifying the dimensions, adding a bookcase or a small cupboard on the top or drawers in the lower part, etc. An interpretation of the roll-top desk that was found notably in Germany was a small writing table fitted with a semicylindrical slatted cover that could be opened from both sides so that the writing surface could be used simultaneously by two people facing each other. Some French *secrétaires* had even more complex mechanisms. The *bureau capucin* (or *table à la Bourgogne*), for instance, was an apparently simple writing table whose flat top divided into two parts: one unfolded to form the writing surface, while the other, comprised of storage compartments and hidden inside the table's body, needed to be raised by means of a ratchet.

The smaller *secrétaires* were often used by women. As Goodman (2009) has demonstrated, the practice of writing letters and the development of epistolary skills became central to the performance of womanhood in elite circles. Accordingly, in addition to the transformation of existing tables through the inclusion of inkstands and other writing implements, new types of furniture and related goods were created to support this new practice (Goodman 2009: 161–246). This was the case, for instance, with the *bonheur du jour*, a small table fitted with shelves or a shallow filing cabinet on the top. A variation of the men's *bureau à gradin*, it was created toward 1760 and was adopted notably in England and in Germany. Women also used various small writing desks and easily movable multipurpose combination tables, thanks to which letter writing was always at hand.

As argued by Goodman, despite their structural differences writing desks contributed to the articulation of a new search for sincerity, friendship, and self-expression that rested in the very fact of writing personal letters by oneself, thus eliminating the mediation of a secretary (i.e., the person) to whom letters used to be dictated (2011: 183–5). Moreover, because they provided secure storage for personal belongings—namely, letters—thanks to locks and secret compartments, writing desks were part of a new conception of privacy. Opened to household staff and visitors, the wealthy eighteenth-century domestic interior was more a semipublic environment than a private space as understood today. Carolyn Sargentson has underlined that, in these conditions, such a piece of furniture provided "small secure spaces within larger [unlocked] ones," thus protecting oneself not only from outside intruders but chiefly from insiders (2011: 226).

Finally, while the secret compartments and complex mechanisms that were used for writing desks contributed to what Sargentson has termed the "performance of secrecy," they were also in continuity with this epoch's fascination for, and engagement with, technology and mechanical devices. This interest is especially visible in the importance given to clocks. These could be small or monumental, mark the time, date, and sometimes even the phases of the moon, feature a barometer, or play music. They could be placed anywhere— some were even integrated into furniture or the paneling—as long as they could be seen and heard.

READING

During the eighteenth century, reading books, for instruction or pleasure, became increasingly popular. Not only were more people (including women) reading, they were reading both more than before and a greater variety of titles, as books, especially small easily handled ones, became more readily available. Whether practiced as part of a group or individually, reading was part of a larger social performance. As Peter Björn Kerber has pointed out, "in order to gain and maintain social acceptance, it was equally important to read, to be known to read, and to be known as well-read" (2011: 75). Unsurprisingly, pieces of furniture related to books were numerous during this period.

Bookcases appeared in England toward the last quarter of the seventeenth century (Bouzin 2000). Twelve freestanding bookcases, commissioned by Samuel Pepys (1633–1703) beginning in 1666, are today preserved at Magdalene College in Cambridge. However, it is only from 1750 that they became regular pieces of furniture within wealthy French homes. Bookcases could be found either as part of another piece of furniture, such as the bureau, for instance, or standing completely independently.[10] The latter, of which numerous variations existed, were frequently designed by architects, especially in England. Some bookcases consisted only of a low body surmounted by a marble top and comprising shelves enclosed behind doors. Others were divided into two parts: a lower body with plain doors to store heavy books, and an upper body with screens or glass doors. This allowed luxurious bindings to be seen, as the display of books contributed to showcasing the owner's wealth and knowledge. Popular in England, breakfront bookcases were widespread during the second half of the century. To reach the higher shelves, especially in the case of built-in library bookcases, library chairs and stools that transformed into a stepladder were designed in England.

Furthermore, dressing tables, writing desks, women's small metamorphic tables, as well as almost all combination pieces of furniture, often provided a bookrest, notably on the reverse side of a mirror or as a tilting writing surface. A reading and writing table designed by Martin Carlin (*c.* 1730–85), today at the Wallace Collection, is fitted with a tilting and rotating porcelain top that can be raised to the desired height thanks to a sophisticated system of toothed wheels and ratchets hidden in the table's body (accession no. F327). Such tables were also fitted with inside drawers and retractable candlestands.

NEEDLEWORK

The practice of needlework by women had been deemed morally worthy since the Renaissance for, as recalled by Rozsika Parker, it enabled the poorest to earn a living and offered the richest a means to earn their honor (1984: 62). Furthermore, it was widely agreed that, by occupying the mind, needlework both saved women from idleness and disciplined their bodies, thus contributing to instill self-control and humility—two of the virtues that defined femininity. However, if the importance given to needlework in women's education might appear as a means to enslave them into domestic activities, it was also a way to legitimize, by making it "safely feminine," an education "which might otherwise have been deemed dangerously masculine" (73).

Yet, addressing the stereotypical connections between female needlework and domesticity—the professional realm of embroidery was mostly dominated by men in Europe at the time—Nicole Pellegrin has underlined that eighteenth-century Frenchmen, amongst them colonels and officers, did not systematically despise amateur needlework (1999: 765). Some handled the needle just as well as the sword and embroidered in the salons. This practice was recorded by many contemporaries such as Philip Thicknesse who, in praising healthy French drinking behavior, noted: "while the Englishman is earning disease and misery at his bottle, the Frenchman is embroidering a gown, or knitting a handkerchief for his mistress" (1777: 99).

Besides if, as argued by Madame Campan, needlework taught young ladies "this calm and measured bearing, which serves both modesty and graces" (1824: 175),[11] such elegance and self control might also have been fostered by proximity to the furniture used while working. Indeed, to live with and move around writing, reading, and work tables was not an easy task when dressed with voluminous and restrictive hooped skirts. Hellman has argued that to share space with these delicate pieces of furniture "and the flaming, spillable, or breakable items they were meant to support—was both an opportunity and a risk: one might highlight one's gestural virtuosity, or betray a lack of control" (1999: 423–4).

Women's work tables often closely resembled their reading tables—when they were not combined in a single piece of furniture. Many had a raised border surrounding the top, commonly in pierced metal, to prevent balls of wool and

FIGURE 3.1 Sewing Box on Stand (England), *c.* 1780–1800, pine veneered with satinwood, rosewood, holly and box, ivory, gilded metal, silk velvet (lining). Photograph courtesy of the Musée des beaux-arts de Montréal.

silk from falling. This was the case of the *tricoteuse*, for instance, a simple table fitted with one or two shelves connecting the legs. The *chiffonnière*, a more elaborate table in use during the second half of the century, had a square or round top that, in the most luxurious cases, was made of a Sèvres porcelain plaque. Standing high on its feet, it was usually fitted with between one and three drawers (to store a piece of work or conceal writing implements) and often had a shelf connecting the legs. Square, rectangular, oval, or even kidney-shaped work tables were found throughout Europe and the United States (Figure 3.1). Many were fitted with a deep storage basket (usually made of fabric) that looked as if it was suspended underneath the table's body.

PLAYING GAMES

While letter writing, reading, or needlework could be performed in intimate circles or alone—although in the wealthy eighteenth-century domestic interior one was seldom, if ever, alone—other activities fostered larger social gatherings. In England, for instance, assemblies were occasions for persons of both sexes to meet and play games, drink tea, have supper, and so on, in other words to engage in a wide range of pursuits that could be held in one or many rooms, depending on the number of guests.

Gambling was widespread amongst every class of society. However, Thomas M. Kavanagh has demonstrated its remarkable significance within the aristocracy, where it was "seen by the courtier as an activity centered not on money and financial gain but on affirming one's basic ethics and identity" (1993: 39). As a social practice that was prohibited but tolerated, gambling—and chiefly high-stakes gambling—was the occasion to show one's detachment from money as a commodity and thus to affirm one's status as being above mere financial wealth. Indeed, it was unsuitable for a "true" noble "to play with the primary intention of winning money; to cheat; or, when losing, to act in such a way as to reveal an inordinate attachment to money" (38). However, eighteenth-century nobility, particularly in France, was not homogeneous and so neither was the understanding of the symbolism of gambling. For the bourgeoisie, whose financial success allowed them to challenge blood hierarchy by buying titles of nobility, social status was built on money and its management. Accordingly, as Kavanagh has argued, the awareness of the wagers' monetary value encouraged the bourgeoisie morally to condemn gambling as the "pure circulation of money," and, by the same token, to deny the very source of its newly acquired power within society (56).

Nevertheless, countless tables were designed specifically for playing cards and other games based either on skill or chance. Typical English card tables had a square folding and fabric-covered top with projecting rounded corners to hold candlesticks as well as small cavities to hold tokens or outlays. When the top was folded, the frame retracted on itself like an accordion following the "concertina" action, and the table could be pushed against the wall to be used as a side table. Circular or pentagonal tables with a central cavity to hold the counters were used to play a game of chance named *cavagnole*. The same kind of table could also be used to play *brelan*, a card game on which *bouillote* is based. Other card games such as *piquet* and *quadrille* were played on rectangular and square tables with a hole at each angle, while triangular tables were used to play *tri*, a game similar to whist, or *hombre*. Mechanical game tables were also designed, such as one by Roentgen, now at the Metropolitan Museum of Art, which combines a top to play cards, one to play chess, and a concealed backgammon box (accession no. 2007.42.1a-e,.2a-o, aa-n).

Sets of matching chairs and card tables were designed, while cabriolet seats or light chairs (discussed below) could also easily be gathered around a gaming table. In addition, seats such as the *voyeuse* were developed especially for playing games. Various seating types—including chairs, armchairs, and *bergères*—could be transformed into *voyeuses*, whose distinctive feature was the back's padded upper rail on which one could lean one's elbows while watching the game. In the case of the *voyeuse-ponteuse*, the upper rail opened to hold one's bet. While *voyeuses* allowed for close proximity between the viewer and the player (the former leaning on the seat's upper rail and looking over the shoulder of the latter), another type of seat was designed for the viewer alone (Figure 3.2). Sometimes called *voyelle*, this seat looked similar to a praying stool (*prie-dieu*)—but how different in its purpose! It had a tall narrow back surmounted by an upholstered rail to support the elbows, and a low seat whose height and shape were gender specific: a man would sit astride on a saddle-shaped seat, while a woman would kneel on a broader and even lower seat. This latter type could also be called *voyeuse à genoux*.

HAVING TEA AND EATING

The consumption of coffee and chocolate, introduced in Europe as early as the sixteenth century, and tea, imported by Dutch merchants from the seventeenth, increased during the eighteenth century. In England, tea drinking and its widespread rituals were associated with social distinction and genteel behavior (Smart Martin 2011). However, as Stacey Sloboda has noted, if the tea table was linked to "polite conversation," it could simultaneously be equated with "deleterious gossip" (2010: 138). Furthermore, tea drinking entailed thorny colonial issues, as the importation of tea leaves owed much to the growing presence of European empires in Asia. Likewise, the production and trade in coffee and cocoa—not to mention the sugar with which all these beverages were consumed—was largely based on slavery, notably in the American colonies.[12]

Nevertheless, the ever-expanding demand for these imported beverages encouraged the production of a great variety of implements and appropriate pieces of furniture. The tea table was central, physically and symbolically, insofar as, as Anna Smart Martin has demonstrated, it supported the pleasure and the performance of drinking tea by providing a "stage" for both the teapot and the action (2011: 174). Rectangular tea tables' tops were usually

FIGURE 3.2 *Voyelle* (France), *c*. 1760–5, wood, cane, leather, brass. Photograph courtesy of the Musée des beaux-arts de Montréal.

surrounded by a raised border to prevent the tea service from sliding off when the table was carried around. An unusual rectangular shape produced in Boston was the "turret-top" table whose perimeter was bordered by semicircular projections, probably to place cups and saucers. The tripod tea table with a circular, sometimes rotating, top was especially popular in England and the United States before it was adopted in France. This type prevailed during the second half of the century and, according to Smart Martin, it fostered a sense of intimacy by authorizing people to gather around on a more equal basis (177). Many of these were fitted with a "bird cage" support underneath the top, which allowed it to be conveniently tilted to a vertical position when the table was not in use. As a complement to the tea table, a tripod kettle stand could be used to hold a kettle filled with hot water.

Other types of tables were used to eat or to ensure the service of food and drinks while gathering in small groups. Introduced in the mid-eighteenth century and used to eat breakfast or light meals, the Pembroke table had a tripartite top: a fixed central part fitted with a drawer in the apron and, on each side, a hinged flap supported by brackets. The "butterfly table," which could be described as halfway between the Pembroke and the gateleg table, was widespread in the United States during the first decades of the century. Considered distinctively American in its form, this table rested on four turned legs connected by turned stretchers and owed its name to the moveable vertical brackets that supported the semicircular hinged leaves and whose profile evoked butterfly wings. Other English drop-leaf breakfast tables had, in their central part underneath a shallow drawer, a compartment enclosed in wooden fretwork or brass wirework; this design made it possible to store food and, perhaps, to preserve it from the dogs.

Light tables fitted with shelves were also used to serve food. They enabled a small party to avoid the presence of servants and to sit close together, thus encouraging a new sense of conviviality and intimacy. They could also be a necessity to compensate for the lack of servants: fortunes were sometimes lost as swiftly as they had been gained, as was the case in France, for instance, following the collapse in 1720 of John Law's economic system. French *tables servantes* and their English counterparts, the dumbwaiters, were given various shapes. A typical dumbwaiter, as introduced in the 1740s, consisted of a central stile supporting two or three circular (sometimes revolving) shelves and resting on a tripod base. The French *rafraîchissoir*[13] was more elaborate: in addition to the shelves connecting the legs and the drawers underneath the top, it was equipped with metal basins to keep bottles of wine in fresh water or in ice, just as the two examples depicted in *Le souper fin* (c. 1780) engraved after Moreau le Jeune (1741–1814) (Victoria and Albert Museum, accession no. E.485–1972).

Larger groups were entertained in the formal dining room, which became increasingly common in wealthy houses during the eighteenth century. This was especially the case in England, where the dining room was also a place for men to debate, take political decisions, and drink after women had retired to the drawing room.

Dining tables had existed for centuries in Europe. However, they were now designed in matching sets with chairs and other pieces of furniture. Tables could be extended, often by adding leaves that were stored separately rather than fixed to the table's top, as had been the case with drop-leaf tables and draw tables—a type introduced during the late seventeenth century. In France, it was under English influence that, from the last decades of the century, stationary extendable dining tables were produced by cabinetmakers.

Although the dining table occupied the center of the room, the key piece of furniture of the dining room was the sideboard. Robert Adam redesigned the sideboard by adding two cupboard-like pedestals at each end of a matching central body in the form of a long table. However, it was only toward the last decade of the century that, thanks to Hepplewhite, these three separate units were combined into one piece that provided both storage and display space for tableware. This type of sideboard, which added solemnity to the room's décor and contributed to its unity, was so fashionable that small versions were produced for humbler households. Furthermore, Adam's dining room sets were commonly complemented by a matching wine cooler, sometimes placed under the sideboard's central part, and urns standing on the pedestals. They were either filled with water or designed as boxes to store cutlery. Dumbwaiters, side tables of various shapes, and round-top pedestal tables or candlestands were also used in the dining room.

SOCIABILITY AND COMFORT: A FURTHER LOOK AT SEATS

Whatever the occasion, the socializing process occurring in the domestic interior would have remained incomplete without a large variety of stools, chairs, armchairs, and other pieces of furniture designed for sitting. Indeed, the eighteenth century is often considered to be the age of seats. Based on the study of French inventories, Daniel Roche has stressed that seats, especially chairs, were ubiquitous even in less privileged households (1997: 205–8). However, to sit on a chair is not "natural" and it is a difficult task to transform the constraints it imposes on the body and the posture into a source of comfort. In France, *chaisiers*—joiners specialized in the making of chairs and armchairs—imagined a multitude of new models that partook of a new desire for comfort while contributing to the development of a new "art" of sitting.

Around 1720, the profile of seats began to change. Backs were lower, chair rails had a slightly protruding curve in the front, and stretchers had completely disappeared by 1730 (except for long or heavy seats). In the case of armchairs, armrests were flared outward and set back from the front legs, a feature that might have been introduced to accommodate the wide hooped skirts fashionable during this period (armrests were brought back in line with the front legs only at the end of the century). Furthermore, it was also during the first decades of the century that arm pads (*manchettes*) were added to armrests.

Chairs and armchairs known as *à la reine* are characterized by their flat, slightly slanted, backs that are separated from their low, somewhat trapeze-shaped, seats (about 40 centimeters high for the chair and a little lower for the armchair). Thus named toward 1730, conceivably in tribute to Queen Maria Leszczyńska who seemed to have appreciated them, these seats remained in use throughout the century (Bouzin 2000; Deflassieux 2005: 275). Often part of architectural furniture and intended to be placed against the wall, they played a prominent role in the symmetrical organization of a room.

The *bergère*, a more comfortable type of armchair popular in France from 1725, had a thick removable cushion on the seat and closed upholstered sides. Often made in pairs, and thus perfectly suited for conversation, this seat came in various profiles and was in fact derived from the *fauteuil en confessionnal*. The latter, just as the wing armchairs already common in seventeenth-century England, had a high back and "wings," stretching on each side from the back's upper rail to the armrest, convenient to protect the sitter from drafts. Wing armchairs, or easy chairs, with rolled arms were popular in the United States as well. The Martha Washington or lolling armchair, a US type developed from English models, was in use during the second half of the century. It had an upholstered tall back connected to the seat and open arms traditionally made of visible wood (e.g., Winterthur Museum, accession no. 1957.0882.001). Another type of French comfortable seat was the *duchesse*, a lounging armchair that resembled a *bergère* with an elongated seat to stretch the sitter's legs. While the *duchesse en bateau*'s seat was fitted at both ends with backs of different heights, the *duchesse brisée* was "broken" into two or three parts that could be used together as a single seat or separately.

One of the most striking developments regarding eighteenth-century seating is probably the wide variety of shapes that were created for the backs. In France, backs could, for instance, be fully upholstered or have an exposed wooden frame, cartouche-shaped with curved outlines, in medallion, or square, rectangle, or gondola-shaped. Toward the end of the century, forms freely inspired from furniture in use during antiquity were also produced, such as backs with a backward scroll and *en bandeau*, that is, made of a large crosspiece of wood joining the back's stiles. In England, backs could be upholstered or in carved exposed wood, with a central splat, intricate open work, or oval-, shield-, and heart-shaped, as, for instance, the ones drawn in Hepplewhite's style. English neoclassical designs were reinterpreted throughout Europe, notably in Germany, Italy, and even France. Of course, they were also to be found in the United States, where Windsor seats of various shapes, known since the seventeenth century and made of dowels tenoned in a solid wooden seat to form the back and legs, became very common from mid-century.

Yet, the most innovative back in terms of comfort and convenience was certainly the concave-curved back designed to envelop the sitter. Created by French joiners around 1740 to 1750 and described as the *dossier en hotte* (Roubo 1772: 634), it led to the creation of a new type of seat known as *cabriolet*. Although various seats could be designed *en cabriolet*—for example, the *bergère en cabriolet*—*cabriolet* chairs and armchairs were usually light seats meant to be moved around the room. They could be grouped into convivial clusters that, in addition to being propitious to conversation and confidences, created a certain "disorder" which served as a counterpoint to the formal organization of the room provided by the architectural furniture.

In keeping with the search for comfort, conviviality, and even intimacy, broader seats welcoming more than one person were created. The settee, usually designed to seat two persons, originated in the seventeenth-century tradition of joining together two chair backs, a feature still visible in the bipartite profile of numerous eighteenth-century settees, either upholstered or not. Another type, the French *tête-à-tête*—later known as *marquise*—was a *bergère* with an enlarged seat for two persons. Supported by six or eight feet, the *canapé*, whose width could reach over two meters, had one upholstered back and upholstered or open armrests at each end of the seat. A variation of this type, the *canapé à confidante*, had a corner seat added at each end. Paradoxically, the backs of the corner seats formed an outward-looking angle with the back of the central part of this *canapé* so that, while at least three people could be seated next to each other, they were facing different directions. In spite of its name, this seat's configuration might not have encouraged intimate conversation.

From mid-century, numerous and sometimes very subtle variations of the *canapé* were created. The sofa is a case in point, for this name was—and still is—often used as a synonym for *canapé*. Despite their similitude, the sofa usually had a lower seat, entirely upholstered back and armrests without any apparent wood, and was sometimes fitted with cushions. Yet, just as the *canapé*, it was meant to be placed against the wall. As a matter of fact, most of these large seats were part of architectural or, as termed by Verlet, seat-furniture (discussed above). They were commonly placed underneath a mirror or facing the chimneypiece and their profiles matched the room's paneling (Verlet 1982: 80). A rare, yet telling example of this is described by Roubo who observes that the sofa's back was arched when intended to be placed against a curved wall or niche (1772: 652).

The impressive variety in the names of seats meant to be used as daybeds points both to "the whim or the cupidity of workmen and merchants" (Roubo 1772: 652) and to the lure of exoticism. Indeed, just as the name sofa came

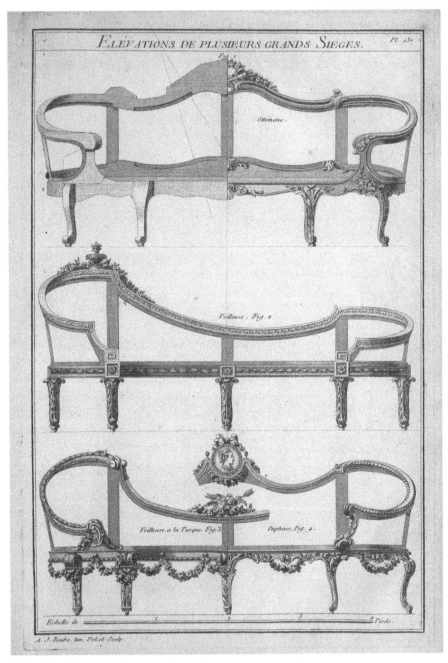

FIGURE 3.3 "Élévations de plusieurs grands sièges," showing an *ottomane*, a *veilleuse*, and half of a *veilleuse à la turque* and of a *paphose*, plate 237 from André Jacob Roubo (1772). Courtesy of The Miriam and Ira D. Wallach Division of Art, Prints and Photographs: Art & Architecture Collection, The New York Public Library. Photograph courtesy of the New York Library Digital Collections.

from the Arabic word *soffah* meaning a raised portion of the floor covered with carpets and cushions (OED Online n.d.), alternative forms had names evoking faraway lands and were in the spirit of the "Turkish style" in vogue during the second half of the century. Among them, the *ottomane* had an elongated oval seat with enveloping armrests, the *paphose* looked just the same but with a kidney-shape seat, the *turquoise* had two symmetrical armrests flanking a central oval-shaped back, the *veilleuse* had two enveloping armrests of different heights joined by the back's oblique upper rail, while the *sultane* had no back and two scrolled arms (Figure 3.3).

SLEEPING

The day's last occupation was to sleep. Servants and guards usually slept on easily disassembled trestle beds that could be stored during the day. Far from being reserved solely for military purposes, portable beds could also be used by aristocrats while traveling, a practice reminiscent of the medieval custom of carrying furniture from one castle to the other. The most sophisticated beds were of two types: *de bout* or *à la française*, with the headboard placed against the wall as in the case of the traditional four-poster bed; and *de travers*, that is with one side of the bed placed parallel to the wall.

In France, four-poster beds were still found in the provinces and the colonies. At court, the *lit à la duchesse*, which appeared in the mid-seventeenth century, was still in use in great bedchambers. It had a low headboard placed against the wall, no foot, no post, and the canopy, which was fixed to the wall, extended over the entire length of the bed. However, *lits de travers*, of which several variations existed, were preferred in private bedrooms where they were often placed in a niche. The *lit à la polonaise*, created around 1740, was crowned by a canopy slightly shorter than the bed and supported by curved iron rods attached to the corners of the head- and footboards. This structure was entirely covered by fabric. The *lit à la turque* had scrolled head- and footboards that were sometimes joined by a slightly higher back placed against the wall. Draperies, spreading from the canopy that was fixed to the wall, surrounded both ends of the bed. The *lit à la romaine* was similar, with, however, a smaller square or rectangular canopy covered with less fabric. Designs for similar types identified as "field beds" were included by Chippendale in his *Director* (1762: plate XLIX).

In England, beds with slender posts, prominent canopies, and heavy, usually sophisticated, draping were common at the beginning of the century. Although draping became more sober during the following decades, beds with massive, profusely carved canopies and abundant draping were still designed for bedchambers, such as the one created by Robert Adam for Osterley Park House at the end of the 1770s. Following the craze for *chinoiserie*, beds with a pagoda-shaped canopy resting on four posts and a headboard ornamented with fretwork were designed as well. From mid-century more attention was granted to carved posts—either cylindrical or of square section—which usually rested on a lower section of a different shape.

Serving tables were also designed to stand beside the bed during the night (they were usually stored during the day). Fitted with shelves, with or without doors, they were used to store writing implements, a book, or a chamber pot. The *table d'en-cas*, higher, larger, and fitted with a sliding shutter, was used to keep a light snack, just "in case" of hunger during the night. The *somno*, a bedside table in the form of a cylindrical or, more frequently in France, rectangular pedestal with a door and a small drawer underneath the top, was among the few novelties created at the turn of the nineteenth century.

Indeed, changes in furniture were mainly stylistic during this period. In France, for instance, the sociopolitical turmoil and economic instability of the French Revolution were not favorable to the development of new types of furniture. Yet, neither the French historical context, nor the growing industrialization of England, and the transformations in the means of production that followed both the drastic changes in the guild systems and the increasing use of machinery, marked the definitive ending of eighteenth-century furniture. On the one hand, the outflow of French cabinetmakers looking for new patrons, as well as the sale of pieces of furniture seized by revolutionaries—notably in the United States where they were bought by the ruling class of this new country—continued to ensure the dissemination of French eighteenth-century types. On the other hand, the already fashionable neoclassical forms, notably those disseminated through English furniture pattern books and archaeological discoveries, continued to be much in favor throughout Europe. As a matter of fact, the general interest in historical design that was to prevail during the nineteenth century was already perceptible, notably in the adaptation of furniture dating from antiquity. This was the case, for instance, of the various reinterpretations of the Greek *klismos'* saber legs, or of the use of the *athénienne*, a Greco-Roman-inspired tripod table used either as a perfume burner, a container for plants, a work table, or a washhand stand. On the whole, the contributions of the eighteenth century to the development of furniture were not only unprecedented; they were to remain crucial for the years to come.

CHAPTER FOUR

The Domestic Setting

ANTONIA BRODIE

The eighteenth century saw profound changes in the way that people across Europe, from the "middling sort" to the highest in the land, perceived and used the places in which they lived. Changing patterns of hospitality, and new fashions in entertaining altered the size and shape, finishes and furnishings of the principal rooms in the houses of the elite. In lesser dwellings, architectural innovations and improvements in lighting and heating resulted in reconfigured living spaces. In addition, advances in the domestic manufacture of textiles, ceramics, and glass, and greater awareness and availability of imported materials such as mahogany transformed the look and feel of European domestic interiors.

During the eighteenth century, the number of people working outside the home increased as bureaucracy, manufacturing, and retail expanded, bringing new ideas about domesticity and its value into play. As domesticity became more valuable, so too did the creation of a setting for it, emphasizing the importance of decoration as an expression of care for family and friends. These new ideas promoted a comfortable informal aesthetic, which was embraced by the middle classes, and can be seen in the rise of upholstered seating and the innovations in heating and lighting discussed below. Nobles and royalty still sought palatial splendor, but increasingly this was recognized as a political statement rather than an agreeable way to live, and as a consequence suites of smaller rooms were created alongside magnificent public spaces in the houses of the great.

Other cultural shifts likewise directed the ways in which rooms were decorated and used. The scientific, philosophical, and political enquiry of the Enlightenment had far-reaching consequences, shaping public life and education for many Europeans, especially the better-off in northern and western Europe.

The French Revolution of 1789 was by far the most dramatic outcome of Enlightenment thinking, but the writings of Rousseau and Voltaire, Kant and Hutton also influenced more broadly how people saw themselves and their world. The rejection of superstition and a growing emphasis upon the value of reason, promoting rational explanations for natural phenomena affected the ways in which many chose to live. A growing awareness of the individual encouraged a desire for privacy and intimacy that allowed greater introspection and self-awareness. The emergence of "politeness," a behavioral, moral, and aesthetic code that promoted elegance and moderation in all things shaped attitudes toward expenditure and consumption, advancing the popularity of restrained classicism, which embodied these ideals more successfully than the extravagant baroque or the playful rococo.

EIGHTEENTH-CENTURY DOMESTIC INTERIORS: THE EVIDENCE

All manner of information about interior decoration and the acquisition of furnishings in the eighteenth century can be found in letters, diaries, travel journals, account books, bills, receipts, and inventories. Visual sources such as prints, drawings, paintings, and architectural plans provide clues about particular decorative schemes while a wide range of objects produced for consumers of all social classes survive in public and private collections across the globe. These tell stories about colors and materials, manufacturing techniques, and changing forms and taste, even when more precise details about their past owners are obscure. A much smaller number of pieces by known makers or for identified patrons also exist, linking specific individuals, their houses and their furnishings.

Visual sources can offer unique snapshots of particular interiors, freezing them in time and recording the positioning of objects and their relation to one another. Even taking into account the likelihood of an artist improving upon reality or inserting objects for symbolic purposes, images still provide information about color schemes and finishes that have a limited life span and are frequently renewed. Details of wall coverings and upholstery, both of which were vitally important and expensive facets of decorative schemes in the eighteenth century, often only survive in images. Images also convey impressions of interiors; whether they were warm and welcoming, or stately and imposing. Such impressions are intensely subjective, but they add another layer to any interpretation of the decoration of an interior, giving some sense of how it might have felt to use a room.

To create a rounded picture of any particular interior demands the survival of several different types of evidence; a single source is rarely sufficient. Written sources such as inventories, bills, accounts books, letters, and diaries illuminate the when, where, who, and how much, and can also give an impression of the meanings and values ascribed to interiors and the objects they contained by their owners or by an interested audience. Often, however, written material lacks the detailed description that might make it possible to conjure an accurate picture of a long-gone artifact or decorative scheme, or to identify similar surviving examples. This is at least partly because we, as twenty-first-century onlookers, lack the wide-ranging knowledge of available products and the sophisticated vocabulary with which eighteenth-century consumers differentiated between similar types of goods.[1] The subtly nuanced ways in which colors were described, and the differences in individuals' perception of color, have a similar impact upon our ability to recreate interiors from written descriptions, and also make it difficult to identify surviving objects precisely, given the changes wrought by time on pigments (Lowengard 2006: ch. 6).

Even in well-documented houses with largely untouched furnishings such as Rosenborg Castle in Copenhagen, Denmark, it is often difficult to align a description with an object because inventory descriptions are often so imprecise. Only infrequently can we be sure that the furnishings described in inventories correspond directly to surviving objects, as in the case of the carved and gilded shelves for displaying china mentioned in the inventory taken of the contents of Drayton House in the Midlands of England in 1710 as one of "Two Guilt Hanging Shelves" in the Spangle Room. This object is very distinctive and still in the room where it was listed in 1710 today (Snodin et al. 2009: cat. 176). Most of those objects that can be linked definitively with a particular person or place were made by exceptional artisans for royal or noble clients. The German cabinetmaker and entrepreneur David Roentgen, for example, made extraordinary mechanical cabinets for, among others, Frederick William II of Prussia and Catherine the Great (Koeppe 2012). There are also, however, a smaller number of less grand items about which a surprising amount is known, because of the lucky survival of associated documentary evidence. One such object is the painted cabinet decorated by Katherine Conolly for her great-niece in the late 1730s and still on display at Conolly's former home, Castletown, just outside Dublin in Ireland. Katherine Conolly was a very rich and influential member of the Irish ruling class, and her commissioning and decoration of this cabinet as a gift for a valued relative is illustrative of the care that furnishings could express (Barnard 2004: 79–80; Knight of Glin and Peill 2007: 6–7).

Changing fashions, the wear and tear of everyday use, and the passage of time mean that intact eighteenth-century interiors are few and far between. Such interiors are particularly rare in continental Europe because of successive wars and violent political upheaval that have resulted in the destruction of buildings and their contents. The long-standing campaigns by successive curators of the palaces of Versailles outside Paris and Pavlovsk in Saint Petersburg, for example, to identify and repatriate items dispersed as a consequence of political turmoil, illustrate how difficult it can be to recreate eighteenth-century interiors.

A few decorative schemes that were created during this period, however, still exist in what is believed to be more or less their original form. Some of these interiors, like those of the Neue Kammern in the Sanssouci Park at Potsdam in Germany or Headfort House near Kells in Ireland, have been stripped of their movable furnishings but are still most instructive, providing information about, among other things, proportion, color, fireplaces, doors, and the relationship between floor, walls, and ceiling. The late rococo interiors of the Neue Kammern, for example, show the complementary use of marquetry, jasper, and lacquer for paneling. Other interiors, however, like those of Dumfries House in Scotland, retain many of their original furnishings. The carved and gilded pier glasses and pelmets, suites of chairs and a mahogany library table all by Thomas Chippendale, Axminster carpets and steel fire furniture by David Robertson offer a glimpse of the nature of the eighteenth-century domestic interior as a whole and the density, richness, and quality of its contents, which are difficult to judge from written sources. Only extensive documentation, for instance the archives of the Crichton family that survive for Dumfries House, make it truly possible to assert confidently that movable furnishings are original to a house (Christie's London 2007: 1:7–29).

Although most of the eighteenth-century interiors that survive are still in situ, there are a number which have been removed from their original locations and can now be seen reassembled in other buildings, particularly in museums. There has long been a tradition among the well-to-do of reusing expensive architectural elements such as paneling and fireplaces, moving them when a building was repaired or destroyed (Harris 2007: 2–12). The trade in architectural antiques boomed in the late nineteenth and early twentieth centuries, responding to growing demand in the United States for European decorative arts and made possible by widespread redevelopment of the major cities of Europe and the reduced circumstances of many landed families. "Period Rooms" as they are known, are evocative and atmospheric, but present numerous problems as evidence. The removal of the paneling from its original context has often been the sole reason for its survival, and as such the room represents valuable fragments of lost buildings and interior schemes. Nonetheless, the scope for alteration and reconfiguration presented by the redeployment of architectural elements means that particularly careful interpretation and evaluation is required when using a "period room" as anything other than suggestive of an eighteenth-century interior. Nearly all of the French eighteenth-century paneled rooms now held by the Metropolitan Museum in New York are cataloged as having "later additions," meaning that they were adjusted to fit spaces other than those they were originally made for.

TRANSFORMING THE INTERIOR:
ROOM USE AND LAYOUT

From the late sixteenth century a trend toward the creation of smaller rooms defined by function, rather than the large multipurpose spaces of the medieval and Renaissance house, in particular the hall, can be seen in the homes of the better-off across Europe. The gallery first appeared in France in the fourteenth century, and the cabinet in the fifteenth in the townhouses built by the very wealthy, rather than in great country houses and palaces, which were less innovative in their layouts (Gady 2011: 55–81). Gradually this fashion was adopted by all those who could afford anything beyond a single room, and resulted in the development of new ideas about how rooms should be used, their size and scale, and their arrangement within the home, as described below.

Throughout the Middle Ages the ability to offer hospitality to all comers was a potent symbol of wealth and status, and played an important role in maintaining the relationship between the nobility and their dependants. The provision of meals and beds for large numbers of itinerant travelers year round placed a considerable burden on lordly householders and had a significant impact on the shape and layout of the houses of the aristocracy. Substantial halls, which could accommodate many people at mealtimes and could be used as dormitories at night, were the norm. The lord ate on a raised platform at one end of the hall, or, sometimes, in a small private room away from the hurly-burly of the main dining hall (Girouard 1978: 84–104). As the nature of the contract between the nobility and their vassals became less formal and this relationship shifted from homage toward patronage, a reduction in open-handed hospitality made it possible to alter the layout and function of the principal rooms in the noble house. Dining was transformed from a public activity in the entrance hall to an intimate pastime and this leap can be seen very clearly in the emergence of separate dining rooms along with new furnishings for them (John 2013). The concept of dining as a select entertainment for a group of one's peers, rather than a broader spectacle, seems to have emerged in the fashionable *salons* of Paris in the later seventeenth century, where nonhierarchical serve-yourself meals were all the rage (Braudel 2002: 222; Pinkard 2009: 87–93). In his memoirs of the French court in the 1760s and 1770s, the comte Dufort de Cheverny discusses casual *soupers* and formal *diners*. The widespread use of folding tables in Parisian homes, however, suggests that although the nature of dining changed, for many people this did not result in the creation of a dedicated space for this activity (Pardailhé-Galabrun 1991: 95–7).

Not only dining, but also sleeping, moved out of the main living area, with bedrooms reserved for sleeping appearing in many houses, although beds also continued to be placed in other rooms, especially those intended for servants

(Pardailhé-Galabrun 1991: 73–83). Beds were generally placed facing the windows and in the homes of the elite were sometimes set within an alcove. The bed was an important site of display, an opportunity to use large quantities of fashionable and expensive textiles, and the decoration of bedchambers often emphasized this by using textiles or imported wallpaper to cover the walls too.

The main entertaining space in larger houses became a room for sitting and participating in a range of fashionable leisure activities including receiving visitors and conversing, drinking tea and coffee, reading, needlework, letter writing, and playing music and card games. Upholstered seat furniture, small occasional tables, writing and games tables all facilitated these modes of sociability, and engendered new ideas about physical ease. Called the drawing room in Britain and the *salon* in France, a fine example of this new kind of room can be found at Longford Castle in Wiltshire, with its original velvet wall covering and carved and upholstered chairs by Giles Grendey.

As activity-specific rooms developed so too did corridors. These allowed movement around a house without passing through any of the rooms and effectively separated the social and service functions of a house. Complex and carefully divided service areas also moved much of the daily business of the household away from the rooms used by the family and reduced contact between masters and servants.[2] There were advantages to these new arrangements—corridors made it easier to close rooms off to provide privacy and prevent draughts while smaller rooms were easier and less expensive to heat. In reconfigured older buildings, however, this often resulted in awkwardly shaped and ill-proportioned rooms. The rooms at Audley End in eastern England created by Robert Adam for Sir John Griffin Griffin in the 1760s, for example, were slotted into a house built in the first decades of the seventeenth century, and lack the high ceilings of new-built Adam interiors. Likewise, the remodeling in 1749 of the early sixteenth-century manoir de Kernault in Brittany in western France by Parisian architect Forestier Le Jeune combined Renaissance beamed ceilings with rococo paneling (Girouard 2000: 138–9).

Throughout the eighteenth century the majority of Europeans still did most of their cooking over an open fire. In the homes of the less well-off, for example, the cooking hearth was the fireplace of their single all-purpose room, although dedicated kitchens were the norm in the houses of the wealthy. In great houses, kitchens were often located in separate buildings, and built with high ceilings to minimize smokiness and the risk of fire, while in grand city dwellings kitchens were often in the basement, although many urban residents rarely cooked at home, relying instead on cook-shops and taverns to provide them with hot food (Roche 1998: 617). Fixed equipment, such as ovens and built-in stoves, appear infrequently in inventories and it is therefore difficult to tell how widespread they were, but it is clear that a wide range of pots, pans, griddles, and braziers were commonly used for cooking in households of all types (Pardailhé-Galabrun 1991: 83–7). Evidence about the appearance of kitchens, and the finishes of their walls and floors, is very limited, suggesting that these rooms were spartan, with limewashed walls and a dirt or stone floor.

Changes in room distribution and layout also affected the great eighteenth-century palaces of Europe, among them the Catherine and Alexander Palaces at Tsarskoye Tselo near Saint Petersburg in Russia, the Palazzina di Caccia at Stupinigi near Turin in northern Italy, and the Schönbrunn Palace in Vienna, Austria, though with very different results from those that determined the disposition of the London townhouse and the Parisian *hôtel particulier* (Stewart 2009; Gady 2011). These palaces, magnificent monuments to the ambition and power of their creators, were vast and complex buildings. They reflected the formal and elaborate nature of court life, the often rigid protocol that defined daily routines, and were carefully calibrated to emphasize and reinforce distinctions in social status. Throughout the period, both new and remodeled palaces shared a plan that mirrored the formality and control of the court. Sequences or *enfilades* of state rooms of ever-increasing luxuriousness radiated out from an impressive central staircase. Large public rooms near the staircase led into smaller rooms used for receiving important visitors and sleeping. In some instances, as at Sanssouci near Potsdam, each chamber had an adjoining servants' room to ensure high levels of service and maximum comfort at all times.

At the far end of the *enfilade,* and usually accessible only from the bedchamber, was the cabinet or closet, a small private chamber used for study, relaxation, and entertaining small numbers of carefully selected guests. As an ostensibly private space to which a privileged circle was admitted, the cabinet was an ideal arena for experimenting with new fashions in collecting and in interior decoration. Here exotic materials, outlandish natural history specimens, and choice prints and paintings could be displayed. Chinoiserie cabinets like that at the Villa della Regina outside Turin, sometimes incorporating lacquer or imitation lacquer paneling, were popular, while the extravagant use of glass and gilding in the cabinet of Frederick IV at Rosenborg Castle near Copenhagen in Denmark was a more unusual expression of this trend. In this rarefied space, individuals could enjoy their surroundings and share them with people whose opinions they valued and whose discretion they could trust.

Identifying the reason for innovations in interior layout is problematic. The development of corridors and the emergence of rooms dedicated to particular activities may have been the result of changes in domestic life, and the adoption of "politeness" by the upper echelons of society (Brewer 1997: 101–3, 111–13). The pursuits most closely associated with the "polite" way of life were all sedentary, and would have been positively unpleasant in cold, drafty rooms. An increase in domestic sociability, especially among women, therefore may well have had an impact upon the disposition of rooms. Certainly it altered the forms of furniture, resulting in the proliferation of small tables and small upholstered chairs for facilitating these activities. It has been argued that certain kinds of new mechanical furniture, like the writing desks of Jean-François Oeben, allowed the performance of sophisticated displays of knowledge and elegance as part of this domestic sociability, the interior forming a showcase for its inhabitants and their recreation (Hellman 1999).

Another interpretation of the widespread alterations in domestic layouts, dubbed "the birth of intimacy" by cultural historian Annik Pardailhé-Galabrun, characterizes these changes as part of a quest for increased privacy. As Pardailhé-Galabrun relates, a desire for privacy reflected the rise of individualism and a move toward greater separation of the wide-ranging activities that took place in the home (Pardailhé-Galabrun 1991; see also Chartier 1989). This assessment, however, places a very twenty-first-century emphasis on the value of privacy. As the social historian John Crowley points out, this results in a "questionable circularity"; suggesting that changes that produced increased opportunities for solitude are proof that desire for privacy was the motivating force behind those changes, even though they also had other effects.[3] Most people continued to live in buildings erected decades, if not centuries, before these shifts took place and very few had either the means or the desire to alter their abode to reflect changing architectural fashions. Nor is it clear the extent to which access to private space was a priority even for those individuals who could shape their surroundings more actively. It is likely therefore that changes in the relationship between the rich and those who served them, new fashions in entertaining and socializing, and technological improvements to fireplaces and windows contributed to these architectural shifts, to at least the same, if not a greater degree, than any desire for privacy.

NEW FASHIONS IN INTERIOR DECORATION: WALLS, FLOORS, AND CEILINGS

The furnishings chosen by eighteenth-century consumers reflect their attempts to reconcile conflicting practical and aesthetic ideals, for if fashion and magnificence mattered, so too did convenience, cost, and longevity. Contemporary descriptions reveal that visitors were finely attuned to the messages that interiors could convey about their owners and their perceptions of their own wealth, taste, and status. Criticism fell upon those whose homes failed to reflect how others saw them. John Loveday was very scathing about the furnishings of the Earl of Pembroke's house at Wilton: "There are no fine Beds, Chairs, Glasses &c here. The Wainscot common, small Pannels of a Lead Colour. The Tapestry of which there is no great quantity, has all small Figures" (Markham n.d.: 55).

Awareness of this reality played a significant role in shaping fashions in furnishings within particular social groups, as Amanda Vickery (2006) has shown in her assessment of the wallpaper choices of middle-class English consumers. "Suitability" was a watchword across social boundaries, and the selection of furnishings appropriate to the individual's pocket and view of her or his own place in the world formed the bedrock of all decisions about interior decoration.

This emphasis on the importance of appropriateness had its origins in classical antiquity, and can be traced to the principle of *decor,* variously translated as decorum or suitability, presented by the Roman author Vitruvius in *De Architectura* written during the first twenty-five years of the first century CE, and rediscovered by architects such as Leon Battista Alberti during the fifteenth century. *Decor* was an essential component in fulfilling the three elements identified by Vitruvius as the fundamental requirements of architecture: beauty, utility, and strength (Hart and Hicks 1998: 3). Applying Vitruvian principles to interiors was difficult, however. The adjustments that were necessary to adapt classical architecture, developed in a Mediterranean climate, to the weather of northern Europe—double-height entrance halls rather than atria, glass windows, corridors instead of cloisters—give some indications of the kind of difficulties that faced homeowners in pursuit of Vitruvian *decor* inside and out. In the absence of clear guidelines explaining what was and was not appropriate, individuals had to determine for themselves how best to decorate their homes, using a variety of different methods to explore the available options.

Carefully observing the furnishings choices of those of a similar status and income when visiting provided valuable indicators of what might be considered appropriate, and also of different ways to furnish rooms of particular proportions and aspect.[4] Trying to imagine how a room might look before embarking on any kind of expenditure on decoration was an important step in the process of making choices that fulfilled an individual's practical, aesthetic, and aspirational requirements. Seeing the homes of others could make this task easier and prevent expensive mistakes, which were difficult to rectify. An essential part of understanding what was and was not appropriate was knowing where in an interior to spend money and where to save. Some things could be neatly contrived for minimal outlay while others demanded lavish expenditure. Even for the very rich, value for money was important, and while creating interiors that positively reflected one's status was a vital aspect of furnishing suitably, overspending was generally viewed as evidence of poor judgment and delusions of grandeur. The derogatory comments of Robert Harley, 1st Earl of Oxford, about the new house built by his political rival Robert Walpole, at Houghton in Norfolk illustrates this attitude. "I think it neither magnificent or beautiful. There is a very great expense without either judgement or taste [...] I dare say had the money which has been laid out here, nay and much less, been put into the hands of a man of taste and understanding there would have been a much finer house, and better rooms and greater."[5]

The first impression created by any interior is largely a consequence of the ways in which the walls are decorated. In the first half of the eighteenth century, wood paneling was the most common finish in the homes of the better-off, providing insulation and protection against damp and insects. Paneling was almost always painted, though the range of paint colors was extremely limited. There was a strict hierarchy of shades based on the expense of the ingredients required to formulate the paint. Earth-based browns and yellows were cheapest, but green, red, and blue mineral-based colors were more costly. Paneling varied from the very plain, as seen in the early eighteenth-century merchants houses of Spitalfields in London, to elaborately carved like that at the Château de Villette in Burgundy. Paneling could also be decorated with stucco relief, which created an effect very similar to that of Wedgwood basalt wares. In some instances, as with Christophe Huet's painted decorations for the Grande Singerie at the Château de Chantilly, the paneling set the tone for all of the furnishings, while William Kent's use of a plain dado in the Saloon at Holkham Hall in Norfolk instead provided a neutral backdrop to substantial carved and gilded furniture, a dramatic upper wall covering, and an imposing cornice and ceiling.

In the first half of the eighteenth century, high-quality plasterwork was still molded by hand, allowing a riot of highly sculptural decoration (Casey and Lucey 2012). Sometimes used as a frame for figurative paintings on walls and ceilings, plasterwork was often a feature in its own right, left white or gilded with flat areas painted a contrasting color. The development of oil-based composition plaster in the 1760s resulted in the widespread use of molds to cast low-relief plasterwork, which was especially well suited to creating neoclassical ceilings using repeated architectural motifs of the kind popularized by the Adam Brothers in Britain. Composition plaster was also to revolutionize the manufacture of picture frames, making highly decorative frames available to a mass market.

Printed or painted paper for walls was an increasingly popular choice as the century progressed. Large hand-painted scenes on paper, intended for screens, were first imported from China in the late seventeenth century but were pasted directly onto walls by European consumers. The popularity of these colorful and exotic wares resulted in the development of papers with large-scale patterns intended explicitly for export and for use as wallpaper. These expensive papers made a splash in the homes of the wealthy, while domestically produced wood-block-printed papers were more modestly priced and less showy, favoring stripes and small floral patterns (Hoskins 2005). As with textiles, more neutral designs of this kind dated more slowly and consequently needed to be replaced only when they began to look shabby. At the very end of the eighteenth century, complex wood-block-printed panoramas were produced by manufactories established by Joseph Dufour and Jean Zuber in France, replicating the murals and large-scale paintings favored by the rich (Prache and de Bruignac-La Hougue 2016). Although panoramic wallpaper was never cheap, it was less expensive than hiring a first-rate artist.

As discussed below, textile wall coverings *en suite* with the upholstery and window dressings were a fashionable option for the rich, but the cost of textiles was such that this was out of the question for the vast majority. In fact, the textile components were the costliest elements of most decorative schemes at the beginning of the eighteenth century, and as such offered an opportunity for impressive display. Maximilian Emanuel of Bavaria's spectacular commission in 1722–4 of no fewer than twelve military tapestries from the Brussels maker Judocus de Vos is a fine example. These were intended for the newly completed Schleissheim castle near Munich and illustrate the perceived power of tapestry as a medium for the expression of monarchical self-belief (Campbell 2007: cat. 57). Likewise, the sumptuous bed of cloth-of-gold brocaded with delicate flowers commissioned by João V of Portugal from The Hague for his marriage to Maria Anna of Austria in 1708 reflected João's sense of himself as the "Sun King" of Portugal (Delaforce 2002: 42).[6] By the end of the century the range of textiles available to the average European consumer had greatly expanded, and as a consequence it was no longer necessary to concentrate domestic spending in this area to the same degree (Roche 1994; Shammas 1994).

Textiles were still tremendously important in the creation of an interior, however, and were used for covering walls and floors, upholstering seat furniture and beds, and dressing windows and even occasionally doors. The development of more sophisticated upholstery techniques, such as the creation of removable chair seat, back, and arm pads, known as *à chassis*, which made it possible to change the textile elements of a room seasonally or according to fashion, resulted in an increase in the quantity of upholstered furniture purchased by the rich (DeJean 2009: 121–2). Grand suites of upholstered seat furniture incorporating stools, chairs, armchairs, and settees that coordinated with the wall covering and window dressing of an interior pulled the focus of attention firmly back to textiles. A set of twelve armchairs and two settees with frames by Nicolas-Quinibert Foliot and upholstered in Beauvais tapestry *en suite* with four hangings depicting Les Amours des Dieux was commissioned by Baron Johann Ernst Berstorff for his house in Copenhagen while acting as ambassador to the court of Versailles in the 1740s. Several of the chairs are now in the collection of the Metropolitan Museum of Art in New York (Plate 15). The importance still attached to high-quality furnishing textiles in the later eighteenth century is perhaps best exemplified by the silks depicting birds by Philippe Lasalle, the most famous of the Lyonnais designer-manufacturers, delivered to Catherine the Great of Russia in 1778 and 1780 for the decoration of the Lyon Drawing Room at the Palace of Tsarskoye Selo, and shortly after copied by Ivan Lazarevich Lazarev in Frianovo (Fryanovo) near Moscow (Lekhovich 2009; Miller 2009). These silks were so desirable they were worth copying (Plate 16).

While the appeal of expensive, top-quality textiles like those produced by Lasalle did not diminish, the availability of less costly domestically manufactured and imported cottons of all sorts altered both the appearance and the atmosphere of European homes (Crill 2008; Grant 2010). Cotton was lighter and easier to wash than the wool or silk-based textiles most commonly used, and the printed patterns and bright colors of imported textiles and those imitating them appeared fresh and new. The description given by Henriette-Lucy Dillon, later Madame de la Tour du Pin, of the "delightful apartment furnished in perfect style" at La Folie Joyeuse in Montfermeil to the east of Paris where she resided during the fortnight before her wedding in May 1770 gives some impression of this: "the hangings were of Indian cloth or calico, patterned with trees, flower-laden branches, fruits and birds against a buff-colored ground, and lined throughout with fine green silk" (de la Tour du Pin [1969] 1999: 65). The combination of calico and silk here, however, indicates that appearance rather than cheapness was the reason for this particular decorative choice.

Across Europe, the majority of floors remained uncovered throughout the eighteenth century. In most cases this was a question of expense, though the elaborate parquet, ceramic tiles, or patterned stone flooring preferred by the rich were intended to be seen. Painted floor cloths were widely used to cover floorboards in houses of all statuses, being a practical alternative to carpet for the less smart regions of elite houses as well as affordable for the less well-off. Most floor cloths were professionally produced, painted on oil cloth, and followed the geometric designs popular for tiling (Fawcett 1998: 161–2; Ayres 2003: 93–100). Carpets from Persia and Turkey gradually became sufficiently available in Europe that by the early eighteenth century they were no longer considered uniquely precious and started to be used as floor coverings, rather than being reserved for use on tables and sideboards as they had been in the previous two centuries. This shift appears to have occurred earlier in Britain than in continental Europe, perhaps as a consequence of strong historic trading links between Britain and the Levant (Völker 2009). Carpets had been produced in Spain from the Middle Ages, but were not manufactured in the rest of Europe before the sixteenth century (Sherrill 1996: 16). By the eighteenth century, however, embroidered, knotted pile and tapestry-woven floor coverings were being made by a number of European factories, both in imitation of Persian and Turkish examples, but also using European decorative motifs. Carpets of all sorts were expensive and were only seen in the homes of the rich (Sherrill 1996).

FASHION AND THE MARKET

Merchants, artisans, and shops were important sources of information about the wide range of furnishings that were available (Sargentson 1996; Walsh 2006: 151–78). Shopping, therefore, could be seen to be as much part of a process of research as entertainment and opportunities for sociability. Increasingly, even makers of luxury goods produced items speculatively as well as to order, not only to encourage impulse purchases but also to provide examples of the kinds of wares that might be obtainable.[7] The development of ornament prints, depictions of interiors, and volumes such as Thomas Chippendale's *Director* (see the Introduction and Chapter 7 in this volume) should be viewed in this context as further ways of showing the consumer the endless range of decoration and furnishing possibilities.

Recognizably modern marketing practices such as newspaper advertising developed during this period as the Rothschild Collection of European trade cards shows, and fueled consumer demand for an ever-wider range of domestic goods. Manufacturers produced constantly changing versions of the same commodities to encourage repeat purchasing, often prompted by increasingly market-savvy shopkeepers who knew their customers and what they wanted. In Paris, the *marchands-merciers*, dealers in luxury goods of all kinds, created new hybrid products that incorporated different materials, such as the Asian lacquer and Sèvres plaques in the cabinets of Martin Carlin. By circumventing the restrictive guild system and employing a range of materials, they popularized a new kind of retail experience (Robinson 1986; Sargentson 1996: 44–61). Fashions in interior decoration moved more slowly than those for clothing, however, and although novelty was an important factor in prompting impulse purchases of smaller objects such as ceramic figures and silver "toys" it is clear that many items were bought upon setting up home and were expected to last a lifetime (Vickery 1998: 167). The majority of furniture fell into this category for most people, although it would appear that some pieces, painted backstools, for example, were considered cheap enough for regular renewal. Nonetheless, the fact that many people bought the furniture that they would live with for the rest of their lives comparatively young, meant that few people inhabited rooms that were highly fashionable for very long. Modish furnishings were for the very rich who could afford to renew schemes regularly. Textiles, which were subject to wear and tear, were replaced with more contemporary designs—chairs reupholstered, new curtains bought—though the popularity of single-color damasks and stripes, both less likely to date than more graphic and colorful designs, shows how middling householders sought out more neutral options to avoid the pitfalls of quickly outmoded high-fashion decorative schemes. Paint, and increasingly wallpaper, were also used as a means of signaling awareness of fashion without necessarily adopting the latest trends. Suitability was again a prime consideration, encouraging consumers to choose furnishings that reflected current fashions but would not date before they needed replacing.

In an age when national identities in Europe were neither geographically clear nor culturally distinct, to identify styles in interior decoration in national terms is somewhat arbitrary. Nonetheless, although court cultures across Europe had many common elements and were becoming increasingly similar throughout the eighteenth century, regional tastes and fashions in interior decoration were still very much in evidence. Freedom to travel and experience the sights, sounds, and tastes of other countries profoundly affected the outlook of many eighteenth-century men and women. Tsar Peter the Great's visit to the empty Het Loo Palace in the Netherlands in 1717 inspired the layout of his palace and gardens at Peterhof and Monplaisir, and directly influenced the tiled kitchens there (Vernova 1996). The free flow of objects and people might have created a homogenized Europe-wide court taste, but in spite of greater access and exposure to broader European fashions, distinct regional styles continued to flourish. New design ideas were adapted to suit local aesthetic preferences shaped by tradition, climate, and way of life. Diverse artistic and artisanal traditions and disparate cultures of consumption produced a wide range of different objects rather than an homogeneous world of goods. The differences between northern and southern Italian interpretations of the rococo style, and the widely disparate interiors and furniture they produced, is an excellent case in point (Fioratti 2004: 133–95). The lavishly gilded octagonal mirror closet of the Palazzo Isnardi di Caraglio (now Palazzo Solaro del Borgo) in Turin with a graphic parquetry floor (Plate 17), displays the extravagances of northern Italian rococo, while the colorful and exuberant ballroom of the Palazzo Alliata di Pietratagliata in Palermo with its magnificent tiled floor reflects the southern Italian interpretation of the style to suit local tastes and climate.

It is also apparent that consumers from different regions had clear ideas about the geographical origins of particular styles and object-types, and that there were strong associations between certain places and specific kinds of goods which varied from country to country. Thus in France, plain mahogany furniture was known as à l'anglais. Some of these connections were clearly historical and related to long-standing trade arrangements. The origins of other links between goods and places are less obvious, but again seem firmly entrenched in the popular consciousness. This is perhaps surprising given the very limited range of imported goods available to the vast majority of the population at this date. It does, however, illustrate the impact of trade upon Europeans, and the extent to which this influenced their perceptions of the nature of goods.

Before the early seventeenth century, goods from the Far East made their way slowly to Europe over land, and consequently only those items that were not snapped up by consumers en route ever made it as far north as the Netherlands and Britain. Silks, which were precious and easier to transport, were imported in greater quantity through the trading states of the Levant, Italy, and the Balkans, but fragile porcelain and bulky lacquer furniture were only rarely seen. Evidence of the preciousness of porcelain can be seen in the way that those rare examples that fell into European hands were often decorated with gold and silver mounts, and regularly appear in portraits and descriptions of cabinets of curiosities (Alcorn 1993: 1: cats. 19 and 24). Through the efforts of the Dutch East India Company, the Vereenigde Oostindische Compagnie in Dutch or VOC, porcelain and lacquer from the Far East became more widely available in the Netherlands in the early seventeenth century and gradually spread across Europe. Much admired and imitated, Japanese and Chinese porcelain and lacquerware were initially available only at auction, and then from a limited number of dealers in major cities. At first a rare luxury, by the beginning of the eighteenth century blue and white decorated porcelain from Jingdezhen in China, and the multicolored Kakiemon wares from Arita in Japan were familiar, widely available, and much more affordable. In many circles, porcelain replaced silver as the material of choice for dining wares, and as it became more affordable and more widely available it began also to replace pewter and stoneware. Prized for its whiteness, its vibrant and sophisticated decoration, and its hardness and impermeability, oriental porcelain was bought by the wealthy in great quantities, some for use and some for display. Those items not intended for daily use were gathered together to decorate dedicated spaces often known as "China" cabinets. This practice, particularly common among elite women, has received considerable attention from scholars, perhaps because it presents a feminine parallel to the collections of fine art associated with men (Impey and Marschner 1998). Large collections of porcelain were also amassed by men such as Christian IV of Denmark at the Rosenborg Slott in Copenhagen, and Augustus the Strong of Poland in his Japanese Palace outside Dresden. After years of experimentation, European manufactories such as Meissen, St Cloud, and Chelsea began to make imitation soft-paste porcelain, and these new wares increasingly replaced silver as the material for plates and dishes. The incorporation of ceramics into paneling became fashionable in the mid-eighteenth century, an example of which survives in the Gabinete de Porcelana at the Aranjuez Palace outside Madrid (Plate 18). The multicolored high-relief ceramic plaques were made at the nearby Buen Retiro manufactory between 1760 and 1765. The quest for porcelain can be seen as typical of the Enlightenment; examination and collection followed by experimentation and production. An opportunity to explore the world through materials.

FIGURE 4.1 An engraving of the fireplace in the Cabinet of Comte Bielenski, designed by Juste-Aurèle Meissonnier in 1734 and published in Paris in 1748. Photograph courtesy of agefotostock/Alamy Stock Photo.

NEW TECHNOLOGIES AND THEIR IMPACT UPON DECORATION

Heating, or lack of it, profoundly affected the ways in which rooms were used, and thus how they were furnished and decorated. Not all rooms were heated, even in the homes of the wealthiest, and in northern Europe parts of larger houses were often shut up during the colder months to make the most of what heating there was. Some houses were designed with this practice in mind, with large north-facing rooms without heating provision for summer use and, separated by a corridor, smaller rooms with stoves or fireplaces facing south for use in the winter.

Traditionally, the fireplace was the focus of a room, both in architectural and social terms, and chimneypieces and fire furniture were created with this in mind. Carved wood and, increasingly, marble were the preferred materials and varied from restrained surrounds with unadorned projecting bolection molding to rococo extravagances like those depicted by Juste-Aurèle Meissonnier (Figure 4.1). Marble surrounds were sometimes purchased on trips to Italy and sent home, as illustrated by the examples inventoried after the capture of the ship *Westmorland* in 1779 (Sánchez-Jágurgui and Wilcox 2012: 258–62). In eighteenth-century Britain the rich burnt coal, and this altered the shape of fire grates, which became smaller and shallower, often with an integrated fire back. Early eighteenth-century examples are made of wrought iron and rare, but by the second half of the century cast-iron grates were being mass produced by manufacturers such as Carron and the Coalbrookdale Iron Works (Edwards 1954: 2:68–70). Wood-burning, which was the norm in the rest of Europe, required different equipment. Andirons or fire dogs were necessary for supporting logs and allowing air to circulate around them, while a thick iron fireback protected the rear of the fireplace and radiated heat from the fire back into the room. Both andirons and firebacks could be highly decorative (Plate 19), as is illustrated by the exceedingly handsome pair of gilt-bronze andirons depicting a cat and a poodle seated on classical-style stools attributed to Phillipe Caffieri the younger and now in the Rijksmuseum in Amsterdam (BK-16903-A), or the fine cast-iron fireback with the arms of Louis-Alexandre de Bourbon, comte de Toulouse now in the J. Paul Getty Museum in Los Angeles.[8]

In much of northern Europe, large floor to ceiling stoves, usually occupying the corner of a room, became the norm and these were often tiled to aid cleaning and conserve heat. Two fine rococo stoves dating from 1768 survive at Stiftsgården, the Norwegian royal family's residence in Trondheim. Stoves of this type also became popular in the dining rooms of French châteaux in the second half of the eighteenth century, perhaps because they did not emit smoke, which might interfere with eating, although they were not adopted in other rooms (Girouard 2000: 144–5). Stoves do seem, however, to have been considered appropriate for smaller, less formal rooms, and their absence from state apartments, where substantial marble chimneypieces of the type popular across Europe were the norm, is notable. The sumptuous interiors of the Esterházy Palace at Fertőd in Hungary, however, which date from the 1760s, show how these two forms of heating could be elegantly combined (Plate 20). Portable braziers for burning charcoal to provide additional warmth in large rooms were also common, especially in Spain where they were used to heat the *estrado,* a raised platform in a small parlor on which the ladies of the house sat upon cushions to socialize (Fuchs 2011: 14–15).

Improvements and expansion in the glass industry, which made it possible to glaze larger windows, meant that many interiors were less dark in the eighteenth century than they had been in earlier times (Louw 1991). The difficulties of providing lighting outside the hours of daylight, however, remained (Ekirch 2005: 90–111). Firelight continued to provide minimal illumination in the majority of homes, but where additional lighting was desired and could be afforded, there were three main ways of achieving it. Burning wax, either beeswax or tallow in the form of candles or rushlights; burning oil in lamps; or burning tree spills. Beeswax candles were costly but gave a clean, clear light and smelled good. Tallow candles were much cheaper to produce but provided less light, smoked, and smelled bad. Candlesticks, for placing on a surface, and chambersticks, for carrying, could be made in a variety of materials according to taste and pocket. Wall sconces, sometimes with a mirrored or polished backing plate to reflect more light, could play an important part in decorative schemes, providing a strongly three-dimensional sculptural element that emphasized the carving on paneling and furniture. Ceiling-mounted chandeliers and lanterns were the province of the well-to-do, requiring not only money to acquire but also a high ceiling from which to hang the light fitting.

The nature and qualities of oil burnt in lamps varied across Europe, with animal fat or fish oil burnt in Scotland and olive oil burnt in southern Italy. Until the 1780s the majority of oil lamps were of the "open" type, with a wick lying in a pool of oil, which gave little light and smoked a great deal. In 1780, however, Swiss scientist Aimé Argand patented a cylinder oil lamp which significantly increased the illumination provided by a single wick and was safer and less smoky than the open version (Edwards 1954: 2:278–81). Argand lamps quickly became fashionable and were produced in a wide range of materials and finishes. Their popularity prompted other manufacturers to attempt to make their own models, infringing Argand's patent and resulting in a number of court cases and professional feuds, most notably with the English entrepreneur Matthew Boulton (Dickinson 1937: 127–30).

In the homes of the wealthy, mirror glass became more widely used than it had been in the previous century when Venetian glassworkers still had a monopoly on mirror production. In 1665 a mirror factory was established in Paris by

Louis XIV's finance minister, Jean-Baptiste Colbert, employing experienced mirror-workers enticed from Venice, who quickly developed techniques for producing larger, stronger mirrors than ever before. The construction of the Galerie des Glaces at the Palace of Versailles outside Paris, completed in 1684, was made possible by these technological developments, which were quickly copied in other European glass manufactories (Melchoir-Bonnet 2001: 73–6). In emulation of Louis XIV, paneling incorporating large quantities of mirror glass became a feature of luxurious interiors, and was especially popular in small, intimate rooms used for select entertaining, such as cabinets. The spectacularly restored mirror cabinets at the Episcopal Palace in Würzburg and at the Palazzo Isnardi di Caraglio in Turin show the impact that such spaces could have, and the extent to which the mirror reflected candlelight.

CONCLUSION

During the course of the eighteenth century significant innovations in the way that domestic spaces across Europe were used and laid out profoundly influenced the ways that interiors were decorated and furnished. Smaller rooms, linked by corridors and defined by use became commonplace, while reception areas such as entrance halls and staircases became more imposing, with separate service areas and staircases tucked away for servants to carry out the business of the house. Improved heating and lighting made these smaller rooms pleasant places to spend time, both shaped by and facilitating modes of sociability that defined eighteenth-century culture.

Textiles and ceramics imported from Asia inspired interior fashions and galvanized European manufacturers to produce a wider range of goods to appeal to all sectors of the market. Distinct regional styles of architecture and decoration defined by tradition and climate persisted despite increased trade and cultural exchange. Tiles from Spain and the Netherlands looked different and were used differently from each other. Paint, paneling, plasterwork, and wallpaper were exploited in myriad European homes to create diverse effects throughout the century.

CHAPTER FIVE

The Public Setting

JEFFREY COLLINS

PUBLIC VERSUS PRIVATE: A SHIFTING DISTINCTION

In an influential study, social theorist Jürgen Habermas identified the bourgeois public sphere (*Öffentlichkeit*) as a "child of the eighteenth century" ([1962] 1991: xviii). For Habermas, between 1700 and 1800 Europe underwent a decisive shift from feudal and monarchical forms of authority based on displays of inherited status to a bourgeois social and political order grounded in civic discourse and predicated on the free circulation of commodities, information, and ideas. While this new public realm operated virtually through newspapers, gazettes, and the Republic of Letters, it was anchored physically in newly arisen social spaces including British coffeehouses, French salons, and German *Tischgesellschaften*, "table societies" whose very name acknowledges their material underpinnings (Habermas [1962] 1991: 30, 32–7; Melton 2001). Scholars of eighteenth-century Western furniture, by contrast, have paid more attention to the burgeoning private sphere, stressing the rise of new, more comfortable forms and styles suited for domestic settings (Pardailhé-Galabrun 1991; Hellman 1999; DeJean 2009; cf. Habermas [1962] 1991: 11, 43–51). Differential survival has also played a role, since furniture designed for public spaces has often succumbed to hard use or proved less appealing to collectors. Ironically, today's public museums of art and design (including ever-popular "period rooms") thus largely exhibit "private" objects, while "public" furnishings, when they survive, remain the province of historical societies or living-history museums.

Despite these limitations, furniture from public settings, here defined to include everything outside the domestic realm offers distinct advantages for research. On the one hand, its acquisition, maintenance, and disposal have often left archival traces; on the other, its comparatively greater visibility and accessibility to contemporary audiences invite scholars to engage a broader range of users, including subaltern groups, than do objects destined for private homes. What is more, public furniture's direct role in civic and communal activity makes it a powerful barometer of changes in social practices and attitudes. Despite its challenges, a focus on objects made for and used in public settings in Europe and its colonies reveals furniture's centrality to multiple sectors of eighteenth-century life, from the traditional and established to the radical and new.

SITES OF REFRESHMENT AND SOCIABILITY

Taverns and coffeehouses

As hubs of commercial, social, and political exchange, "public houses" including inns, ordinaries, taverns, alehouses, and brandy shops loom large in accounts of eighteenth-century sociability and associated historical developments (Melton 2001: ch. 7). Although their furnishings have rarely been preserved, public spaces of this kind, and the interactions they fostered, may be reconstructed through contemporary documents and images (Graham 1994: fig. 3; Clayton 2003: figs. 3, 4; Cowan 2005: 79–80, figs. 36, 37). In colonial Boston, Massachusetts, probate inventories reveal that most taverns contained just one or two "long" (trestle or refectory-style) or "oval" (drop-leaf) tables per room, suggesting "fluid, integrated groups of drinkers rather than distinct subgroups" (Conroy 1995: 18, 88; Clayton 2003: 13). Seating, by contrast, followed the more general shift away from the communal benches, forms, and stools typical of sixteenth- and seventeenth-century interiors toward individual chairs. In 1698, Boston's Blue Anchor Tavern still offered seven benches alongside forty-seven chairs; three decades later, the nearby Sign of the Sun boasted ninety-three chairs, thirteen of which were "new," six with covers of "Turkey work," and the rest with seats of rush or leather, plus one (presumably coveted) "easy chair" (Conroy 1995: 87, 89, 119).

This pattern corresponds to the tavern furniture depicted by Boston-born painter Joseph Greenwood during a sojourn in the 1750s in Surinam (now Suriname), a Dutch plantation colony in northeastern South America and an important entrepôt for New England merchants (Plate 21) (Crawford 2018). In a large room (almost certainly a tavern in Paramaribo) furnished with a mirror and a lantern clock, seven bibulous traders, several of whom went on to prominence in the American Revolution, gather around a large drop-leaf table supplied with ladderback chairs with rush seats, one of which has fallen and broken in the foreground. Behind them, three more genteel patrons play cards at a smaller table fitted with a white cloth, while further revelers dance at the right and an attendant of African descent (likely enslaved) distributes punch from a central counter. The global uniformity of British pub furnishings became the stuff of satire. In 1753 London's weekly newspaper *The World* described one purported Grand Tourist's delight at finding a "very good billiard-table and very good company" at Rome's "English coffee-house," which he far preferred to the company of foreigners (Mead 1914: 392). That travelers appreciated familiar trappings is confirmed by the Scottish painter David Allan's view of a similar Roman café complete with a tripod stand, billiard table, and longcase clock to comfort homesick Britons (*c.* 1775; National Gallery of Scotland, D 4497 M; Wilton and Bignamini 1996: 115, cat. 72, illustrated).

The introduction of coffee by traders returning from the Levant expanded both the range of public houses and their furnishings. Despite the beverage's exotic roots, Europe's early coffeehouses—first established in Oxford in 1650, followed quickly by London (1652), Dublin (1664), Paris (1672), Hamburg (1677), Vienna (1685), and Leipzig (1694)—retained the refectory tables, benches, and settles associated with taverns, as depicted in a well-known gouache drawing of a London coffeehouse interior of *c.* 1700 (spuriously dated 1668), now in the British Museum (accession no. 1931,0613.2; see also Melton 2001: 247; Clayton 2003: 10, 17, 22–6; Cowan 2005: 115). As one London broadside of 1674 explained, egalitarian furnishings were part of coffeehouses' appeal:

First, Gentry, Tradesmen, all are welcome hither,
And may without Affront sit down Together:
Pre-eminence of Place, none here should Mind,
But take the next fit Seat that he can find:
Nor need any, if Finer Persons come,
Rise up for to assigne to them his Room.
                                        (Clayton 2003: 26; Cowan 2005: 102–3)

Conversation was encouraged by racks for the books, newspapers, and gazettes that turned coffeehouses into "penny universities"; some topical journals, such as London's *Tatler* (1709–11) and *Spectator* (1711–12 and 1714), claimed to gather their material from debates conducted over coffeehouse tables. At Daniel Button's coffeehouse in Covent Garden, where their editors Richard Steele and Joseph Addison convened a "little Senate" of like-minded friends from 1712, a marble letter box adorned with the mouth of a lion allowed authors to deposit anonymous manuscripts; as Addison explained in *The Guardian* for July 3, 1713, "Whatever the Lion swallows I shall digest for the use of the publick." Coffeehouse tables were also ideal for exhibiting curiosities and "gimcracks" for public auction (Cowan 2005: 120–38, fig. 22).

Garraways, near London's Royal Exchange, kept an upstairs sale room with a small rostrum and wooden seats, while the coffee room at Lloyd's, heart of the marine insurance trade, included a "pulpit" for announcing shipping news (Clayton 2003: 24, 51, 61, 64, figs. 15, 18).

In Europe's increasingly populous cities, coffeehouses doubled as refuges from cramped private quarters. One visitor to London in the 1720s noted that "a Man is sooner ask'd about his Coffee-House than his Lodgings" (Clayton 2003: 22). A decade later, one regular praised Mrs. George Carterwright for her comfortable establishment in Dublin:

> Her coffee's fresh and fresh her tea,
> Sweet her cream, ptizan, and whea [...]
> Next her bar's a magic chair,
> Oft I'm charm'd in sitting there.
>
> (Kennedy 2010: 30)

Fancier locales played up coffee's exotic associations through equipment, décor, or costumes that evoked its Eastern origins. Others, like the genteel café pictured in a French treatise of 1702 by the Chevalier de Mailly (*Les entretiens des cafés de Paris et les différens qui y surviennient*, published in Trevoux by Étienne Ganeau), evoked a luxurious private salon, complete with upholstered chairs, framed paintings, a mirror, a chandelier, and potted plants. Over the course of the century, coffeehouse furnishings became increasingly genteel and individualized. By the 1720s, Boston's upscale Crown Coffee House stocked leather-covered chairs, paintings, prints, "prospective Glasses," a japanned eight-day clock, silver punch bowls, brass candlesticks, and over a thousand clay pipes (Conroy 1995: 88–95). By the 1780s, London's tonier establishments offered semi-enclosed dining booths with tablecloths, braziers, and/or privacy curtains (Clayton 2003: 24; Cowan 2005: 181–3, figs. 10, 11, 33, 34). These amenities were likely inspired by the restaurants that had begun to emerge a decade earlier in Paris, proposing not just new types of food but new methods of dining. By replacing the cook-caterer's shared *table d'hôte* with customized service in separate rooms or alcoves furnished on a domestic model, the restaurant became "a public roof over a series of private tables," as historian Rebecca Spang has termed it, redefining the boundaries between individual and collective experience (2000: 7–8, 55–7, 68–70, 86).

CLUBS AND ASSOCIATIONS

Like cafés, voluntary clubs and associations proliferated during the eighteenth century and offered important venues for (semi-)public life (Clark 2000: 128, fig. 4.1). One such club, founded in 1753 by Liverpool merchants and customs officials, jokingly claimed to be running the small town of Sefton to which it repaired for Sunday meals, appointing a town clerk, recorder, bailiffs, aldermen, and chaplain and renting a corporate pew in Sefton Church with a special box for its "mayor" (Saxton 1948). Although exclusive by definition, clubs routinely met in public houses, sometimes in dedicated rooms whose furnishings reflected members' interests. In Cheshire, the local Jacobite club equipped its premises with chairs covered with remnants of the cloak Charles I wore to his execution (Graham 1994: 20; Clark 2000: 247).

Evocative—indeed, parodic—accoutrements were embraced by the Society of Dilettanti, an elite group of former Grand Tourists who convened at London's Bedford Head Tavern in 1732 to blend "friendly and social intercourse" with "promotion of the Arts," including archaeology. Club furnishings reflected the members' love of liquid refreshment: as Horace Walpole quipped, membership's "nominal qualification was having been in Italy, and the real one, being drunk." In 1736 the Dilettanti commissioned a mahogany casket, supplied by sculptor Thomas Adye to designs by members Sir James Gray and George Knapton, to contain "The Book of Forfeitures and Dinner money," as well as "the Box containing money for the current services" (Redford 2008: 7). Topped with an ivory figure of the god of wine, it was modeled on the so-called Tomb of Bacchus, an ancient porphyry sarcophagus linked with drunken rituals of the "Bentvueghels," Rome's society of Dutch and Flemish artists (Clark 2000: 247, plate 14; Redford 2008: 6–7, fig. 4; Kelly 2009: 39–41, fig. 23; Collins 2019: 576–7, fig. 30.3).[1] Three years later, woodworker Elka Haddock delivered a satyr-legged "sella curulis" for the society's president, who was cloaked in a wine-red toga for pseudo-religious initiation ceremonies (Hayward 1977: 489; Graham 1994: 66–8, fig. 88; Redford 2008: 5–6). Even more rakish was a temple-form mahogany ballot box centered on a cask straddled by a personification of Justitia. As Jason Kelly notes, "This drunken Justice was a playful allusion to the haze of the Dilettanti's alcoholic revels as well as a sexual reference," since voting on new members required the insertion of balloting balls between Justitia's legs (Plate 22) (Clark 2000: 247, plate 15; Redford 2008: 6, fig. 3; Kelly 2009: 41, fig. 25).

Symbolic furniture was central to Freemasonry, an international network of lodges that the German dramatist Gotthold Ephraim Lessing linked to the very birth of bourgeois society (Habermas [1962] 1991: 35; Melton 2001: ch. 8). Rooted in medieval masons' guilds but nurtured in taverns and coffeehouses, the fraternal order took form in London in 1717 and quickly spread to Ireland, France, Italy, Germany, and British North America. Three surviving masters' chairs from colonial Virginia, perhaps commissioned by the royal governor, deploy tools of the building trade as metaphors for personal and societal regeneration (Graham 1994: 64–6, 71–2, figs. 14, 87, 93, 94, 135; Howlett 1996; Hurst and Prown 1997: 188–201, cats. 53–5).

The most elaborate was crafted of painted and parcel-gilt mahogany by the British-born cabinetmaker and Freemason Benjamin Bucktrout (1744–1812), perhaps for the Grand Lodge convened in Williamsburg's Raleigh Tavern in 1777 (Colonial Williamsburg, accession no. 1983–317; Howlett 1996: illustrated; Hurst and Prown 1997: 192–9, cat. 54, illustrated). Adapting a "French Chair" from the 1754 edition of Thomas Chippendale's *Director*, Bucktrout added a tall back composed of Corinthian pilasters topped by the sun, the moon, and a bust of the worshipful master. Between them float symbols of the order's three degrees, including the hinged gauge of the Entered Apprentice (for dividing the day among work, study, and sleep), the level and plumb of the Journeyman or Fellowcraft (for measuring out justice and mercy), and the compass and trowel of the Master, who guards moral boundaries and unites the lodge in brotherly love (Howlett 1996: 203–4, 208–25; Hurst and Prown 1997: 192). The rusticated arch at the top originally bore a crown in honor of the king (Howlett 1996: 225–6; Hurst and Prown 1997: 194). Standing five feet high, this grandiloquent throne aggrandized its worshipful occupant while encapsulating the order's core tenets.

SITES OF EDUCATION

Libraries and schools

Secretive as it was, Freemasonry reflected the eighteenth century's stress on moral and intellectual improvement. Libraries, once the purview of the court, the church, or private families, welcomed a wider group of patrons in dramatic reading rooms that abandoned the semi-enclosed stalls and chained books typical of medieval and Renaissance libraries in favor of wall-mounted bookshelves that embellished and unified the space. The most ambitious, including Rome's Biblioteca Casanatense, opened by the Dominicans in 1701, and Biblioteca Lancisiana, founded in 1711 by Pope Clement XI's personal physician, included mezzanine balconies to expand the available shelving. At the sumptuous Biblioteca Joanina at the University of Coimbra, Portugal (1720s), the balcony rests on downward-tapering *estipites*, whereas the imposing Biblioteca dei Girolamini in Naples (1727–36) recesses the upper story behind a balustraded gallery. At Bologna's Institute of Sciences and Arts, Pope Benedict XIV commissioned two-story walnut bookcases designed by sculptor Ercole Lelli, completed in 1756, which maximize book storage by tucking shallow alcoves under the projecting mezzanines (Collins 2016: 391–2, plate 26). Britain adopted the new trend, described as "à la moderne" by one writer in 1703 (Petroski 1999: 139), in projects including the Codrington Library at All Souls College, Oxford, designed by Nicholas Hawksmoor and completed by James Gibbs in 1751, and the neo-Palladian library of Christ Church College, Oxford, completed in 1772. Rome's Biblioteca Angelica, completed in the 1760s by woodworker Nicola Fagioli, added a vertiginous second balcony to access a third level of bookcases. The trend reached its height in French architect Étienne-Louis Boullée's unrealized project of 1785 to remodel the royal library in Paris, first opened to the public in 1692. Boullée envisioned an immense, top-lit reading room—"a glorious amphitheater of books," according to a contemporary commentator—complete with four stepped tiers of open shelves browsed by toga-clad scholars and furnished with a Greek-inspired, klismos-form stool (The Morgan Library and Museum, New York, accession no. 2017.17).

Antiquity was an important inspiration for Amsterdam's Felix Meritis Society, founded in 1776 to promote "happiness through merit" and opened twelve years later in a temple-fronted building on the Keizersgracht. Dedicated to promoting the arts, letters, sciences, and commerce, its facilities included a life-drawing classroom with stepped risers surrounded a platform for posing models, a solution already adopted at the Académie Royale de Peinture et de Sculpture in Paris, housed at the Louvre since 1692, and Bologna's Accademia Clementina, established at the Institute in 1712 (Williams 2019: 178–9, fig. 10.3; Collins 2016: 393–5, fig. 16.2).[2] Felix Meritis also benefited from an oval concert hall, an astronomical observatory, and a physics classroom fitted with curving bleachers inspired by ancient theaters. Similar in Paris, architect Jacques Gondoin modeled the semidomed, semicircular dissection hall at Paris's École de Chirurgie (1764) on the Greek theater recently discovered at Herculaneum, part of a concerted embrace of ancient prototypes for modern educational purposes. Hierarchy still obtained, and whereas bench seating in the cavea was open to the public every morning and afternoon, professors and prestigious guests were accommodated in plush chairs of Gondoin's design, with neoclassical hoof feet (Gondoin 1780: 10).[3] In a similar way, seats on the *gradins* at Paris' art academy (not all equally desirable or well lit) were allocated by precedence, the sons of academicians choosing first according to their fathers' rank, followed by prize-winning students in descending order of accomplishment, and finally by those pupils "without connections or decorations" (Williams 2019: 179–80).

Museums

Appropriate furnishings were essential for the new public or publicly oriented museums, which sought models in a variety of contexts. In 1742, Benedict XIV commissioned Italy's first public "Museum of Human Anatomy or Internal and External Anthropometry," unveiled a decade later at the Institute in Bologna primarily for the benefit of artists but also of medical students and the curious public. The project's promoter, Ercole Lelli, was an anatomical sculptor who in 1734 had carved two *écorché* (flayed) figures of linden wood to support the lector's chair at the anatomical theater of Bologna's Archiginnasio. Lelli's elaborate showcases for the new "Camera della Notomia," centered on four pairs of life-size wax statues in successive stages of dissection, recalled contemporary natural history cabinets, including those at the Institute, and pharmacies, such as the roughly contemporary Ospedale degli Incurabili in Naples. Project drawings (Figure 5.1) show his attempt to facilitate intensive study by surrounding viewers with a syncopated curtain of glass combining flat cases for small specimens with projecting "nicchie" or "custodie" for his figures, which rotated for ease of inspection.[4] "Crystalline shrines of the anatomized body," as Rebecca Messbarger terms them, Lelli's vitrines fostered "the Enlightenment cult of science" in a setting that recalled a chapel filled with sculptured saints (Messbarger 2010: 8–10, 20–51 [esp. 46–8], figs. 14, 25–6; Collins 2016). Similar sacristy-style cabinets, glazed and topped with portraits

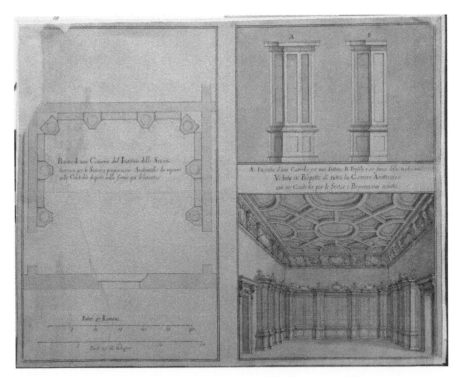

FIGURE 5.1 Attributed to Ercole Lelli (Italian, 1702–66), drawings for display cabinets in the "Camera della Notomia" at the Instituto delle Scienze e delle Arti, Palazzo Poggi, Bologna, late 1740s, pen and ink with brown and pink washes. Archivio di Stato di Bologna, Assunteria di Istituto, Diversorum, busta 10, no. 2 (bis). Photograph courtesy of Jeffrey Collins.

of famous surgeons, graced the anatomical museum Benedict established at Rome's hospital of S. Spirito in Sassia, displaying medical and obstetric models collected from across Europe (Collins 2004: 226–7, fig. 134).

Other museum furnishings looked to aristocratic models. Paris's first public art gallery, opened at the Luxembourg Palace from 1750 to 1779, displayed vases of agate and porphyry atop a suite of marble-topped tables supplied by the Garde-Meuble de la Couronne, the department of the king's household responsible for movable furnishings. These princely fixtures, similar to those deployed in French royal palaces, created a suitably opulent setting for some 120 paintings and drawings chosen from the royal collection, adorned with gilt frames and hung against green cloth as in the annual Salon exhibitions at the Louvre (McClellan 1994: 13 and 218, n. 1). Three decades later, Louis XVI outfitted the new museum being established at the Louvre (a project conceived in 1776 but not realized until 1792), with a pair of sumptuous cabinets purchased from the collections of the duc d'Aumont in 1782 (Meyer 2002: 1: 212–15, cat. 53, illustrated). Crafted by Joseph Baumhauer in the late 1760s, these objects (now at Versailles) were themselves museum pieces, incorporating panels of Boulle marquetry and mosaics depicting birds and flowers in *pietra dura* (inlaid semiprecious stones) harvested from older furnishings made under Louis XIV. On public display at the Louvre, perhaps housing medals or other mementos of royal history, these cabinets recalled the glories of the *Roi Soleil,* a high point in French history and a focus of national nostalgia.

As a beacon of cultural tourism, Rome occupied a special place in the development of museums and museum furnishings. Emblematic are the impressive pair of bronze tables crafted in 1742 by pontifical founder Francesco Giardoni (1692–1757), to an unknown architect's design, for the main hall of Rome's new Capitoline Museum of ancient sculpture. Conceived to support tops crafted from polychrome mosaic pavements unearthed at Emperor Hadrian's Villa—valuable antiquities in their own right—the tables (now displayed in the Pinacoteca) combine baroque motifs such as female masks and foliate stretchers with winged-lion monopodia inspired by ancient furniture (González-Palacios in Bowron and Rishel 2000: 165, cat. 42). These striking designs prompted a vogue for similar tables in gilt wood, including a pair for the Quirinal Palace and an example featured in Pompeo Batoni's double portrait of Emperor Joseph II and his younger brother, the Grand Duke of Tuscany, who visited the Eternal City in 1769 (Kunsthistorisches Museum, Vienna).

Lion monopodia reappear in the striking quartet of cabinets crafted in exotic hardwoods by papal goldsmith Luigi Valadier and the Tyrolean cabinet maker Andrea Mimmi between 1780 and 1782 for the Vatican's Museo Profano, dedicated to the display of smaller antiquities including cameos, ivories, and statuettes (Figure 5.2; Collins 2004: 73–4, fig. 34; Cornini and Lega 2013: 30–1, 59–73).[5] Unlike the fanciful beasts on the Capitoline

FIGURE 5.2 Andrea Mimmi (born South Tyrol, active in Rome second half of the eighteenth century) after designs by Luigi Valadier (Roman, 1726–85), display cabinet (one of four) for the Museo Profano (then part of the Library), Vatican Palace, Rome, 1780–2, veneered in tropical hardwoods including *giallo angelino* and red sandalwood, with gilt-bronze mounts. Photograph courtesy of Jeffrey Collins.

tables, these snarling protomes are among the earliest literal transcriptions of a classical prototype in modern furniture; described in Valadier's bill as, "carved in the antique taste," they are directly modeled on an ancient Roman table leg (*trapezophoros*) in floriated alabaster, purchased for the nearby Pio-Clementino Museum in 1779 from the estate of Giovanni Battista Piranesi (González-Palacios 2018: 259–63 and 287–9, figs. 6.1–6.4). Even more expressive of the museum's ethos are two colossal bronze display tables commissioned by Pius VI in 1789 for the main hall of the Vatican Library. Executed by Paolo Spagna and Vincenzo Pacetti to designs by Giuseppe Valadier (son of Luigi) and painter Christoph Unterberger, each features a massive granite top carried by twelve figures of Hercules (perhaps inspired by ancient silenes at villa Albani) bearing reliefs chronicling the pontiff's heroic labors. These naturally include his enrichment of the museum, his 1783 visit in the company of Gustav III of Sweden, and his triumphant re-erection of three ancient Egyptian obelisks (Collins 2004: 81–2, figs. 41–2, ch. 4, and 193–219; González-Palacios 2018: 456–65, figs. 10.3 and 10.4).

The rise in museum visitorship also sparked more practical furnishings. Inspecting the Vatican's famous *Stanze* (an apartment frescoed in the early sixteenth century by Raphael and his school) in 1721, the English painter and essayist Jonathan Richardson bemoaned the poor lighting but was delighted to find a stepped viewing "Machine" in the Hall of Constantine, "on which one sits Commodiously to observe those parts of the Works which otherwise would be too remote from the eye" (Richardson and Richardson 1722: 195–7). Eighty years later, the French painter Hubert Robert depicted a similar elevated platform in a view of the Grand Gallery of the Louvre, to assist a budding artist copy an Old Master (McClellan 1994: 139, fig. 53). Robert includes protective railings, proposed in his 1780s project for adapting the palace gallery for public display (McClellan 1994: 55, fig. 24). More elaborate guardrails shielded the Pio-Clementino's precious ancient pavements, including a mahogany barrier in the rich Cabinet of the Masks that reproduced the Egyptian telamons guarding the museum's entrance. Comfort was not forgotten, and the same room obliged tired tourists with benches constructed of rare (if hard) porphyry slabs on giltwood frames (Collins 2004: 179–80, fig. 105, and 319, n. 88). Artists made do with rough-hewn stools, judging from contemporary views, although the *sgabello* pulled up to an easel in Johann Zoffany's famous view of the Tribuna at the Uffizi of the 1770s (Royal Collection) bears the Medici arms and a striped cushion. To the left, the Honorable Felton Hervey enjoys a luxurious velvet armchair and Charles Loraine Smith an upholstered backstool, perhaps similar to the chair of crimson velvet the Grand Duke provided, along with a scaffold and easel, to the German artist Johann Christian Mannlich while copying Raphael's *Madonna della Seggiola* at Palazzo Pitti in 1770 (Mannlich 1989–93: 2:10).

SITES OF RECREATION AND COMMERCE

The eighteenth-century transformation of theaters and opera houses from annexes of the court into commercial enterprises dependent on public subscription had concomitant effects on their layout, decoration, and furnishing (Habermas [1962] 1991: 38–9; Melton 2001: ch. 5). Some did double duty as reception spaces. In 1747, France's ambassador to the Holy See, Cardinal Fréderique Jérôme de La Rochefoucauld, staged a cantata at Rome's Teatro Argentina to celebrate the remarriage of the Dauphin, avoiding legal restrictions on female performers by transforming the auditorium into a sumptuous festival hall adorned with a lavish carpet and plush armchairs for fellow princes of the church (Kerber 2017: 95–100, fig. 112). The doge of Venice likewise engaged the Teatro San Benedetto in 1782 to host a state luncheon for the "Counts of the North," at which Grand Duke Paul Petrovich of Russia and his wife Maria Feodorovna (traveling incognito) dined onstage with selected guests as spectators watched from the boxes (Wilton and Bignamini 1996: 191, cat. 141, illustrated). Parterres, previously unfurnished, increasingly received fixed seating. In Naples, as British traveler Samuel Sharp observed, music lovers had the choice of nearly six hundred comfortable places in the pit of the Teatro di San Carlo, each "with arms resembling a large elbow chair." Those in the first four wide rows boasted the added convenience of a lockable seat that "lifts up like the lid of a box," allowing seasonal subscribers to come and go without disturbing patrons in spots hired by the night (Sharp 1766: 84–5).

The real action was in the pricier boxes or loges, which doubled as miniature drawing rooms. As Sharp explained, "The *Neapolitan* quality rarely dine or sup with one another, and many of them hardly ever visit, but at the Opera." Rather than attending to the performance, the gentlemen "run about from box to box" while the ladies conversed, played cards, or regaled their company "with iced fruits and sweet-meats" (Sharp 1766: 82–3). Charles Burney noted that each box at Milan's ducal theater seated "six persons [...] facing each other," with a separate inner room complete with fireplace "and all conveniences for refreshments and cards." In Venice, Sarah Bentham noted that each box was furnished with blinds and a commode chair (Sweet 2012: 39–40). Burney added that those wishing to gamble would find on the fourth tier "a *pharo* table, on each side of the house," which no doubt contributed to the "abominable" noise during performances (1771: 81–2). Yet boxes were also spaces of intimacy, as seen in Jean-Michel Moreau the Younger's 1777 drawing of an encounter in one such "petite loge" at the top of a Parisian theater, part of a project documenting fashionable clothing and furnishings (Rothschild Collections, Waddesdon Manor, accession no. 203.2004, cat. 44).[6] Under a leering ram's head, a wealthy "sybarite" welcomes a young dancer and her duenna to a plush love nest whose pier glass, gilt-bronze wall lights, upholstered *fauteuils*, and two layers of privacy curtains create a secluded space of seduction at the very heart of public life.

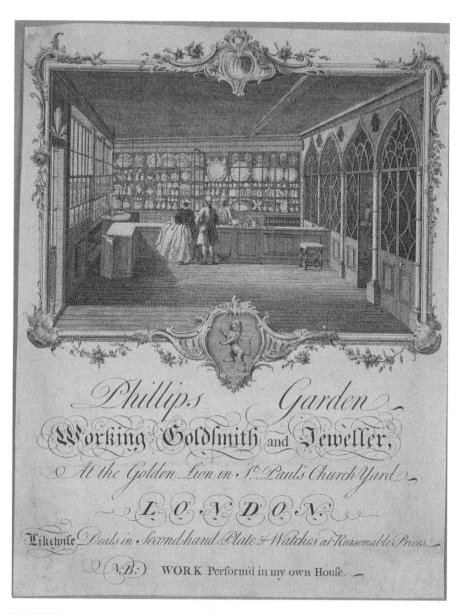

FIGURE 5.3 Attributed to Francis Garden, Trade card of Phillips Garden, working goldsmith and jeweler, at the Golden Lion in St. Paul's Churchyard, London, *c.* 1750s, etching with engraved lettering, 27.6 × 21.4 centimeters. Photograph © The Trustees of the British Museum.

Europe's growing bourgeoisie sparked new attention to the outfitting of shops, especially those purveying luxury goods. As the British jeweler Joseph Brasbridge reflected, "The great secret [...] is to expose enough to excite curiosity, and to conceal enough to leave curiosity ungratified" (Brasbridge 1824: 51). This was the strategy of the fashionable establishment at 3, quai de Bourbon, on Paris's Île Saint-Louis, whose handsome oak front, supplied by *menuisier* Étienne Séjournant in 1776, showcased the latest temptations behind broad areas of glazing (Kisluk-Grosheide and Munger 2010: 38–9, cat. 7). No less enticing was the antiquary's shop in Naples captured in a 1798 image of Prince Augustus Frederick (later Duke of Sussex) and British envoy and collector Sir William Hamilton inspecting open shelves stacked with ancient vases and souvenir gouaches (Wilton and Bignamini 1996: 217, cat. 164, illustrated).

It was London, however, that most travelers praised for the "Brillancy and Shew" of its emporia (Reverend William Cole in 1765 quoted in Kisluk-Grosheide and Munger 2010: 38–9). The Prussian officer and historian Johann Wilhelm von Archenholz averred that "Nothing can be more superb than the silver-smiths' shops" in London's fashionable West End, groaning with elegant goods elegantly displayed. (Archenholz 1789: 1:151). The 1760 contract between John Parker and Edward Wakelin lists the numerous "presses, counters, drawers, shew glasses, and looking glasses" furnishing their shop in Panton Street. Brasbridge lured customers by presenting "gold buttons and trinkets" in a cotton-lined case, whereas jeweler Henry Ellis of Exeter filled his window with "a horizontal showcase [...] which held my gold chains, seals and keys" (Clifford 2004: 41, figs. 29, 30). So proud was London goldsmith Phillips Garden of his shop near St. Paul's that he depicted its interior on his trade card (Figure 5.3). Glazed cupboards display waiters, tureens, and other holloware, while removable drawers contain flatware and assorted "toys." To the right, four Gothick Revival windows light the workshop where his stylish merchandise took shape.

SITES OF WORSHIP

Despite the expansion of secular institutions, religious settings remained primary venues of public life for many eighteenth-century Europeans. Worship was not the only draw; as one correspondent complained to London's *Universal Spectator* in 1734,

> *Churches* were for People to shew their *fine Cloaths* in, their *Diamonds*, *Rings*, *Toupees*, and *Snuff-Boxes*; every thing but their Devotion: Here some whisper, nod, bow, ogle, kneel, and laugh; others look about, frown, are concern'd, affronted with their Gallants, seem serious with their *Lovers*, and trifling with their *God*.

(Friedman 2011: 87)

Church furnishings reflected this overlap, some echoing domestic forms and others, such as the *Liedtafeln* (customizable signboards) installed in Lübeck's Marienkirche following the publication of Buxtehude's new hymnal in 1701, distinctly ecclesiastical (Range 2012: 199–201, fig. 8.1). Whatever their inspiration, the wooden fittings supplied by joiners and cabinet makers worked in tandem with sacred architecture to shape worshippers' experience.

SEATING FOR CLERGY AND CONGREGANTS

In churches, as in homes, where, how, and even whether one sat reflected and reinforced social hierarchy. Popes and bishops enjoyed elevated thrones in the apse or choir, sometimes as part of elaborate stalls that continued to be built in ceremonial settings throughout the eighteenth century, especially in Catholic and Anglican contexts. The classicizing oak stalls unveiled at St. Paul's Cathedral in London in 1697, designed by Sir Christopher Wren (1632–1723) with limewood reliefs by the Dutch-born sculptor Grinling Gibbons (1648–1721), incorporated towering organ cases as well as a velvet-hung *cathedra* of carved walnut for the bishop, a crimson velvet armchair for the dean, and seats for the Lord Mayor and members of the Corporation of London. Cathedral canons were housed in tiered enclosures, following medieval models, behind which rear "closets" (resembling high-sided theater boxes) accommodated their wives and children (Bond 1910: 82–4; Graham 1994: 17, 26–7, figs. 20, 21, 35; Friedman 2011: 64, fig. 305).

Even richer were the lavish stalls created by woodworker Pedro Muñoz between 1719 and 1722 for the cathedral of the wealthy city of Puebla in the Viceroyalty of New Spain (today in Mexico). Containing 103 seats, this imposing construction was enriched with elaborate intarsia of bone and precious tropical hardwoods forming complex interlace patterns that were once interpreted as *mudéjar* echoes of Spain's Muslim past, transported to the New World (Plate 23). In fact, some of these elaborate knot motifs derive from garden designs published by Georg Andreas Böckler (*Architectura curiosa nova*, Nuremberg, 1664) and Jan van der Groen (*Den nederlandtsen hovenier*, Amsterdam, 1669 and 1721) as well as in architectural decoration by Hans Vredeman de Vries (see Volume 3, Chapter 8 in this series), a reminder of the importance of books and prints as vectors of design inspiration. Here, these parquetry parterres have liturgical functions and could have inspired connections with the gardens of Eden and Gethsemane. With their rich coloration, botanical diversity, and riot of geometric patterns, these stalls create a mesmerizing *hortus conclusus* at the heart of the vast nave (Díaz Cayeros 2012: 38–50, 56–60, 67–9, 241–58).[7]

In more modest houses of worship, seats for presiding clergy followed or adapted domestic fashions. The combined armchair and lectern at the parish church of St. Lawrence at West Wycombe, Buckinghamshire, crafted in rosewood around 1765, echoed designs by Thomas Chippendale, with the addition of a crowning dove (Randall 1980: 81, fig. 89). The sturdy oak armchair in the chancel at Upton, Cambridgeshire (inscribed "Joane Browne / Want Not / A.D. 1700"), likely originated as a household object gifted for its air of antiquity (Bond 1910: 126–7; Graham 1994: 29; Howard 2004: 154, fig. 151). The neo-Gothic sanctuary chairs at Shobdon Church, Heredfordshire, designed around 1755 by William Kent and/or Richard Bateman, reflect the appeal of older styles to suggest a historical pedigree (Graham 1994: 27–8, fig. 36; Friedman 2011: 215–17). A Gothic idiom was also chosen for the chaplain's chair designed by Robert Adam around 1780 for Alnwick Castle in Northumberland. "Of an antique Form, painted white with gold Ornaments," according to a contemporary inventory, the chair's trefoil arches, crocketed pinnacles, and seraphim handrests evoke the Percy family's antiquity in concert with the chapel's neo-medieval décor (Harris 2001: 91, fig. 136).

Seating for prominent laymen was distinguished through form, material, and color. A heraldic canopy marked the mayor's pew constructed at Blandford Forum, Dorset, in 1748 (Randall 1980: 58, 64, fig. 65), while the governor's pew designed by James "Athenian" Stuart and William Newton about 1780 for the Royal Naval College at Greenwich was graced with dolphin-form railings (Bristol 2006: 372–3, figs. 8–25, 8–26, 8–27). Upholstery was a sure sign of status. The Duke of Chandos's chapel at Cannons House, Middlesex, boasted crimson velvet chairs and cushions trimmed with lace (dispersed at auction in 1747); four decades later, the sovereign's stall at St. George's Chapel, Windsor, was richly covered with purple velvet and cloth of gold (Friedman 2011: 64, 66, and fig. 503). At Alnwick, nine wheel-back chairs painted in gold and white with green velvet cushions were reserved for family members in a carpeted alcove, while guests sat less comfortably on twenty-four silk-upholstered stools. Such luxury shocked the future clergyman James Plumptre, who recorded his indignation in 1799 "at seeing the *House of prayer*, turned into the *House of ostentation of the Percy family*" (Harris 2001: 91–2; Friedman 2011: 255–8). The residents of colonial Conway, Massachusetts, took similar exception to the pretensions of a Tory landowner who insisted on occupying his own armchair near the deacon. Arriving late one Sunday, he found it missing and, "much to his own disgust and to the satisfaction of the audience," was obliged to sit "side by side with the common people." A few years later, his chair was found "on the top of Dr. Hamilton's hill hanging in a hemlock'" (Rice 1867: 32, n.).

Congregational seating, introduced in the later Middle Ages, was far from universal in the eighteenth century. Edward Wright, who accompanied the future Earl of Macclesfield to Italy in the 1720s, noted that the Romans

have no Pews in their Churches, and 'tis a great advantage to the prospect [...]. For by this means, at the entrance, you have one clear uninterrupted view, quite to the further end. The People kneel upon the bare Marble; only Ladies of the first Quality, and Ambassadors Ladies, have Cushions.

(Wright 1730: 203)

An exception was made for the Lenten sermon season, when the authorities filled "the middle of the Church with Benches, and stretch a Canopy of Canvas quite over Preacher and People, a little higher than the Pulpit, partly for warmth, and partly to assist the voice." Seating was equally makeshift in some Lutheran churches. Folding chairs remained in use in Amsterdam (Spicer 2012a: 475, fig. 16.9), while an English visitor to Cape Town noted the custom of using chairs instead of pews, which he attributed to "the scarcity of wood in this colony when at its first foundation every man provided his own seat" (467). In Lutheran Norway, by contrast, fixed seating enforced social discipline by separating male and female commoners across the aisle or, if unmarried, in transept galleries. The families of clergy, military officers, royal household staff, and rich burghers commanded places of honor behind the choir screen or in raised, privately constructed pews facing the pulpit (Ekroll 2012: 283, 299). Similar divisions marked the rural parish church at Jõelähtme in Estonia, where a survey taken around 1730 recorded the German elite in the chancel, other Germans in the nave, and the Estonian populace in the upper galleries (Kodres 2012: 343 and fig. 13.5). In colonial Massachusetts, meetinghouses were seated by criteria including age, wealth, "honor," "usefulness," and "qualification," such as military or civic office. Race also played a major role, with Blacks and Indigenous converts, despite having full religious privileges, restricted to the rearmost benches or the balcony (Dinkin 1988: 410–13).

In many Anglo-American churches, social segregation was promoted through enclosed or box pews, which remained popular throughout the eighteenth century and whose rents helped fund the parish. The Mock Corporation of Sefton rebuilt its pew from scratch in 1772, while the residents of the Hall in Northorpe, Lincolnshire, maintained a separate pew for their dogs until the early nineteenth century (Saxton 1948: 84–5, plates xxvii, xxviii; Randall 1980: 57–8; Graham 1994: 19; Friedman 2011: 53). While tenants might customize these Sabbath precincts with locks, cushions, partitions, or even stoves, the authorities at Holy Trinity in Guildford, Surrey, stipulated that pews could only be lined in green, "except those belonging to the Bishop and [...] Corporation" (Friedman 2011: 53, 56, 66). Just as in houses of entertainment, pews were priced by desirability, sometimes forcing church leaders to choose between plans that maximized revenue and those that accommodated the greatest numbers (Friedman 2011: 53–4). New churches, by contrast, favored uniform bench pews, especially in structures with innovative ground plans (e.g., Friedman 2011: 507, 578, 585, figs. 41, 580, 582, 677, 678, 689, 690). In Poland, both the centralized Lutheran church of the Holy Cross at Poznań (constructed from 1777 to 1786 to designs by Anton Höhne) and the circular "Evangelical-Augsburg" church of the Holy Trinity in Warsaw (built between 1777 and 1781 to designs by Simon Gottlieb Zug) featured concentric pews recalling contemporary theaters (Harasimowicz 2012: 432–43, figs. 15.13–15, 17–19).

FURNITURE FOR PREACHING AND LITURGY

In both Catholic and Protestant contexts, the Reformation's emphasis on preaching and scripture lent prominence to furniture for public address. Among the century's most daring "oratorial machines," as Jonathan Swift called them in his satirical *Tale of a Tub* (London, 1704), is the cantilevered pulpit designed by painter and architect Charles de Wailly (1729–98) for the Parisian church of St. Sulpice in 1789. Accessed by twin staircases rising between two piers, the pulpit soars over the congregation like the Montgolfier brothers' hot-air balloon, first demonstrated six years earlier.[8] Anglican communities on both sides of the Atlantic also favored elevated pulpits, sometimes of stepped design incorporating desks for the reader and clerk (Randall 1980: 70, 76, 78, figs. 78, 79). At Greenwich, James Stuart modeled the novel tholos-shaped lectern on the choragic monument of Lysicrates he had published in *The Antiquities of Athens* (London, 1762); originally set on axis, this Greek-style pulpit was later embellished with medallions in Coade stone (a matte-finished stoneware developed *c.* 1770) depicting the Acts of the Apostles after designs by Benjamin West (1738–1820) (Bristol 2006: 372; Weber 2006a: 457–61, figs. 10–78, 10–79, 10–80). Some pulpits swiveled to avoid favoritism: as John Wesley noted in 1781, the wheeled lectern in the octagonal chapel of Sheffield's Shrewsbury Hospital was "shifted once a quarter, that all the pews may face it in their turns" (Friedman 2011: 102). Lutheran pulpits might be combined with the altar or organ and embellished with sculpture. The lavish lectern at St. Jacob's Church in Augsburg, installed in 1705, culminated in a two-meter-high golden angel; the slightly later pulpit in the city's Evangelische Ulrichskirche was crowned by John the Baptist, with gilded figures of the Evangelists and a canopy supported by flying angels (Gray 2012: 57; Spicer 2012: 473–4, fig 16.8). In Cape Town, in the 1780s, German sculptor Anton Anreith adorned the pulpit with a swan and "two-well-carved Herculean figures, coloured to resemble bronze," symbolizing Luther's eloquence and strength. (Spicer 2012: 466, fig. 16.5).

The eighteenth century's most elaborate sculptured pulpits were created for preaching orders in the Catholic southern Netherlands (roughly present-day Belgium), who embraced theatrical furnishings to engage and instruct their listeners. The elaborate oak pulpit completed by Michiel Frans van der Voort the Elder (1667–1737) in 1713 for the Cistercian abbey church of Saint Bernard near Antwerp (later moved to the city's cathedral; Fierens 1943: 18–19, plate IX) evokes the Garden of Eden, with railings in the form of tree branches and birds perched on trunk-shaped newels. Overhead, a trumpeting angel descends toward a tent-shaped sounding board held aloft by flying putti, perhaps inspired by the famous canopied bed of Princess Maria Mancini Colonna, designed by Johann Paul Schor, that Van der Voort may have seen in Rome between 1690 and 1693 (see Volume 3, Chapter 8 in this series). Van der Voort's subsequent pulpit for the Norbertine priory church of Onze-Lieve-Vrouw van Leliëndaal (Plate 24) (now at St. Rombout's Cathedral, Mechelen; Fierens 1943: 19–20, plate XII), executed between 1721 and 1723 with the assistance of Theodoor Verhaegen, is even more dramatic, depicting the moment at which Saint Norbert of Xanten, in the midst of a moral conversion, falls from his horse below a rocky outcropping. To the preacher's left, Satan slithers toward Eve in the form of a serpent amid a tangle of foliage, while to his right a crucifix completes God's plan of salvation and blooming lilies evoke the church's dedication. The pulpit's functional components—rustic "stone" steps, a preacher's rostrum wreathed in rocks and vines, and a sounding board sprouting a thicket of shrubbery—are subsumed into a *theatrum sacrum* (sacred theater) that integrates furniture with sculpture and vivifies the power of faith (van Eck 2012: 378). By mid-century, this baroque impulse was waning, and the pulpit carved by Laurent Delvaux (1696–1778) for St. Bavo's Cathedral in Ghent, depicting Truth Revealed by Time, reasserts a visual distinction between the oaken supporting structure and the sculptural elements added in real or fictive marble (Fierens 1943: 23–4, plate XVIII).

Eighteenth-century altars varied by confession as well as budget and materials. The cherub-headed altar table and aedicular reredos designed by Nicholas Hawksmoor in 1728 for St. George's, Bloomsbury, London, recalled Catholic stone altars, here rendered in an early use of West Indian mahogany (Bowett 1999). In smaller Anglican churches, communion tables followed domestic models. The stylish example at Rye, Sussex (*c.* 1740; see Randall 1980: 123, 128, fig. 147), adopts the Vitruvian scroll moldings, acanthus-scroll skirt, and lion-form cabriole legs favored by William Kent, its sacred purpose marked only by the central angel's head. Furniture for baptism also blended secular and sacred elements. For the medieval church at Ringsaker, Norway, woodcarver Lars Jenssen Borg supplied a baroque-style font in 1704, supported by a sculptured putto and set within a balustraded enclosure bearing the royal monogram (Snodin and Llewellyn 2009: 222–3 and cat. 51, 52, illustrated; Ekroll 2012: 301–2). James Gibbs's *Book of Architecture* (London, 1728, plate 146) likewise provided six designs for cisterns on pedestals "which may also serve for Fonts"; in a similar way, the marble font at St. George's in Hanover Square, London, mounted on casters and kept under the communion table, reminded one nineteenth-century observer of a wine cooler (Friedman 2011: 90; see *The Ecclesiologist*, 2 [1843]: 141). The neoclassical oak font designed by Robert Adam in 1763 for the neo-Gothic church of St. Mary Magdalene at Croome d'Abitot near Worcester features spiral flutes, acanthus leaves, and lion-paw feet, perhaps suggesting a repurposed ancient bronze. The same year, Sir Francis Dashwood (a prominent member of the Dilettanti) ordered a wooden font for West Wycombe inspired by an Etruscan bronze tripod, complete with doves imitating the famous ancient mosaic at the Capitoline (Randall 1980: 54; Friedman 2011: 87–90, fig. 174). The evocation of ancient metalwork may also explain the choice of Wedgwood's black basalt ware for four baptismal fonts supplied between 1778 and 1788 for parish churches in Hertfordshire, Bedfordshire, and Shropshire (Kelly 1965: 104–8, figs. 48–50; Randall 1980: 50, figs. 44, 54).

SYNAGOGUE FURNITURE

Liturgical furniture was equally important in Jewish worship, which accorded special honor to the chest or ark (*Aron Kodesh*) housing the Torah scrolls, and the elevated desk (bimah) from which they were read to the congregation (Buxton 1981: 387–94; Krinsky [1985] 1996: 21–6). Some eighteenth-century arks were crowned with tablets of the Law and/ or sculptured rays, evoking divine illumination and perhaps the radiance of Moses in descending from Mount Sinai. The towering ark constructed in Berlin in 1710 was set against a window for similar effect (Krinsky [1985] 1996: 49–50 and 261–2, fig. 118). Others evoked the ancient tabernacle by incorporating twisted or "Solomonic" columns also popular in Catholic contexts (see Plate 23). In rural Germany and Poland, including the late eighteenth-century wooden synagogue at Wołpa (in present-day Belarus), the ark was frequently given visual emphasis through carved and painted ornament rich in mystical significance (Krinsky [1985] 1996: 57–8; Hubka 2003: 31, fig. 70). Bimahs likewise drew attention through ornamental railings, pillars, or canopies. The octagonal bimah at Gwoździec, Poland, erected in 1731, bore an elaborate open lantern, while the pillars of the twelve-sided example at Wołpa extended up to the vaulted roof (Buxton 1981: 391 and fig. 512; Krinsky [1985] 1996: 225–30; Hubka 2003: 29–31 and fig. 25). Eighteenth-century drawings of the modest Swiss synagogues at Endingen and Lengnau show the bimah surrounded by rows of portable reading stands, of which an elaborately carved example from the Polish town of Jablonów is preserved at the Museum of Ethnography and Craft in Lviv, Ukraine (Krinsky [1985] 1996: 280–2, figs 131–2; Hubka 2003: 38, fig. 37).

As in churches, synagogue seating reflected social structure. In smaller communities where space was at a premium, seats were restricted to a few places of honor below the bimah, as at Gwoździec, and/or a bench ringing the walls (Hubka 2003: 31, 37). The unusually well preserved synagogue constructed by London's Sephardic community at Bevis Marks to designs by Quaker architect Joseph Avis, completed in 1701, retains nearly all of its original furniture, including twenty banister-backed pews flanking the processional axis between the ark, here a façade-like, pedimented structure set beneath a broad window, and the bimah, its curved railing marked by Solomonic turnings (Plate 25). Three generations later, London's "Great" or Ashkenazic synagogue (completed in 1791 as the third building on the site, destroyed in the Second World War) surrounded the bimah with rentable bench seating for five hundred men and a large communal pew for the poor (Krinsky [1985] 1996: 22, 412–17, fig. 243; Friedman 2011: 41–2, figs. 33, 34). Women, when they attended at all, were typically confined to annexes or balconies, as in London and in the spacious synagogue at Livorno, which added a second matroneum in the 1780s to accommodate the thriving community. Controversy ensued when members objected to the labeling of specific zones for wives and daughters of the most prominent families, a move that was ultimately rescinded (Krinsky [1985] 1996: 352–3). In Dutch Suriname, the increase in Eurafrican *congregantes*, mixed-race offspring of Jewish planters and enslaved Africans led to a 1754 edict banning *congregantes* and their European spouses from the coveted seats between the pillars and restricting them to the mourner's bench (Ben-Ur 2007: 190). In the synagogues of the Comtat Venaissin, then part of the Papal State, seats of honor were reserved for Elijah, the prophet believed to have ascended to heaven in a whirlwind. Miniature armchairs set into a niche in the wall near the ark (at Carpentras, rebuilt in 1741) or atop a cloud-shaped corner bracket (at Cavaillon, constructed from 1772 to 1774) suggested the prophet's spiritual presence during circumcisions and expressed the community's longing for his return at the end of days (Krinsky [1985] 1996: 238–42, fig. 104).

SITES OF GOVERNMENT AND ADMINISTRATION

Furniture for state apartments

Like church furniture, palace fittings filled both practical and symbolic roles, particularly in apartments devoted to rituals of state. Even if popular access was often restricted in practice, such rooms constituted public-facing stages for the performance of power, on which splendor, symmetry, and precedent trumped considerations of comfort. In Rome around 1750, British traveler Sacheverell Stevens was surprised to find the pope's palace at Montecavallo on the Quirinal Hill filled with old-fashioned wooden seating including *sgabelli*, *cassepanche* (storage or chest-benches), and faldstools (purchases of which are documented in palace accounts earlier in the century) rather than upholstered chairs, although he did admit that "some few were beautifully varnished" (that is, painted) with the current pontifical arms (Stevens 1756: 219; González-Palacios 2010: 120–4,

128–9). Matching suites of such furniture reinforced institutional identity. Under Clement XI, orders included new pedestals (*sgabelloni*) for displaying the pontifical busts in the long gallery at the Quirinal (1704); thirty-six gilded, leather-covered armorial chairs for the Congregation of the Sacra Consulta (a judicial branch of the Curia) (1707); and new frames for the cardinals' portraits at villa Belvedere (1716; González-Palacios 2010: 120, 126, 128).

Expressive furniture anchored the state rooms of Rome's great family palaces, where baldachins, thrones, console tables, mirrors, and candlestands announced inhabitants' rank and communicated their character (González-Palacios 2010: 106; see my discussion of the Brustolon mirror in Volume 3, Chapter 8 in this series). Military men might favor trophy-laden state beds and prie-dieux like those published by Filippo Passarini in his *Nuove inventioni d'ornamenti* of 1698 (see my discussion of Passarini in Volume 3, Chapter 8 in this series), or the similarly bellicose console table, supported by a weapon-wielding lion, illustrated in Giovanni Giardini's *Diversi disegni* of 1714 (Walker and Hammond 1999: 185, cat. 53, illustrated). Other objects mobilized the owner's coat of arms, such as a number of console tables created for the princely Borghese family and ornamented with their heraldic eagle and/or dragon (González-Palacios in Bowron and Rishel 2000: 173–4, cats. 58, 59, illustrated). Even bookcases melded practical and expressive functions. For Prince Giovanni Battista Rospigliosi, whose family owed its prominence to the election of his uncle Cardinal Giulio Rospigliosi as Clement IX (1667–9), architect Nicola Michetti conceived two monumental examples around 1715 for the family's palace on the Quirinal, steps from the pope's residence (Plate 26). Appropriately, their upper sections (with broken pediments centered by cartouches originally adorned with the family *stemma*) invoke baroque church façades, altars, or even reliquary cabinets from the age of Borromini; the supporting stands are draped in tasseled lambrequins, originating in the scarves or mantling adorning knight's helmets and frequently used in liturgical settings. This combination of motifs, together with their size and luxury, announced the Rospigliosi's literal and dynastic proximity to pontifical power (Wolfram Koeppe in Kisluk-Grosheide et al. 2006: 90–1, cat. 33).

The expansion of educational travel, particularly the Grand Tour, helped diffuse Italian modes throughout the Continent. Inspired by the grandeur observed at Continental courts, returning British aristocrats commissioned foreign-trained artists and architects such as William Kent to design Italian-style hall benches, consoles, mirrors, and seating to complement collections of antique statues and Old Master paintings (Weber 2013, Collins 2013: 260). Among the most extravagant are the four gilded sofas John Linnell supplied to Baron Scarsdale for the drawing room of the Curzon family seat at Kedleston Hall in Derbyshire from 1762. The suite's writhing mermen, mermaids, tritons, sea nymphs, and dolphins, invoking Britain's recent maritime victories over the French in the Seven Years War, troubled some contemporaries. "Tho very magnificent," worried the Duchess of Northumberland in 1766, "I think these frames rather too heavy"; two years later Horace Walpole dismissed them as "settees supported by gilt fishes and sea gods absurdly like the King's coach." The observation was perceptive, since Linnell had signaled Curzon's rise at court by incorporating ideas first developed for George III's coronation (Jackson-Stops 1985: 273–4, cat. 194, illustrated).

Across the English Channel, Louis XIV's investment in luxury industries, combined with the French court's tradition of public accessibility, made Versailles a touchstone for the furnishing of eighteenth-century state rooms. Official etiquette demanded adherence to tradition, and as late as 1769 France's royal wardrobe (Garde-Meuble de la Couronne) commissioned 144 old-fashioned giltwood stools (*pliants* or *ployants*) for the dauphine Marie Antoinette. Initially divided into separate summer and winter sets, the suite comprised twenty-four for her state bedroom and 120 for her games room, since protocol demanded (despite the future queen's own preferences) that only she had the right to a chair. When the stools were refurbished in 1786, the provision of interchangeable seat frames allowed the Garde-Meuble to send half the set, after regilding, to the king's state bedrooms at Versailles and Compiègne. Having escaped the revolutionary sales, the king's stools were reemployed at the Luxembourg Palace during the Directory before beginning a fourth tour of duty in Empress Josephine's Grand Salon at the Palace of Laeken, near Brussels (Meyer 2002: 1:33–4). Yet the court was not immune from changing taste, and Louis XV eagerly replaced his great-grandfather's ponderous cabinets-on-stands with more "convenient" commodes, particularly in his private spaces. These included a richly mounted medal chest crafted by cabinetmaker Antoine-Robert Gaudreaus (*c.* 1682–1746) in 1738 for the king's study (later sent, with matching corner cupboards, to the royal library), as well as dozens of elaborate commodes veneered in tropical hardwoods (*bois des Indes*) or costly Asian lacquers.

As Versailles's largest state room, the "Grande Galerie" or Hall of Mirrors (inaugurated in 1684) exemplifies the challenges of decorating and maintaining a heavily trafficked space that was "clearly designed for public consumption and was no longer restricted to the court" (Kisluk-Grosheide and Rondot 2018: 5). Besides facilitating indoor exercise, the gallery hosted diplomatic and dynastic events such as the Persian and Turkish embassies of 1715 and 1742, the "Yew Tree Ball" of 1745, and celebrations of the future Louis XVI's marriage to Archduchess Marie Antoinette of Austria in 1770. In December 1751, the department of the Menus-Plaisirs honored the birth of an heir to the Dauphin by lighting six thousand wax candles in twenty-four temporary chandeliers and four giltwood stands; "thus furnished," noted the Parmese ambassador, "this gallery is the most beautiful thing I've seen in the world and, indeed, in the universe" (Baulez 2007a: 77–8, my translation). On ordinary evenings, light came from *torchères* or *guéridons* set between twelve agate and alabaster tables (Tessin 1926: 281; Baulez 2007b: 86–7). In 1690, after the Sun King's original suite of solid silver furniture was melted to pay for the War of the League of Augsburg, the Hall of Mirrors received sixteen of the sixty more economical but still imposing giltwood *guéridons* supplied to the king's state apartment. These stands were joined in 1695 by sixteen stools and four benches with silver embroidery and gold fringe, and again in 1708 by surplus stools relocated from the Salon of Diana. It was not long before several covers and all the fringes had been stolen, occasioning the stools' reupholstery in less costly crimson velvet with gold piping; soon after, thirty straw-stuffed benches covered in red floral *moquette* (wool velvet) were added to accommodate overflow from concerts in the Salon de la Paix. By mid-century, Sacheverell Stevens found the gallery's furniture "much soiled" and inferior in "neatness and cleanliness" to English state rooms. The situation was addressed in 1762 by the delivery of forty plainer stools with green-painted frames and vintage Savonnerie carpet covers, which were replaced again in 1790 with twenty-four still simpler white-painted stools sent from Paris. The now outmoded *guéridons* were substituted in 1769 with six neoclassical examples shaped as maidens holding cornucopias (designed by sculptor Augusin Pajou) and six in the form of antique candelabra festooned by putti (designed by architect Jacques Gondoin; Stevens 1756: 40; Souchal 1962: 76; Meyer 2002: 1:48–9, cat. 8; Baulez 2007b: 88–90; Saule 2007: 57; Maës 2013: para. 78). At Versailles, as in palaces throughout Europe, the challenge was to maintain appearances on an ever-shrinking budget.

Chairs of state: From palace to legislature

Despite the continuing importance of state beds, no furniture announces power like a throne; as Celia Fiennes observed at Windsor in 1698, "some of these fooleries are requisite sometimes to create admiration and regard to keep up the state of a kingdom and nation" (Graham 1994: 44–5). At Versailles, Louis XIV's silver-clad throne survived until 1709, when it too was replaced with a giltwood model the Sun King dismissed as an ordinary armchair. Normally kept in the Hall of Apollo, it was moved to a tall dais in the Hall of Mirrors for the Persian embassy of 1715, an expedient repeated for Louis XV's reception of the Turkish ambassador Said Efendi in 1742 (Saule 2007: 68; Maës 2013: paras. 66–8). Perhaps showing its age, it was replaced the next year with an ambitious rococo throne by sculptors Sébastien-Antoine and Paul-Ambroise Slodtz, incorporating lion masks (sketched by British architect William Chambers around 1750) and palm branches recalling King Solomon's temple in Jerusalem (Maës 2013: paras. 108–13, 143–55). France's rivals were not to be outdone, and in 1742 the Holy Roman Emperor Charles VII commissioned a Parisian craftsman, likely following designs from sculptor Jean Martin de Bruyne, to supply the throne for his coronation in Frankfurt (Baarsen 2007: 108, fig. 8). Even the Dutch, France's erstwhile enemies, ordered French-style thrones to mark the elevation of Prince William IV as Stadholder in 1747. The walnut example supplied by chairmaker Gerrit Hutte and sculptor Pieter van Dijck for the Court of Justice in The Hague retains its original upholstery of green velvet embroidered in silver, the back capped by projecting rococo cartouches displaying the arms of Zeeland, Holland, and West Friesland (Baarsen 2007: 104–5, fig. 5; 2008: 160, fig. 20). The most exuberant thrones were the often imaginary versions included in official portraits, loaded with symbols expressing the ruler's virtues. (See also chapter 8 in this volume.) Among the grandest is the uncomfortable-looking chair depicted in Antoine-François Callet's state portrait of Louis XVI, complete with winged lions, branches of laurel, lictors' fasces, and a sculptured personification of Justice.

In Britain, the constitutional monarchy inaugurated in 1688 tempered displays of royal power, and in contrast to Continental norms, the armchair featured in Godfrey Kneller's 1716 state portrait of George I would look at home in any patrician's study (National Portrait Gallery, London, 5174). Yet thrones remained essential props at coronations, their forms reflecting the political climate. Whereas earlier Stuart thrones had followed classical x-frame models, Queen Anne's comparatively modest coronation chair of 1702 for Westminster Abbey (now at Hatfield House) elaborated a domestic template (Graham 1994: 47–8, fig. 63). Twelve years later, for George I, chairmaker Richard Roberts revived the bound captives from Charles II's throne at Windsor, here celebrating the Hanoverian triumph over Catholic tyranny (Graham 1994: 45; Bowett 2005). The multiple state chairs delivered by royal chairmaker Katherine Naish for the coronation of George III and Queen Charlotte in 1761 are particularly well documented and suggest the complexities of such events (Roberts 1989: 63). For the coronation proper, at Westminster Abbey, Naish delivered gilded thrones for the king and queen, each carved with a Kentian "Lyons Paw & Face on each foot" and upholstered in brocaded silk with gold tassels and fringe (Roberts 1989: 64, fig. 1; Graham 1994: 48–9, fig. 64; Salmon 2013: 323–5, figs. 13.11, 13.12). Naish also provided eight simpler "State Chairs" of walnut with "large Scrole Elbows" and matching footstools, two for the sovereigns to use while listening to the sermon, and six in color-coded velvet (not quite correct, according to some observers) for the accompanying civil and ecclesiastical authorities. Naish's collective charge for the chair frames (£22) was dwarfed by the cost of the fabric (£143), trimmings (£302), and assembly (£36), a reminder that the largest expense of prestige seating lay in the textiles. For the ensuing ceremony at the House of Lords, Naish delivered a less lavish gilded throne, flanked by "High Stools" for parliamentary officials and a red velvet canopy of state costing over £800 to embroider, mount, and trim with "treble gilt rich lace" fringe. The proceedings concluded near the House of Commons, where Naish supplied a third, lion-less throne whose parcel-gilt walnut frame and less costly velvet covers were calibrated to the venue's lesser prestige (Roberts 1989: 63–6).

Two surviving ceremonial chairs from the Capitol at Williamsburg, Virginia, Britain's most populous colony in mainland North America, suggest furniture's role in projecting power overseas. Closest to monarchic models is a high-backed mahogany armchair likely used by royal governors in their council chamber (Colonial Williamsburg, 1930–215). Like the thrones discussed above, the chair's unusual proportions, with a seat height of approximately sixty-six centimeters as opposed to the more usual forty-three, literally elevated the king's deputy and required a footstool (now lost) to keep his legs from dangling in the air. Though once thought to have been made in Virginia, the chair was more likely crafted in London in the 1750s and imported for the governor's use, along with carved and painted coats of arms and iron warming stoves. Its metropolitan features, including serpentine arms with acanthus-carved supports and carved lion-head terminals, as well as cabriole legs with C-scroll carvings and hairy paw feet, inspired a range of adaptations by Williamsburg craftsmen. Similar echoes of the mother country marked the architectonic speaker's chair in the elective House of Burgesses, whose form and placement evoke its prototype in London's House of Commons (Colonial Williamsburg, 1933–504 [L]). This imposing chair, however, was crafted locally of Virginia black walnut and tulip poplar, its awkward grafting of curved arms and legs onto a rectilinear aedicule originally adorned with the royal arms suggesting the brewing tension between a distant, foreign authority and the colonists' demands for self-determination.

Furniture's role in revealing political structures was on view at the fateful meeting of the Estates General convened at Versailles on May 5, 1789, at a moment of fiscal and philosophical crisis. Reflecting the ancien regime, phalanxes of benches segregated representatives of the clergy, nobility, and commoners (the largest group, set farthest from the throne) from the king, enthroned under a canopy, and the royal ministers presiding from a central table.[9] Even if later engravings aggrandized the spectacle, the event convinced many French subjects that society should no longer be divided into competing classes marked by inherited rights and privileges. As the situation decayed, the king's furniture itself was seized and auctioned off as national property or reassigned new functions in the whirlwind of governments that followed the monarchy's fall. Several dozen such pieces, including desks and chairs confiscated from the royal family, the *emigrés*, and those condemned by the revolutionary authorities, bear the brand "ASSNAT" marking furnishings employed by the National Assembly created on June 17, 1789.[10]

Like their predecessors, the revolutionary authorities grasped furniture's symbolic value and sought new models to promote republican values. By late 1792 the painter Jacques-Louis David, already commissioned by the Committee of Public Safety to design new national costumes for government officials, the military, and French citizens, was called on to convert the former theater at the Tuileries Palace into a chamber for the National Convention. He turned to the established joiner Georges Jacob (1739–1814), from whom he had commissioned innovative studio furniture and who had previously supplied benches (*banquettes*) and stools (*tabourets*) for the first Assembly of Notables convened at Versailles in 1787 (Lefuel 1923: 144). David conceived the president's curule-form armchair, upholstered in purple, but tapped the young architects Charles Percier and Pierre-François-Léonard Fontaine to design the president's desk, supported by winged griffons, the speaker's tribune ornamented with gilt-bronze crowns, two sleek secretary's desks with gilded capitals and twin argand lamps, stalls for the 760 deputies, and benches for the public (145–6). Percier and Fontaine's designs, executed in gleaming mahogany by Jacob, drew explicitly on antique models in a style identified as "Etruscan," perhaps to stress its pre-imperial associations. Jacob's employment for the new state continued, and in October 1794 he received 3,030 livres for furniture and chairs for the members of the Committees of General Security and of Public Safety, where David's friendship insulated him during the Terror (Lefuel 1923: 80–3). Further orders included sixty additional desks in walnut with black-painted filing cabinets at 160 livres apiece, following a model at the Garde-Meuble. In 1798 the firm billed the succeeding Council of Five Hundred at the Palais-Bourbon for ten mahogany chairs "of a new form," with pierced tripod-shaped splats and back supports inlaid with Etruscan ornaments in brass; a dozen mahogany stools (*tabourets*) also of novel shape, with feet terminating in the heads of geese; and thirty-six mahogany chairs for the conference hall (Ledoux-Lebard 1984: 284; Samoyault 2009: 25, fig. 21).

Although the objects supplied to the Convention have not been identified, their innovations were embraced by private patrons including Napoleon Bonaparte, who ordered a similar chair for his house in rue de la Victoire around 1797, later gifted to his personal physician (Plate 27) (Samoyault 2009: 26–7, figs. 25, 29; Garric 2016: 279, cat. 77).[11] While its winged lion protomes revive now-familiar Roman models, the chair's broad proportions, raked back, plain arm supports, and expanse of uncarved mahogany strike a new tone. Though some versions incorporate the trellis-form splats Jacob debuted in seating delivered to the Queen's Dairy at Rambouillet in 1787, these chairs' rear saber legs and deep, concave backrest, inspired by Greek *klismoi* known from painted pottery and funerary reliefs, inaugurated a new masculine mode that appealed to France's new cultural and political leaders.[12] Public and private spheres again intersected, as officials invoked the power of the state in their private studies, while Jacob, former supplier to the crown, used his design skills, business acumen, and political connections to navigate the transition from royal to republican regime. With the dissolution of the guilds in 1791, his shop embraced previously restricted techniques and materials, becoming one of the most successful suppliers of furniture of all kinds under the Directory and the Consulate, and, under the leadership of his talented son François-Honoré-Georges Jacob-Desmalter (1770–1841), a tastemaker during the empire.

* * *

By the time of the French Revolution, the influence of the public, public opinion, and the public sphere was acknowledged throughout Europe. 'Publizität," as one German satire put it, was "The magic word before whose power / even the people's masters cower" (Habermas [1962] 1991: 70). The sites and objects surveyed here only hint at the proliferating material culture that supported and, indeed, helped produce a public sphere on which we still rely. Further research is needed on the furnishings of other emerging public arenas such as law courts, legislatures, lending libraries, schools, and city parks, as well as hybrid forms like coaches and omnibuses that were, in a sense, public furniture on the move. Greater attention should also be paid to the ways furniture functioned publicly in lesser-studied areas of Europe and in Europe's expanding dominions overseas. What is clear is that eighteenth-century audiences understood that sitting around a common table, whether in a coffeehouse or a committee, fostered different modes of thought and expression than kneeling before a throne or altar. And it was precisely the optimism that society could be improved through material means that led eighteenth-century designers and consumers to value public furniture, understood in its broadest sense, as catalysts of change.

CHAPTER SIX

Exhibition and Display

FRÉDÉRIC DASSAS

The role of furniture within an art collection increased considerably in importance during the eighteenth century. Together with the "fine" arts, furniture played a key part in the development of a decorative architectural system devised for the presentation of paintings, sculpture, and other precious objects, which reached a high point at this time. This furniture comprised pieces that were specifically earmarked for the purpose of presenting, showcasing, or housing the art collection in question—as well as those that were essential to the overall layout of spaces and, thereby, in supporting the enjoyment of visitors. Above and beyond examining furniture in isolation, therefore, it is vital to consider its relationship to collections of art, inasmuch as it appears that it was through their integration within such collections that pieces of furniture first acquired the status of extraordinary *objets d'art* in their own right in the eighteenth century. Yet while it is true to say that the eighteenth century witnessed a crucial step forward in considering the "decorative" arts on a par with the "fine" arts, this did not outlast the birth and growth of great public institutions, which did not consider furniture as "collectable" in its own right, at the beginning of the nineteenth century. The aim of this chapter, then, is to examine the three reasons for the presence of furniture in an art collection in the eighteenth century: first, as works of art appreciated in their own right, as examples of excellence in craftsmanship or for the rarity of their materials; second, as a way of displaying or preserving the objects of the collection; and finally, as an integral element of the decorative scheme lending its splendor to the display of the works of art.

IDENTIFYING "COLLECTABLE" FURNITURE: SOURCES

Inventories

The first evidence dealt with here regarding the status of furniture and related objects within private possessions is that found in probate inventories. These inventories simply consist of different lists of items. The two more important are the first, which is a room-by-room description of the deceased's main residence, and the last, which is a list of the deceased's papers. In between are "specialized" lists that might deal with other residences belonging to the deceased, books, linen, clothes, silver, or money, some of them requiring the competence of a specific expert to estimate the value. If necessary, lists dealing with tools, jewels, scientific instruments, or *effets précieux* (valuable objects, including paintings, sculpture, and other works of art) will be included. While the reasoning behind the organization of the goods in these inventories into different categories is not always apparent and may simply reflect the various areas of expertise of those valuing the objects or preparing them for sale, a hierarchy among the possessions of the deceased is nonetheless always revealed. Thus, when the furniture and works of art appear together room-by-room in the main appraisal, this reveals little interest in the works of art, which are generally of low value. However, when the works of art are listed and valued separately by another expert, it suggests that they may be considered an art collection. The differentiation between pictures and other works of art (marble and bronze sculpture, vases and columns, furniture, furnishing bronzes, etc.) within the *effets précieux* is rarer, but nevertheless allows us to identify those furnishings of outstanding status, as distinct from everyday items. It goes without saying that those items of furniture not listed among the *effets précieux* were not considered "collectable."

As the century progressed, furniture enjoyed a growing presence in the sections of inventories devoted to *effets précieux*. Before 1750, even when we have examples of items belonging to collections differentiated from the rest of the personal effects, exceptional furniture was not listed with these, but rather in solidarity with everyday furniture. In the inventory of Pierre Thomé (d.1710), *trésorier général des galères*, paintings, marble, and small bronzes were valued alongside everyday furniture, Boulle furniture, marble tables, chandeliers, and gilt bronzes, mirrors, curtains, and wall hangings.[1] In 1722, by contrast, in the house of Pierre Gruyn, a former *garde du trésor royal*, the porcelains, bronzes, and pictures were appraised separately from everyday objects; yet the deceased's remarkable pieces of Boulle furniture were not categorized separately from the rest of the furniture.[2] In 1737, the *marchand-mercier* Thomas-Joachim Hébert (1687–1773) went to the house of the comtesse de Verrue (1670–1736) to value the chandeliers and, separately, the porcelain, jewels, and various works of art (sconces, rock crystal and porcelain candelabra, a porcelain clock, bronze figures, snuffboxes, rings and medallions, etc.). He did not include any furniture with these.[3] Three years later, the inventory of the huge collection of Pierre Crozat (1661–1740) dealt separately with pictures and certain sculptures, prints, and engraved gems. All the other contents of the *hôtel*, including everyday furniture, marble tables, Boulle furniture, chandeliers, and gilt bronzes, were treated without differentiation.[4]

Inventories of great collections made during the second half of the eighteenth century reveal the more frequent inclusion of part of the furniture with the works of art, as shown in the following examples. In 1759, in the house of the art collector Marcellin de Selle (1704–59), the paintings were valued by the painter Pierre Rémy (1724–98) but it was the *marchand-mercier* Martin Hennebert (d.1770) who proceeded to value the porcelains and bronzes as well as the marquetry furniture in the *cabinet* (a room of this name) of the master of the house. This group of items included furniture by André Charles Boulle (1642–1732) and Charles Cressent (1685–1768), clocks, chandeliers, and porphyry vases.[5] The appraisal of the huge collection of Jean de Julienne, in 1766, was made on the advice of Pierre Rémy and Claude François Julliot (1727–94). It was divided into three large assemblages: everyday furniture, "pictures, drawings and other curiosities," and *effets précieux*. It is now in the latter section that Boulle furniture is to be found, together with lacquer furniture, marble tables, porcelain, lacquer objects, and gilt bronzes.[6] In 1776, the same hierarchy is found with the possessions of the financier and collector Paul Randon de Boisset (1706–76).[7] In the inventory of Augustin Blondel de Gagny (1695–1776), also compiled in 1776, the *effets précieux* and furniture are now entirely transferred to the domain of works of art.[8] The same principle is found in 1785 at the house of Bailli de Breteuil,[9] then in 1791 at the house of the duc de Praslin, where the pictures and objects were valued by the dealer Alexandre Joseph Paillet (1743–1814).[10]

Auction catalogs

Sale catalogs, often embellished with commentary, allow one to discern more precisely the nature of the objects thought worthy of arousing the interest of collectors. That of the sale of Louis-Augustin Angran de Fonspertuis dates from 1747.[11] It is the first one to accord a more prominent place to *objets d'art* and furniture. The section that is dedicated to "rock crystal and porcelain chandeliers, clocks of taste, and other *meubles curieux & composés*" comprises seventeen lots. It follows porcelains, bronzes, and lacquer objects and precedes pictures, drawings, prints, and shells. The introductory paragraph justifies, because of the improving quality of Parisian production, the integration of the finest furniture within the body of the collection:

> It is not without reason that one can place certain pieces of furniture and jewellery produced nowadays within the rank of objects of "curiosity". Taste has become so refined in France, that one only desires that which is distinguished and perfect. In emulation of the most scrupulous execution, artists of lesser works daily increase the imagination and variety of one piece after the other.[12]

In 1756, it was written in the duc de Tallard sale catalog that "the furniture decorating the apartments [...] could compete with the masterpieces of art that we admired in forming the most magnificent assemblage imaginable."[13] A separate section is dedicated to *meubles précieux* (valuable furniture). It amounts to forty-nine lots and is divided between marble tables; rock crystal chandeliers; clocks; furniture decorated with lacquer, *pietra dura*, Boulle and veneered wood marquetry; a large oak bookcase decorated with sculptures; and three tapestry hangings.

In 1767, the catalog of the Jean de Jullienne sale marks a new stage in the importance accorded to objects and the recognition of furniture as an autonomous category within the collection.[14] The catalog is divided into two parts: the first is dedicated to pictures, drawings, prints, and sculptures, the second to "porcelains of superior quality [...], old lacquers, rich Boule [*sic*] furniture, and *bijoux* [items such as snuffboxes, fans, watches, etc.]."[15] An entire section is then dedicated to *meubles curieux* (exceptional furniture), signaling the emergence of this new category, distinct from crystal chandeliers and marble tables. It contains thirty-eight lots of furniture decorated with either Boulle marquetry, Florentine stone (i.e., *pietra dura*) or lacquer. From the 1770s onward, large sales rich in works of decorative arts multiplied, and furniture found a place all of its own within these. In 1777, for example, the third part of the Paul Randon de Boisset sale was entirely dedicated to "marbles, jaspers, agates, old porcelains [...], and *effets précieux* including old lacquers, rich Boule [*sic*] furniture, chandeliers, lights and sconces of gilt bronze."[16] Lacquers, *meubles curieux de marqueterie* (exceptional marquetry furniture), and marble tables were described in three separate sections, with the last two alone amounting to some sixty lots. In the same year, in the Blondel de Gagny sale,[17] a large section entitled *meubles précieux*[18] grouped together chandeliers, lacquer and marquetry furniture, clocks, and other gilt bronzes. It began by differentiating chandeliers and "works of the famous Boule [*sic*]" from the rest. It included lacquer and *ébénisterie* (cabinetmaking) furniture, among which a stand attributed to Charles Cressent (1685–1768); marble tabletops; clocks, lights, and candelabra; various small pieces of furniture in different materials; objects in lacquer, stucco, soapstone, and enamel; as well as two tapestries and a harpsichord by the Flemish Ruckers family of instrument makers.

At the end of the century, one finds in the duc de Praslin's sale catalog of 1793 marble vases, agates, "rich marquetry furniture by Boulle and others of this type," bronze mounts and porcelains.[19] Mahogany furniture, novelly, was the subject of a separate section. In 1797, in the sale of Laurent Grimod de La Reynière, mahogany furniture was also specifically mentioned, although separately from "marquetry furniture of Boulle and others of this type."[20]

Travel guides

Descriptions given in travelers' guides paint portraits of collections in situ and provide insight into furniture's function within the arrangement of a collection as a whole.

Hébert's *Dictionnaire pittoresque et historique de Paris, Versailles, Marly, Triano* (1766: 1:36), provides a highly detailed description of the interiors of the Hôtel Blondel de Gagny, an exceptional portrait of one of the most beautiful collections of the century, including its almost complete set of furniture.[21] In the first room in the enfilade looking out onto the Place Vendôme, a commode surmounted by a pier glass, both by Boulle, is placed against the far wall. *Amphitrite* by the sculptor Michel Anguier (1612–86) is placed on the commode between vases in Egyptian green marble and two porcelain fish mounted with candle branches. At the side of the windows are two Boulle candlestands surmounted with candelabra. The center of the room is occupied by a table with lumachelle marble (with distinctive markings from fossilized shells) bearing bronze sculptures, vases of Egyptian green marble, and porcelains. The sconces are also by Boulle. In the salon that follows, two lacquer corner cupboards occupy the far end. Two Boulle commodes are placed against the right-hand wall, on which are placed porphyry vases, antique bronzes, and small pieces of *bleu celeste* porcelain representing different animals. One console table in Boulle marquetry is placed next to the chimney. In the center of the room there is a large table of alabaster on which many porcelains are displayed, amongst which is a large *bleu celeste* nacelle (probably a kind of large bowl) enriched with a gilt-bronze mount executed by Jean-Baptiste Vassou (1739–1807). The music room is entered from and forms the last part of the enfilade. A side table with an Egyptian green marble top is placed between the windows, supporting two faceted Kakiemon porcelain urns and three pieces of celadon porcelain. A second side table, an *armoire* (cupboard) fitted with partitions, and a clock with the movement by the Parisian family of Thuret are attributed to Boulle; and the ensemble is completed with a Ruckers harpsichord and screen painted by Jean-Antoine Watteau (1684–1721).

Twenty years later, the *Guide des amateurs et des étrangers voyageurs à Paris*, published by Luc-Vincent Thiéry (1734–1822), gives us a glimpse of several major collections. We will limit ourselves here to the descriptions of three *salons* belonging to some personalities at the court who were installed in the Faubourg Saint-Germain district of Paris. The Baron de Besenval (1721–94), former *Inspecteur general des gardes suisses et grisons*, was close to Marie Antoinette and installed in the far west of the rue de Grenelle. In his salon, a tabletop of porphyry rests on a "superbe pied doré" and displays an antique bronze and some porcelains. A second table in Egyptian marble is placed on a stand of Boulle marquetry, embellished with a figure of white marble, vases mounted in Spanish brocatelle and porcelains. Sculptures are displayed on one pair of Boulle furniture (the collection includes three pairs). Two pedestals (*gaines à tablier*), also by Boulle, are used for mounted vases. The corner cupboards are in lacquer, covered with oriental alabaster tops, and used to carry porcelains. One commode, also of lacquer, with a top of Turquin Blue marble, is covered with Chinese and Sèvres porcelain (Thiéry 1787: 2:575).

In the house of the duc de Brissac, governor of Paris, also in the rue de Grenelle, the first *salon* is hung with crimson damask and set aside for the display of his collection of pictures. Two large Boulle bookcases, now preserved at the Château de Versailles, flanked a bust of Louis XIV, enriched with agate draperies and gilt-bronze ornaments and were used to present porcelain and agate vases, all enhanced with gilt-bronze mounts. A commode with an Egyptian marble top is placed between the windows and surmounted by porcelains and lumachelle vases, mounted with candelabra, placed either side of a bronze Moses. Some other bookcases, smaller in size, are used to display porcelain that, now with bronze mounts, has been transformed into incense burners and candelabra (Thiéry 1787: 2:570).

Further west, the comte de Vaudreuil, *grand fauconnier de France* and intimate with the Duchesse de Polignac, friend of the Queen, was installed in the rue de la Chaise. The salon, in which are displayed *Hercules and Omphale* by François Boucher (1703–70) (Pushkin State Museum of Fine Arts, Moscow), *The Death of the Children of Bethel* by Laurent de La Hyre (1606–56) (Musée des Beaux-Arts, Arras), and the *Bacchanalia in front of a terminal figure of Pan* by Nicolas Poussin (1594–1665) (National Gallery, London) on a background of green wallpaper is filled all around with sumptuous furniture: a pair of small cabinets decorated with *pietra dura*, other pieces of large furniture covered with Boulle marquetry, all coming from the workshop of Joseph Baumhauer, called Joseph (d.1772), a pair of glazed bookcases in three parts, also with Boulle marquetry but the work of *ébéniste* Étienne Levasseur (1721–98), and a large lacquer commode. All were used to display vases, candelabras, and especially sculptures by François Girardon (1628–1715), Clodion (1738–1814), Jean-Pierre-Antoine Tassaert (1727–88), and Le Breton (Thiéry 1787: 2:546).

Images of interiors

Some views of interiors, sources that are all too rare for this period, complete this section. These are often disappointing with regard to furniture. *The Concert in a Salon* of *circa* 1720 by Nicolas Lancret (Munich, Alte Pinacothek) supposedly shows us the interior of the gallery in Pierre Crozat's *Hôtel*; but aside from conveying the majesty of the room, the abundance of chairs, and presence of lofty pedestals displaying busts, it provides us with little information. The interiors of the businessman, patron and collector Jean de Jullienne (1686–1766), are much simpler in character. Unfortunately, the illustrations of the *Catalogue des tableaux de Jean de Julienne*, preserved in the Pierpont Morgan Library (Tillerot 2011), barely feature any furniture at all. One exception is "*Cabinet* preceding the gallery" featuring a large console table with a marble top installed under a sculpted pier glass, a pedestal, and tall bookcase surmounted by three oriental porcelain vases (Figure 6.1). The most famous (and complete) views of a Parisian collection are those of the Hôtel Choiseul on the Choiseul box, which we owe to the paintbrush of Louis-Nicolas Van Blarenberghe (1716–94). The duc de Choiseul does not seem to have been particularly interested in furniture and those pieces that are represented are extremely luxurious but exclusively everyday examples: high-quality modern furniture and rows of chairs set out along the dado (Plate 28). Likewise, the walls of Blondel de Gagny's bedchamber, as they appear in a drawing preserved in the Louvre

FIGURE 6.1 *Catalogue des tableaux de Jean de Julienne*. Two views (28 & 29) of the same room. The Morgan Library & Museum, 1966.8. Purchased as the gift of the Fellows. Photograph courtesy of the Morgan Library & Museum.

FIGURE 6.2 Gabriel de Saint-Aubin. Gallery of the Hôtel Randon de Boisset, 1777.
Red and black chalk, black ink, 200 × 157 mm. Musée des Arts décoratifs, Lyons.
Photograph courtesy of ART Collection/Alamy Stock Photo.

(Musée du Louvre, Département des arts graphiques, accession no. 32746), are
covered with pictures. Occupying a place of prominence in front of the bed is
the Rape of Europa by Noël-Nicholas Coypel (1690–1734), which the inventory
records in the room. The collector's furniture is concentrated in the enfilades
of rooms installed in the main building overlooking the Place de Vendôme, and
also in the wing over the courtyard. In addition to the bed with a tester, one

notices a fall-front desk, which is described amongst other things as being of "ancient lacquer," a screen, comfortable chairs, and a bureau, possibly by Boulle as mentioned in written sources.

The portrait of *The Baron de Besenval in his Salon de Compagnie* (National Gallery, London) is a closely centered painting and very precise document of the interior of his house. The master of the house, seated at the corner of the fireplace, is nonchalantly leaning on a screen of Chinese paper. On the chimneypiece are placed a garniture of delicate pieces of celadon porcelain, mounted in gilt bronze. In the hearth, the andirons are decorated with sphinxes and satyrs' heads. In the background one can make out the presence of an *armoire basse* (or low cupboard) in Boulle marquetry. The view of the gallery of the Hôtel Randon de Boisset (Musée des Arts décoratifs, Lyon), meanwhile, is of particular interest to our subject. It shows us the symmetrical arrangement of the picture-hang, the rhythm underneath created by the column shafts displaying the vases, one wall responding to another, and by brackets in the upper part supporting other vases. Between the columns are console tables in large numbers, loaded with vases and sculptures (Figure 6.2). Not one chair is represented. Finally, a cross-section of the gallery in the project for the Hôtel Lebrun (*c.* 1786) preserved in the Archives Nationales (Pradère 2014), provides a hypothetical and highly systematized picture of the display of a collection, and the role of furniture within this. The picture hang is perfectly symmetrical. In the lower part rhythm is generated by a suite of three support pieces of furniture, each one surmounted by vases or sculpture, flanked with seats and pedestals on which busts are placed.

FURNITURE'S STATUS WITHIN COLLECTIONS

The furniture mentioned in the above documents fits into three categories: as collectable in its own right, for housing or displaying part of a collection, or as part of the decorative scheme within which the collection is displayed. This division is only a means of analysis; it is through their capacity to accumulate these characteristics that certain types of furniture became obligatory pieces in every grand collection. A low cabinet, a pedestal in Boulle marquetry, or a marble table could be appreciated by a collector for their own qualities through their capacity to house or display vases, stone or marble sculptures, or porcelain, and because they contributed a sense of balance and nobility to the walls of a salon or gallery all at the same time.

What is collectable furniture?

Certain pieces of furniture are undoubtedly sought after because of their own merits. As a general category, "marble tables" feature in all the great collections.

The term can be misleading and must be understood as referring above all to tabletops and not their supports. In the finest examples, "marble" may refer to any of the most sought after stones: porphyry, serpentine, alabaster, *verde* and *giallo antico*, as well as compositions in *pietra dura*. The salon of Lenoir de Breuil, in the rue Montmatre, had a remarkably large concentration of these in the years preceding the Revolution, including five porphyry tables, of which the first was placed between the windows and the others formed two pairs: one with a Boulle marquetry stand, the other in a round form resting on feet of gilt bronze. A table of Egyptian green marble was placed on a support of Boulle marquetry, while the center of the room was occupied by a round alabaster table, also on a support of Boulle marquetry (Thiéry 1787: 1:454; Samoyault 1972). As with pictures and sculptures, such beautiful pieces of furniture passed from one collection to another. The pair of flamed alabaster tables resting on ebony feet embellished with *pietra dura* that Randon de Boisset had bought in Rome and that, in the 1776 inventory,[22] were mentioned in the gallery of the *hôtel* in the rue Neuve-des-Capucines, would pass successively into the collections of the duchesse de Mazarin, the duc d'Aumont, and the comte de Vaudreuil before featuring in the Coclers sale of 1789. They were sold for 1,520 livres in 1777, 2,410 and 2,415 livres in 1781 and 1782, respectively, and 2,000 livres in 1787, all large sums of money for the time. Objects such as these have been dispersed and it is relatively seldom that one can identify them. For example, of the seven tables bought by the Crown in 1782 from the collection of the duc d'Aumont, none can now be identified.

Boulle furniture was collectable furniture par excellence. It was appreciated for the originality of its compositions, the richness of the bronzes and the gilding, and the virtuosity of the marquetry work. The work of André-Charles Boulle rapidly came to be regarded as a kind of souvenir of the reign of Louis XIV. The artist himself, who died in 1732, had regarded the birth of rococo with indifference. This attitude began to prove advantageous from the end of the 1740s when fashion shifted to a revival of interest in Louis XIV so that by the 1770s there was a true vogue for Boulle furniture. This phenomenon was, to a large part, the result of merchants stimulating trade through their purchases. They not only sparked the creation of new pieces of furniture in this style but also, and perhaps more importantly, inspired those they advised in the purchase of works of art to acquire Boulle pieces (Pradère 2005).

The repeated mentions of the name of this *ébéniste* raises a number of issues because the word "Boulle" carried a variety of connotations (Dassas 2012). Perhaps inevitably, the esteem in which Boulle furniture was held led to the repeated use of this maker's name, even for pieces not made by him. One finds in the 1747 Angran de Fonspertuis sale, for example, the explicit mention of "Boulle the elder," who can only be André-Charles Boulle. In the 1782 Radix de Sainte-Foy sale, meanwhile, the editors of the catalog clearly distinguish

PLATE 1 Recreation of Marie-Antoinette's private room, Versailles. Photograph courtesy of Myrabella/Wikimedia Commons.

PLATE 2 Commode by André Charles Boulle. The Jack and Belle Linsky Collection, 1982/The Metropolitan Museum of Art. Photograph courtesy of the Metropolitan Museum of Art.

PLATE 3 *Bureau du Roi* (the King's desk), also known as Louis XV's roll-top secretary, designed between 1760 and 1769, Cabinet intérieur du Roi, in the Palace of Versailles. Photograph courtesy of the Palace of Versailles/Wikimedia Commons.

PLATE 4 Portrait of Monsieur de Lavoisier and his Wife, chemist Marie-Anne
Pierrette Paulze by Jacques-Louis David, 1788. Purchase, Mr. and Mrs. Charles
Wrightsman Gift, in honor of Everett Fahy, 1977/The Metropolitan Museum of
Art. Photograph courtesy of the Metropolitan Museum of Art.

PLATE 5 Bernard II van Risenburgh, Double Desk, *c*. 1750. Gift of J. Paul Getty. Photograph courtesy of the J. Paul Getty Museum.

PLATE 6 Jean-François Oeben, Mechanical Table, 1761–3. The Jack and Belle Linsky Collection, 1982/The Metropolitan Museum of Art. Photograph courtesy of the Metropolitan Museum of Art.

PLATE 7 Adam Weisweiler, Commode, 1790. Gift of Mr. and Mrs. Charles Wrightsman, 1977/Metropolitan Museum of Art. Photograph courtesy of the Metropolitan Museum of Art. Object no. 1977.1.12.

PLATE 8 Small-scale model for a bed, 1772. Wax models such as this one were often made as presentation models for clients. They show part of the process used by artists and cabinetmakers in developing the design. This is a rare survival. Photograph © RMN-Grand Palais (Louvre Museum)/Franck Raux.

PLATE 9 François Etienne Calla, small-scale educational model, c. 1783, Paris, showing a typical cabinetmaking workshop of the time with an array of hand tools. © Musée des arts et métiers-Cnam, Paris. Photography by Sylvain Pelly.

PLATE 10 Elias Martin (1739–1818), oil on canvas of a marquetry workshop in England, late eighteenth century. The Swedish National Art Museum in Stockholm.

PLATE 11 Bernard II van Risenburgh, Commode (France), *c.* 1740–45, oak veneered with panels of Chinese Coromandel lacquer and European black-lacquered veneer, gilt-bronze mounts, brèche d'Alep marble top. The Lesley and Emma Sheafer Collection, Bequest of Emma A. Sheafer, 1973/The Metropolitan Museum of Art. Photograph courtesy of the Metropolitan Museum of Art.

PLATE 12 High chest (probably Concord, Massachusetts), *c.* 1769–76, cherry, soft maple, white pine, brass. Gift of Henry Francis du Pont, 1952.256. Photograph courtesy of the Winterthur Museum/Wikimedia Commons.

PLATE 13 Attributed to Michael Kimmel, Writing cabinet, 1750–5, Dresden, Saxony. © Victoria and Albert Museum, London. Photograph courtesy of the Victoria and Albert Museum.

PLATE 14 The Salon de la Princesse de Soubise, hôtel de Soubise, Paris. Interiors designed by Germain Boffrand, 1735–40. Photograph courtesy of Photo 12/Alamy Stock Photo.

PLATE 15 Armchair (*fauteuil à la reine*) (part of a set); frame by Nicolas-Quinibert Foliot. Purchase, Martha Baird Rockefeller Gift, 1966/The Metropolitan Museum of Art. Photograph courtesy of the Metropolitan Museum of Art.

PLATE 16 Silk brocade after a design by Philippe de Lasalle, 1773–7. Photograph courtesy of agefotostock/Alamy Stock Photo.

PLATE 17 The octagonal mirrored room at the Palazzo Isnardi di Caraglio, Turin. The Palazzo was designed by architect Benedetto Alfieri, 1739–40. Photograph courtesy of DeAgostini/A. DE GREGORIO/Getty Images.

PLATE 18 The Porcelain Cabinet at the Palacio Real de Aranjuez, incorporating ceramics designed by Giuseppe Gricci and made at the Buen Retiro factory in Madrid, 1760–5. Photograph courtesy of Ljuba Brank/Wikimedia Commons.

PLATE 19 One of a pair of andirons made by Jacques Caffieri in 1752 and now in the Cleveland Museum of Art. Photograph courtesy of Artokoloro/Alamy Stock Photo.

PLATE 20 A bedroom incorporating a ceramic stove in the Esterházy Palace, Fertőd. Photograph courtesy of John Elk III/Alamy Stock Photo.

PLATE 21 John Greenwood (American, 1727–92), *Sea Captains Carousing in Surinam*, *c.* 1752–8, oil on bed ticking, 37¾ × 75¼ inches (95.9 × 191.1 centimeters). © Museum Purchase. St Louis Art Museum. Photograph courtesy of the St Louis Art Museum.

PLATE 22 Thomas Adye (British, active 1730–53), Balloting box, 1737–8, Honduras mahogany and gilt bronze, 42.5 × 40.4 × 21 centimeters. Reproduced by kind permission of the Society of Dilettanti, London.

PLATE 23 Workshop of Pedro Muñoz, Choir stalls, Cathedral of Puebla, Mexico, 1719–22, detail showing a parterre design on the left and a pattern from Hans Vredeman de Vries in the middle; inlaid Solomonic columns, evocative of the Jewish Temple in Jerusalem, divide the lower seats. Ebony, granadillo, caoba, tapincerán, encarnado, gateado, camote, Naranjo, palo amarillo, quebranta hachas (jabín, Florida fishpoison tree), cedro (Spanish cedar). Photograph courtesy of Carlos Varillas.

PLATE 24 Michiel van de Voort the Elder (Flemish, 1667–1737), with the assistance of Theodoor Verhaegen (Flemish, 1700–54), pulpit for the Norbertine priory church of Onze-Lieve-Vrouw van Leliëndaal, Mechelen, 1721–3. Transferred in 1809 to St. Rombout's Cathedral, Mechelen, and adapted by sculptor Jan-Frans Van Geel (Flemish 1756–1830). Carved oak. Photograph © Ad Meskens/Wikimedia Commons.

PLATE 25 Interior of Bevis Marks Synagogue, London, completed 1701 to designs by Joseph Avis, showing original bimah (left foreground), pews, ark, and women's gallery. Photograph courtesy of David Jackson/Caroe Architecture Ltd.

PLATE 26 Bookcase (one of a pair) from Palazzo Rospigliosi, Rome, design attributed to Nicola Michetti (Italian, d.1759), *c.* 1715, walnut and poplar, 159 × 24 × 94 inches (403.9 × 61 × 238.8 centimeters). Gift of Madame Lilliana Teruzzi, 1969, Metropolitan Museum of Art, New York (47.100.270). Photograph courtesy of the Metropolitan Museum of Art.

PLATE 27 Attributed to Georges Jacob (French, 1739–1814), Desk chair (*fauteuil de bureau*), *c.* 1797, mahogany, copper, leather, 37¾ × 29⅛ × 18⅞ inches (96 × 74 × 48 centimeters). Châteaux de Malmaison et Bois-Préau, Reuil-Malmaison, don baron Rabusson-Corvisart, 1950, M. M. 50.61.1. Photograph courtesy of Jeffrey Collins.

PLATE 28 Van Blarenberghe, Choiseul box bottom, premier cabinet. Scan of F.J.B. Watson, "Choiseul Boxes," reprint from A. Kenneth Snowman (ed.), *Eighteenth Century Gold Boxes of Europe* (Boston Book and Art Shop, 1966). Photograph courtesy of Wikimedia Commons.

PLATE 29 Teschen table (also known as the Europe table). Photograph courtesy of DeAgostini/G. DAGLI ORTI/Getty Images.

PLATE 30 Eight-light chandelier, gilded and enamelled bronze, gold inlays.© Musée du Louvre, Dist. RMN-Grand Palais/Thierry Ollivier. Photograph courtesy of the Musée du Louvre.

PLATE 31 Badminton Cabinet, commissioned by Henry Somerset, 3rd Duke of Beaufort, from the Grand Ducal workshops in Florence in 1726. Photograph courtesy of LIECHTENSTEIN. The Princely Collections, Vaduz–Vienna.

PLATE 32 Houghton Hall. View taken during the 2014 exhibition. Reproduced in the catalog. Photograph © Houghton Hall.

PLATE 33 Pier table, *c.* 1768. The Ethel Morrison Van Derlip Fund/Minneapolis Institute of Art. Photograph courtesy of the Minneapolis Institute of Art.

PLATE 34 Design for the Grande Galerie in the Louvre by Hubert Robert. Photograph courtesy of Photo Josse/Leemage /Corbis/Getty Images.

PLATE 35 S. Hooper, *A common council man of Candlestick Ward and his wife on a visit to Mr. Deputy at his modern built villa near Clapham* (1771). Photograph courtesy of the Lewis Walpole Library, Yale University.

PLATE 36 William Kent (designer), One of a pair of pier tables for Chiswick House, London, 1727–32. Photograph courtesy of Chivalrick1/Wikimedia Commons.

PLATE 37 William Hallett Sr. (attrib.), The Pomfret Cabinet shown with original painted decoration and heraldry, c. 1752–3. Photograph courtesy of Lucy Wood.

PLATE 38 Joseph-Siffrein Duplessis, *Louis XVI of France in Coronation Robes*, 1779. Photograph courtesy of Wikimedia Commons.

PLATE 39 Presumed portrait of Madame de Franqueville and her children. Photograph courtesy of the Musée des beaux-arts de Montréal.

PLATE 40 Ange Laurent de La Live de Jully, probably 1759. Samuel H. Kress Collection/ National Gallery of Art. Photograph courtesy of the National Gallery of Art.

PLATE 41 *The Toilette of Venus*, 1751. Bequest of William K. Vanderbilt, 1920/The Metropolitan Museum of Art. Photograph courtesy of the Metropolitan Museum of Art.

PLATE 42 *Before*, 1730–1, William Hogarth. Photograph courtesy of the J. Paul Getty Museum.

pieces of furniture "by Boule" from those of the "Boulle type."[23] In the 1793 Choiseul-Praslin sale, furthermore, these distinctions multiply, specifying alongside works by "the famous Boule [sic]" or "by Boulle," other categories that are less prestigious: "Boule [sic] marquetry" and "in the style of Boule [sic]." This last included those productions by "some very clever craftsmen who followed the manner of Boulle."[24] One is sometimes surprised by the nature of the works that one finds under these different descriptions. In the collection of the *trésorier general de la Marine*, Marcellin de Selle, for instance, the works described as by "Boule the elder" included a chinoiserie *armoire*, even though chinoiserie does not appear to fit with his style. In 1782, in the collection of the duc d'Aumont the name of Boulle is associated with a pair of magnificent cabinets from the collection of Louis XIV to which we will return, but which owes nothing to the master. Two small cabinets decorated in *pietra dura*, recent works by Joseph Baumhauer of which the Louvre holds two examples,[25] were included in the same sale, as in the sales of Radix de Sainte-Foy (1782) and the comte de Vaudreuil (1787), under the heading "Boulle type," which indicates a remarkably wide acceptance of the term.

Grand "Boulle" furniture is found in one collection after another, and mention is often made of different collectors who appreciated it. So it is that a piece "embellished in a superior manner," decorated with a bas-relief illustrating Apollo and Marsyas, passed successively through the hands of La Live de Jully, Randon de Boisset, and the Baron de Saint-Jullien;[26] and that the famous secretaire preserved today in the British Royal Collection had been found successively in the collections of the comte du Luc, the comte de Vaudreuil, and in the following century, the future King George IV (Royal British Collections, Windsor Castle, RCIN 29945). From the second half of the eighteenth century onward, such pieces of furniture had obviously acquired a degree of prestige, illustrating their status as true works of art within art collections.

The status of other types of *ébénisterie* is more ambiguous. Fine lacquer and *pietra dura* pieces of furniture were undoubtedly judged worthy of featuring legitimately in a collection, but one must note the virtual absence of furniture decorated with porcelain plaques in collectors' interiors in the eighteenth century. Although very expensive, they were probably judged too frivolous. The case of Cressent deserves special mention. Even if he did not equal Boulle in glory, he was undoubtedly sought after. His name appeared in numerous collections. The most famous is that of Marcellin de Selle, although Bonnier de La Mosson, Blondel de Gagny, Marin de La Haye, the duc de Richelieu, and Haranc de Presle also possessed furniture by him (Pradère 2003). Cressent's reputation at the end of the century was sufficiently high that in the 1793 Choiseul-Praslin sale catalog, mention is made of "an ancient marquetry bureau [...] Cressent type."[27]

Grand examples of horology were also much sought-after and highly expensive items, with clocks by or attributed to Boulle esteemed and valued in the same way as his furniture. Boulle's production of clocks follows a small number of "models" or "types," subject to a vast number of variations but always easily recognizable. Among these models are the *Michelangelo*, the *Parques* (Three Fates), the *Lampe antique*, the *Enlèvement de Cybèle*, and the *Temps couché*. The collector Randon de Boisset (1708–76) himself possessed a remarkable number of these models: a *Parques* with figures after Nicolas Coustou (1658–1733), a *Michelangelo* (an example that had featured in the collection of Jean de Jullienne), a *Lampe antique*, and an *Enlèvement de Cybèle*. One finds these same models owned by a number of other collectors, such as the duc de Bourbon, La Live de Jully, and Grimod de La Reynière, while the model described as *Temps couché* was in the collection of Louis Antoine Crozat de Thiers (1699–1770). The great model featuring the chariot of Apollo (Château de Chantilly, Musée Condé, and Munich, Residenz) and attributed to Boulle featured in the collection of Blondel de Gagny.

The presence of splendid marquetery clock cases distinguishes the finest collections of the century. Among the most celebrated are those executed by Alexandre Jean Oppenordt (1639–1715) and by Jean-Pierre Latz (*c.* 1691–1754) to house the planispheric mechanisms of Michel Stollewerck (Wallace Collection and J.P. Getty Museum); the bronze case by Jacques Caffieri (1678–1755) housing Claude-Simeon Passemant's mechanism executed for the king at Versailles (Château de Versailles); the spectacular *Pendule de la Création du Monde* (Musée du Louvre, Paris), also housing a Passemant astronomical mechanism; and finally, those produced later by Balthazar Lieutaud (1720–80) for the mechanisms of Ferdinand Berthoud (1727–1807) (Musée du Louvre, Paris; Frick Collection, New York). Yet again the collection of the duc d'Aumont can be cited as an example. At the moment of dispersal it included four clocks valued at over 1,000 livres. The first, with its movement by Berthoud in a monumental case probably executed by Oppenordt to a design by Berain at the beginning of the century, was bought for 1,400 livres by the Parisian merchant Vincent Donjeux. A huge dial-case destined to be integrated into a section of paneling, also with a mechanism by Berthoud and bronzes executed by Pierre Gouthière (1732–1813), was sold for 3,799 livres. A third, with a mahogany case and a particularly sophisticated mechanism, the work of Robert Robin (1741–99), was bought by Claude Baudard de Sainte-James (1738–87) for 443 livres. The final example was the work of Digue and came from the bedchamber of Louis XV. The duc had inherited it by right of his position as *premier gentilhomme de la chambre* at the death of the sovereign in 1774. It was sold for 1,600 livres.[28]

Furniture in the service of collections

Furniture used specifically for the display of collections includes an enormous variety of types. Of these, the great cabinets on stands, notable for their glittering decoration utilizing semiprecious stones, gilt bronze, ivory, ebony, and pewter, among other things, and suitable for housing treasures, seem destined to rank among the most collectable pieces of furniture. In fact, one finds them in all the great collections. In French collections, these are often attributed to Boulle and can frequently be linked to the main models that left his workshop. Most of the time these are fairly late examples of relatively modest dimensions; the older monumental cabinets do not seem to have been particularly favored. However, the dispersal of cabinets from the royal collection in the middle of the century (Castelluccio 2007) did arouse the interest of merchants, who wanted to salvage and reuse the materials with which they were made. As a result, the only traces of royal monumental cabinets found in the years that followed relate to the two *"grandissimes* cabinets" by Domenico Cucci (1635–1704), with twisted columns on a lapis lazuli ground, probably acquired by the duc d'Aumont and attributed to Boulle in the d'Aumont sale catalog.[29] It is probably significant that such pieces of furniture were owned by a collector who is known for his lack of interest in painting. The excessive size of cabinets of this type was generally deemed incompatible with the hanging of pictures because it provided an obstacle to their appreciation. In addition, their style was probably regarded as archaic. It is rare for the contents of the cabinets to be recorded with any precision. The description made of those belonging to the great Boulle marquetry cabinets in the gallery of the Hôtel Grimod de La Reynière reveals the passion of the owner of the house for semiprecious stones and gold boxes: plaques of agate, pitted tortoiseshell, inlays of ivory, fragments of lacquer embellished with Burgos stone, malachite, jasper, and fossilized wood were placed next to small military compositions painted in oil, the assemblage coming from dismantled boxes or parts of boxes waiting to be mounted.[30] While this cabinet clearly contained a collection of valuable small objects, it goes without saying that a cabinet is capable of containing all sorts of objects or documents, whether precious or not.

The versatile nature of these cabinets stands in contrast to the specialized functions of a number of other kinds of furniture. Collections of medals, for example, both noble and scholarly in nature, inspired exceptional furniture creations. The *cabinet des médailles* of Louis XIV, for instance, was one of the wonders of Versailles. Alexandre-Jean Oppenordt executed the furniture placed against the lower part of the walls of the room that contained part of the collection and the large table which occupied the center of the room. For Louis XV, the Parisian *ébéniste* Antoine Gaudreau (*c.* 1680–1746) delivered a medal cabinet and a pair of corner cupboards, which still decorate the king's inner *cabinet* at Versailles today. Once again, it is not surprising to see the work of Boulle and Cressent singled out. Boulle supplied the *médaillier* now preserved at the Ashmolean Museum in Oxford, which became one of the most famous models for *armoires basses*, subsequently abundantly replicated. The medal cabinets decorated with caduceus motifs in the J.P. Getty Museum (84. DA.858) and in the Hermitage (МБ 423) are also large examples. The medal coffers belonging to the duc de Bourbon (Bibliothèque Nationale, Paris), by contrast, are the smallest. There exist others, of intermediate format and different decoration (Rezidensmuseum, Munich; Altebestand Ab.; Wallace Collection, London, F20). Cressent's most famous medal cabinet was made for the duc d'Orléans (Bibliothèque Nationale, Paris, accession no. 55.702), but he supplied another remarkable model, of which Marcellin de Selle possessed an example, the evidence of which is provided by the pair currently preserved in the Gulbenkian collection in Lisbon (accession no. 2368).

Scientific and natural history collections also gave rise to remarkable furniture creations. The shell cabinet of Ange-Laurent La Live de Jully (1725–79), which matched his bureau and filing cabinet, was placed in the *cabinet flamand* of his *hôtel*. It should be noted that although this piece is described in the 1770 sale of the collection, it is not mentioned in the 1764 published description of the collection in which the Boulle bookcase installed in the next room is the subject of a laudatory note (de La Live de Jully 1764). The shell cabinet of Louis-Augustin Angran de Fonspertius (1719–84) was in lacquer with inlays of soapstone and fourteen drawers. Placed in his *cabinet des Indes* in 1747, it housed several hundred shells.[31] Jean de Jullienne placed his cabinet of Coromandel lacquer with eight drawers in the room that led to his gallery.[32] François Boucher's shell cabinet had been executed by Jean-François Oeben (1721–63) and decorated with bronze mounts by Caffieri,[33] like that of La Live de Jully. The pair of shell cabinets decorated with purple wood veneer and probably forming part of Pajot d'Ons-en-Bray's *cabinet* is a fine example of these all too rare pieces of furniture (Christie's London 2005b).

Mineralogy cabinets belong to the same category as furniture destined for specific types of collections. It should be pointed out, though, that the taste for stones goes far beyond the strict framework of furniture. It is deserving of a specific study including, in addition to marble tops and *pietra dura* (always highly favored by Parisian collectors), all kinds of ornamental vases, columns, and pedestals, often richly ornamented with gilt bronze, as well as the mineralogical snuff boxes described as "bijoux" and found in many collections. The so-called Teschen table (Table de Breteuil), which recently entered the collections of the Louvre, is one example of the application of mineralogical categorization to furniture (Plate 29). The most spectacular mineral cabinet, meanwhile, is that preserved at the Château de Chantilly, presented by Gustave

III of Sweden to the prince de Condé and made by Georg Haupt. It reminds us of the importance of scientific collections at the time and what the history of furniture owes them.

The term "bookcase" covers at least two types of fairly different furniture. The great bookcases placed against walls are the most ambitious examples. They can be extremely *deluxe*. The most famous example is the one mentioned above, which featured in the collections of La Live de Jully, sold by the prominent Parisian *marchand-mercier* Lazare Duvaux (1703–58) in 1756 for 12,000 livres. It decorated the great salon in the *hôtel* in the rue de Ménars and was made up of a suite of large glass cupboards separated by pilasters that were decorated with panels of Boulle marquetry, its upper part designed for the display of sculpture. Bernard II van Risenburgh (known as BVRB), Cressent, and Jean-François Leleu (1729–1807) have provided other examples of these enfilades of *ébénisterie* intended to decorate an entire room. Bookcases of more modest dimensions might be no higher than human chest height. Those with three doors, derived from the model that Boulle delivered to the prince de Condé at Chantilly (Musée du Louvre, OA 5461 and OA 5466), experienced an extraordinary success and might be considered the type of furniture typically made to please collectors. It not only preserved the collections that it housed and displayed them to their best advantage (with objects placed on top of the furniture), but also formed a brilliant ornament to the whole collection, enriching it with the quality of its marquetry and bronze mounts. As the century progressed, further replicas and variations left the workshops of Jean-Louis Faizelot-Delorme, Joseph Baumhauer, and Etienne Levasseur, having been produced on the initiative of the great *marchands-merciers*, of whom the foremost were Julliot and Lebrun.

One should say a word about glass display cases and bell jars of various shapes, intended to protect the most fragile objects from dust and the clumsiness of visitors. The use of simple glass bell jars was widespread. Descriptions mention them frequently, the journal of Lazare Devaux noting acquisitions made by Madame de Pompadour[34] and the duc d'Aumont, the latter making a purchase in 1756 of a small glazed gilt bronze frame to house a "pagoda from the Indies."[35] There were also large display cases. The gallery of Jean de Jullienne contained six table-cases with glass tops for displaying his natural history collections in pigeonhole compartments. The most famous object of this type was probably the glazed lacquer showcase executed by Riesener for Marie Antoinette and delivered in 1781 to her great inner *cabinet* at Versailles.[36] It was destined to house the queen's collection of lacquer.

Further, one can consider the different types of supports, bases, pedestals, consoles, and stands as belonging to a genre all its own. Here again, Boulle had been remarkably creative, producing several superb models of stands and pedestals; the universally successful *gaine à tablier* model, abundantly reproduced throughout the century, being the most famous example of this (Figure 6.3). Although table stands in general could be in Boulle marquetry,

FIGURE 6.3 Pedestal in Boulle marquetery, attributed to André Charles Boulle, Paris, before 1715. Grünes Gewölbe, Staatliche Kunstsammlungen Dresden. Photo: Dirk Weber.

gilt wood was more common. The marble or bronze stands are the richest. The duc d'Aumont possessed two tables with porphyry stands that were bought by Marie Antoinette for the impressive sum of 24,000 livres.[37] In the case of cabinets or marble tabletops on stands, the stand itself was often considered as a simple accessory and it is rare for its value to be stated. It is, however, the case that the three table stands in the collection of Bonnier de La Maison, carved by "le sieur Pelletier,"[38] qualified as masterpieces of sculpture and were sold for 1,935 livres.[39] The Louvre also preserves a pair of stands of beautiful quality that come from the collection of the duc d'Aumont, unfortunately deprived of their original tabletops (Musée du Louvre, Département des objets d'art, Paris, OA 9461 and GME 1670).

It goes without saying that different kinds of *meuble d'appui* mentioned above (cupboards, bookcases, and cabinets) could, alongside their main purpose, also play a role in the display of works of art when vases, small bronzes, busts, terracotta, and porcelains of all types were placed on top of them. For example, an entire section of the inventory taken in 1791 after the death of the duc de Praslin in the *cabinet à l'italienne* within his *hôtel* in the rue de Bourbon, currently the rue de Lille, is dedicated to the appraisal of "porcelains, marble vases and other precious objects which decorate the top of the bookcase".[40]

Accompanying the collection

A comparison between the description made by Hébert of the rooms in which the Blondel de Cagny collection was displayed and other information that we possess about the collection is instructive with regard to the items of furniture that Hébert excluded in a systematic manner, namely, seating. The inventory of the Blondel de Cagny collection does something similar, amalgamating the *ébénisterie* almost entirely with the rest of the collection. The remaining items in each room include the hangings, curtains, seating and, depending on the room, some lanterns, fire grates, candle sconces, and a few pieces of furniture, all grouped together in one entry. These compact appraisals nonetheless represent high valuations: 3,000 or 4,000 livres for the remaining contents of the main rooms in the wing apartment, including two Beauvais tapestries; 1,464 livres for that of the *salon cramoisi* (crimson room). To have a more accurate idea of the quality and diversity of furniture displayed alongside the works of art of the collection, it is vital to add the full content of this inventory to Hébert's description, given earlier: in the second room of the enfilade overlooking the square, a complete set consisting of six armchairs, a sofa, two *bergères*, and a screen, all upholstered in crimson damask that matches the wall hangings and curtains in a luxurious way; and in the music room, four armchairs and two chairs covered with green damask, also matching the wall hangings and curtains, completed with four armchairs and two *bergères* covered in a rich brocade of gold and silver. The same approach to furniture holds for Thiéry's description of the great salon of the comte de Vaudreuil, which fails to mention the splendid set of seats executed by George Jacob (1739–1814) that was still there right up to the dispersal of the collection in 1787.[41]

All the collections mentioned here were displayed in rooms, galleries, and apartments following the decorative principles of the period for the arrangement of interiors, in which seating furniture played a major role. According to these principles, the walls were divided horizontally. The upper section was devoted to textiles, mirrors, or richly carved panels. Below this, the dadoes, usually embellished only by the sober design of molded frameworks, necessitated the mass and balance of seating furniture, along with that of tables, pedestals, or more elaborate examples of *ébénisterie*. Indeed, it is in this area that the procession of *armoires basses*, bookcases, and low cabinets, so frequently mentioned, took place. The tops of these pieces displayed sculptures and objects that, like the paintings placed above, stood out against the background of richly colored textiles.

The vertical rhythms were no less important than the horizontal divisions. These arose from the emphasis placed on a certain number of axes, which created symmetries that imposed themselves on the disposition of furniture as well as on the hanging of paintings or the placing of any other significant component of the room. Tables of carved wood, closely linked to the architectural framework, were strictly confined to the centers of walls, corners, and piers, with mirrors placed above them. Works of *ebénisterie*, usually more freely distributed about a room, could be used to complement carved pieces or to substitute for them. Each large piece of furniture constituted a high point in the rhythm, and had to be flanked by narrower objects such as seats, busts on pedestals, sculptures, columns, or vases. Such an arrangement, in uniting the furniture occupying the lower level with the paintings placed above, provides the canonic model of a collector's display. It is this principle that informs the cross-section of the gallery in the project for the hotel Lebrun example mentioned above.

One should say a word about lighting, in particular chandeliers, an indispensable accompaniment to the whole collection, although by their fixed nature they do not, strictly speaking, form part of the furniture. One example, the small enamel copper chandelier today in the collections of the Louvre and probably formerly in the collections of Jean de Jullienne and Augustin Blondel de Gagny, was clearly considered "collectable" already in the eighteenth century (Plate 30) (Musée du Louvre, Département des objets d'art, OA 9940). The most beautiful chandeliers in rock crystal, meanwhile, reached considerable prices. They were often the object of specific appraisals and benefited from commentaries added to the catalogs. The chandeliers appraised by Hébert that belonged to the comtesse de Verrue reached the sum of 52,800 livres.[42] The "magnificent rock crystal chandelier," mentioned in the sale of the collections of the duc de Tallard in 1756, was sold for the sum of 16,000 livres.[43] That of Blondel de Gagny reached 18,000 livres.[44] Bronze chandeliers, especially if they were attributed to Boulle, were particularly in favor. The introduction to the Tallard sale catalog gave a revealing indication of the attention paid to the quality of their light, the harmful effects of which one feared when it was too glaring. It specifies that these chandeliers "are much more suitable for *cabinets* [rooms in which collections are arranged], where one avoids as much as possible using mirrors in places destined for pictures. One crystal chandelier would become too bright, and would break the beautiful harmony, which the lover of painting seeks for his assemblage of masterpieces of art."[45] The beauty of the light thus succeeds in perfecting the "beautiful harmony" of the effects created between the display of works of art and the installation of furniture, brought together in an elaborate decorative framework that is entirely conceived to receive and enhance them, and to delight visitors who have come to contemplate them.

A CENTURY OF CULTURAL AND ARTISTIC EXCHANGES

Generalizations about what was going on in Paris cannot be applied too rigorously on a European scale. However, it contributes to shedding light on the essential characteristics: the links between art and furniture of a highly luxurious nature developed in a comparable way and the same rules applied to the creation and display of the great collections of Europe. The attraction of rare materials, rich compositions, and products from afar, the constant marriage between paintings, sculpture, and furniture constituted the same shared heritage of intellectual and aesthetic references.

The princely collectors of Europe

In the eighteenth century, the world of collecting was a privileged meeting point between artistic centers across the continent, acting as a counterpoint to the evolution of styles and specific activities of the great centers of creation. As with architecture, the dialogue that took place among the great princely collections affirmed the grandeur of sovereign houses. International relationships were a result of family links, which united Madrid with Naples, Florence with Mannheim, London with Herrenhausen, Parma with Versailles. After the death of Louis XIV, France no longer boasted a king-collector but Augustus II and then Augustus III at Dresden,[46] the Electors Max-Emannuel and Karl Albrecht in Munich,[47] Friedrich II in Berlin,[48] Stanislas Poniatowski in Warsaw, and Catherine II at Saint Petersburg,[49] all perpetuated the tradition. They launched prestigious manufactories, issued commissions, and their agents criss-crossed Europe on the lookout for favorable opportunities offered by the art market.

The Versailles model cast its shadow across everything for part of the century. One needs to go back to the middle years of the reign of Louis XIV to see the full picture. In the *Grand Appartement* silver furniture, porphyry vases, monumental cabinets decorated with *pietra dura*, and marble tables were assembled, surrounded by the principal classical sculptures and a selection of masterpieces from the painting collection. In the king's private apartments, and likewise in those of the Dauphin on the lower floor, visitors admitted to contemplate them found canvasses by the great masters, together with Boulle marquetry furniture, clocks decorated with precious stones, rare books, small bronzes, filigrees, agates and crystals, and porcelain. Although the silver furniture of the Grands Appartments had already been melted down in 1689 to help fund the Nine Years War. The contents of the Grand Dauphin's *cabinets* would not be dispersed until after his death in 1711, and the king's *appartement de collectionneur* remained intact until the end of his reign in 1715. A recent exhibition paid homage to the history of the great collections of silver furniture, dominated by the legendary and tragic destruction of Louis XIV's silver masterpieces.[50]

Remarkable princely commissions of silver furniture that one should see as continuations of the above trends at Versailles, were made even in the first quarter of the century. Northern Europe was particularly active. The most famous creations were a result of the initiatives of Frederick IV and then Christian VI of Denmark for Rosenborg Castle and the royal palace of Copenhagen. For the sumptuous Dresden of Augustus the Strong, comparable pieces were delivered until about 1720 from Augsburg workshops. Until the 1730s Friedrich Wilhelm I of Prussia, stimulated by rivalry with his Saxon neighbor, issued exceptional commissions that were destined for the audience chamber and throne room at the royal palace in Berlin. Unfortunately, these did not survive the melting down ordered by Friedrich II in 1745 to meet his needs in the Silesian Wars. Production in Augsburg continued until after the 1750s. The surprising candlestands, inlaid with Meissen porcelain and delivered about 1730 to the *Reiche Zimmern* in the Munich Residenz for the Elector Karl Albrecht, provide evidence of how this taste endured until the rococo style.

Furniture decorated with *pietra dura*, the production of which was dominated at the beginning of the century by the workshops of the Grand Duke of Florence, was almost as regal in character. Production carried on in Florence until the 1730s, and was prolonged following the demise of the Medici dynasty after being transferred to Naples and Spain, owing to the initiative of Charles de Bourbon, who successively ruled in Naples and then Madrid.[51] Two exceptional pieces of furniture, destined for abroad, marked out the first half of the century: the monumental cabinet executed between 1707 and 1709 and offered by Cosimo III de' Medici to his son-in-law Johannes von Neuburg, Elector Palatinate (Palazzo Pitti, Florence), and that made about twenty years later, as a result of the initiative of the young Duke of Beaufort, who had it in mind for his seat at Badminton (Princes of Lichtenstein collections, Vienna). It is noteworthy that this piece of furniture, probably the last great masterpiece of its kind, left the workshops in Florence as the result of an order issued by an English aristocrat, connoisseur of Italy, collector, and talented designer with a passion for architecture, and who undertook to give his country residence the appearance on the exterior of a Roman palazzo (Plate 31) (Gomme 1984: 163–82). The Badminton cabinet followed another famous present in England from Cosimo III: the cabinet offered in 1681 to the 5th Earl of Exeter on the occasion of his journey to Florence and to this day preserved at Burghley House. Both take the place in the long sequence of masterpieces of Italian furniture that formed part of the collections of English collectors between the end of the seventeenth century and the beginning of the nineteenth. Beside *pietra dura* from Florence, English collections also featured articles produced in Rome, even older and the origin of which was not always identified. The finest Roman cabinet was installed by the banker Henry Hoare (1705–85) in his residence at Stourhead, to accompany the classical sculptures and the paintings by Carlo Maratta (1625–1713), Denis Calvaert (*c.* 1540–1619), Carlo Docli (1616–86), and Poussin. To display it, he had a pedestal made in 1743 in the form of a triumphal arch decorated with reproductions of modern Roman monuments (Jervis and Dodd 2015: 156).

The affirmation of British taste

The growing interest amongst English collectors for furniture decorated with *pietra dura* provides evidence of an evolution in taste that was born amidst exchanges between Italy and England, and profoundly transformed the relationships between architecture, collections, and interior decoration during the second quarter of the century. The curator and historian John Harris has proposed the possible role played by the antiquary and art collector John Talman (1677–1726) in the origin of ideas amongst the English about the integration of furniture collections into coherent decorative assemblages (Harris 1985: 211–16). Leaving London for Italy in July 1709, Talman was accompanied by the young painter William Kent (1695–1748).[52] Kent lived in Italy from 1709 until 1719. Beyond his activities as an art agent in the service of rich English collectors, he dedicated himself to a systematic study of architecture, the decorative arts, and garden design, which he used to promote himself as a designer once he returned home. Kent and his most enlightened patrons shared a number of objectives: to give to the collections bought in Florence, Rome, or Naples a framework worthy of housing them; to create residences that bore witness to the erudition and taste of their owners; and to allow the works of art to act as living witnesses of the grandeur of the civilization which gave birth to them.

From the 1720s, Kent designed interiors at Houghton Hall, Chiswick House, and Holkham Hall, decorating the ceilings and supplying furniture designs. These interiors were intended to house exceptional collections, gathered, in the case of Chiswick and Holkham, by true connoisseurs. In designing furniture in a new style, Kent sought inspiration in the best Italian and French models, whether of décor or furniture, amongst these, most probably, the gallery of the Palazzo Colonna in Rome with its spectacular richly sculpted gilt-wood side tables, the Palazzo Pitti in Florence, the Louvre in Paris, and some of the most recent creations of André-Charles Boulle. While Kent was not the only creator of furniture at Chiswick House, one finds his inspiration everywhere, though the furniture has since been dispersed and today is found mostly at Chatsworth House in Derbyshire (Rosoman 1985: 663–77). There one can admire the *pietra dura* tabletop with its stand terminating in eagles with spread wings, which was placed in the *Blue Velvet Room* at Chiswick, still accompanied by its pair of pedestals, also decorated with stones. The great side tables with their splendid *putti* and a series of mahogany seats, all coming from Chiswick House's octagonal hall, are also at Chatsworth. All these attest to the same formal inventiveness, the same ornamental fecundity, and above all, a taste, new to England, for the three-dimensional. The furniture of Houghton, by contrast, is still in situ. A recent exhibition reunited it with the paintings from the collections of Robert Walpole, which had graced the house in the past.[53] Through these examples one grasps the extent of the new relationship established between furniture, decoration, and collections in England: furniture is specifically designed to be worthy of the masterpieces next to which it is placed and forms an integral part of the architectural decoration conceived, from floor to ceiling, to display the paintings to their best advantage (Plate 32).

From Rome to Athens and from Paris to London: Disseminating ancient forms

The relationship between Italy and London was by no means exclusive. Rome was the purveyor par excellence of antique material, particularly rare marbles, the ancient quarries of which were no longer identified. Rome not only supplied paintings and classical sculpture but also tables, vases and columns of marble, and mosaics both ancient and modern. Mentions in Paris sales catalogs of Roman discoveries or vases executed in Rome are frequent, especially in the catalogs of the Randon de Boisset and the duc d'Aumont sales. Rome in the 1740s was a melting-pot from which the most innovative creations emerged. The new and close relationship established there between architecture, the decorative arts, and art collections profoundly influenced the evolution of taste in the second half of the century. In 1742 Pope Benedict XIV donated to the Capitoline Museum a pair of tables created during the preceding decade whose stands had been executed by Francesco Giardoni (1692–1757) to display mosaics from Hadrian's Villa (González-Palacios 2004: 181). In terms of style, these tables departed radically from such recent models as the tables executed for the nephews of Clement XII and now in Palazzo Corsini (163–4). In three ways, the Capitoline tables heralded new trends that were to remain essential characteristics of further artistic development: through the archaeological provenance of their tops; through their design, which anticipated the creations of Piranesi; and through their inclusion in one of the earliest public collections in Europe.

The depth of influence exercised by artists who had gathered in Rome during the 1740s and later scattered across Europe has already been underlined in other studies (Eriksen 1974; Brunel 1976). The celebrated furniture executed for the *cabinet* of La Live de Jully in 1756, after designs by Louis-Joseph Le Lorrain (1715–59), who returned from Rome in 1749, is one of the most characteristic manifestations of this phenomenon. Announced in the 1770 sales catalog as having been executed "in imitation of works by the famous Boulle," it perfectly reflects the mixture between archaeological quotations, creative fantasies, and the will to impose a radically new style which marks the first attempts by Parisian neoclassicists in the domain of furniture.

In England, the first champion this archaeological historicism was James Stuart (1713–88), who traveled as far as Greece and passed through Paris in 1755 before returning to London.[54] Stuart does not occupy a place in the history of the decorative arts comparable to that of Robert Adam during the following decade, but his role was essential: both as a precocious disseminator of the repertoire of forms that he had personally brought back, and as an introducer to England of innovations from within the milieu of Paris. As with the Capitoline table and La Live de Jully's furniture, the context of Stuart's creations is characterized by the conjunction of an archaeological interest and the presence of art collections. Called to Kedleston Hall in 1757 by Nathaniel Curzon, who had works of art brought from the Continent that were to be displayed in his residence, Stuart supplied drawings of tables and tripod candelabra, which were probably the first attempts in using archaeological material in the realm of English furniture. For the hall of Newby Hall—where he would be, as at Kedleston, supplanted by Adam—he provided designs for an organ case and fireplace incorporating tripods, Doric pilasters, and Ionic columns that show the same originality. Stuart also designed pedestals in the antique style, an obligatory feature in every collector's interior at the time, stylistically close to contemporary Parisian creations and to those that William Chambers (1722–96) provided for the plaster cast gallery at Richmond House, Whitehall, in about 1759 (Kenworthy-Browne 2009: 40–9; Goodison 1990: 67–89). Finally, at Spencer House he directly took inspiration from his own drawings of classical motifs and ornaments made in Greece, creating candelabra, seats, and lanterns.

Between neo-Gothic and neoclassicism

At the very moment when the endeavors of artists and collectors, who were enamored with archaeology, blossomed in a spectacular way, English patrons embarked on paths hitherto unexplored. Beginning in 1748, Horace Walpole (1717–97), son of the man who built Houghton, undertook to transform a modest residence on the outskirts of London into an experimental laboratory of neo-Gothic taste.[55] Strawberry Hill was at the same time an aesthetic experience, an intellectual adventure and a setting for the most diverse collections. Walpole was more interested in England and the Middle Ages than Italy and antiquity. He gathered together works of art and pieces of historical evidence to which he added personal commissions, in the conception of which he frequently participated. Erudition and fantasy presided over this unique blend of taste, which clearly acknowledged the importance of furniture within the process of gathering architecture, interior decoration, collections, and commissions into one all-encompassing project. Walpole ordered a chest with Boulle marquetry from Paris and believed he was preserving chairs that had belonged to Cardinal Wolsey. In the Great Parlour, neo-Gothic chairs and mirrors, executed by William Hallet (1707–81) (Figure 6.4), were placed side by side with a miniatures cabinet of Palladian inspiration and a neo-Gothic drawings cabinet. At the beginning of the 1760s he solicited from the architect Robert Adam (1728–92) a design for a bed derived from a drawing of the vaults in the Henry VII Chapel at Westminster Abbey and asked him to draw inspiration from the monument of Edward the Confessor in conceiving a chimneypiece (Wilton-Ely 2011: 3–14). Whether they are classical or medieval in inspiration, such schemes, always full of historical or archaeological associations, only reach their full significance through their connection with the collection, which is at the origin of their creation.

The case of Horace Walpole serves as an example of the precocious interest amongst English collectors in a type of furniture that we have seen triumph in the interiors of Parisian collectors: that of Boulle furniture. We return to this so as to emphasize that its success was not only limited to Parisian collections. In Germany, for example, traditional affinities with metal marquetry provided a receptive setting for Boulle's work. Augustus II in Dresden and Max II Emanuel in Munich issued commissions for and included Boulle furniture in their collections. It is also probable that La Live de Jully's great bookcase was offered without any success to a German collector, possibly Friedrich II himself. In terms of Boulle furniture, nonetheless, it was England, in the second half of the eighteenth century, that was destined to shine as it made its entry into the world of French furniture collecting. One does not precisely know the circumstances in which the great Cucci cabinets, sold by the Crown, entered the collections of the Duke of Northumberland, but some years later the departure of one of

FIGURE 6.4 Richard Bentley and Horace Walpole, designers, William Hallett, maker, Chair of Gothic pattern from Strawberry Hill, *c.* 1755. Photograph courtesy of the Lewis Walpole Library, Yale University.

the Boulle cabinets in the collection of the duc de Tallard for England is better documented. Featuring as lot no. 1032 in this collector's sale in 1756, it was bought by the merchant Rémy "for England" (Demetrescu 2014: 30–59). This mention constitutes a vitally important chronological marker as the first piece of evidence in the history of the route to England taken by Boulle furniture coming from French collections.

With the appearance of the earliest creations of Robert Adam in the 1760s, the link between architectural décor, collections and furniture became even closer. After returning from Italy in 1758, Adam set about reforming the taste of his contemporaries by integrating his Roman experience with the design of interior decoration. This consisted in the liquidation of the Palladian heritage, too much marked by the heaviness of Roman baroque, and instead a turn toward the recent archaeological discoveries that revealed the interior decoration of the ancient Romans, all in the spirit of creative liberty inspired by Piranesi. Adam's success was immense. Like Kent, he worked for aristocrats who had traveled through Italy, where they had ordered antiquities and paintings that would be displayed in their English homes, and it is not surprising to find the dialogue between furniture and collections, especially of antiquities, at the heart of Adam's preoccupations as well. Following on the heels of Stuart, Adam was called to Kedleston Hall where he intervened as much in the external architecture of the house as in the interior decoration and designs for furniture. He established precise plans for picture hanging in the main rooms (Russell 1989: 143–53), and the importance of the classical sculpture collection spurred him on to provide a vital space for sculpture. At Newby Hall, furthermore, Adam was for the most part the author of the furniture designs and from the 1760s onward conceived an entire gallery completely dedicated to the splendid collection of classical statues assembled by William Wedell (1737–92) (Middleton 1986: 48–60). Sculpture enjoyed the same remarkable treatment in the décor of the hall and antechamber of Syon House, the interiors of which Adam completely transformed for the Duke of Northumberland in the same years.

In Italy, the 1769 publication *Diverse Maniere d'Adornare I Cammini* comprises Piranesi's major contribution to the domain of the decorative arts and provides evidence of the persistent vigor of the Roman milieu right up to the last quarter of the century. Amongst the plates in the compilation one finds a model for the tables executed at the same time for one of the nephews of Pope Benedict XIII, Piranesi's compatriot from Venice and dedicatee of the work, of which two examples are known (Rijksmuseum, Amsterdam, BK-1971-14, and Institute of Arts, Minneapolis) (Plate 33). In these designs, classical motifs are transformed by the originality of the composition and a profusion of ornament characteristic of the Venetian who, in the preface to this work, exhorts his reader to find "new ornaments and manners." Piranesi's influence on Roman creations remained strong after his death in 1778 right up to the end of the following decade, as evidenced by tables with mosaic tops inspired by those in Hadrian's Villa, executed in Rome under the direction of Francesco de Belli between 1786 and 1788 and destined for Stanislas Poniatowski, King of Poland (González-Palacios 2004: 218).

In a comparable spirit, the transformation of the Borghese palace was carried out in the early 1770s, under the direction of the architect Antonio Asprucci (1723–1808), following the marriage between Prince Marcantonio Borghese and Anna Salviati in 1768 (González-Palacios 2004: 340). Asprucci's intervention resulted amongst other things in the *Galeria Terrena*, an enfilade of rooms destined to house the masterpieces of the princely collection. In the third room stood the celebrated great "jasper table." Its bronze stand, featuring caryatids executed in the preceding century by the sculptor Alessandro Algardi (1598–1654), had been completely transformed by the silversmith Luigi Valadier (1726–85). Next to it, a pair of sculpted wood tables, probably executed to a design by Asprucci (1723–1808), supported tabletops made from ancient mosaics. In the seventh room, porphyry dominated: a pair of dodecagonal tables and a pair of candelabra, both created by Valadier, were placed next to sixteen imperial busts, their heads of porphyry embellished with draperies of various coloured marbles. Around the stem of the candelabra stood three feminine figures derived from three famous antique models, among them the *Venus Callipyge*, then preserved in the Villa Farnesina, Rome. Such an example provides remarkable evidence of how precociously classicizing compositions were created in Rome and of the literal transposition of motifs taken from the classical repertoire in the creation of furniture. Finally, in the eighth room Roman *pietra dura* tabletops were displayed, their stands borrowing from both the Capitoline tables, created three decades earlier, and the caryatides of Algardi's jasper table (González-Palacios 2003: 89–99).

Toward the museum

The end of the eighteenth century is marked by a radical break. In France, the considerable purchases made by the Crown in 1782 at the duc d'Aumont's sale, part of which is still preserved at the Louvre, had been executed with the creation of the future museum in mind. This acquisition consisted of vases, columns, and marble tables, then considered indispensable complements to a collection of paintings and sculpture, as illustrated in the imagined *Grande Galerie* of the Louvre by the landscape painter Hubert Robert (1733–1808) (Plate 34). Not long afterward, however, the decorative arts were excluded from art collections. The desire to rationalize collections according to technique and school, as well as the constraints of public display, engaged the nascent study of museums in ways of thinking that had no room for furniture. In parallel, the rupture caused by the Revolution gave French decorative arts a new historical and aesthetic significance. From the 1780s onward the Prince of Wales had contributed to the introduction of French fashions to England, entrusting the furnishing of his residence at Carlton House to Henry Holland (1745–1806), an architect especially receptive to French taste. The prince solicited the advice of the Parisian *marchand-mercier*, Dominique Daguerre, collected Flemish paintings as Parisian collectors had done passionately throughout the century, and ordered furniture from Parisian craftsmen.[56] In doing this, the future George IV radically turned away from the style inherited from Robert Adam and reconnected with the endeavors of designers such as Stuart or Chambers.[57] The prestige that suddenly accrued to artifacts which could evoke the memory of the *ancien régime* accentuated this trend. Rapidly, furniture enriched with porcelain plaques, Boulle marquetry, oriental lacquer, or *pietra dura* panels as well as mounted objects that had assured the triumph of the great Parisian *marchands-merciers* before the Revolution flowed across the Channel. They were soon accompanied by vestiges of the court at Versailles, such as furniture by Riesener, Carlin, or Benneman, rightly or wrongly associated with the former sovereigns and their entourage.

The subsequent course of the relationship between eighteenth-century furniture and art collections is conditioned by those ruptures described in the previous paragraph, which swiftly rejected as *passé* the practices of the century that had just ended. In France, the seizure of property belonging to émigré aristocrats carried out by the revolutionary administration resulted in a considerable artistic heritage entering national collections. Thus, Boulle furniture, marble tables, mounted objects, and rare clocks, all reflecting the practices of Parisian collectors of the time, accumulated for some years in national depots. Items that were not restituted or sold would serve to furnish official palaces until they were increasingly handed over toward the end of the nineteenth century to museums, which were more suitable for their display. The former royal palaces, Versailles, Fontainebleau, or Compiègne, were obvious repositories for royal furniture, and the Louvre became the privileged destination for works that came from Parisian private collections. Several very beautiful pieces of furniture were then reunited, in the same museum, with the paintings and sculptures that had preceded them for a century on this path, but at a distance, in a separate department, without, anymore, rubbing shoulders with them directly and in a spirit that had nothing in common with the one that had presided over their initial gathering in the interiors of Parisian collectors who loved outstanding pieces of furniture.

CHAPTER SEVEN

Furniture and Architecture

PETER N. LINDFIELD

The appearance and character of British furniture, arguably one of the most dynamic and rich regions for furniture design, changed dramatically over the course of the eighteenth century. New woods came to prominence—mahogany offered fresh possibilities for carved and pierced decoration, and satinwood provided flame-like surface patterns (Bowett 2012: 120–9, 218–21)—but more significant were the repeated changes in fashionable design: "English Baroque" (what William Kent designed for eighteenth-century "Palladian" interiors); rococo; Gothic; chinoiserie; neoclassical; and antiquarian (Ward-Jackson 1958; Wainwright 1989). As these labels suggest, a lot of these furniture styles were modeled upon, inspired by, or intended to ape architecture, architectural forms, structures, structural motifs, and/or ornament. Architecture consequently had a significant impact upon the design of eighteenth-century British furniture. Fashionable furniture designers and makers, including Britain's most renowned designer-maker Thomas Chippendale the Elder (Gilbert 1978), as well as, among many others, William Hallett Sr. (Wood 2005) (Victoria and Albert Museum [hereafter V&A], London, W.48–1934) and the Royal cabinetmaking firm of Vile and Cobb (V&A, W.11:1 to 135-1963), were designing, promoting, and producing explicitly architectural or architecturally informed furniture during the eighteenth century according to these different tastes, or modes. Such architectural furniture—this is furniture made to resemble the form, ornament, and/or structure of architecture—was not only designed by cabinetmakers, carvers, and craftsmen such as Chippendale, Robert Manwaring, and Ince and Mayhew; architects were also active in the field and proposed anything up to and including whole interior schemes, encompassing wall decoration as well as moveable and fixed furniture. William Kent, James "Athenian" Stuart, Robert Adam, and James Wyatt, for example, are well known for their architectural work, but they are also notable for their furniture designs (Harris 2001; Weber 2006b, 2013; Robinson 2012). In some instances, architects worked with renowned upholders, as is the case with Adam, who "subcontracted" the creation of his furniture, such as the pieces for Sir Lawrence Dundas's London town house, 19 Arlington Street (Gilbert 1978, 1997), and for Sir Rowland Winn's country pile, Nostell Priory, Yorkshire (Boynton and Goodison 1969a, b; Gilbert 1978) to Chippendale. Cabinetmakers, consequently, were exposed directly to architects' idiosyncratic interpretations of furniture design, and this interaction surely offered non-architectural craftsmen further guidance, or hints, for designing architectural furniture. There exists, consequently, a tension and connection between the types of professional creating architecture-inspired furniture in eighteenth-century Britain: practicing architects who also turned their hands to creating furniture as part of their work on clients' houses, and cabinetmakers and designers who applied what could, at worst, be a vague understanding of current or past architectural styles to their practice.

Some architects believed their bespoke furniture to be superior to that designed and produced by mainstream upholders and cabinetmaking firms such as Gillows (Stuart 2008), whose designs were potentially ubiquitous and either incompatible or only vaguely related to the architectural settings. By designing one-off pieces of furniture, architects could maintain the tone and exclusivity of their interiors, which can be seen particularly in the work of Robert Adam and James Wyatt, considered later. Adam, nevertheless, reused designs—for example the Gothic throne at Alnwick Castle, Northumberland, was earlier used for Croome Court's church, Worcestershire (Harris 2001; Lindfield 2017a)—which compromises this exclusivity. William Porden, architect and surveyor to the 2nd Earl Grosvenor, exemplifies the reason for creating bespoke architectural furniture at the turn of the nineteenth century. He criticized heavily Gillows's neoclassical furniture proposed for Eaton Hall, Chester, a house that he personally designed and redeveloped in an "exclusive" Gothic style for the Earl from 1802 (Lindfield 2013). Circumventing Gillows's apparently poor, "pedestrian," and ubiquitous neoclassical chairs (Metropolitan Museum of Art, New York, 38.37.24–5), Porden interfered and he proposed his own designs (Lindfield 2012, 2017b):

> sending two of those [furniture drawings] I have prepared and will send Mr Gillows if I can get them that your Lordship may decide between them and the work of a mere Mechanic. [...] I do not by this interference mean to prejudice your Lordship against Mr Gillow who is an excellent Workman, and able to execute whatever may be directed, but I see nothing that distinguishes him as a man of superior taste.
>
> (Grosvenor Family Archive, Chester, 9/278, November 23, 1807: 1r)

This could have numerous benefits for both architect and patron: the architect would increase the value of his commission; designs were chargeable, and it would also allow him to realise a house's interior according to his architectural and aesthetic vision, assuming the client was happy to go along with this, as was the case for Porden at Eaton. By going through the architect, the house's owner would be spared dealing with an additional firm. There were, of course, also disadvantages to this arrangement as architects generally were not as experienced, or even trained, in designing furniture and their understanding of manufacturing techniques—what was physically possible—was limited in comparison with cabinetmakers or other craftsmen; this necessitated their subcontracting of work to other firms.

The relevance and application of architectural forms and styles to eighteenth-century furniture is consequently bound with the century's shifting aesthetic predilections and directed not only by professional furniture designers and furniture makers, but architects themselves. The rapidity of these shifting fashions was criticized at the time, including by Adam Smith in his *Theory of Moral Sentiments* (1759: 373–6) and S. Hooper's engraving, *A common council man of Candlestick Ward and his wife on a visit to Mr. Deputy at his modern built villa near Clapham* from 1771 (Lewis Walpole Library, Farmington, CT, 771.11.01.02+) (Plate 35). Smith argued that the fleeting fashions generated waste:

> The modes of dress and furniture are continually changing, and that fashion appearing ridiculous to-day which was admired five years ago, we are experimentally convinced that it owed its vogue chiefly or entirely to custom and fashion.
>
> (Smith 1759: 374)

And the ridiculousness of these numerous, briefly in-vogue styles as applied to furniture and architecture in eighteenth-century Britain is articulated in Hooper's plate where the classical, Gothic and Chinese styles are incoherently set cheek by jowl in the "new built villa." Irrespective of these various styles, a common thread uniting eighteenth-century British furniture is the introduction of architectural forms. This chapter outlines and assesses the changing and occasionally surprising architectural themes and forms governing both fashionable mainstream and idiosyncratic bespoke furniture in eighteenth-century Britain. It consequently expands upon Jill Leaver's important, progressive and wide-ranging study, *Architects' Designs for Furniture*, by exploring a broader range of designers and craftsmen, along with amateur and gentlemen architect-designers responsible for eighteenth-century architectural furniture (Lever 1982).

ARCHITECTURE'S RELEVANCE TO EIGHTEENTH-CENTURY FURNITURE DESIGN

Architecture was promoted in Georgian Britain (1714–1830) as an important and highly relevant subject, not only for those designing buildings but also for those creating furniture. It was recommended by designers such as Thomas Chippendale that designers producing fashionable furniture should study architecture. Batty Langley, known primarily for his infamous 1741–2 pattern-book on Gothic design, *Ancient Architecture: Restored and Improved by Rules and Proportions* (Lindfield 2014b: 142–55), also advocates architecture's relevance to furniture design, especially in bookcases. In his 1740 treatise, *The City and Country Builder's, and Workman's Treasury of Designs*, he delineates, for example, "Tuscan" (plates CLVII–CLVIII), "Dorick" (plates CLIX–CLX), and "Ionick" (plate CLXI) bookcases. Defending his decision to promote architecturally informed and inspired furniture, he writes that:

> When a Gentleman applies himself, with a good Design of a Book Case, &c. made by an able Architect, to most of the Masters in this Trade [cabinetmakers]; they instantly condemn it; and alledge [*sic*], that 'tis not possible to make Cabinet Works look well, that are proportioned by the Rules of Architecture; because, they say, that the Members will be too large and heavy, &c. whereas the real Truth is, they do not understand, How to proportion and work the Members of those Designs; and therefore advise the Unwary, to accept of such *Stuff*, as their poor crazy Capacities will enable them to make.
>
> (Langley 1740: 23)

Architecture also comes to the fore in the preface and introductory plates to each edition of Chippendale's *The Gentleman and Cabinet-Maker's Director* (1754, 1755, and 1762), the period's leading and arguably most influential furniture pattern-book (Gilbert 1978):

> OF all the ARTS which are either improved or ornamented by Architecture, that of CABINET-MAKING is not only the most useful and ornamental, but capable of receiving as great assistance from it as any whatever. I have therefore prefixed to the following designs a short explanation of the five Orders. Without an acquaintance with this science, and some knowledge of the rules of Perspective, the Cabinet-maker cannot make the designs of his work intelligible, nor shew, in a little compass, the whole conduct and effect of the piece. These, therefore, ought to be carefully studied by everyone who would excel in this branch, since they are the very soul and basis of his art.
>
> (Chippendale 1754: iii)

The first eight plates of each edition of the *Director* are dedicated to classical architecture's five Orders and their various technicalities. Each Order is delineated individually and with precise attention to proportion and detail, which each plate's description enumerates at length (Figure 7.1). This matches classical architecture's importance and high status in eighteenth-century Britain courtesy of its connection to antiquity, and its rationalized and mathematical rules and proportions. Classicism was, of course, particularly relevant to this century given the intellectual and cultural phenomenon of the Grand Tour—a tour where Britons (primarily, but not exclusively gentlemen aristocrats) traveled to the Continent to "experience" and learn from classical antiquity; they brought back with them a deeper understanding of the classical past's literature, culture, and particularly relevant for this chapter, architecture. Portraits painted of these gentlemen by artists such as Pompeo Batoni (1708–87), for instance, his *c.* 1760–5 *Portrait of a Young Man* (Metropolitan Museum of Art, New York, 03.37.1), place these travelers within the architectural and intellectual context of classical antiquity, and reveal the importance of classicism's architectural context and fabric to this acculturation. Architects, including Adam, went on the Grand Tour as well, and in Adam's case this had a significant impact upon his architectural commissions and furniture designs once he returned to England: a comparison between his pre-Grand Tour work at Dumfries House, Ayrshire, and post-Grand Tour work at Kedleston Hall, Derbyshire, illustrate this point especially well. Exemplary of classicism's intellectual and aesthetic importance in eighteenth-century Britain is Alexander Gerard's 1759 assessment of classical architecture in comparison with Gothic:

> The profusion of ornament, bestowed on the *parts*, in *Gothic* structures, may please one who has not acquired enlargement of mind, sufficient for conceiving at one view their relation to the *whole*; but no sooner is this acquired, than he perceives superior elegance in the more *simple* symmetry and proportion of *Grecian* architecture [...] WHERE refinement is wanting, taste must be coarse and vulgar.
>
> (Gerard 1759: 122–7)

Those with a cultured, "enlarged mind" to use Gerard's terminology, accepted this reasserted foreign style of architecture as appropriate to eighteenth-century Britain's progressive and current political, economic, and social climate. Horace Walpole (1717–97), author, letter-writer, nominally politician, aesthetician, the last son of Sir Robert Walpole (1676–1745)—Britain's first "Prime Minister"— was eighteenth-century Britain's arch-Gothicist (Snodin 2009), he illustrates how classical architecture was visually, culturally, and intellectually appealing to an age where the Grand Tour of the Continent was a cornerstone of aristocratic and aspirational culture:

FIGURE 7.1 Thomas Chippendale (designer), Composite Order, 1753. Rogers Fund, 1920/The Metropolitan Museum of Art. Photograph courtesy of the Metropolitan Museum of Art.

If two Architects of equal Genius & Taste, or one man possessing both, & without the least degree of partiality was ordered to build Two buildings, (& supporting him unlimited in expense) one in the Grecian & one in the Gothic style, I think, the Gothic w[oul]d strike most at first, the Grecian would please the longest. But I believe this approbation would in some measure flow from the Impossibility of not connecting with Grecian & Roman Architecture, the ideals of the Greeks & Romans, who invented & inhabited that kind of building.

(Lewis Walpole Library, Farmington, 49 2615, I, 52)

Walpole was not the only one who celebrated the relevance of classicism's connection with the past and relevance to the eighteenth-century present. As has been identified already, Gerard theorized classicism's relevance. This was not limited simply to intellectual commentators, such as Walpole and Gerard, but also craftsmen. Celebrating classical architecture's rationalized and mathematical precision, Chippendale describes the Composite Order as follows:

Take any determined Height, as in the CORINTHIAN Order, and divide it into five parts, one Part shall be the Height of the Pedestal, the other four Parts must be divided into five Parts as before; one of them is the Height of the Entablature: The Height of the Capital is one Module, and ten Parts: The Column diminishes; of its Semi-diameter on each Side, from one third Part of the Height. The Dimensions are as in the CORINTHIAN Order.

(Chippendale 1754: 3)

The remaining three prefatory architectural plates in the *Director* delineate the Orders' bases, and one offers guidance for "drawing the spiral lines of the volute of the Ionick Order" (Figure 7.2) (Chippendale 1754: 4). Although these exact details and architectural principles are not incorporated directly into Chippendale's furniture designs in his *Director*, this guidance demonstrates the relevance of architectural forms and principles to intellectualized and architecturally informed furniture in the period.

Despite changes in style during the eighteenth century, the centrality of the Classical Orders of architecture remained constant. Chippendale's advocacy of the Orders, for example, came at the height of rococo in 1750s Britain, and most of the *Director*'s designs follow this style (Gilbert 1978). Nearly fifty years after Chippendale's *Director* first appeared, Thomas Sheraton (1751–1806), a late eighteenth-century advocate of a pared-back form of classical design, also commended an understanding of the Orders to cabinetmakers and designers in his *Cabinet-Maker and Upholsterer's Drawing-Book* (1793): classical architecture and its rules of proportion were still of relevance to the

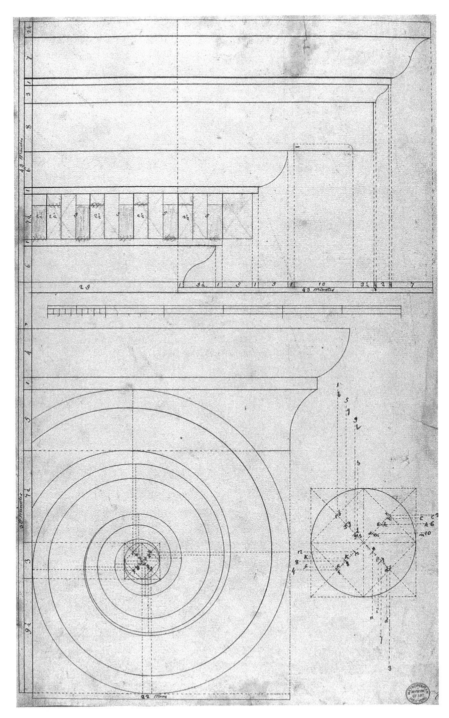

FIGURE 7.2 Thomas Chippendale (designer), Rule for Drawing the Spiral Lines of the Volute of the Ionic Order, 1753. Rogers Fund, 1920/The Metropolitan Museum of Art. Photograph courtesy of the Metropolitan Museum of Art.

furniture designing and making industries, especially so since neoclassicism was the prevailing style at the time. Justifying his delineation of the Orders, beyond their aesthetic and intellectual currency, Sheraton writes that "the knowledge of these particulars must ever be considered as essential parts of good drawing, in which architecture is often introduced, and sometimes makes the principal figure" (1793: 1:121). This knowledge, he continues, is relevant to the Georgian cabinetmaker and designer:

> As many cabinet-makers, and even some ingenious upholsterers, are found desirous of having a knowledge of the five orders, and the proportions of the several frontispieces, I thought an attempt of this sort would be favorably received, as it undoubtedly tends to make the work more generally useful, and will prevent the trouble and expense of having recourse to other books on the subject. And this has not been merely my own opinion, but the sentiment of some well-wishers, who desired me to let the orders have a place in my book.
>
> (Sheraton 1793: 1:121)

The revised and expanded third edition of a treatise by the architect Sir William Chambers (1723–96) *On the Decorative Part of Civil Architecture* (1791) also emphasizes the relevance of architecture to the decorative arts widely conceived:

> An art [architecture] so variously conducive to the happiness of man, to the wealth, lure and safety of nations; naturally commands protection and encouragement: in effect, it appears, that in all civilized times, and well-regulated governments, it has been much attended to, and promoted with unremitting assiduity; and the perfectioning of other arts, has ever been a certain consequence: for where building is encouraged; painting, sculpture, and all the inferior branches of decorative workmanship, much flourish of course; and these, have an influence on manufactures, even to the minutest mechanic productions; for design is of universal benefit, and stamps additional value on the most trifling performances, the importance of which, to a commercial people, is obvious; it requires no illustration.
>
> (Chambers 1791: iii)

Architecture's relevance to eighteenth-century furniture, consequently, appears to extend beyond the work of architects to include designers, artists, and craftsmen; even non-overtly architectural eighteenth-century furniture appears to have been conditioned by an understanding of architectural forms and principles. The remainder of this chapter traces the architectural influences upon eighteenth-century furniture according to style and chronology.

KENT AND FURNITURE FIT FOR NEO-PALLADIAN INTERIORS

Fashionable architecture in early eighteenth-century Britain, as promoted by a select number of architects, especially Colen Campbell of Boghole and Urchany (1676–1729), Richard Boyle, 3rd Earl of Burlington and 4th Earl of Cork (1694–1753), William Kent (*c.* 1686–1748), and James Paine (1745–1829), favored an especially distinctive form of classicism. These architects and gentlemen connoisseurs reinvigorated a type of classicism promoted by Andrea Palladio (1508–80) that Inigo Jones (1573–1652) brought to England in the seventeenth century. Palladio is known for his sixteenth-century villas, *palazzi*, and basilica in the Veneto, Italy, the designs for which were circulated in his architectural treatise *I Quattro Libri dell' Architettura* (1570) (Hart 2011; Pisani 2015). Palladio provided copious details about the minutiae of classical architecture, including its proportions, and the treatise details his as well as ancient classical architecture. The four-book work also delineates buildings' internal elevations—colonnades, constellations of niches, door surrounds, entablature friezes, and moldings. There is not, however, any mention or depiction of furniture. Neo-Palladian designers could refer to Palladio's *I Quattro Libri* for architectural references and guidance, but the treatise was of no direct help when it came to providing comprehensive interior furnishing programs (Lever 1982: 14).

Overcoming this lack of guidance and precedence, Kent, a painter, designer, and "architect," applied the mass of, and architectural details found in, this architecture to produce furniture fit for his clients upon his return to England under the sponsorship of Lord Burlington. These architectural traditions were also combined with Italian furniture that he saw during his ten-year residence in Italy (1709–19) such as *cassoni* Metropolitan Museum of Art, New York, 45.67.2), as well as seventeenth-century baroque furniture (Weber 2013: 449–67). Some types of furniture that are naturally architectural or architectonic in form and appearance, such as cabinets, beds, tables, and bookcases, were rendered with architectural forms in a straightforward manner such as proposed by Langley (1740: plate CLXIV) and Chippendale (1754: plates LX–LXIX). Important pieces of such microarchitectural furniture can be found among the pieces Kent designed for Sir Robert Walpole's neo-Palladian country seat, Houghton Hall, Norfolk, newly constructed between 1725 and 1732. One of his notable contributions to the house relevant to this chapter is the *c.* 1732 State Bed made for the Green Velvet Bedchamber (V&A, W.58-2002). "Four-poster" tester beds are naturally architectural, and Kent modeled this bed's ornamental features upon suitably relevant forms from the language of classical architecture: the tester's external facing, for example, is presented as an entablature. A pair of dilated shells—typical of Kent's oeuvre and derived from seventeenth-century furniture—is bracketed out from a pedimented tablet flanked by volute scrolls on the headboard that creates a temple-like façade akin to the buildings of the Italian architect and theorist Leon Battista Alberti (1404–72), such as at Santa Maria Novella, Florence. The underside of the Houghton State Bed tester is also rendered in architectural terms, with the concentric oval moldings responding to classical ornament in the house. The headboard's broken pediment, crested by a shell, responds precisely to, and reflects the architectural forms found in, Kent's overmantels in Houghton's Stone Hall and Great Dining Room, as well as the pier glass design used in the Green Drawing Room. Shells are found readily in Kent's work at the juncture of broken pediments or scrolls, and this device, a leitmotif of his oeuvre, is exhibited by his seat furniture and tables at Chiswick House; Devonshire House, Richmond House and Wanstead House, London; Hampton Court Palace, Surrey; Holkham Hall and Raynham Hall, Norfolk; and Rousham Hall, Oxfordshire (Weber 2013: 469–507).

Perhaps also designed by Kent is the Walpole Cabinet (V&A, W.52:1, 2-1925), made for Sir Robert's son, Horace Walpole, that displayed ivory plaques collected during his Grand Tour of the Continent. Made originally for Walpole's London townhouse on Arlington Street, it was transferred to his well-known Gothic villa in Strawberry Hill, Twickenham, and installed in the house's Tribune (Figure 7.3) (Lewis Walpole Library, Farmington, 789.00.00.73dr++). The cabinet's noticeable features are the pedimented cresting—Walpole's personally differentiated coat of arms in a cartouche decorates the tympanum, the carved decoration set within the cabinet's triangular temple-derived apex—topped with the figures of three of Walpole's artistic heroes: Inigo Jones; the celebrated court painter and diplomat Rubens (1577–1640); and the sculptor François Duquesnoy (1597–1643) (Walpole 1784: 56; Snodin 2009: 317). Save for the baroque-style armorial cartouche, this cabinet lacks the energy and playfulness of Kent's other classically inspired furniture, such as the suite of mahogany hall chairs c. 1727–32 for the Gallery at Chiswick House where the back's geometric temple façade connects with sinuous and matted scrolling arms and volute-like canted front legs (Weber 2013: 484–7). The cabinet is, nevertheless, associated with Kent: Walpole is thought to have designed the cabinet with the assistance of Kent in 1743.

Architecture had a significant impact upon Kent's furniture designs, although as the Houghton State Bed's headboard and the Chiswick hall chairs demonstrate, classical architecture's forms and motifs were presented in a distinctly new, idiosyncratic, even imaginative, manner given that no exact models existed. Their reconfiguration of classical forms is, nevertheless, restrained in comparison with other pieces designed by Kent. A poignant example of this are his pair of 1727–32 pier tables for Lord Burlington's Palladian villa, Chiswick House (Plate 36) (V&A, W.14 to: 2-1971). Although they essentially follow a clearly

FIGURE 7.3 John Carter, The cabinet of miniatures and enamels *c.* 1784, 32.6 x 27.5 cm, Watercolour. Photograph courtesy of the Lewis Walpole Library, Yale University.

defined set piece of classical design, the Corinthian capital, all that remains of the capital is the outline: the capital's constituent ornament is either substituted for other decorative forms or recomposed to create new patterns; the mass of acanthus fronds that should shroud the Corinthian capital are pared back to just two that delineate the table's outline and replace the corner volutes; the abacus is not plain but rather executed as dentil molding; the astragal—glazing bar—is similarly "enhanced" and decorated with a band of Greek key molding; and the fluted shaft swells out to the pedestal base. The pier tables' form and ornament complement Chiswick's architectural simplicity, classicism, and ornate decorative schemes, but unlike the Houghton State Bed, this table illustrates Kent's penchant for generating distinctive and original artistic creations based upon, but not limited to, the ornamental language and formality of classicism. His 1731 design for a side table at Houghton Hall is exemplary of this imaginative reworking of classical forms and it is representative of numerous of his tables (Figure 7.4) (V&A, 8156). The design employs the same concave fluted columns as used in the Chiswick pier table, and its frieze is coherently architectural, however one of the main features—the barbed S-scroll—that connects the fluted columns and frieze, introduces another of Kent's principal decorative forms: a fish scale-like pattern, known as matting, applied to otherwise plain surface, and which Palladio illustrates in his *Quattro Libri* (Palladio 1570: IV, 58). A pair of *torchères* designed by Kent and carved by John Boson for Chiswick's Garden Room further exemplifies this imaginative deployment of classical forms; the *torchères* are rigorously architectural and modeled upon terms with an Ionic fluted platform above the head, and decorated with Kent-like matting and acanthus fronds and with appropriately robust volute feet (V&A, W.47A/2,3-1962). Whilst these *torchères* demonstrate Kent's direct engagement with recognizable classical motifs, they also illustrate his reconfiguration of the forms for dynamic and decorative effect. There are, consequently, two very distinct ways in which classical architectural forms were used in structural ways and ornamental details.

Kent's distinctively weighty style of classical furniture was circulated in John Vardy's 1744 publication *Some Designs of Mr Inigo Jones and Mr Wm Kent*, and the plates delineate both the Chiswick pier table (Vardy 1744: plate 40) (Plate 36) and the Houghton side table (Vardy 1744: plate 41) (Figure 7.4). Plates 42 and 43 illustrate his seat furniture; the settle at the top of plate 43 effectively paraphrases classical paneling fielded with acanthus molding, and the cresting is a modification of the familiar broken pediment motif centering on an upturned shell as found on the Houghton State Bed's headboard. The chairs on this and the subsequent plate reveal Kent's persistent use of matting, robust scrollwork, and term-like legs. These leitmotifs are manifest in the work of several of Kent's contemporaries, including Benjamin Goodison (*c.* 1700–76), whose pair of *c.* 1754–6 settees for the Great Room at the Earl of Guilford's house in Grosvenor Square, London, includes Kent-like volute-cabriole legs and scrolled arms faced with acanthus fronds and matting (V&A, W.8-1964). Matthias Lock, who is better known for his accomplished rococo designs for carved decoration, also engaged with Kent's weighty form of "Palladian" furniture. The pair of pier tables on his pencil sketch (V&A, 2848:98) feature classical friezes—fluted

FIGURE 7.4 William Kent (designer), John Boson (carver), Design for a Pier Table for Houghton Hall, Norfolk, 1731. Bequest of W. Gedney Beatty, 1941/The Metropolitan Museum of Art. Photograph courtesy of the Metropolitan Museum of Art.

(upper) and Vitruvian scroll (lower)—even though the upper table has fully developed rococo cabriole legs and apron. The simplicity of the Vitruvian scroll molding on the lower proposal, together with the volute legs ornamented with acanthus fronds and a line of tapering husks offers close comparison with Kent's own work, such as the window for the barge of the Prince of Wales (Kent and Jones 1744: plate 53). This selection of early eighteenth-century furniture demonstrates a clearly defined and imaginative redeployment of classical forms spearheaded by Kent to create a style appropriate to the early eighteenth century.

ROCOCO: THE ANTITHESIS OF ARCHITECTURE?

The rococo, known as "the modern" (Chippendale 1754: title page), or "contrast" (Simon 2003: 42) in mid-eighteenth-century Britain, was brought over from the Continent by Huguenot craftsmen escaping persecution (Snodin 1984: 27–73). Gathering in London, especially around Old Slaughter's Coffee House (Girouard 1966a: 58–61), and with the formation of the St. Martin's Lane Academy, a school in London organized by William Hogarth (1697–1764) where artists and craftsmen gained an understanding of, and training in, the new style of the rococo (Girouard 1966b: 224–7), British decorative arts embraced and followed a decidedly idiosyncratic reinterpretation of the French style (Snodin 1984; Lindfield 2015a), which included Chinese and Gothic sub-versions of the style peculiar to Britain. Characterized by organic flowing design, C- and S-scrollwork and the appearance of dripping wax, the rococo abandons symmetry and architectonic stability—it has, in fact, been described as anti-architectonic (Osborne and Jordan 2017)—in favor of asymmetric equilibrium (Ward-Jackson 1958: 8–9). The style's antithetical and anti-architectural nature was intolerable to some. Isaac Ware, for example, in his *A Complete Body of Architecture* (1756), laments rococo's popularity in Britain: "we have seen architecture, a science founded upon the soundest principles, disgraced by ignorant caprice; and fashion very lately has attempted, and it were well if we could not say attempts now, to undermine and destroy it by the caprice of *France*" (Ware 1756: 447). He continues:

> it is our misfortune to see at this time, an unmeaning scrawl of (C's) inverted, turned, and hooked together, take place of *Greek* and *Roman* elegance, even in our most expensive decorations. This is not because the possessor thinks there is or can be elegance in such found weak ill-jointed and unmeaning figures: it is because it is *French*; and fashion commands that whatever is *French* is to be admired as fine: the two words (so low are *Britons* sunk) mean the same thing!
>
> (Ware 1756: 447)

These statements contradict Ware's involvement with William Hogarth running the St. Martin's Lane Academy (the primary "school" for the rococo in England), and his later rococo-styled Boudoir, French, and Music rooms at Chesterfield House, London (1748–9), which are the most authentically French interiors of the British rococo (White 1986: 175–6). Ware, however, is keen—after having been paid for his work—to trace his particularly successful rococo rooms to Lord Chesterfield's personal taste and requirement rather than his own preferences: the rococo, he writes,

> is the reigning taste of the present time in *London*, a taste which tends to the *discouragement* of all good and regular architecture, but which the builder will be often under a necessity to comply with, for he must follow the fancy of the proprietor, not his own judgement.
>
> (Ware 1756: 295)

Ware, consequently, was pragmatic and particularly good at the style when he was called upon to work in the mode.

Despite the accomplishment of Ware's work at Chesterfield House, the rococo was not a particularly easy style to master and some craftsmen were not as adept at it; instruction manuals were issued to assist those that were, perhaps, unable to receive direct tuition in the asymmetric style that ran contrary to traditional principles of design. Matthias Lock included detailed instructions for inexperienced craftsmen on how to develop an S-curve into a *raffle* leaf—acanthus-based C- and S-scrolls—in a range of his pattern books (Lock 1740, 1770). Despite following published designs, some craftsmen were unable the execute the patterns with a convincing amount of balance and harmony, such as a suite of *c*. 1750s chairs sold at Croft Castle, Herefordshire, in 2002 (Sotheby's 2002: lot 17, 24–5) that attempt to replicate a relatively straightforward plate from Chippendale's *Director* (Chippendale 1754: plate 21; Lindfield 2016: 117–20). Although rococo's acanthus scrollwork derives from classical traditions, it nevertheless lacked the latter's inherent formalities and set forms, or "pillars" of design. Architecture had no real place in the rococo—hence called anti-architectonic—however some of Britain's most talented rococo designers and craftsmen, including John Linnell (1729–96) (Hayward and Kirkham 1980: 2–3), Thomas Johnson (1714–78) (Johnson 1793: 1, 2, 5, 11), and Thomas Chippendale (Gilbert 1978), willfully and repeatedly wove architecture into their work to create a distinctively British reinterpretation and reapplication of rococo's forms and principles.

The typical vocabulary of architectural elements found in the British rococo can be found in Linnell's designs and include angular cornices (V&A, E.168-1929); stylized and contorted columns (V&A, E.165-1929); steps and balustrades (V&A, E.187-1929); colonnades (V&A, E.220-1929); reeded moldings wrapped with spiraled acanthus leaves (V&A, E.93-1929); and canopies and pediments (V&A, E.148-1929, E.205-1929, E.202-1929, E.221-1929). Like Thomas Johnson (V&A, E.3778-1903) and Matthias Lock (V&A, 2553), Linnell incorporated barn-like structures effortlessly and seamlessly into his asymmetric designs for mirrors (V&A, E.165-1929). These mostly, but not always, subtle and coded architectural details can be found in a surprising number of rococo designs (Ward-Jackson 1958). Although published designs are primarily speculative, the architectural motifs and forms identified in these hypothetical drawings and published plates can also be found in executed furniture from the period, such as Johnson's *c*. 1750–60 pier glass (V&A, W.23-1949) and *c*. 1760–5 girandole (V&A, W.48-1952), as well as an anonymous *c*. 1760 pier glass (Metropolitan Museum of Art, New York, 55.43.1,.2).

The rococo also overlapped with other architectural traditions: the chinoiserie and the Gothic. The first had been a not uncommon sight in seventeenth-century houses (Porter 2010) given the popularity of Chinese-inspired cabinets on stands (V&A, W.9-1936). During the 1750s, Chinese ornament, or that considered to represent Chinese applied design and architecture, was incorporated directly into the rococo's sprawling C- and S-curved compositions. Frets—pierced geometric railings—were especially popular in affording rococo furniture oriental and architectural overtones. Chippendale's design for a Chinese Bed (Figure 7.5) (Metropolitan Museum of Art, New York, 20.40.1(35), blue paper, p. 40) demonstrates this architectural reworking of the rococo given its pagoda-roof, bells, and blind fretwork in its canopy. This architectural scheme is finished with C-scrolls on the lower edge and the headboard is decorated with an exclusively rococo-composition of C- and S-scrollwork so that this overtly Chinese-architectural scheme retains an affiliation with the prevailing taste for organic forms. Chippendale's design for Chinese Chairs (Metropolitan Museum of Art, New York, 20.40.1(23), blue paper, p. 27) illustrates how the pierced fretwork affords otherwise rococo-style parlor chairs—articulated by the stretchers and backs' crestings—a visually contradictory style. For more overtly architectural furniture in rectilinear, volumetric terms, such as cabinets and china cases, these forms— pagodas, bells, geometric fretwork-like glazing bars—are applied as surface ornament to create a chinoiserie effect, and as with his design for a Chinese bed, sprinkled with rococo ornament to afford it a modern 1750s identity, such as the dramatic China Case (Metropolitan Museum of Art, New York, 20.40.2(88); blue paper, p. 202).

Gothic forms were also popular at this point in the eighteenth century, and motifs derived from medieval architecture were incorporated willfully and repeatedly into fashionable rococo furniture designs. One-third of the plates

FIGURE 7.5 Thomas Chippendale (designer), Chinese Bed, 1753. Rogers Fund, 1920/ The Metropolitan Museum of Art. Photograph courtesy of the Metropolitan Museum of Art.

FIGURE 7.6 Thomas Chippendale (designer), Pier Glass for Coplestone Warre
Bampfylde at Hestercombe, Somerset, *c*. 1765. Rogers Fund, 1920/The Metropolitan
Museum of Art. Photograph courtesy of the Metropolitan Museum of Art.

in each edition of Chippendale's *Director* are either explicitly Gothic—and identified as such—or include Gothic forms (Lindfield 2016: 110, 228–9, 230–1). More so than with Chinese forms, however, these Gothic shapes appear as architecture proper and include arcading, pinnacles, finials, lancet windows, and piercing. The rococo-Gothic nevertheless ignored the formalities of Gothic architecture, including the relationship between pinnacles, finials, crockets, gabled ends, and fenestration, and were used instead as a decorative gloss right through to a robustly architectural armature upon which rococo scrollwork sits and from which it springs. This is illustrated by one of Chippendale's designs for pier glass frames, where a clustered column and two registers of trefoil pedants delineate the glass's border, and around which rococo scrolls writhe (Metropolitan Museum of Art, New York, 20.40.1(63), blue paper, p. 78). Gothic's armature could be, and was, converted entirely into rococo scrollwork to form astragals, fenestration, and cresting in Chippendale's design for a desk and bookcase (Metropolitan Museum of Art, New York, 20.40.2(32); blue paper, p. 143), or his unpublished though executed *c.* 1765 pier glass design for Coplestone Warre Bampfylde's house, Hestercombe, Somerset (Figure 7.6) (Metropolitan Museum of Art, New York, 20.40.1(68), blue paper, p. 83; see Lindfield 2015b: 452–6; Legate 2016: 904). This Gothic rewriting of the rococo was facilitated by the two styles' complementary shapes: the ogee arch and S-scroll are prime examples of this.

Chippendale was not alone in Gothicizing the rococo; the styles were combined by other cabinetmakers and designers working at the time. An underlying Gothic structure is evident in the left-hand design of Ince and Mayhew's *Lady's Secretary's* (Ince and Mayhew 1762: plate 18), and Lock's design for a girandole is equally modeled upon medieval-derived shapes (V&A, 2848:88). Despite his proficiency with rococo forms and asymmetry, John Linnell's two traced attempts at combining rococo and Gothic forms are particularly unsuccessful: the rococo and Gothic forms do not sit well with each other and appear disjointed in comparison with the especially coherent designs proposed by Chippendale, Lock, and Ince and Mayhew discussed here. Even though the rococo jettisoned architectural forms, precision, and proportion in favor of organic shapes and equilibrium, something Ware articulated in his *Complete Body of Architecture* (1756), mid-eighteenth-century British craftsmen and designers wove architectural features repeatedly into their work.

CHINESE AND GOTHIC FURNITURE PROPER

Whilst Chinese and Gothic forms were introduced into mid-eighteenth-century rococo furniture without compromising the host style's organic qualities, these two modes were also expressed on their own in more explicitly architectural terms. Linnell's 1754 Chinese-styled bed, suite of armchairs and dressing table designed and made for the 4th Duke and Duchess of Beaufort's Chinese Bedroom at Badminton House, South Gloucestershire, exemplifies this (V&A, W.143:1 to 26-1921, W.33-1990, W.34-1990, W.55:1 to 24-1952). The bed's headboard, made from three panels of Chinoiserie fretwork, and the grand pagoda tester finished with contorted dragons at the orthogonals are equally as architectural as the *en suite* armchairs whose arms and backs enclose an almost identical repertoire of fretwork (Hayward 1969). Fretwork also punctuates the front of the dressing table, with the center bay's japanned decoration reinforcing the architectural and narrative aspects of the style that are equally evident in Chippendale's 1771 suite for the Chinese Bedroom at Nostell Priory, Yorkshire. Chippendale's Chinese furniture for Nostell Priory includes a pier glass replete with fretwork, Ho-Ho birds, and a pagoda canopy (Nostell Priory, NT 959753), a suite of japanned chairs with fretwork beneath the arms (Nostell Priory, NT 9597490), and a japanned clothes press (Nostell Priory, NT 959752). He also produced the 1775–8 japanned clothes press (V&A, W.22:1 to 8-1917) and corner cupboard (V&A, W.24:1, 2-1917) for David Garrick's villa on the Thames (Gilbert 1978). Fashionable interpretations of Chinese design such as the Nostell pier glass (Nostell Priory, NT 959753) also benefited from an increasing understanding of Chinese design as collated and presented in Sir William Chambers' treatise, *Designs of Chinese Buildings, Furniture, Dresses, Machines and Utensils* (1757).

Although overtly architectural Gothic design also proliferated in the 1750s, the style is especially manifest in furniture designed by William Kent from the 1730s. For his 1731–6 refurbishment of York Minster, Kent proposed furniture, including the pulpit and stalls (York Minster Library, York, YM/F1140/2, YM/F239) (Friedman 1995: 81–4). These designs are dominated by a bold use of blind windows with ogee heads, ogee-pendent friezes and faceted responds. Although the interior plasterwork and furniture of Shobdon Church, Herefordshire, respond directly to Kent's Gothic furniture, there is no evidence to suggest that he supplied designs for it prior to his death in 1748. Dicky Bateman (*c.* 1705–74), friend of Horace Walpole, superintended its reconstruction between 1752 and 1756 (Colvin 2009; Lindfield 2016: 70–5). Shobdon's pulpit and celebrant thrones in particular reflect Kent's Gothic style: the pulpit imitates his York Minster design and the thrones incorporate some of the most distinctive facets of Kent's architectural and furniture designs: vase-like legs, robust scrolled arms, and organic finials. These details were available to readers of Vardy's 1744 collation of Kent's and Jones's designs: models for the thrones' legs and arms are found on plate 43, the finials are delineated on plates 48 and 49, and the York Minster pulpit is found on plate 51. It is possible, consequently, that Shobdon's Kentian furniture could have been derived exclusively from consulting Vardy's pattern-book. As I have shown recently, the Countess of Pomfret's *c.* 1752–3 polychrome Gothic cabinet (Plate 37), made perhaps by William Hallett Sr. for Easton Neston, Northamptonshire, was effectively cobbled together from various motifs incorporated into Kent's York Minster pulpit. These Gothic forms were, nevertheless, recomposed and applied to an overtly architectural framework that resembles closely the Countess's subsequently designed and realized Gothic town house on Arlington Street, London, where a central-gabled façade is flanked by octagonal piers crested by onion domes (Harris 1991; Freeman 2012; Hawkes 2013; Lindfield 2014a).

Overtly architectural Gothic furniture was designed and made for Walpole's medievalist "castle" of his "ancestors," Strawberry Hill, Twickenham, in the 1750s and 1760s. Designed by Walpole and his group of mainly amateur and gentlemen architects, this furniture represents a distinctly original presentation of the Gothic aesthetic. For the parlor Walpole and Richard Bentley designed a suite of eight ebonized chairs (Walpole 1973: 181–2)—black was chosen specifically because it represents the color of aged furniture, and especially because it imitated the color of the turned ebony furniture that he adored and termed the "true black blood" (Walpole 1941: 77; Wainwright 1985). The chairs are notable for their backs that are modeled upon an ecclesiastical window, however the tracery's exact form is stylized and the presence of reticulations beneath the double-ogee head's shoulders does not follow medieval precedent. Arranged around the parlor's perimeter, these chairs effectively punctuate the room's walls akin to tracery windows in church walls. A pair of pier glasses designed by Walpole himself for the parlor are also modeled upon ecclesiastical windows. This was a logical decision as they complement the chairs, but at the same time they are original as medieval looking glasses of this size simply did not exist.

Equally architectural was the parlor's table designed by Bentley and mounted with Sicilian jasper (Walpole 1784: 4). Like the chairs and pier glasses, this table is ebonized, and this self-consciously historicist finish matches the table's Gothic decoration that it confined primarily to the table's frieze that is composed of repeating septafoil-cusped ogee arches finished with trefoil stops, and above and behind which runs a band of repeating trefoil-headed lancets within panels. The table's legs are spiral-turned and are thus akin to the "true black blood" that Walpole first wrote about after having seen a suite at Esher Place, Surrey, a Gothic Revival house designed c. 1733 by William Kent for Henry Pelham (1694–1754) (Harris 1989; Lindfield 2014b: 147–9). In August 1752 Walpole wrote that

> The true original chairs were all sold [...] there are nothing now but Halsey-chairs, not adapted to the squareness of a Gothic dowager's rump. And by the way I do not see how the uneasiness and uncomfortableness of a coronation-chair can be any objection with you: every chair that is easy is modern, and

unknown to our ancestors. As I remember, there were certain low chairs, that looked like ebony, at Esher, and were old and pretty.

(Gray 1935: 364)

John Chute (1701–76) of the Vyne, Hampshire, designed Strawberry Hill's Library presses following an explicitly architectural model (Lewis Walpole Library, Farmington, 49 3490 Folio, 5): the pulpitum side door from Old St. Paul's Cathedral, London, which was depicted in Dugdale's *Old St Paul's* (Dugdale 1716: plate opp. p. 146; Walpole 1784: 33). Walpole was concerned with antiquarian and architectural coherence, and consequently rejected two alternate schemes by Bentley for the Library bookcases because they quite simply did not look convincingly medieval, or "proper," and his proposal for the room's chimneypiece that was overtly architectural though only modeled loosely upon the tomb canopy of Edmund Crouchback, Westminster Abbey, London (Lewis Walpole Library, Farmington, 49 3584, 36–8). In December 1753, Walpole addresses directly the unacceptably imaginative aspects of Bentley's proposals, suggesting an evolving understanding of the medieval had infiltrated eighteenth-century Gothic design:

> For the library, it cannot have the Strawberry imprimatur: the double arches and double pinnacles are most ungraceful; and the doors below the book-cases in Mr Chute's design had a conventual look, which yours totally wants. For this time, we shall put your genius in commission, and, like some regents, execute our own plan without minding our sovereign. For the chimney, I do not wonder you missed our instructions: we could not contrive to understand them ourselves; and therefore, determining nothing but to have the old picture stuck in a thicket of pinnacles, we left it to you to find out the how. I believe it will be very difficult; but as I suppose *facere quia impossibile est*, is full as easy as *credere*, why—you must do it.
>
> (Walpole 1973: 157–8)

Many other pieces of architectural furniture were produced for Strawberry Hill, but Walpole's villa is hardly the only repository of such furniture in the eighteenth century. Equally Gothic chairs were designed for Arbury Hall, Warwickshire, *c*. 1760, the newly Gothicized family seat of Sir Roger Newdigate (1719–1806) (Lindfield 2016: 164–5), and also a suite of chairs provided by Newdigate for the newly decorated and refashioned Hall at University College, Oxford, that he superintended in the 1760s (Cox 2012; Lindfield 2016: 165–7). Henry Emlyn (1729–1815) also designed architectural chairs for St. George's Chapel, Windsor Castle, Berkshire, to correspond with his restoration of the Chapel from 1773 (Roberts 1976–7). Emlyn increased the number of choir stalls in the chapel with remarkable accuracy, but of more relevance to this chapter is the suite of chairs he designed and made in 1785 for the Monarch's Closet on the north side of St. George's sanctuary. They are essentially of a standard shield-back pattern included in pattern-books, such as George Hepplewhite's *The Cabinet-Maker and Upholsterer's Guide* (1794: 1–7, 9), however the typical neoclassical forms are substituted with Gothic window tracery and ornamented with fleur-de-lis, Tudor roses and the Garter badge, and crested with a suitably architectural crocketed "ogee flip" (Lindfield 2016: 177–9). Whilst these chairs and those in Strawberry Hill's parlor and University College's hall are clearly and obviously Gothic, they also follow different fashions: neoclassical, antiquarian, and rococo, respectively. The application of medieval architectural forms in eighteenth-century furniture was mediated frequently by other styles, as illustrated by these two examples.

There was a shift toward increasingly architectural representations of medieval form in the third edition of Chippendale's *Director* (1762). Whilst some new plates in the third edition (Chippendale 1762: plate XIV) match the first edition's overtly decorative combination of Gothic and rococo forms (Chippendale 1754: plate 14), increasingly architectural renditions of medieval motifs— not diluted by other nonarchitectural or non-Gothic styles—are apparent. The back, seat rail, and legs on the left-most chair on plate XVII, *Hall Chairs*, are entirely architectural—the back is modeled upon a four-light tracery window—and the sexfoil-cusped back of the middle chair on plate XXV, *Designs of Chairs*, approaches a rose window. This shift is particularly noticeable when the modifications to plate LXXI, *Library Bookcase*, from the first edition of the *Director* is compared with its updated rendition in the third, 1762 edition of the *Director* as plate XCVII. In the first edition, the bookcase's astragals imitate Gothic tracery—trefoil and ogee-headed lancets—along with pinnacles and finials akin to Chippendale's rococo-Gothic pier glass design for Copleston Warre Bampfylde at Hestercombe House mentioned above (Metropolitan Museum of Art, New York, 20.40.1(68), blue paper, p. 83; see Lindfield 2015b: 452–6) but in rococo scrollwork. In the third edition these rococo forms have been replaced by rigid architectural motifs—rococo scrollwork is nowhere to be seen. Especially representative of this shift in fashionable Gothic furniture design in the 1762 edition of Chippendale's *Director* is plate CVI, *A Gothic Organ*, which is notable for its overtly architectural cresting, especially its crocketed onion dome that imitates some of the most impressive monuments of Perpendicular Gothic architecture, such as Henry VII's Chapel, Westminster Abbey, and King's College Chapel, Cambridge (Chippendale 1762: plate CVI). Chippendale was not the only designer promoting overtly architectural Gothic furniture; this style can also be seen in other pattern-books from the period, including Ince and Mayhew's *Universal System of Household Furniture* (1762: plates LXIII, LXXXVI) and the Society of Upholsterers and Cabinet-Makers' *Household Furniture in the Genteel Taste* (1763: plates 52, 72).

NEOCLASSICISM

Fashionable furniture shifted back to classical precepts in 1760s Britain, though this new incarnation of classical design—neoclassicism—was of a significantly different character to early eighteenth-century classicism, or the baroque, as promoted by William Kent. Neoclassical furniture was influenced directly by archaeological discoveries made in Italy and eastern Europe during the eighteenth century, including Herculaneum (from 1738) and Pompeii (1748). Architects and designers traveled to these sites, as well as to other remains of classical and Renaissance architecture, such as Diocletian's Palace, Split, Croatia, which Robert Adam visited and surveyed with Charles-Louis Clérisseau in 1757 and about which he published a survey and reconstruction (Adam 1764). The discoveries at Herculaneum and Pompeii were also disseminated to a wider audience through the plates of *Le antichità di Ercolano esposte* (1755–92), which helped advance a "new" form of classicism.

In 1762 Chippendale issued the third edition of his *Director*. Whilst some plates were reissued in their original or modified states, 106 new designs were introduced; consequently, 53 percent of the plates were new. There were very few explicitly neoclassical proposals in these new designs; perhaps the most notable are plate CXIX, *A Toylet Table* (Figure 7.7), and plate CXLVII, *Terms for Bustos &c.*, but these designs still retain a significant amount of rococo scrollwork. Christopher Gilbert, the late authority on Chippendale, on the other hand suggests that neoclassical forms were introduced progressively in the third edition's plates:

> There are no Neo-Classical elements in the editions of [the *Director* from] 1754 and 1755 and the fashionable furniture he supplied to Dumfries House in 1759 contains no hint of imminent change. Chippendale's introduction of Neo-Classical motifs can be chronicled by noting the imprints on plates in which they appear [in the 1762 edition], the annual totals being—2 (1759); 7 (1760); 7 (1761); and 2 (1762). Accordingly, Chippendale's furniture designs reveal Neo-Classical precepts at least three years before Robert Adam's first essay in the style.
>
> (Gilbert 1978: 119)

Irrespective of the exact number of neoclassical plates in the *Director*, Chippendale appears to have been slow to embrace neoclassicism in print, yet his firm supplied a significant amount of neoclassical furniture to country houses, including Nostell Priory (1766–85), and Harewood House, Yorkshire (1767–78) (Gilbert 1978). Chippendale's clothes press for Nostell, supplied in 1769, is ornamented with tapering lines of husks on the press's front corners, and volute scrolls decorated with acanthus leaves (Nostell Priory, NT 959763). The suite of eight hall chairs (Nostell Priory, NT

FIGURE 7.7 Thomas Chippendale (designer), A Toylet Table, *c.* 1760. Rogers Fund, 1920/The Metropolitan Museum of Art. Photograph courtesy of the Metropolitan Museum of Art.

959702) supplied by Chippendale to Nostell in 1775 demonstrates a more comprehensive form of neoclassical decoration with *paterae*, bands of fluted decoration, rib-and-sail ovals, and filament-like strings of connected husks encircling and delineating the larger ornament. Less overtly architectural in underlying form, though decorated with motifs used throughout Adam's neoclassical schemes, is the suite of chairs and sofas designed by Robert Adam and executed by Chippendale for Sir Lawrence Dundas in 1764–5 (V&A, W.1-1937). The chair and sofa frames are carved with the scrolled filaments, husks, and griffins very much like those Adam studied in Rome, and as especially represented by a tripod stand that Adam drew whilst on the Continent *c*. 1755 (Sir John Soane Museum London, Adam Volume 57/44). Adam's furniture, in comparison with this seat furniture, tends to be more robust in form, but equally as ornate in surface ornament, as is illustrated by his dining room sideboard arrangement for Kedleston Hall, Derbyshire, designed in 1762 (Kedleston Hall, Derbyshire, NT 109264, NT 109450), with its squared-off legs and apron frieze composed of repeating swags. The Kimbolton Cabinet, made 1771–6 by Ince and Mayhew following Adam's design as part of his work on the Manchester's house, Kimbolton Castle, Cambridgeshire, is intended entirely for the display of Florentine *pietra dura* panels made by Baccio Cappelli in 1709 (V&A, W.43-1949). With Ionic-tapered legs, *ormolu* Corinthian pilasters, and repeating marquetry borders of sinuous and interconnected classical leaf-work and swagged husks, the mounts and surface effects broadly reveal the opulence of Adam's neoclassical furniture. Whilst the Kimbolton Cabinet is subtle with its delicate ornamental and architectural surface decoration, Adam's 1777 State Bed for Osterley Park, London (Osterley Park, NT 771784), and the associated half-lunette commodes (Osterley Park, NT 771768–9), celebrate neoclassical ornament in lustrous terms with the marked contrast between ormolu mounts and the marquetry base.

Mainstream cabinetmakers were also recommended designs that simulate Adam's opulent work but at a more modest cost in pattern-books, such as George Hepplewhite's *The Cabinet-Maker and Upholsterer's Guide*. Whilst pared back, most of the chair designs incorporate neoclassical vases and swagged filaments (Hepplewhite 1794: plates 4–8), while sideboard tables and their associated pedestals are strewn with arabesque-neoclassical scrollwork, bands of fluting, alternating *paterae* and panels, tapered pilasters, and draped filaments (plates 31–6), which can also be found on tabletops (plates 61–6), beds (plates 98–101), and girandoles and pier glasses (plates 113–18). The close relationship between the designs in Hepplewhite's *Guide*, the work of Gillows and James Wyatt's architectural practice and furniture has been addressed recently and reveals a consistent application of architectural forms in late eighteenth-century English fashionable furniture (Robinson 2012: 126).

Adam also worked in a distinct form of neoclassical design, particularly at Osterley Park in 1774 for the Etruscan Room. As I indicated in this chapter's introduction, Adam designed the room's decorative aspects, ranging from the ornament painted on its walls, ceiling, and even furniture. The Etruscan room, consequently, is an *en suite* scheme. The source for the room, Raphael's *logetta* at the Vatican, connects classical ornament—vases, sphinx, and anthemion—with filament-like husks in a restrained, bichromatic color scheme. This ornamental scheme is applied also to the chairs that Adam designed for the room; the filament-husks run around the legs and rails, and the splat is painted with a stylized reinterpretation of the wall's decoration (Osterley Park, NT 771792). The chair's overall form, however, does not directly and overtly acknowledge the most ambitious and decorative facets of neoclassical design, which were carved with intricate surface decoration, as with Adam's commodes discussed above.

CODA

Architects, furniture-designers, furniture makers, and gentlemen connoisseurs were, throughout the eighteenth century, proposing and creating fixed and moveable furniture based upon, and suitable for, architectural and architecturally ornamented interiors. The numerous styles available to these designers and makers does not disguise the repeated and often highly imaginative application of architectural elements, motifs, and structures into furniture throughout the course of the century. Their incorporation into furniture varied depending upon whether the designer was a trained architect, furniture designer, or a designer in more general terms. Architecture remained essential to nineteenth-century furniture design as well, particularly with the Greek Revival led by Thomas Hope, the Egyptian Revival, the Romanesque Revival as exhibited at Penrhyn Castle, Gwynedd, and the Gothic Revival. Despite the widespread and direct influence of architecture upon furniture design in the eighteenth century, A.W.N. Pugin (1812–52), codesigner of the New Palace of Westminster with Charles Barry (1795–1860) following the Great Fire of 1834 (Atterbury 1995; Hill 2007; Shenton 2016), criticized directly the way in which aspects of medieval architecture were copied and incorporated directly into furniture:

> In pointed decoration *too much* is generally attempted; every room in what is called a Gothic house must be fitted with niches, pinnacles, groining, tracery, and tabernacle work, after the manner of a chantry chapel [...]. These observations apply equally to furniture;—upholsterers seem to think that nothing can be Gothic unless it is found in some church. Hence your modern man designs a sofa or occasional table from details culled out of Britton's Cathedrals, and all the ordinary articles of furniture, which require to be simple and convenient, are made not only very expensive but very

uneasy. We find diminutive flying buttresses about an armchair; every thing
is crocketed with angular projections, innumerable mitres, sharp ornaments,
and turreted extremities. A man who remains any length of time in a modern
Gothic room, and escapes without being wounded by some of its minutiæ,
may consider himself extremely fortunate. There are often as many pinnacles
and gablets about a pierglass frame as are to be found in an ordinary church,
and not unfrequently the whole canopy of a tomb has been transformed for
the purpose, as at Strawberry Hill.

(Pugin 1841: 40)

There was no fixed way to create furniture inspired by architecture in eighteenth-
century Britain, and as Pugin's comment quoted here shows, the ways in which
this architectural context was harnessed not only evolved but could vary from
designer to designer and craftsman to craftsman. It is apparent, however, that
architectural forms, motifs, and ornaments were crucial to eighteenth-century
England's fashionable furniture.

CHAPTER EIGHT

Visual Representations

MICHAËL DECROSSAS AND SYLVAIN CORDIER

ORNAMENT PRINTS AS MODELS AND DISSEMINATORS OF TASTE

Fashion is the tyrant of good taste.

—Blondel ([1771] 2002: 463)

Ornament prints, the first type of visual representation considered here, were fundamental to the creation, development, and dissemination of the decorative arts throughout the whole of the eighteenth century. This type of engraving, though, is not easy to define and has long been unfairly viewed as of secondary importance. This opinion has largely resulted from the historiography and the legacy of scholars such as Fiske Kimball who were certainly pioneers, but who, according to Marianne Roland Michel, "played a modest part in the study of ornament, when considered on its own" (Michel 1982; Kimball 1949).

Ornament prints as a fashionable pastime

The intensive publication of ornament prints, which is characteristic of the entire eighteenth century, is a response to the context, evident from the end of the seventeenth century but with profound modifications, in which lifestyle, interior arrangements, and a newly discovered concern for comfort brought about a taste for decoration or for the "gracious *badinage* amongst ornaments from within," as the architect Pierre Alexis Delamaire (1737) wrote (Scott 1995; Scott and Cherry 2005; Michel 2015). Ornament became a fashionable pastime, nurtured by various specialist publications with large circulations such as *L'Homme du Monde éclairé par les Arts* (Blondel 1774: 63–81); or periodicals such as the *Gazette de Littérature, des Sciences et des Arts*; the *Gazette*; the *Avant-courreur*; the *Journal des sçavans*, among others. Above all, though, this fashion was championed by the gazette and literary magazine *Nouveau Mercure* (1717–21), later the *Mercure de France* (1724–61), which published, for example, several letters *Sur l'Amour & la connoissance des Beaux Arts*, in which the author noted: "Nothing escapes the notice of the intelligent man. Mirrors, chandeliers, candle stands, their forms, their qualities, as well as different table tops of precious marbles, cabinets, lacquer chests and other enticements from Japan, Bronzes and marble figurines, expensive Porcelains, clocks and other works in marquetry: Carpets, beds, furniture of taste."[1]

The *Mercure* itself was particularly keen, as it often noted, "to grasp everything which could give birth to the love of and taste for Fine Arts."[2] It described, for example, the works of artisans, such as, in 1734, a silver dining service by Ballin;[3] the decoration of a house in the rue d'Anjou, Fauxbourg Saint-Honoré in Paris built to the designs of Pierre Contant d'Ivry (1698–1777) with paintings by Le Maire and sculptures by Martin;[4] and a large *cabinet* with *boiserie* (woodwork decoration), destined to be placed in a magnificent castle near the city of Warsaw belonging to Count Bialinski. This last was "conceived, designed and brought to fruition by the efforts and under the supervision of M. Meisonnier, whose talents are so well known and have earned him the position of *Dessinateur ordinaire du Cabinet du Roy*."[5] The *cabinet* had been executed in Paris before being despatched, and its elements were subsequently engraved and published in the *Oeuvre* of the artist (Meissonnier, *c.* 1735). But as these reviews were not illustrated, the descriptions of the décor and advice remained too obscure, no doubt, to be of much practical use to the reader.

The Taste for engravings

Publishers of and dealers in prints, as well as authors, however, were quick to understand the advantages they could draw from this interest in interior decoration. The engravings, whether individual or, more often, placed in compilations, became the means for the uniform spreading of taste, changes in fashion, and specific inventions. The images themselves can be divided into "motifs," including scrolls, acanthus leaves, rosettes, etc., and "forms," such as joinery, goldsmith work, clocks, chandeliers, locks, and embroideries.

Some *marchands-merciers*, dealers in the decorative arts, whose role in the evolution of taste is now well known, were important agents in the spread (or sometimes, indeed, the vulgarization) of taste, by catering for the best artists and craftsmen whose ideas they engraved or had engraved by others. This is the case with the Chereau, Mariette, and Langlois dynasties, or personalities such as Pierre Aveline (1656–1772), or even Gabriel Huquier (1695–1772). The latter, a dealer, collector, publisher, and engraver as well as a designer, painter, and member of the *Académie de Saint-Luc* in Paris, published not only most of the great rococo artists such as Watteau, Gillot, Boucher, Charpentier, Lajoue, Oudry, Meissonnier, and Contant d'Ivry but also numerous craftsmen such as Bellay (active in Paris 1734–47) and Dominique Pineau (1718–86).

All these publications were aimed at two categories of buyers: one comprising art dealers, artists, and craftsmen; the other those who commissioned the art. The first category had reason to follow fashion and also found in it an easy source of inspiration. They could elaborate on fashion and return their own drawings to those who had published the engravings that had originally inspired them (Decrossas 2018). Being at the same time didactic and practical, the engravings offered a huge repertoire of ideas to choose from, allowing artists and designers to play at reapplication, adaptation, transposition, associations and combinations, and contributing to the success of the productions of this period (Jackson 2017). The *menuisier*'s domain was one of the most fertile for prints. In these, authors took care to give all necessary indications to make the work easier. For example, in his compilation *Plans et elevations d'armoires et buffets* (c. 1740–55), F. Cornille supplied on every plate all the necessary details for reproduction including scale, frontal views, details about paneling, and ornaments to copy. In *The Gentleman and Cabinet-maker's Director* (1754), Thomas Chippendale, on plate IX *Chairs in perspective*, also gives details on how to reproduce these, placing the chair-back into a perspectival grid and providing additional plates that suggest variants for legs and seats as well as chair-backs.[6]

For the art dealers, the purchase of plates represented a far from inconsiderable investment. The price of the *Livre d'Ornements* (1751) by the goldsmith Pierre Germain, for instance, was offered at two livres for eleven plates. Another example is the *Livre d'Echantillons* preserved in the Jacques Doucet Collection in the library of the Institut national d'histoire de l'art, Paris. This includes a list of the different series and prints it contains, including one on bookbinding, at their respective prices,[7] and shows that the cost of making the volume came to fifty-two livres and thirteen sols.[8]

But far from catering solely for art dealers who could propose fashionable models to their clients, the ornament prints that came from the best masters were aimed at those who commissioned the art themselves and were anxious to remain up to date with the latest evolutions in taste. It was necessary to respond to the insistence on novelty from this demanding but heterogeneous

FIGURE 8.1 Work by Juste-Aurèle Meissonnier (French, Turin, 1695–1750, Paris). Rogers Fund, 1918/The Metropolitan Museum of Art. Photograph courtesy of the Metropolitan Museum of Art.

clientele, and also to stimulate and direct their choice, not to mention taste, with the illustrations and descriptions given in journals and gazettes, whilst also proposing various ensembles. The idea was to offer models to the potential client in the form of both elevations and cross-sections, such as for paneling or furniture placed in arrangements, as suggested by *Divers dessins de menuiserie pour la decoration des apartments presentement à la mode* (*c.* 1750). For those who commissioned the interiors, these prints illustrated the ideals in fashionable décor, all the more powerful if the engravings were connected with a celebrated artist, for instance Oppenord, Boffrand, Meissonnier (Figure 8.1), or Contant d'Ivry, Dumont, Delafosse, Neufforge, etc. For a detail or to search for the latest piece of fashionable furniture, ornament, or current taste, one could consult the same engravings as a dealer. Thomas Chippendale (1718–79), for example took care to specify in the preface to the 1754 first edition of his *Gentleman and Cabinet-Maker's Director* that "The Title-Page has already called the following work, *The Gentleman and Cabinet-maker's Director,* as calculated to assist the one in the choice, and the other in the execution of the design; which are so contrived, that if no one drawing should singly answer the Gentleman's taste, there will yet be found a variety of hints sufficient to construct a new one" (1754: 3). In the third edition that came out in French eight years later, the information was apparent from the title onward: *Le guide du tapissier, de l'ébéniste, et de tous ceux qui travaillent en meubles: comme aussi celui des honnêtes gens qui en font faire* (the guide for the upholsterer, *ébéniste,* and all those who work in furniture and likewise for the honorable people that have it made) (Chippendale 1762).

Nevertheless, certain series seem to have been made specifically for the needs of the *Homme du monde* (Man of the World). These engravings were based on genuine typologies and models in joinery and cabinetmaking, stretching from chairs to commodes and including not only tables, bureaux, *secrétaires* (writing desks), corner-cupboards, *chiffoniers,* etc., but also bronze mounts for furniture, clocks, andirons, sconces, candlestands, chandeliers, and incense burners. The thirty-one design booklets after Juste-Nathan François Boucher (1736–82), published in about 1780 by Le Père and Avaulez, listed, in series of six plates, different variations of the same furniture.[9] For example, the *secrétaire,* an invention of this period, might be *à pente* (sloping), *à tombeau* (tomblike or resembling sarcophagi), *à cylinder* (roll-top), *à panse* (bellylike), or *en armoire* (wardrobe). It appeared in different guises in booklets nine, ten, and eighteen. For the commode, that emblematic piece of furniture, the author also offered two suites (booklets seven and eight) in models *à la dauphine, à l'italienne, à la provençale, à la polonaise, à l'imperiale, à l'antique, à la reine, à la françoise* (Figure 8.2), *à la romaine, à la chancelière,* and two models *à l'anglois.* Endowed with these precious pieces of information, the "consumer" could choose a model

FIGURE 8.2 *Commode à la Françoise*, no. 44. Photograph courtesy of Art World/ Alamy Stock Photo.

and any variations before approaching a dealer, intermediary, or producer, so as to have it made according to his preferences.

The dissemination of prints

It is difficult to trace the channels, networks, and intermediaries through which these prints were disseminated. Clearly, contemporary journalists understood the importance of advertising because *Le Mercure*, in 1726, published in its Foreword: "We invite merchants and engravers to inform us about new prints so as to advertise them in an advantageous manner."[10] But if advertisements for ornament prints found their place among engravings of *interpretations*, one ends up establishing the fact that they were above all engravings of "motifs." These advertisements gave pride of place to prints by Watteau,[11] and to a lesser extent Boucher, Lajoue, or Mondon. The appearance of the latter's *trophies*, *rocailles*, and *plaques*, *Le Mercure* noted in April 1736, result in "the complete enrichment of naturally grouped figures, varied and contrasted with taste [...] engraved by Le Sieur Aveline [and], dedicated to le Prince de Carignan, who honours the author with his protection; a most weighty approval which must convey a highly favourable idea of the talents, merit and the works of sieur Mondon."[12]

Prints dealing with décor only attracted attention in the gazettes and magazines, however, when they appeared in books of architecture, such as the 1745 treatise *Livre d'architecture* by Germain Boffrand, published by the bookseller Guillaume Cavelier, which included "a chapter on interior decorations, apartments and furnishing schemes."[13] It is again the case with Jean-François de Neufforge's 1756 *Recueil élémentaire d'architecture*, which *Le Mercure* states "contained different designs for the interior decoration of buildings."[14] Prints of *objets d'art*, starting with those of new furniture, do not really appear in *Le Mercure*. Nevertheless, in April 1756 an advertisement appeared in *Le Mercure* for "a Book of table feet invented and engraved by Pineau," published by Huquier;[15] and, in the *Gazette de France* of March 6, 1789, the first booklet of new beds at "Chereau, rue S. Jacques" was announced.[16] These advertisements were above all a means for publishers of and dealers in prints to make themselves known. A description of his business made by Gabriel Huquier (1695–1772), for example, in *Le Mercure* of April 1737, and repeated in numerous issues, states:

> It will easily be seen from the quantity of new prints which fill this article that the presses of copper-plate engravings are no less busy in Paris than in this bookshop; we can even add that the Sciences find less profit in these than the arts do in others; amongst the Merchants and engravers in burin and acid, no new prints of any kind appear as frequently as those of Mr Huquier; he engraves them himself with intelligence and does a great trade in them.[17]

Finally, publishers had to rely on their own networks, the importance of which continued to grow during the eighteenth century, to disseminate their prints.[18] These networks included, in the first place, merchants. On a number of points these associations require further research and analysis with regard to ornament prints. Nonetheless, *l'Architecture Françoise* (1727), published by Jean and Pierre-Jean Mariette, and *l'Architecture à la Mode* (*c.* 1738), a publication begun by Nicolas II Langlois and continued by Jean and Pierre-Jean Mariette, are fairly emblematic. Sometimes these books spread forms and tastes in architecture as much as in ornament, and they reached a wide public far beyond the Kingdom of France, as two volumes of *l'Architecture à la Mode* show, having been bound in leather in the eighteenth century bearing the ex libris of the Portuguese family of the Conde de Óbidos.[19] We do not know what channels this work traveled through, but there is an enormous potential field of research on a global scale aimed at identifying the networks these merchants belonged to and the way in which they obtained the engraved plates. Examining the inventories of the contents of shops, something that still remains to be done with regard to ornament prints, is one way forward.

The second network is that of the publishers themselves who, in reissuing copies of prints, played a considerable role in spreading taste. Here, too, research still largely remains to be done. The Englishman Richard Brookshaw (*c.* 1736–after 1800), as an example, published ornamental vases after those by Juste-Nathan

François Boucher originally published in Paris by Geneviève-Marguerite Chéreau (1755–82) (*A New Book of Vases Designed by Boucher* 1771; *Nouveau Livre de Vases par F. Bo...*, c. 1755–68). The most important center for the reissuing of prints, though, was Augsburg in Germany, which played an important part in spreading ornament prints throughout central and eastern Europe. Several figures distinguished themselves here, notably Johann Georg Merz (1694–1762), Martin Engelbrecht (1684–1756), Johann Georg Hertel (1719–68), Johann Jakob Haid (1704–67), and Johann Martin Will (1727–1806). The latter published furniture prints after Juste-Nathan François Boucher, sometimes combining several engravings from the original edition onto the same plate (Victoria and Albert Museum, London, accession no. 24888:4) (Figure 8.3).

The work involved both in copying and circulating prints had a direct impact on these centers' own production. Prints illustrating examples of the rococo style (*rocaille*) are particularly revealing of this. Models by Meissonnier, Pineau, and others influenced numerous designers who exaggerated their characteristics and proposed their own versions, which contributed to the success of these forms in

FIGURE 8.3 Juste-Nathan Boucher (after), *Theil* (Chairs), an etching depicting two designs for chairs decorated with acanthus leaves and beading and upholstered with vertically striped fabric. From a series of German copies after French designs, here Boucher's designs for furniture and interior and exterior decoration. German copies published by Johann Martin Will. Victoria and Albert Museum, London, accession no. 24888:4. Photograph courtesy of the Victoria and Albert Museum, London.

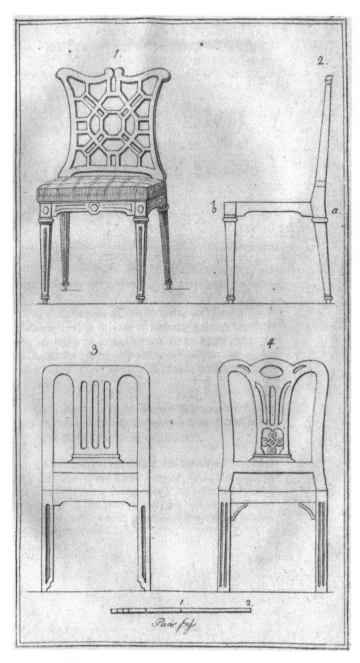

FIGURE 8.4 *Journal des Luxus und der Moden*, "Ameublement. Moderne Stühle"
March 1787. Photograph courtesy of the German Research Foundation/Duchess Anna
Amalia Library Weimar.

central Europe. The example of the commodes designed and engraved by Franz Xavier Habermann (1721–96) and published in Augsburg by Johann Georg Hertel is particularly telling and seems to illustrate perfectly the criticism of Blondel at the beginning of this chapter, showing how the fashion for rococo ornament has resulted in a very impractical set of designs (Blondel [1771] 2002: 463).

During the last decades of the century, a new way of disseminating ornament prints appeared, namely, fashion magazines. Their launch was sometimes fairly chaotic, perhaps because of their ambition to cover current taste in everything from clothing to interior decoration, paneling, and furniture by *menuisiers* and *ébénistes*. Their innovation was the inclusion of additional and more complex copper engravings to illustrate the descriptions in the texts. The first of these appeared in bimonthly issues in Paris from 1785 onward by way of subscription under the title of *Cabinet des modes*,[20] published by François Dubuisson. The prospectus stated that it would "aim itself at the principal bookshops of France and Europe" and that it would offer to "Artists, Manufacturers and Merchants of all kinds a more prompt and more considerable sale, in revealing objects and making them known; to the Lovers of Art it would offer the enjoyment they were searching for." It was rapidly copied and imitated in France and Europe (Van Dijk). The following year in Weimar, Germany, Friedrich Melchior Kraus began publishing the monthly *Journal des Luxus und der Moden* (1787–1812), on the same principle. In March 1787, he published a plate, accompanied by a notice in the rubric "Ameublement", with a description and explanation of three English modern chairs (Figure 8.4). "Da man in einem geschmackvoll meublierten bürgerlichen hauße bey weitem nicht so mancherley formen von Stühle nothig hat, als in einem palais oder Schloße, so liefern wir hier, auf Taf. 9. drey der einfachsten und schönste" (In a tastefully furnished middle-class house one needs far fewer types of chairs than one does in a Palace or Castle, and so we provide here, in Plate 9, three of the most simple and beautiful examples). All these models, although simplified, were drawn from those of Chippendale, who was always fashionable.

Print collectors

The interest in ornament plates, which met the demands of buyers fascinated with fashion, had another effect. These plates became, like the engravings of paintings by the great masters, an element of curiosity that one wanted to have in one's *cabinet*, or portfolios, or bound in books (Decrossas and Grivel 2014: 262–76).

If at the beginning of the century the collector Antoine-Joseph Dézalier d'Argenville (1680–1765), in his *Lettre sur le choix & l'arrangement d'un Cabinet de curieux*, mentioned in his section on prints that he make separate volumes for illustrations of architectural elements, ornaments, theater decorations, animals, hunting and maritime themes, geography, topography, the costume of different nations, *pièces noires* (a kind of print not engraved in the usual way and with a smoky appearance), and modern minor masters, he still principally concerned himself with old masters of the sixteenth and seventeenth centuries (Dézalier d'Argenville 1727). But the attention of amateurs and collectors of the eighteenth century seems to have rapidly turned toward contemporary masters, probably spurred on by editors who proposed rare subjects to them. One sees it in the editorial work done on the posthumous publication of the *Oeuvres* of Oppenord in the 1750s (Oppenord, *c.* 1749–61). Oppenord's style was no longer fashionable but either at the request of the publisher Huquier, if not actually by Huquier himself, Lajoue's landscapes were incorporated into Oppenord's interior designs (Michel 1984: 158–61). Such additions could be of no use to the art dealer, artist, or craftsman, or to someone looking for models to be created. But this approach, in aiming to make the work more valuable, could win over the collectors.

FURNITURE WITHIN THE FINE ARTS

Through a selection of examples drawn from Western iconography of the eighteenth century, this section sets out to shed light on the function of furniture within the domain of the fine arts. First, we will turn to the place occupied by furniture in the iconographic language of the portrait.

Seated or standing: The state portrait

In producing the full-length portrait in 1701 of King Louis XIV, originally destined for the court of Philip V of Spain, the grandson of the king of France, the artist Hyacinthe Rigaud (1659–1743) put forward a model of royal portraiture that was bound to impose itself on his contemporaries and later generations of artists and monarchs (Figure 8.5). Rigaud's Louis XIV thus serves as an introduction to how the eighteenth century would stand in the complex question of how to represent political reality through symbolism. The staging and posture adopted by the king would be repeated by the adult Louis XV in the latter's 1730 portrait by Rigaud and his 1760 portrait by Louis-Michel van Loo (1707–71). Similarly, Louis XVI was painted by Joseph-Siffrein Duplessis (1725–1802) in 1777 and Antoine-François Callet (1741–1823) in 1779 in this way (Plate 38).

Rigaud's portrait of Louis XIV skillfully throws into relief the question of the function of seating as an element in the representation of the sovereign. The king, standing upright, is placed at the top of some steps to a throne (throne here meaning the entire architectural structure including the armchair), crowned with a large canopy. His posture is dynamic because he appears to be advancing slowly but surely toward what seems to be the hand of justice in ivory, placed on a stool with a cushion on his right, an effective allusion to the

FIGURE 8.5 Portrait by Hyacinthe Rigaud of Louis XIV of France, 1701. Oil on canvas, 103 × 76 5/16 inches. Photograph courtesy of Musée du Louvre/Wikimedia Commons.

good progress of the reign of a sacred monarch. The giltwood armchair is placed behind the body of the sovereign and at first glance constitutes the focal point of the throne, creating the impression of being a place of power that only belongs to the king. Yet it is treated with striking discretion. As an obvious symbol and at the same time a shadowy object, it only seems to act as a companion. One would, in fact, be tempted to understand its presence as a negation of the theatrical display here that constitutes the dynamic posture of the royal person advancing along the paths set by God. The armchair in the background is, in fact, placed there to emphasize that the sovereign deliberately does not take his place there. On the contrary, this particularly lavish seat, in carved and gilded wood, expresses the idea that the royal image defines itself not as a static figure but instead as something dynamic progressing toward the fulfilment of the association between the political and the sacred. The standing position should then be seen to represent a certain concept of monarchic authority through visibly disconnecting the king's person from his chair.

The perpetuation of this pose by Louis XIV's successors sheds light on the use of official space in France under the *ancien régime*: the throne at Versailles only enjoyed a relative prestige, and did not express the sacredness of the monarchy in the same way as the king's bed. Admittedly the throne is a formal object, utilized during diplomatic receptions laid on for ambassadors, these taking place within the context of the royal bedchamber or, on some occasions, in the Hall of Mirrors. The setting of the armchair part of the throne, though, changed within official daily life, eventually integrating the space of the State Apartments of Versailles as part of a long evolution throughout the eighteenth century, which favored the seating designed by the Slodtz brothers for Louis XV.[21]

This gradual process of integration into the State Apartments went hand in hand with an equally slow evolution that one could term the "heritage factor" of the seating component of the throne. Although it served as a splendid piece of stage setting under Louis XV and Louis XVI, the throne was not a sacred object in its own right. It did not "make" a king, and it did not possess the ability to confer the nobility of royal functions. Louis XIV appears to have maintained a distance from the throne, as witnessed by Rigaud's portrait. It is therefore interesting to note that if Rigaud's composition for royal portraiture continued to be used by Louis XV and Louis XVI, it was to place the sovereigns systematically in stage settings different from that of the throne, and more exactly in places that were not real. What the royal portrait in France of the eighteenth century teaches us is that it is precisely the lack of historical authenticity of the throne that speaks effectively for the authority of the monarch. In other words, authority rests in the person rather than the object, and this is why the pose of Louis XIV is also adopted by his great-grandson and great-great-grandson.

The choice of throne depicted was also a question of aesthetic and stylistic conventions, since they often were imaginary pieces: the one in the Van Loo portrait of Louis XV painted at the end of his reign refers to the beginnings of neoclassicism while the true throne actually used at Versailles is older and in the rococo style, supplied by the Slodtz brothers (Maës 2013). The one in the 1779 portrait of Louis XVI by Antoine-François Callet refers to the spirit of antiquity found in the designs of Jean-Démosthène Dugourc (1749–1825) and is not connected with reality at Versailles. Or, instead of an imagined chair, the artist might have utilized a functional chair of secondary importance, as was the case with Duplessis's 1777 portrait of Louis XVI, where the painter had at his disposal a beautiful giltwood chair, a little out of fashion, that came from the furnishings of the inner apartments of the king. This seat then was a real object, but it was not a state chair. Whether fantasy or reality, this variety of forms in chairs ends up reminding one that they had been included above all else in the iconographic program to recall that royalty saw itself as a body standing upright rather than on a fixed throne.

The dynamic and powerful theatrical setting of the Louis XIV model devised by Rigaud imposed itself beyond the frontiers of France. This was as much a result of the installation of the House of Bourbon on several thrones of Europe as of the effectiveness of the message it conveyed. As a result, the positioning of the seat beside the sovereign in portraits began to establish itself in one court after the other, thus offering an interesting catalog of forms and fashions throughout the eighteenth century.

European seated portraits: From Louis XV in his minority to the popes

Alongside his image of Louis XIV standing in front of his throne, Rigaud presented a second interpretation of monarchy, perfectly legitimate from a political point of view, in the form of the young Louis XV seated in the armchair part of his throne. These two contrasting proposals, painted by the same artist and separated by fourteen years, offer two ways of understanding the monarchy of France of the *ancien régime*, reflecting visually on the political characteristics and stakes involved. If the adult Louis XIV, aware of his authority over monarchic Europe in 1701, deserved to be depicted standing, Louis XV is seated because he is a minor. The seat is no longer a secondary participant in the representation but the obvious means of evoking the legitimacy of the authority of the sitter, who was too young to rule and thus the government acted in his name. The iconographic function of the throne as a receptacle for the sovereign's body is interesting, because it aims to make the furniture an accessory in active support of the sacredness of the king's person. Louis XV, with his index finger pointing toward the right, adopts an imperious position. This authority, though, needs a symbolic buttress. The seat and seated posture symbolize both the legitimate monarchic framework and the relevance of the principle of regency, while at the same time anticipating the portrait that would later appear, showing the king standing upright.

An interesting parallel could be made with another portrait of a child prince, that of Archduke Francis of Austria, painted by Anton Raphael Mengs (1728–79) in 1770 (Figure 8.6). The little prince, future Emperor Francis I, holds himself upright in his child's clothes. He makes a gesture of authority with his right hand, with the index finger pointed toward the left of the spectator, while he leans with his other hand on the seat of a lavish rococo armchair in

FIGURE 8.6 Portrait by Anton Raphael Mengs of Archduke Francis I of Austria and II of the Holy Roman Empire (1768–1835), who would become Emperor of the Holy Roman Empire and also of Austria. Photograph courtesy of the National Museum of the Prado/ Wikimedia Commons.

gilded wood. In contrast with Rigaud, fifty years earlier, Mengs thinks in a very different manner about the function of the seat to invoke his model's minority. In representing his model standing in front of an armchair visibly too large for him to take his place on it, he illustrates the disproportion between the child's body and the symbols of adult power. Louis XV was seated on an armchair his size, a piece of furniture that is as respectful to his age as it is to his status as sovereign. The little archduke, however, is a child to whose power the world has not yet submitted.

The seated posture is also characteristic of another powerful institution, the Catholic Church. It is interesting to comment on this subject through the example from the end of the century of Pius VI. Through examining the official representation of the pontiff, the art historian Jeffrey Collins has noticed the place assigned to furniture in creating the image of the pope. Two portraits are of particular interest in this respect. The first, of 1775 by Giovanni Domenico Porta, is both an election portrait and the first image of the new pontiff (Collins 2004: fig. 9). Pius VI is seated in a giltwood armchair surmounted by his coat of arms, the model of which, being out of fashion, harks back to the chair represented in the official portrait of his predecessor, Clement XIV. If one should see in this seat an obvious visual tool of the principle of continuity, as Collins sets out to do, one notices that the artist modifies this idea of continuity through the portrait's background. While the chair on which Pius VI is seated symbolizes immediate continuity through the succession that had just taken place in 1775, immemorial continuity is shown by the presence of the throne of Saint Peter, the *cathedra Petri*, in the background of the portrait. The juxtaposition of these two chairs in the portrait should be interpreted in association with the two objects in the foreground. In front of the monumental *cathedra* there is a tiara, the triple crown of the Vicar of Christ. In front of the secular armchair, there is in the hand of the new pope the letter in paper indicating his name and his place in the history of mankind.

Another portrait of the same pontiff, painted by Pompeo Batoni (1708–87) in 1775–6, is worthy of attention—one in which Pius VI takes his place in the armchair that Mengs had represented some years before in his 1758 portrait of Clement XIII. In both cases, it is the furniture that reveals the continuity between pontiffs. In Batoni's work, it is the lavish rococo clock that attracts the attention of the viewer, reminding us of the temporal nature of the papal role and the political reality of the life of he who governs.

The aristocratic portrait

The representation of furnishing within the family portrait or genre painting often constitutes an effective way of revealing authority and the problematic nature of power. On this account, *Thomas Wentworth, Earl of Strafford and his family* by Gawen Hamilton (1732, Ottawa, National Gallery of Canada) is a fine example within the context of Hanoverian England.

In 1732, the antiquarian George Vertue described this painting as "in the Conversation manner the disposion [*sic*] genteel & agreeable" (Vertue 1934: 61). In other words, as a clever reorientation of the formal portrait, this conversation piece is more pleasant to look at, yet clearly illustrates the hierarchical relationship between the people present, namely, the Earl, his wife, and their sons, surrounded by retainers. The representation of certain pieces of furniture is very revealing about the function of these objects, enabling one to understand what the scene is evoking. One notices that the division between the sexes into two spaces—the left masculine and the right feminine—is associated with the presence of two pieces of furniture: on the male side a lavish armchair of carved giltwood crowned with the Earl's coronet on which the head of the family and holder of the title sits. On the female side stands a small tea table around which the Countess sits with her female companions. That which is intimate and agreeable (the female side) responds to the official world of political duties (the male side), the armchair and table acting within a strict system of social representation. The education of the young heir, William Wentworth (1722–91) and the requirement that he take up his position in the male sphere is clearly represented by the woman guiding him toward his father.

The Montreal Museum of Fine Arts preserves an interesting family portrait of 1712 by the French artist François de Troy (1645–1730), presumed to be of widowed Madame de Franqueville and her children (Plate 39). The picture shows the magisterial role played by seating within the social hierarchy of a French aristocratic house of the early eighteenth century. One notices that the painter manages two spaces, the interior of the château and the terrace where Madame de Franqueville is seated. The former is placed in the background, as the presence of the portrait of the deceased husband and father shows. Under this portrait one notices the presence of armchairs with large scrolled armrests, covered in blue velvet. The seat of authority is thus associated with the portrait of the head of the family.

On the terrace is deployed the greater part of the scene. One finds here the mother of the family, her two daughters and sons, accompanied by an enslaved African boy attending to the youngest daughter, and a number of chairs. Madame de Franqueville sits on one of the same chairs as the set visible in the house beneath the portrait of her husband. One notices on her right a chair with the same upholstery but without armrests, and therefore of less important status: it is tempting to see this as a symbol of transfer of authority. The widow has left her own chair to take her place in the armchair of her husband, until the time when her young son reaches his majority. Moreover her son has arisen from a small folding chair so as to squeeze the hand of his mother against his cheek as a sign of homage. The sky in the background seems to indicate the colors of the morning: it is the dawn of a new rule.

The portrait of the collector: furniture as a mark of taste

Portraits of collectors provide an exceptionally fine corpus of representation of objects and pieces of furniture that serve as props for the social and historic status of the sitter. One famous eighteenth-century example is the 1759 portrait of the financier and patron Ange-Laurent de La Live de Jully (1725–79) by Jean-Baptiste Greuze (Washington, National Art Gallery) (Plate 40). An eminent figure in the field of French taste during the 1750s, La Live published in 1764 descriptions of certain pieces of furniture intended to accompany his collections of paintings and *objets d'art* in his historic *Catalogue historique du cabinet de peintre et sculpture Françoise de M. de Lalive*. The author describes his Flemish *cabinet*, which was to receive and enhance his non-French pictures: "this *cabinet* is decorated with furniture made in the antique style, or to use a word which is currently very much over-used, in the *gout grec* [Greek taste] [...]. The furniture has been executed to the designs of Le Lorrain, a painter of the *Académie*, who died a few years ago in Russia" (de La Live de Jully 1764: 110–11). It was these pieces of furniture with which La Live had wished to surround himself in his portrait of 1759. In it, one clearly recognizes a large bureau in ebony with gilt bronze ornaments, the work of the *ébéniste* Joseph Baumhauer (d.1772) and the sculptor and bronze-founder Philippe Caffieri (1714–74). It is today housed in the Château de Chantilly. The accompanying chair, on which La Live is seated, can no longer be traced but one recognizes within it the perfect stylistic relationship with the bureau. The nature of these exceptional pieces of furniture, which had been the engines of the first manifestations of the *goût grec* in Parisian circles during the 1750s, provided motivation for the realization of this picture: it is as much a faithful portrait of these pieces as their owner that Greuze realized, and La Live takes on the life of a man of taste, in the aesthetic choices of a collector and issuer of audacious commissions.

Likewise, the great and successive portraits of the Marquise de Pompadour (1721–64), most often known as Madame de Pompadour, represent exciting evidence of the search for social legitimacy on the part of Louis XV's favorite. The furnishings represented around her by artists François Boucher (1703–70), Maurice-Quentin de la Tour (1704–88), and Francois-Hubert Drouais (1727–75) in the course of her twenty-year "reign" over the heart of the king, at first as a mistress and then as a friend, provide points of reference for the inevitable setting of the stage for this fundamentally important personality in the history of taste in France of the eighteenth century.

The first portrait of Madame de Pompadour that François Boucher painted dates from 1750, but is only known to us through two sketches, close to each other in date. The main characteristic of these is the faithful adoption of the rules of princely portraiture, which were notably observed during the same period by Jean-Marc Nattier (1685–1766), in the paintings of the daughters of Louis XV. These two sketches differ in the clothes and furniture of the model, proposing, in the same pose, two ways of celebrating the virtues of the marquise and her role in promoting the arts, literature, science, and music. The first one, preserved in the Louvre, represents her in the ample, cream dressing gown with a bodice tied *à l'espagnole* (in the Spanish fashion) distractedly and pensively trilling on the keys of a lacquer-cased harpsichord (Musée du Louvre, R.F. 2142). The second example, today at Waddesdon Manor, confers exactly the same pose upon her, in a *robe à la française* (dress in the French style), holding a straw hat in one hand and a small medallion in the other, mounted on two rows of pearls, a small jewel, that she is preparing to put on before going out on a promenade (Waddesdon Manor, accession no. 965.1995).

What links the two pictures is the theatrical presentation of the subject. The armchair reminds one of the royal joiner François-Toussaint Foliot's seats, which were to be delivered to the marquise at Château de Bellevue some years later. The 1750 dating of the sketch, however, hinders this being part of this furniture ensemble (Baulez 1991). The most interesting element is the imposing bookcase with glass doors in the background, on which are displayed a sumptuous clock and a beautiful celadon porcelain vase. With a classicizing outline, the bookcase connects this Louis XV interior to the architectural rigors of the large *armoires* (imposing cupboards, used more for display and swagger than storage) by André Charles Boulle (1642–1732), without adopting any of the details of Boulle decoration, as well as to furniture by Étienne Levassueur (1721–98) or Philippe-Claude Montigny (1734–1800), both of whom created copies and pastiches of Boulle furniture in the eighteenth century. The dating of the two canvasses to around 1750, therefore, is surprising: one sees an early piece of neoclassical furniture—*à la grecque*—in other words at least five years before Joseph Baumhauer's creations for La Live de Jully. This bookcase is an evocation of the furniture in the architectural language of the classical grand manner of Louis XIV, a visual element that very much borrows from architecture. With a bookcase filled with books and put at the disposal of a woman of wit, the furniture is also and above all else a true "building" of a personality whose status at the court at Versailles was complex. We find here one of the essential functions of furniture integrated into a portrait that denotes rank: to speak in favor of the authority of the subject and to express the importance of social position.

In 1751, Boucher painted *The Toilette of Venus* (Plate 41) for the bathing quarters of the Château de Bellevue, the subject of which aimed to show the tender moments in the life of the king and his mistress as an elegant invocation of the way of life amongst the gods of Olympus. This picture provides a fine example of furniture as an element in the narrative. In effect, the sumptuous sofa "comes to life," with a curious juxtaposition of the putto in giltwood surrounded by putti in flesh and blood. The viewer awaits the imminent metamorphosis of this cherub into a living being who will take his turn in serving and cajoling his divine mistress. The *Toilette of Venus* thus places a piece of furniture into the mythological iconography where inanimate objects are waiting to come to life. The theme of the painting, without doubt, exercised an influence on Boucher, who gained confidence and five years later executed a new commission to represent the marquise in person.

CHAPTER NINE

Verbal Representations

TESSA MURDOCH

This chapter focuses on verbal representations of furniture and furnishings in England, 1700–1800. A wide range of documentary evidence preserved in family archives reflects the careful stewardship of records for legal and financial reasons justified by the British tradition of inheritance by primogeniture. Descriptions are drawn from inventories, diaries, and letters from patrons, designers, and craftsmen and from a variety of other sources. By mid-century, for example, designs for furniture published by leading cabinetmakers were also accompanied by written descriptions. Among these, the three editions of Thomas Chippendale's *Director* inspired comparable publications by Ince and Mayhew, George Hepplewhite, and Thomas Sheraton. Contemporary novels provide surprisingly vivid descriptions of interior furnishings. The novelist Samuel Richardson, son of a joiner, evidently learned to observe the detail of domestic settings from an early age. Furthermore, before the introduction of street numbering, tradesmen were dependent on suitable shop signs, which dictated advertisements in the form of trade cards and labels. Advertisements in daily newspapers also helped to attract custom. Disposing of furniture by raffle was a novel method of attracting interest in a new product. Archives recording royal and aristocratic family expenditure are a particularly rich source of documentary evidence and include bills from suppliers and remarkable legal documents testifying to unpaid debts at the time of a patron's death.

INVENTORIES

In 1709, after the death of Ralph, 1st Duke of Montagu, the contents of his London and country homes were inventoried by the upholsterer James Gronouse. These documents shed fascinating light on the furnishings selected for different members of the household. In his palatial London home, Montagu House, Bloomsbury, which later housed the British Museum, the late Duke's apartment included a closet (for storing personal accessories and memorabilia), a bed chamber, a drawing room, and an antechamber. His bed was hung with masculine "plad" with window curtains to match; there were three cane chairs with cushions and a cane squab and stool. A pair of walnut stands provided raised platforms for lighting equipment. The fireplace, equipped with a stove grate, fender, shovel, tongs, poker, and brush, was an additional source of light as well as heat during the cold winter months. The only painting in the duke's bedroom was a portrait of Hortense Mancini, Duchess of Mazarin, his close friend and the former mistress of King Charles II. This survives at the duke's principal country seat, Boughton House, Northamptonshire, in its original carved gilded frame provided by the London workshop of the Pelletier family, French refugees from Paris. As Protestants they were forced to leave the French metropolis in 1685; they settled in Amsterdam before moving to establish their London workshop in 1688. They used designs by Daniel Marot (1660–1752) architect to William III and Mary II, trained at the court of Louis XIV under Jean Berain the elder (1637–1711). The duke's Drawing Room provided opportunities for relaxation, with an easy chair upholstered in crimson cloth and a card table. The adjacent Ante-Chamber was furnished with a pier glass between the windows, a pendulum clock, and a clothes-press that indicates that the duke's clothes were stored here; it was in this room that his valet prepared the duke's clothes for the day. The bed in the "Lady's Bed Chamber" had paned damask curtains trimmed with gold and silver fringe with eight chairs and two round stools upholstered to match. The walls were hung with tapestry for warmth and luxury; an easy chair was upholstered with green damask. There was a looking glass with an inlaid frame, a marble table, and a watch clock. The contents of the duchess's bedchamber were more valuable at £191 9s as opposed to the duke's at £18 12s (Murdoch 2006b: 17, 19). Such elaborate beds were often the most expensive items of furniture in the house (Murdoch 2002: 3–9).

The language used in inventories depended on the education of the appraiser and often reflects local pronunciation. Such documents provide information on the range of furnishings supplied for the use of royal guests, the patron, and members of his household. At Boughton House, where the Duke of Montagu's doctor Pierre Silvestre also served as supervisor of building and garden projects, Silvestre had a bed hung with Indian "plod" (plad, intersecting horizontal and vertical stripes in contrasting colors as found in Scottish tartans) with four chairs, a walnut dressing table, and a wainscot close stool with a pewter pan. The contents were valued at £10 9s (Murdoch 2006b: 51–2). Such provision contrasts with the State Bedchamber which was furnished in readiness for a visit from William III. Here the bed with its crimson damask hangings flowered with gold and trimmed with gold fringe was accompanied by six elbow chairs covered with the same damask, and six matted chairs with matching cushions, which lined the room. The window pier was hung with one large looking glass in a glass frame and top, with an inlaid walnut table and stands. Over the chimney another looking glass in three sections canted forward (often described as a "landskip" glass given its horizontal format) helped to reflect both daylight and candlelight. Three pieces of tapestry illustrated scenes from the *Acts of the Apostles* after the cartoons by Raphael. Both the chimney furniture and the door furniture were itemized; the latter described as "a brass lock Staple and two bolts." The total valuation for the contents of this room was £321 11s (53).

In 1743 the Hall at Ditchley, the Oxfordshire home of George Henry Lee, 2nd Earl of Litchfield, was furnished with six richly carved benches partly gilt and a rich slab frame with a "Dove" colored marble slab. The Hall was lit by carved and gilt "compass" side lanterns (with curved upper profiles). The walls were hung with two history paintings and a family group portrait; there was one plaster statue. The total value of the contents was £46 12s (Murdoch 2006b: 148).

This contrasts with the Great Room with its

> two marble tables on rich frames; two glasses 60 by 34 inches, 2 large gilt stands with leather cases, ten mahogany carved chairs with red Morocco leather seats, four elbow chairs similarly upholstered, a needlework screen; 4 whole length pictures, a landscape over the chimney, and a large Turkey carpet.

The "Spring Umbereloes" and rod were window blinds. The total value of the contents of the Great Room was £195 10s 6d (Murdoch 2006b: 149).

The North Dining Room at Holkham, the Norfolk home of Thomas Coke, was furnished in 1760 with fourteen chairs upholstered in red morocco leather; matching crimson window curtains, a painted floor cloth (oil cloth with applied painted patterns that was hard wearing and impervious to spills of food and wine), a mahogany dining table to seat ten that could be expanded with two additional parts. A sideboard marble table of "asbestoes" and porphyry was supported on a gilt frame with brass ornaments. Two mahogany dumb waiters, a small mahogany table, and a canvas screen assisted the servants in delivering the meal; adjacent to the Dining Room, a room behind the buffet was equipped with a mahogany table in two parts to set out desserts, two plate warmers, a mahogany cistern for bottles and frame, one pail for washing glasses and frame (Murdoch 2006b: 215–16).

The housekeeper's room in Thomas Coke's London house in Thanet Street, Bloomsbury, was simply furnished with check hangings to the bedstead, an old dressing table and glass, a mahogany stand, four matted chairs, an old wainscot press, and a walnut tree chest of drawers (Murdoch 2006b: 232). The butler's room was equipped with a bed, a deal (pine) table, a stool, a mahogany tray, a knife tray, a wainscot tray, a plate warmer, a back gammon table, a chess board, a mahogany cistern and stand, and another cistern for ice (234).

At Powderham Castle, Devon, the contents of the Library were listed in an inventory taken on the death of Viscount Courtenay in the summer of 1762; the descriptions identify the woods used, demonstrating the increased recognition of rare hardwoods then sought in contemporary cabinetmaking (Gilbert and Murdoch 1993: 140).

The "Two Manchineel Book Cases carv'd gilded & inlaid with Brass" were supplied by the Exeter-born cabinetmaker John Channon in 1740—the use of the term "Manchineel" is misleading as twentieth-century scientific identification pronounced that the wood was padouk. The name "manchineel" (sometimes written "manchioneel") as well as the specific epithet mancinella is from Spanish *manzanilla* (little apple), from the superficial resemblance of its fruit and leaves to those of an apple tree. A present-day Spanish name is in fact *manzanilla de la muerte*, "little apple of death." This refers to the fact that the poisonous manchineel is one of the most dangerous trees in the world. These spectacular bookcases are embellished with gilt carving and brass inlay and each bear a brass tablet engraved "17 J Channon 40." This signature has led to the assumption that all mid-eighteenth-century English furniture embellished with brass inlay should be attributed to Channon. However, the French taste for furniture of marquetry in brass and pewter created a market for furniture decorated in metal inlay and a number of London-based cabinetmakers supplied furniture thus embellished; they include John Renshaw, J. Graveley, and Frederick Hintz (see Murdoch 1993). Libraries housed scientific instruments and other reference collections such as historical medals. The Powderham library included three other mahogany bookcases, with

> enrich'd & fluted Pilasters; Two Mahogany Do [ditto] plain with close Pediments & carv'd Capitals A Cedar Medal Case Carv'd and Gilded A Marble Chimney Piece & Slab with wood ornaments, Tabernacle, Frame, with a Bust Standing on a Bracket & a Landscape A Large square mahogany Table with fret enrichment, & clawd Feet 8 Mahogany Stools Mahogany Pillar & Claw reading Table Mahogany steps Four green hair silk Damsk Curtains, An Alarum, Orrery, Globes, Telescopes & other Mathematical Instruments.
>
> (Gilbert and Murdoch 1993: 140)

Sir William Courtenay, Channon's patron, listed the contents of the Powderham library in his will as part of

> All my household Goods, pictures and furniture and my Library, Globes and other things in my library and which shall be at my Castle or Mansion house of Powderham shall be deemed as heirlooms and for Ever be Enjoyed as far as the Lord will admit by the person and persons who for the time being shall be in possession of or intitled to the Rents and profits of the same Castle.
>
> (Gilbert and Murdoch 1994: 68)

The creation of the library at Powderham was deemed as an heirloom and established the Courtenays, Earls of Devon, as the ancient county family who claimed descent from Louis VI, King of France. It coincided with the publication of a family history in 1735, in which the author noted that the "Courtenays having been Governors of this County for above Five Hundred Years, as Viscounts and Earls of Devonshire, the chief Affairs of the County did go through their Hands. So that an History of the Family of Courtenay may, in effect, be said to be an History of the County of Devon" (Gilbert and Murdoch 1994: 68).

DIARIES

National variation and regional color is provided by descriptions in diaries. The travel diaries of Celia Fiennes cover the period 1685—c. 1712 and usefully comment on church as well as country house furnishings. In London Fiennes comments on the rebuilt St. Paul's Cathedral, "the choir with curious carved work in wood, the Arch Bishop's seat and the Bishop of London's and Lord Mayor's [...] very finely carv'd and adorned, the alter alsoe with velvet and gold, on the right side is placed a large crimson velvet elbow chaire which is for the Dean" (Fiennes 1982: 223–4). The diary of James Woodforde, the country parson, kept between 1758 and 1802, is dominated by accounts of his diet. On May 16, 1781, he had the "best day of fishing ever." The largest fish he caught was "a Pike which was a Yard long and weighed upwards of thirteen pounds after he was brought home." The following day his guests were quite astonished at the sight of the great pike on the table. "Was obliged to lay him on two of the largest dishes, and was laid on part of the Kitchen Window Shutters covered with a cloth" (Woodforde 1979: 169–70). Such improvisation pales by comparison with James Woodforde's account of gracious entertainment received elsewhere in the country. In August 1783, Woodforde was invited to dine with the Townsends at Honingham "who behaved very genteel to us":

> The drawing Room in which we drank Tea etc was hung with Silk. The Chairs of the same kind of Silk and all the woodwork of them gilded, as were

the Settee's. The looking glass which was the finest and largest I ever saw, cost at secondhand £150.0.0.

> The height of the looking glass was 2.2 meters, and the breadth of it was 1.65 meters. The frame and ornaments were carved and gilded, and it was very handsome (Woodforde 1979: 210).

The large looking glass in the Green Drawing Room at nearby Houghton Hall provides an apt comparison.

In early September, the parson was very impressed by dining with the Bishop of Norwich:

> There were 20 of us at the Table and a very elegant Dinner the Bishop gave us. We had two Courses of 20 Dishes each Course, and a Desert after of 20 Dishes, Madeira, red and white Wines. A most beautiful Artificial Garden in the Centre of the Table remained at Dinner and afterwards, it was one of the prettiest things I ever saw, about a yard long and about 18 Inches wide, in the Middle of which was a high round Temple supported on round Pillars, the Pillars were wreathed round with artificial Flowers—on one side was a Shepherdess on the other a Shepherd, several handsome Urns decorated with artificial Flowers.
>
> (Woodforde 1979: 212)

In November 1789 Parson Woodforde records purchasing secondhand furniture from Willm [William] Hart, a cabinetmaker from Hog Hill, Norwich: "large second hand double-flapped Mohogany Tables, also one second hand Mohogany dressing Table with Drawers, also one new Mohogany Washing-Stand, for all which paid 4.14.6. that is for the 2 Tables 2.12.6. Dressing Table 1.11.6. Mohogany Wash-stand 0.10.6. I think the whole of it to be very cheap" (Woodforde 1979: 363).

LETTERS

The *Purefoy Letters* provide a fascinating insight into the provision of furnishings in London for a manor house in the country, Shalstone, Buckinghamshire (*Purefoy Letters* 1931: 98–125). Henry Purefoy lived with his mother at Shalstone House and the letters document aspects of their everyday lives between 1735 and 1753. Letters to cabinetmakers include correspondence with Mr. Belchier at the sign of the Sun, St. Paul's Church Yard, London. The first, dated Sunday January 11, 1735, apologizes for the delay in replying to one from the cabinetmaker of December 19—the delay occasioned by the "hurry of Xmas." Mr. Purefoy acknowledges the "peice of glasse & bitt of wood for ye drawers wch both do very well. I have ordered Mr Robothom to pay your bill wch is £11 5s when he pays you pray give him a receipt in full" (98–9).

You say you must have £3 16s for a glasse in a gold frame three foot eleven inches & an half long by twenty-four inches, the middle glasse to be thirty one inches long. I do leave it to you if you must have so much. Do it at your leisure but pray let ye glass be true & you shal have your money so soon as I have ye glasse. Tis much against my will you have been out of your money so long.

(Purefoy Letters 1931: 107–8)

The next order placed with Belchier is dated February 8, 1743, and is for "a round neat light mahogany folding table with four legs, two of them to draw out to hold up ye ffolds. It must be four foot two inches wide. Send it (with the price thereof) by Mr Zachary Meads the Bucks carrier who sets out of London on Monday nights & ffriday nights" (Purefoy Letters 1931: 107–8).

On July 18, 1749, Mr. Purefoy acknowledges receipt of a desk (Figure 9.1) from Belchier "but we can't open the Draw but do suppose it opens in the two Slitts down the Legs. I desire you will let me have a lre [letter] next post how to

FIGURE 9.1 Table–desk supplied by John Belchier to Henry Purefoy at Shalstone, Buckinghamshire, 1749. (See Purefoy Letters 1931: plate 11 facing p. 110.) Photograph courtesy of Book Worm/Alamy Stock Photo.

open & manage it, as also what it comes to that I may order you payment." On July 29 a further letter confirms "I have received your Letter & I have found the way of the Writing Table wch stuck together thro' damp" (*Purefoy Letters* 1931: 111).

The brother of one of the maids in the dairy at Shalstone, Mr. Greaves, was a chairmaker who worked in Soho, London, at the sign of the Golden Chair, Warwick Lane, Golden Square. Mr. Purefoy wrote to Greaves, on August 3, 1746:

> Your sister Mary tells mee you can help mee to a second hand sedan chair; if you can meet with one that is strong & tite I desire you will let mee know of it & I will send a friend to look at it. If you have never a second hand one let mee know what you will have for a new one lined with cloath.
>
> (*Purefoy Letters* 1931: 108)

Eventually a sedan chair was bought for eight guineas from Mr. George Vaughan of Coventry Street, off Piccadilly (*Purefoy Letters* 1931: 108).

From the optician George Sterrop, also in St. Paul's Churchyard, Henry Purefoy ordered "a portable Barometer of a Guinea price with an oak case" in June 1752. Purefoy's first letter enquired whether a "portable" barometer "will bear being carried about in that manner [...] on journeys and of the price of one in an oak case with a lock and key & Hinges thereto to put it in." Purefoy has a copy of Sterrop's advertisement, which listed three different prices "Plain mahogany with paper scale 15s, Ditto brasse plate silvered 18s" and a carved version at one guinea. He asks for "one of your printed shop bills of what things you sell, in the oak case with the barometer," demonstrating that such a label might be requested by the client. Henry Purefoy patronized clockmakers in Bicester, Oxfordshire, and Helmdon, Northamptonshire, whom he called on for repairs. He purchased an alarm clock in London from Mr. Mulford in Cursitor's Street in Chancery Lane in February 1744 for £3 15s, but by May 1745, Purefoy complained that "It would not go at all at first & I was forced to send for a clockmaker to put it in order; it performed pretty well but the case is so little, the Pendulum knocks so very hard against the side of it that it will not let me sleep" (*Purefoy Letters* 1931: 112–13).

Mr. Purefoy also bought furniture locally. In July 1736, he wrote to Mr. King a chair-frame maker at the sign of the King & Queen in the local town, Bicester, as follows

> As I understand you make chairs of walnut tree frames with 4 legs without any Barrs for Mr Vaux of Caversfield, if you do such I desire you will come over here in a week's time any morning but Wensday [sic]. I shall want about 20 chairs.
>
> (*Purefoy Letters* 1931: 102–3)

This was followed on October 29, 1736, with a reminder

> I wonder you don't come with my Chairs as you appointed—pray don't faill
> to let mee have them with all convenient speed and let mee have a line or two
> from you how I must get them hither, some times our Teams go that way.
> Direct yours to be left for me at Mr Welchman's at Brackley, one of your
> Town cutlers who keep Brackley market will bring it.
>
> (*Purefoy Letters* 1931)

For Dumfries House, Ayrshire, the architect John Adam demonstrated to his
patron, William, 5th Earl of Dumfries, that planning the furnishing of the
rooms needed to begin as building work gathered momentum; this gave the
architect the opportunity to introduce craftsmen. For the two main reception
rooms, John Adam wrote:

> Between the Windows there should be fine Marble tables with handsome
> frames. From the floor to the underpart of the belt or surbase moulding
> that goes round the room is 2 feet 8 ins and to the top of it is 3 feet which
> dimentions [*sic*] will regulate the height of these frames and tables; and their
> length Ornamental furniture.
>
> (Gilbert 1978: 1:131)

The pier tables were supplied by George Mercer, whose workshop was near
Cavendish Square, London. A bill dated August 6, 1757, for "2 Sienna and 2
Jasper Marble Tables with Carved and Gilt frames, the whole agreed at £88"
was followed by a letter from Mr. Mercer:

> One thing I beg leave to lay before your Lordship, that is when I made
> the Estimate of the Table Frames I only thought of painting but nothing
> of Gilding which cost Twelve guineas. Therefore humbly admit to your
> Lordship to make me such an allowance as you shall think proper. I shall by
> this post write to Messrs. Adams to take care of them until your Lo'p shall
> send Carriages for them.
>
> (Gilbert 1978: 1:13)

At Dumfries, a substantial order for furniture was placed with Thomas
Chippendale, the leading West End cabinetmaker, established in London's
St. Martin's Lane. The 1759 bill includes detailed descriptions of the bedstead:
"a large mahogany double screw'd Bedstead wt. A Dome top ornamented in the
Inside the feetposts fluted & a Palmbranch twisting round & carv'd Capitals
a carv'd headboard a strong burnish'd Rod a lathe bottom & strong triple
wheel castors," which cost £38. The "set of large rich carv'd Cornices cover'd

& covering & laceing the Headboard & Dome" cost £23. For the library, Chippendale supplied a "Table of very fine wood the top cover'd wt. Best black leather, a Writing drawer at one End wt. A double rising slider cover'd, & drawers & cupboards in the sides & strong triple wheel castors"; this cost £22. For the dressing rooms, at a cost of £17,

> a neat mahogany shaving table st. A folding top & a Looking glass to rise wt. a spring & Rack a Cupboard & drawer etc £4; a mahog. Breakfast table of fine wood wt. a Writing drawer & Wirework round & castors etc £6 8s; a Japann'd Cloathes-press wt. folding doors & sliding shelves cover'd wt. marble paper & Bays, aprons & 2 drawers.

In 1763, Chippendale supplied equipment for the butler's use in the dining room: "Two mahogany Oval Cisterns with brass hoops & hands" cost 4 guineas; "2 large mahogany Butlers Trays" cost £1 3s; "a large mahog'y compass teatray wt. a neat cut rim" cost £1 16s; "6 neat mahogany bottle boards with brass rims" cost 9s (Gilbert 1978: 1:136–9).

Pattern books would provide potential patrons with tempting prospects. In 1762, Ince and Mayhew included in their *Universal System of Household Furniture* "A State Bed, with a Dome Tester, which has been executed, and may be esteemed amongst the best in England: the Furniture was Blue Damask, and all the Ornaments in burnish'd gold, and richly fringed" (Ince and Mayhew 1998: plate XXXII, p. 5). The terminology used by Ince and Mayhew almost needs a glossary. The explanations are provided in French and English and the spelling is eccentric. Thus "Lanthorns" not lanterns; "therms" not candlestands; "voiders" not trays; "Lady's Secretary's"; "Gentleman's Repository"; "Lady's Toiletta's," "Lady's Apparatus"; "Ecoineurs"(corner cupboards), "A China Case"; "Burjairs" or "Birjairs" (the French term for a winged armchair); "Illuminaries." The explanations help to define these terms; thus "A Gentleman's Repository; the upper Part or Middle is a Book-case; on each Side is Draws; the Top of the under Part or Middle, is a Desk Drawer; under that either Draws or Cloaths-Press, as shewn by two Designs; on each Side Cupboards" (plate XXI, p. 3).

In 1793 Thomas Sheraton published designs for an "Universal Table" in *The Cabinet-Maker and Upholsterer's Drawing Book*, Part II, Plate XXV:

> The use of this piece is both to answer the purpose of a breakfast and dining-table. When both the leaves are slipped under the bed, it will then serve as a breakfast-table; when one leaf is out, as in this view, it will accommodate five persons as a dining-table, if both are out, it will admit of eight, being near seven feet long, and three feet six inches in width. The drawer is divided into six boxes at each side, as in the plan, and are found useful for different sorts

of tea and sugar, and sometimes for notes, and the like. In this drawer is a slider lined with green cloth to write on. The style of finishing them is plain and simple, with straight tapered legs, socket castors, and an astragal around the frame. This table should be made of particularly good and well-seasoned mahogany, as a great deal depends upon its not being liable to cast. The covers of each box before mentioned, may have an oval of dark wood, and the alphabet cut out of ivory or white wood let into them, as in the plan; or they may be white ovals and black letters, the use of which is to distinguish the contents of each box.

(White 1990: 289)

Accounts of furnishings are to be found in letters. The correspondence between the sisters Lady Louisa Conolly, Sarah, Caroline, Lady Holland and Emily Duchess of Leinster, daughters of the 2nd Duke of Richmond, reflects the interest in French-style furniture supplied by Pierre Langlois (Murdoch 2001: illustrated p. 22). Langlois's trade card dating from about 1759, in fashionable French and English, announces that he "Makes all Sorts of Fine Cabinets and Commodes made & Inlaid in the Politest manner with Brass & Tortoiseshell & Likewise all rich Ornamental Clock Cases, and Chandelier & Lanthorns."[1] The French text is more specific. In addition to commodes, he supplied "Secretaires" (writing desks) and "Encoignures" (corner commodes), which is probably the earliest reference to this French form of furniture being supplied by a maker working in England. Langlois specializes in "Meubles, inscrulez de fleurs en Bois" inlaid with scrolling flowers and repairs "Vielles Ouverages de Marqueteries" (old marquetry).

Lady Louisa Conolly, ensconced in Ireland at Castletown, County Kildare, wrote to her sister Sarah on March 22, 1762, "I have a commode coming over from Mr Langlois that Lady Anne (her mother-in-law) has bespoke for me. It is one of the cheap ones but I shall like it mightily and wish it was to come soon." The following February Lady Anne wrote to her son Thomas Conolly (Louisa's husband), "I hope Lady Louisa will get the commode soon and that she and you will like it. I paid Mr Langlois." A month later Caroline, Lady Holland wrote to Emily, Duchess of Leinster of Louisa Conolly sharing her knowledge of fashionable French furniture:

I hear she likes L'Anglay's inlaid things very much, and I would wish to send her something that might suite some of her rooms, whether commode table, bureau or coins, which to be sure one might vulgarly call corner cupboards, but really they are lovely and finish a room so well. I have two beauties in the Salon at Holland House.[2]

Jane Austen writes from Steventon, Hampshire (her birthplace), on Tuesday January 8, 1799, of Martha Lloyd, sister of Jane's sister-in-law Mary, Mrs. James Austen,

> Martha kindly made room for me in her bed, which was the shut up one in the new nursery. Nurse and the child slept on the floor, and there we all were in some confusion and great comfort. The bed did exceedingly well for us, both to lie awake in and talk till two o'clock, and to sleep in the rest of the night.
>
> (Austen with Hughes-Hallett and Drury 1990: 30)

Such a "shut-up bed," supplied by Thomas Chippendale for the use of David Garrick's household at Hampton, is preserved in the V&A (W.21:1 to 8-1917). The contemporary example illustrated (Figure 9.3a and b) illustrates the drawers by day (Figure 9.2a and b).[3]

FIGURE 9.2 a and b Press bedstead, *c.* 1775. Photograph courtesy of Phillips of Hitchin.

LITERARY DESCRIPTIONS

The novelist Samuel Richardson (1689–1761), born in Derby, the son of a joiner, went to London aged seventeen to join the printing trade. His novels, written in letter form, reflect his father's trade and contain much detailed information about furnishings. His most celebrated novel, *Clarissa*, for example, demonstrates how furniture was used (Richardson [1748] 1926). In the evening, an elbow chair offered support for the sufferer of gout who lent on the back of the chair (vol. I, pp. 35–6). The heroine takes the precaution of locking her bedroom door when she is writing letters (I, 425). Looking, later, for lodgings in London, she arrives in Dover Street and at an inner house overlooking the quiet garden "very genteelest—elegantly furnished with a dining room, two or three handsome bed-chambers—one with a pretty light closet in it, which looks into the little garden, all furnished with taste" (I, 110). The closet is equipped with books including the Gospels, Sermons, Telemachus in French, plays by Steele, Rowe, and Shakespeare, and contemporary drama and poetry, Mrs. Cibber's *The Careless Husband*, Dryden's *Miscellanies*, periodicals including *Tatler*, *Spectator*, *Guardians*, and the literary works of Alexander Pope, Jonathan Swift, and Joseph Addison (II, 194).

Lovelace, Clarissa's rejected suitor, records his frustration at his inability to reach her as he describes her gestures and movements in the context of her furnished rooms.

> I looked through the keyhole at my going by her door, and saw her on her knees, at her bed's feet her head and bosom on the bed, her arms extended and, in an agony she seemed to be sobbing, as I heard at that distance, as if her heart would break.
>
> (II, 514)

"The glass she dressed at, I was ready to break for not giving me the personal image it was wont to reflect of her, whose idea is for ever present with me" (II, 524). Again, in her chamber "sighing over her bed and every piece of furniture in it," Mr. Lovelace cast his "eye towards the drawers of the dressing-glass and saw peep out, as it were in one of the half-drawn drawers, the corner of a letter." He "snatched it out and found it superscribed by her To M. Lovelace" (II, 525). Such bedroom furniture was designed to have locked compartments in which to conceal personal correspondence from prying eyes. In Plate 43 a young woman drags down just such a dressing table as she resists a young man's attempts to drag her onto a bed.

Clarissa's bedroom has window curtains of stuff-damask (a woven fabric with patterns created in satin weave)—better than silk. The bed is in a "pretty taste neat and clean with a silk camlet" (a plain weave worsted cloth). The closet has a print of Saint Cecilia after an Italian master. It is large enough to hold "a cabinet she much values & will have with her wherever she goes—it has many jewels in it of high price" (III, 39–40). The jewel cabinet from Stanton Harcourt, Oxfordshire, is an interesting comparison (Murdoch 1997). When Clarissa faints, she throws up the closet sash for air (III, 40, 42).

As the novel progresses Clarissa moves to

> A horrid hole of a house. The floor was clean. A bed at one corner, with coarse curtains tacked up at the feet to the ceiling, because the curtain rings were broken off, but a coverlid upon it, in tatters and the covers tied upon tassels, that the rents in it might go no further. The windows dark and double barred. Four old Turkey-workd chairs bursten-bottomed the stuffing staring out. An old tottering worm eaten table that had more nails bestowed in mending it to make it stand than the table cost fifty years ago when new. On the mantelpiece was a iron shov up candlestick with a lighted candle in it, an old looking glass cracked through the middle. The chimney—two half tiles in it on one side & one sole one on the other, old half barred stove grate, a stone bottle with yew, southernwood, dried sweet

briar & sprigs of rue in flower. In a dark nook was an old broken bottomed cane couch with a worm eaten leg. And this, then horrid Lovelace, was the bedchamber of the divine Clarissa. She was kneeling in a corner of the room, near the dismal window, against the table on an old baluster of the cane couch, half covered with her handkerchief; her arms crossed upon the table, the forefinger of her right hand in her bible. Paper, pens, ink, lay by her book on the table.

(III, 444)

TRADE CARDS, LABELS, AND ADVERTISEMENTS

Prior to the 1760s, when street numbering was introduced in London, shop signs that often emphasized the speciality of the shops were common. Street numbering was generally adopted by the 1780s, but the shop sign, instead of being resigned to obscurity, found a new use. The designs of shop signs began to be used as decorative devices on bill heads and trade cards. Thus the London cabinetmaker John Brown at the sign of "Three Cover'd Chairs & Walnut Tree on the East Side of St Paul's Church Yard, near the School," advertised in 1729 that he

made and sold Window Blinds of all sorts, painted in Wier, Canvas, Cloth and Sassenet, after the best and most lasting manner ever yet done so that if ever so dull an dirty they will clean with sope and sand and be like new; where may be seen great choice of the same being always about them. Likewise at the same place is made the new fashion Walnut Tree Window seat cases to slip off and on, very much approved of beyond stuff seats.

(Murdoch 1997: 104–8)

In 1730, Brown advertised a move to another building in St. Paul's Church Yard and announced that he stocked "All Sorts of Windsor Garden Chairs of all Sizes painted green or in the Wood," an early reference to this type of chair (Beard and Gilbert 1978: 115). In 1738 he advertised that he

Makes and Sells all sorts of the best & most fashionable Chairs, either Cover'd, Matted,or Can'd. Likewise all Sorts of Cabinet Work, with Sconces, Pier & Chimney-Glasses, Mohogany and other Tables: Blinds for Windows made & Curiously Painted on Canvas, Silk or Wire: Where is good Choise etc best painted of any in London, none excepted. NB. Upholsters work of all Sorts neat & Cheap.

(Heal 1953: 25–6, plate p. 15)

Such information was of necessity condensed on printed labels stuck to the furniture supplied; the only surviving example still serves as a sign post to the supplier and reads "John / Brown / Chair Maker / at ye three Chairs / & Walnut-Tree / ye East Side of / St Paul's" (Gilbert 1996).

In February 1737, the *London Evening Post* announced (Figure 9.3) that

John Renshaw, Cabinet-Maker, in Brook-Street, Holbourn, over-against Gravel-Street, having now finish'd a very curious Desk and Book-Case, which is allow'd, by the Best and most Impartial Judges, to far excel any Thing of the Kind that has ever been made, for its Beauty, Figure and Structure, which are very extraordinary. It chiefly consists of fine Mahogany, embellished with Tortoiseshell, fine Brass Mouldings and Ornaments, with Palasters curiously wrought after the Corinthian Order. The Inside is compos'd in the most beautiful and convenient Manner; and it being propos'd by Several Persons of Distinction to have it raffled for, Mr. Renshaw intends to dispose of it accordingly, at so easy a Rate as 2s. 6d. each Chance, which doth purchase

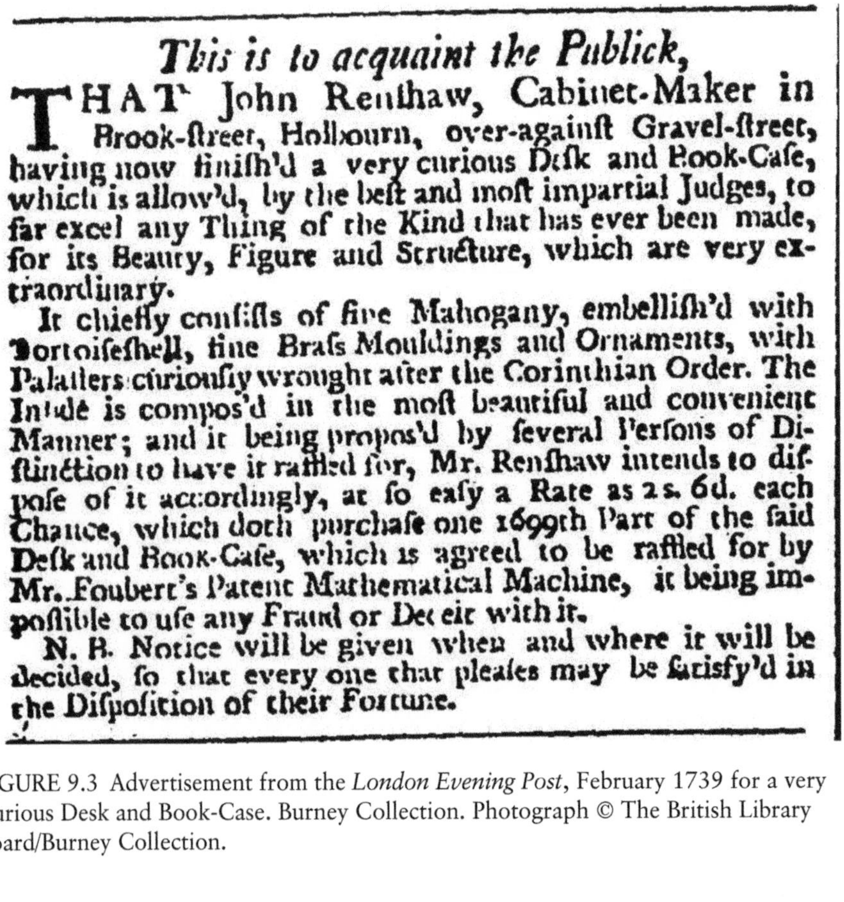

FIGURE 9.3 Advertisement from the *London Evening Post*, February 1739 for a very Curious Desk and Book-Case. Burney Collection. Photograph © The British Library Board/Burney Collection.

one 1699th Part of the said Desk and Book-Case, which is agreed to be raffled for by Mr. Foubert's Patent Mathematical Machine, it being impossible to use any Fraud or Deceit with it.

(Gilbert and Murdoch 1993: 61, fig. 47; 1994: 78–9)

This description is very close to the a desk and bookcase acquired by the Victoria and Albert Museum in 1953 (V&A, W.37:1 to 37-1953).

Lake Young advertised his coach and looking-glass manufactory in James's Street, Covent Garden in 1769 and his warehouse near the pump in Watling Street, London:

Where Merchants, Captains of Ships, Country Chapmen etc may be supply'd on reasonable Terms with all Sorts of Looking Glasses, Vizt. Sconces, Pier & Chimney Glasses, Dressing Boxes & Swingers, in Mahogany, Walnut-tree & Painted, or in rich Carv'd & Gilt Frames, in the neatest Taste & newest fashion. All Sorts of Window Glass, Wholesale and Retail, or for Exportation.

(Heal 1953: 311, plate p. 208)

Covent Garden was by the eighteenth century London's center of coach and carriage making and appropriately situated close to leading cabinetmakers in St. Martin's Lane. This important carriage industry attracted talent from the regions. In about 1785, Henry Clay moved from Birmingham to 18 King Street, Covent Garden. His business had been built on his 1772 patent for "new Improved Paper-ware" and his reputation for papier-mâché products including trays, tea caddies, knife boxes, and dressing cases. His official patent provides a detailed description of the materials and techniques of papier-mâché without using that French term and reads

Making in paper high varnished panels or roofs for coaches, and all sorts of wheel carriages and sedan chairs, pannels for rooms, doors, and cabins of ships, cabinets, book-cases, screens, chimney-pieces, tables, tea-trays, and waiters, by pasting several papers upon boards or plates of regular thicknesses on each side the same until the thicknes required is attained; the edges are cut off or planed until the board or plate appears, and the papers taken off such board or plates are screwed or fastened on boards or plates, and are rendered inflexible by drying in a hot stove, while at the same time they are rubbed with or dipped in oil or varnish, which drenches into them, and secures them from damp, etc. The papers so made are worked in every respect like wood, and into articles such as tea-trays and dressing boxes. The articles may be coated with colour and oils sufficient to make the surface even, and are then japanned and high varnished.

(Gilbert 1996: 22)

A notice of auction of the effects of Thomas Jordan appeared in the *Daily Journal* for Saturday March 22, 1735, and emphasized the quality and range of exotic hardwoods Jordan had turned:

> To acquaint all Gentlemen, Merchants and others, Dealers in Tunbridge and Turnery Ware, that on Wednesday 9th April in Easter Week and the following days, will be sold by Auction, the Entire Stock in Trade of the late Eminent Mr Thomas Jordan, deceased, wholesale Turner, at his Dwelling-House, the Rose and Crown, Snow Hill consisting of very large and most agreeable choice of goods and Toys, in Ivory, Aligarzant, Lignum Vitae, Lemon, Cedar, Manchinele (a West Indian hardwood) Holly and other choice woods. As likewise in the Cabinet Trade fine Mahogany, Walnut-Tree, and other Bookcases, Buroes, Chest-Tables, Pier and Chimney-Glasses, Sconces etc, with a very large quantity of the above mentioned fine woods.
>
> (Burney Newspapers, British Library; *Daily Journal*, March 22, 1735)

The sale of the stock of the recently deceased chair and cabinetmaker Elijah Chupain, "eminent in his Profession for his many new and beautiful designs in the Cabinet way" advertised in the *London Daily Post and General Advertiser* July 27, 1739, from his premises in King Street, Bloomsbury, demonstrates the range of fashionable goods that Chupain supplied although there is no surviving documented record of sales during his lifetime. His stock included

> large Glass Sconces in carv'd and gilt frames, a large Quantity of Mahogany Walnut-tree and other Work; as fine Desks and Bookcases with Glass Doors. Mahogany and Walnut-Tree double Chests with a Desk in them or without: Quadrille Tables, fine Writing-Tables, Spring-Tables, dining, box, Night, Corner, Square and other Tables, a large quantity of Mahogany or Walnut Tree Chairs cover'd or uncovered.
>
> (Burney Newspapers, British Library; *London Daily Post and General Advertsier*, July 27, 1739)

In March 1743, the *Daily Advertiser* carried an advertisement for

> John Chamberlain, at his late Dwelling House the corner of Crown Court, Knave's Acre; consisting of Desks and Bookcases, Desks, Tables, Chests of Drawers, Cloaths Chests, Scrutoires etc in Walnut-Tree, Wainscoat and Mahogany: Pier and Chimney Glasses, Sconces, Chairs, Carpets, Standing Beds (space saving folding beds).with divers other Goods in the Cabinet, Chair and Upholstery Way.
>
> (Burney Newspapers, British Library; *Daily Advertiser*, March 4, 1743)

Cabinetmakers might add their trade card as a label affixed to the furniture they supplied or may have had a simpler, smaller label printed for that purpose. John Belchier who supplied Henry Purefoy with furniture used both in the 1730s. His small printed label was cut circular or square; the fuller label was headed by his shop sign the Sun read

> John Belchier/Cabbinet & Looking Glass-Maker, /at the Sun on the South-side of/St Pauls near Doc'trs – Commons /Grinds & Makes-up./ all sorts of fine Peer and Chim/ney-Glasses, and Glass Sconces,/Likewise all Cabbinet Makers Goods/N.B. Great choise of all Ready Made / at reasonable Rates.
>
> (Gilbert and Murdoch 1994: 68–70, figs. 3–5)

Alternatively, a maker might just affix a manuscript label such as that found on one of the interior drawers of a brass-inlaid padouk desk and bookcase in an English private collection which was inscribed "Antrobus/Fecit 1730." Such a signature might be found on a drawing or print so it is unusual to find such a simple autograph on furniture. The name is associated with Manchester, and a James Antrobus is recorded there in 1725—it is possible that he had migrated to London by 1730, but as yet no documentary evidence has emerged to prove this (Gilbert 1996: 17).

BILLS

Remarkable documentation preserved at Arundel Castle for the decoration of Norfolk House, the London home of the 9th Duke and Duchess of Norfolk, includes itemized bills indicating the cost of carving specific repertoires of ornament. A particular feature of this interior, demolished in 1938, is the paneled Music Room, which was the work of Jean Antoine Cuenot (d.1763) who was paid £2643 3s 8½d for his extensive work in the house between March 5, 1753, and February 24, 1756 (Murdoch 2006a: 54–5). The Music Room is preserved in the British Galleries at the Victoria and Albert Museum, and is entered through one of the original doorways from the Norfolk House Drawing Room. Another Drawing Room doorway is preserved in the Metropolitan Museum of Art, New York. The carving is so elaborate that the different elements were itemized separately. "Pieces of Mosaick with flowers a top" cost £2 1s 6d; the turning of "2 vauzes carv'd with four different ornaments" cost £3 10s; the "two Palm Trees for the tope of the Vauzes" (which no longer survive) cost £3 and the "four Monkies in different postures" cost £19 12s. The "4 large festoons of fruit & flowers supported by the Monkies measure 24 feet" cost £17 6s. Gilding all the ornaments and architraves of these two doorcases came to £31 16s alone. To match the monkey doorways, Cuenot supplied a table with "ornament cut through 3 heads, festoons of Drapery, & a Trophy with festoons of flowers & a Rail between the legs with a Monkey on it." The Chinese Looking Glass now in the York Bedroom, Arundel Castle, was originally made as a "Chimney Trumo Glass Frame" (with a painted panel below the glass in the same frame) for the duchess's Dressing Room at Norfolk House. For this Cuenot charged £8 14s. Three panels of looking glass are back-painted with Chinese pastoral scenes with cattle, sheep, and pigs to remind the Duchess of her farm at Worksop, Nottinghamshire. The glass was an appropriate addition to the "intirely Chinese" interior with its painted "Sattin or Taffity" hangings "in the most Beautiful India Pattern you can Imagine, Curtains & Chairs the same." Even the brass fender and sconces were described as Chinese. This exotic Western style was inspired by furnishings exported through the East India Company understood today as "chinoiserie." Cuenot supplied glass and silvered glass for mirrors. He made branches to support lamps for the hall and staircase that were carved, gilded, and lacquered, and carved two "illuminating lanthorns with an Eagle at the top of each," one of which features in a *Country Life* photograph of the Grand Staircase.

Cuenot also supplied furniture for the 9th Duke and Duchess of Norfolk's great house in Worksop, Nottinghamshire. The bills demonstrate the range of materials and techniques he had mastered. Although he primarily worked as a carver and gilder, Cuenot also supplied carving in ivory and cast work in brass, although he may have subcontracted such tasks. For the Worksop chapel Cuenot carved and gilded in "oyl gold a Tabernacle with 4 graddains & a Reposoir and 10 candlesticks" costing £28 10s. Cuenot supplied the ten nozzles, sockets, and pans for the candlesticks for £1 2s, ivory to lengthen the cross of the crucifix at 8s, and a brass cross 100 × 35.5 × 6.35 centimeters for £4 8s, which survived the Worksop fire of 1761 and is recorded in the chapel there in 1777. He also supplied a "Great table to have been prepar'd for burnish gold" for the Worksop Great Room for £18 17s. Such verbal description served as evidence for the patron's approval of costs incurred prior to settlement of Cuenot's accounts.

LEGAL DOCUMENTS

Auction notices of sales of stock in trade after decease provide insight into the range of furniture provided by the London cabinetmaking trade in the eighteenth century. More detail into business practice is provided by the witness of creditors to the executors of leading patron Ralph, 1st Duke of Montagu. In 1712 Thomas Pelletier of St. Paul's Covent Garden, carver and gilder, appeared before Montagu's executors to explain that his late father Jean Pelletier had provided Montagu with carvers and gilders' work (Murdoch 1998: 372–3). Thomas confirmed that "he lived with and helped his father in the trade from before 1688 until his death" and was privy to the entries made in his book of accounts, which was kept in French. Thomas's brother René, by then of St James's Westminster, who describes himself as engraver, was also living with his father in 1688. René

> did by his father's Direcion from time to time make Entries thereof in his father's Books of Accts & soone after his father's Death bespeak of his Brother Thomas Pelletier severall goods & Things belonging to the Trade of a Carver & Gilder and since his father's Death he has continued to live with his Brother and work at the trade and his Brother did doe severall Carvers and gilders work and finde at the Request and for the Service of the Late Duke severall materials used abt the works. And his Brother also employed him to keep and make entries in his Brothers books of acct of such work and materials And that all the goods and things sold work done and materials provided as well by his father as his Brother are set down. documented.and that he was privy to the doeing the work and finding the materials and Delivery of the greatest part of the goods and believes all the goods and things in the Bill were actually provided sold & delivered by his father and Brother for the use and by direction of the Duke. And that the prices are just and reasonable and as then usually had of other for the like And his father and Brother have at severall times received of the Duke several Sumes although there remained due to his Borther from the Duke's estate £1124.8. He has compared the Bill with the late Duke's Accot in the Book & they agree save only the Account in the Bill is entred in the Book in French and in the Bill in English into which it was translated by his Direcion both which Languages are so well understood by him that he knows by comparing them whether they agree.
>
> (Boughton House. Legal depositions to the Executors of
> Ralph, 1st Duke of Montagu, 1712)

Although the Pelletiers had left France as a Protestant family because of religious persecution, the brothers Thomas and René later fell out of partnership; René claimed that "because he was the best workman and had the Misfortune of not Understanding English" he minded "the work at home" and Thomas minded

> the business abroad wch mostly consisted in Buying up thos Materialls as were necessary to be Worked with & for supplying such psons as they were Employed by & to wait on such psons as had any work to be done as also to call in wt moneys were due to them for any work they had done or for what things they had supplied them with That Rene thinking that he could not rely upon any person better than on a Brother readily agreed the Same without Reducing the same in to Writing.
>
> (Boughton House. Legal depositions to the Executors of
> Ralph, 1st Duke of Montagu, 1712)

The partnership dissolved in March 1711. Thomas Pelletier developed a second career as a dealer and auctioneer and René led a more humble existence as a mounter or mat-maker.

Their brother-in-law was fellow Huguenot John Guilbaud whose trade label is preserved on a writing cabinet in the Geffrye Museum, London. He worked at "the Crown and Looking Glasse in Long Aker," Covent Garden and "Selleth all manner of Cabbinet work and Japan Cabbinets./Large Tables/ Small Suets, all maner of Looking Glasses/Pannells of Glasse/Chimneypeaces/ and all Sorts of Glasse Sconces" (Gilbert 1996: 32). Significantly the label is surmounted by a Royal crown: in 1690 Guilbaud had charged Queen Mary £30 for "two scriptors inlaid with flowers" and in 1691 supplied "a plain scriptoir" for Whitehall Palace (Beard and Gilbert 1978: s.v. "Guilliband, John").

The extensive use of French terms in furniture and furnishings in Europe in the eighteenth century demonstrates the huge debt due to immigrant craftsmen and designers who trained in France and then established their workshops abroad. Terms already mentioned include Birjair (bergere), a winged armchair of a type first introduced in 1725, but taken up by Mayhew and Ince from 1759 and Thomas Chippendale from 1773; Coins (encoignure), a corner cupboard; the French term used by Mayhew and Ince and the English derivation cited by Horace Walpole in his "Description of Strawberry Hill" 1782, where there is a "Coin of Old Japan" in the Gallery—referring to a corner cupboard veneered with Japanese lacquer. The term commode is also of French derivation, first introduced in 1708; it is Thomas Chippendale who takes up the term with his designs for Commode tables. It is rarely acknowledged that the use of the French term mirror (miroire) for looking glass only emerges in the early nineteenth century with Sheraton's 1803 *Cabinet Dictionary* (Edwards 1954: vol. 2, s.v. "Birjair, Coin, Commode and Mirror"). The range of documentary sources for furniture in the long eighteenth century is as varied as it is rich. Combining descriptions in inventories, bills, and advertisements with the vivid accounts of such furniture in use in the eighteenth-century novel provides the human presence needed to bring the furniture to life. With Lovelace we are permitted to look through the keyhole to witness Clarissa's straitened circumstances in those miserably furnished London lodgings, a vivid contrast to the lavish furnishings described in royal bills and aristocratic inventories.

NOTES

Chapter 1

1 Table, Pierre Gole, *c.* 1660 (1986.38.1). Print, Small Bouquets Tied With A Ribbon, Jean-Baptiste Monnoyer, 1656–99 (20.61.2 [21a–22b]); Rogers Fund, 1920, The Metropolitan Museum of Art.

2 It is well known that Antoine Watteau was in fact employed by Audran to paint some of the figures depicted on the paneling.

Chapter 2

1 Tortoiseshell is the common name given to the shell removed from the back carapace of three marine turtle species (hawksbill, green turtle, and loggerhead). No land tortoise was ever used for the manufacture of furniture. While most published works use the word tortoiseshell, the correct term should be turtleshell.

2 Boulle marquetry, also called *Tarsia a incastro* is a marquetry technique named after the eponymous cabinetmaker. The technique was developed for wood marquetry but it is better known as a technique applied to brass and turtleshell. André Charles Boulle (1642–1732) was not the inventor of the technique but his name became synonymous with it and, toward the end of the eighteenth century, his name became the common term for a marquetry of metal and turtleshell. Boulle marquetry was widely used and remained in fashion throughout the eighteenth century, primarily in France and Germany.

3 Mercury gilding: a process for gold plating in which an amalgam of mercury and gold is applied to an object and then exposed to heat to vaporize the mercury and leave the gold behind in a thin layer. Mercury gilding is also called fire gilding.

4 Maurice Cochot, *Mecanique proper a scier en feuilles le bois d'acajou, ou tout autre bois, brevet d'invention de 5 ans, pris le 7 Decembre 1814* (Sawmill to resaw mahogany or any other wood into thin sheets. Patent contracted on December 7, 1814 for 5 years). The date of 1799 is wrongly and repeatedly published in modern literature. The Cochot saw, in cast iron, is still in use today.

5 A somewhat obscure and ambiguous term that seems to have been used, at different times, for very different materials. Also known as *galuchat* and *chagrin*. The word,

along with its French and German equivalents, *chagrin*, is said to derive from the Persian expression *saghari*, which was applied to a leather produced from an ass, and which had an indented grain surface caused by spreading seeds of the common flowering plant goosefoot (*chenopodium*) over the surface of the moist skin, covering the skin with a cloth, and trampling them into the skin. When the skin was dry the seeds were shaken off, leaving the surface of the leather covered with small indentations.

In the seventeenth and early eighteenth centuries, however, the term "shagreen" (or "chagrin") began to be applied to a leather made from sharkskin having a curious grain surface of lozenge-shaped, raised, and spiny scales of minute size, the character of which is difficult to perceive without optical assistance. The term was also applied to the skin of a rayfish (probably Hypolophus sephen), which is covered with round, closely set, calcified papillae resembling small pearls. In its natural form it has been used for many years in both the East and the West for a variety of purposes, including bookbinding; however, in the early years of the eighteenth century it became the practice to grind the surface flat and smooth, leaving only the pattern of small contiguous circles. The leather was dyed from the flesh side so that the dye did not reach the small circles of calcified substance but only colored the epidermis where it could be seen between the circles. This is the leather that for a century has been called "shagreen"; how confusion arose with sharkskin, which is completely different both in character and in appearance, is not clear.

6   The most expensive cabinet ever bought by the royal court of France is a large cabinet acquired by Louis XVI from David Roentgen at the astronomical cost of 96,000 livres.

Chapter 3

1   However, this situation began to change precisely during this period. For a study of furniture in all French social classes, see Pardailhé-Galabrun (1988).
2   See Chapter 1, "Design and Motifs," in this volume.
3   For further details see, among others, Hayward (1965) and Kirkham and Weber (2013).
4   For a survey introduction to Québec's furniture, see Lessard (1999). The Conquest refers to the acquisition of the French North American colonies of Canada by Great Britain during the Seven Years War (1756–63).
5   Verlet makes a second distinction between furniture made by *menuisiers*, a profession resembling that of joiner or carpenter, and by *ébénistes*, cabinetmakers specialized in veneered furniture. This division relates to fabrication techniques and will not be discussed here.
6   This is the case of certain seats, writing tables, cabinets, and screens, for instance.
7   The French word *meuble* refers to something that can be moved (usually a piece of furniture), in contrast to the word *immeuble* defined as an entity that cannot be moved, very often a building.
8   Regarding this ritual see, among others, Hellman (1999) and Chrisman-Campbell (2011).
9   The "public toilette," during which women basically put the final touches to their beauty routine, was in fact preceded by an initial, and entirely private, toilette.
10   Bookcases integrated to the paneling will not be addressed here.
11   My translation from the French original "Les filles ont besoin d'être formées dès leur plus jeune âge à ce maintien calme et posé, qui sert à la fois la modestie et les grâces."

12 Regarding the consumption of tea, coffee, and chocolate in France, see Herda-Mousseaux (2015).

13 The term *rafraîchissoir* also refers to a basin of porcelain or metal with an indented rim used to suspend drinking glasses in cool water.

Chapter 4

1 The glossary of *Noble Households* (Murdoch 2006b) lists no fewer than twenty-two different wool-based textiles, in addition to numerous cottons linens, silks, and blends. Familiarity with different timbers seems also to have been commonplace, suggesting a wider ability to discern subtle differences between similar materials.

2 These changes are described more fully by Girouard (1978, 2000).

3 "For the past twenty years economic and social historians have been emphasizing how propertied households throughout postmedieval northwestern Europe gave increasing priority in their consumption patterns to domestic enhancements that provided more privacy, cleanliness, warmth, and light. Historians usually label these enhancements 'comfort' and, by a questionable circularity, often point to the desire for comfort as an explanation for their development" (Crowley 2000: ix). For an exploration of the historiography of privacy, see Orlin (2007: 9).

4 See Hannah Greig's discussion of the way that Anne, Countess of Strafford chose furnishings for her new London home (2013: 41–4).

5 Tinniswood 1998: 88, quoting from Robert Harley, "Journeys in England," HMC report Portland MSS VI 1901, p. 161.

6 This description of the bed is taken from a letter written by Lady Marow to her daughter Lady Kay, August 26, 1708, who saw it displayed in London, quoted in *Historical Manuscripts Commission Dartmouth Papers*, vol. 3 (1896): 146–7.

7 See for example the trade card of the London upholsterer, Christopher Gibson (VAM 14435–60) illustrated in Beard (1997: plate 195). The card depicts the interior of an idealized upholsterer's shop displaying, among other things, numerous chairs, a canopied bed, a looking glass in a carved frame with candle sconces, bolts of fabric, and heraldic hatchments. There were lots of things to buy here.

8 Rijksmuseum, BK-16903-A&B, *c.* 1770 (Rijksmuseum n.d.); J. Paul Getty Museum, 2004.58, cast iron fireback, French, 1703–25.

Chapter 5

1 The figure of Bacchus was also carved by Adye, whose bill of fifteen guineas (for the casket alone) was settled by the society's secretary on May 1, 1737. The cabinetmaker Christopher Fuhrlohg, to whom it is attributed by Redford (2008: fig. 4, caption), was responsible for completing the rear face of the box in 1780, amid other repairs to the club's regalia (see Hayward 1977: 486, 489).

2 For a view of the life-drawing room (captioned "Teken Zaal / Salle de Dessin"), see the engraving by Reinier Vinkeles and Daniel Vrydag after Pieter Barbiers II and Jacques Kuyper, published in Amsterdam in 1794, of which an impression is held at the Metropolitan Museum of Art, New York, 47.100.270.

3 Two side chairs stamped by Louis Delanois, likely from a different set than the lecturer's armchair pictured in Claude-René-Gabriel Poulleau's engraving and among 21 chaises "pied de biche" recorded at the Ecole in 1911, were sold at Christie's London on June 1, 2020, lot 66.

4 The cases could also be unlocked, per an inventory taken on March 18, 1766, describing statues in "nichj serrati con cristalli, che s'aprono, e chiudono con chiave,

e chiavatura, e che si girano sopra di un perno onde possano voltarsi da tute le parti, ed osservarsi" (Archivio di Stato di Bologna, Assunteria di Istituto, Diversorum, busta 10, no. 2 (bis), "Statue anatomiche in cera formate da Ercole Lelli").

5   In recounting Pius's inspection visit to Valadier's studio, Cracas's *Diario Ordinario* no. 710 (October 20, 1781): 6, described the cabinets as "lavorati di un gusto particolare, e impelliciati di vari legni della Cina, cioè Angelino [perhaps *Andira inermis*, native to Guyana, Brazil, and the West Indies and also known as 'partridge wood' or 'cabbage bark'], e Sandalo rosso [perhaps *Pterocarpus sandalinus*, indigenous to southern India], con suoi piedi, o siano zampe intagliate sul gusto antico."

6   Moreau's drawing was engraved by Jean-Baptiste Patas for the *Troisième suite d'estampes pour servir à l'histoire des mœurs et du costume des François dans le dix-huitième siècle* (Paris, 1783) and republished in 1789 as "La debutante en petite loge" in the *Monument du costume physique et moral de la fin du dix-huitième siècle*. Whereas the original text narrates this as a scene of seduction, the later edition, with a new text by novelist Restif de La Bretonne, recasts it as the story of a generous prince who educates and arranges a good marriage for a young beggar-girl.

7   I am grateful to Patricia Díaz Cayeros for her expertise and generous assistance with obtaining photography.

8   For a finished drawing of de Wailly's second, executed project, see Cooper-Hewitt, Smithsonian Design Museum, 1911-28-293.

9   See, for instance, Isidore-Stanislaus Helman and Charles Monnet, *The Opening of the Estates General 5 May 1789 in the Salle des Menus Plaisirs in Versailles* (Bibliothèque nationale de France, RESERVE QB-370 (9)-FT 4).

10 See, for instance, a Régence-style *bureau plat* of *c.* 1725 in ebony veneer and ebonized wood, bearing this stamp, sold at Sotheby's New York, October 13–14, 2016, lot 249.

11 Lefuel (1923: 346) and Ledoux-Lebard (1984: 284) identify mahogany chairs with Jacob's stamp at the Archives Nationales with those supplied for the National Convention, while Samoyault (2009: 25) judges the archival descriptions too vague for precise identification. For a well-known sheet with five related chair designs, sometimes attributed to Percier, see Ledoux-Lebard (1984: 283) and Samoyault (2009: 25–8, fig. 25).

12 Versions of the "Corvisart" armchair bearing Jacob's stamp as used until at least 1796 have been sold at Beaussant Lefèvre, April 19, 2016, lot 52, and Sotheby's Paris, December 11, 2019, lot 32; an example bearing the stamp used from 1796–1803 was sold at Sotheby's London, May 3, 2012, lot 59. For a chair of identical form stamped by Jean-Baptistie-Claude Sené (1747–1803), who also supplied furniture to the Directory and its officials, see Ledoux-Lebard (1984: 578, illustrated). An identical chair appears in Louis-Léopold Boilly's portrait of the composer François-Adrien Boieldieu, shown in the Salon of 1800 (Museum of Fine Arts of Rouen, accession no. 1905.1.1).

Chapter 6

1   Paris, Archives nationales, Minutier central des notaires parisiens, Etude LXIII, 617, July 28, 1710.

2   Paris, Archives nationales, Minutier central des notaires parisiens, Etude XIV, 255, March 16, 1722.

3   Paris, Archives nationales, Minutier central des notaires parisiens, Etude I, 380, October 12, 1736.

4   Paris, Archives nationales, Minutier central des notaires parisiens, Etude XXX, 278, May 30, 1740.

5   Paris, Archives nationales, Minutier central des notaires parisiens, Etude LX, 327, October 24, 1759.

6   Paris, Archives nationales, Minutier central des notaires parisiens, Etude XXIX, 529, March 25, 1766.

7   Paris, Archives nationales, Minutier central des notaires parisiens, Etude LXXXIV, 546, October 18, 1776.

8   Paris, Archives nationales, Minutier central des notaires parisiens, Etude LVII, 529, July 27, 1776.

9   Paris, Archives nationales, Minutier central des notaires parisiens, Etude LV, 67, August 31, 1785.

10 Paris, Archives nationales, Minutier central des notaires parisiens, Etude LVIII, 547b, December 16, 1791.

11 Reported on March 4, 1748, Lugt no. 682.

12 "Ce n'est pas sans raison que l'on peut mettre certains meubles & certains Bijoux de nos jours au rang des choses curieuses. Le goût est devenu si délicat en France, que l'on ne veut rien que de distingué & de parfait. Dans les moindres ouvrages, les artistes, par émulation, renchérissent journellement les uns fur les autres, tant du côté de l'imagination & de la variété, que de celui de l'exécution la plus scrupuleuse."

13 March 2, 1756, Lugt no. 910.

14 March 30, 1767, Lugt no. 1603.

15 "porcelaines de qualité supérieures [...], anciens laques, riches meubles de Boule, & bijoux."

16 February 27, 1777, Lugt no. 2652.

17 December 10, 1776, Lugt no. 2616.

18 One should note that an editorial incoherence in the title at the top of the page suddenly makes room for the mention of "meubles curieux" at the start of page 207.

19 February 18, 1793, Lugt no. 5005.

20 July 31, 1797, Lugt no. 5643.

21 The information supplied by Hébert's guide are punctiliously completed by that which is in the inventory, cf. infra.

22 Paris, Archives nationales, Minutier central des notaires parisiens, Etude LXXXIV, 546, October 18, 1776 et vente du February 27, 1777, Lugt no. 2652, lot no. 818.

23 April 22, 1784, Lugt no. 3411.

24 Choiseul-Praslin sale, February 18, 1793, Lugt no. 5005.

25 Paris, Musée du Louvre, département des objets d'art, OA 5448–4559.

26 La Live de Jully Sale, March 5, 1770, Lugt no. 1805, lot no. 261; Randon de Boisset Sale, February 27, 1777, Lugt no. 2652, lot no. 788; vente Saint-Julien, June 21, 1784, Lugt no. 3749, lot no. 185. Mentioned in the same way in the sales of Randon de Boisset and Saint Julien.

27 Choiseul-Praslin Sale, February 18, 1793, Lugt no. 5005, lot no. 250.

28 Aumont Sale, December 12, 1782, Lugt no. 3488, lot no. 335.

29 Aumont Sale, December 12, 1782, Lugt no. 3488, lot no. 312.

30 Inventory following the decease of Laurent Grimod de La Reynière, Arch. nat., Min. cent. XX1, 630, 22 germinal An II.

31 Angran de Fonspertuis Sale, March 4, 1748, Lugt no. 682, lot no. 614.

32 Inventory following the decease of Jean de Jullienne, Arch. nat., Min. cent. XXIX, 529, March 25, 1766.

33 Vente Boucher, February 18, 1771, Lugt no. 1895, lot no. 1863.

34 Day-book of Lazare Duvaux, 1753, no. 1454.

35 Day-book of Lazare Duvaux, 1756, no. 2425.

36 *Les laques du Japon, collections de Marie-Antoinette*, Versailles, Musée national des châteaux de Versailles et de Trianon, October 15, 2001–January 7, 2002.

37 Aumont Sale, December 12, 1782, Lugt no. 3488, lot no. 318.

38 Most probably Jean Martin Pelletier, sculptor active in Paris on several major building projects during the years 1720 to 1740, among which the hôtel Bonnier de La Mosson.

39 Bonnier de La Mosson Sale, March 8, 1745, Lugt no. 614, lot no. 939.

40 Inventory following the derath of Renaud César Louis de Choiseul, duc de Praslin, Arch. nat., Min. cent. LVIII, 547b, December 16, 1791.

41 Vente mobilière, Arch. nat., Min. cent. LXXI, 80, September 7, 1787.

42 Inventory following the decease of la Comtesse de Verrue, Arch. nat., Min. cent. 1, 380, October 12, 1736.

43 Vente Tallard, March 22, 1756, Lugt no. 910, lot no. 1010.

44 Vente Blondel de Gagny, December 10, 1776, Lugt no. 2616, lot no. 940.

45 Vente Tallard, March 22, 1756, Lugt no. 910, lot no. 1014.

46 *Splendeurs de la cour de Saxe*, Versailles, Musée national des châteaux de Versailles et de Trianon, on several major projects, January 23–April 23, 2006.

47 *Pracht und Zeremoniell. Die Möbel der Residenz München*, Munich, Residenzmuseum, September 7, 2002–January 6, 2003; Langer 1995.

48 *Friedrich der Grosse. Sammler und Mäzen*, Munich, Kunsthalle, November 28, 1992–February 28, 1993.

49 *Catherine la Grande. Un art pour l'Empire*, Toronto, Musée des Beaux-Arts de l'Ontario, October 1, 2005–January 1, 2006, and Montréal, Musée des Beaux-Arts, February 2–May 7, 2006.

50 *Quand Versailles était meublé d'argent*, Versailles, Musée national des châteaux de Versailles et de Trianon, November 21, 2007–March 9, 2008.

51 *Art of the Royal Court*, The Metropolitan Museum of Art, New York, July 1–September 21, 2008.

52 *William Kent*, Bard Graduate Center, New York, September 20, 2013–February 16, 2014; Victoria and Albert Museum, London, March 22–July 13, 2014.

53 *Houghton Revisited*, Houghton Hall, May 17–September 19, 2013.

54 *James "Athenian" Stuart, 1713–1788*, Victoria and Albert Museum, London; Bard Graduate Center, New York, November 16, 2006–February 11, 2007; London, Victoria and Albert Museum, March 15–June 24, 2007.

55 *Horace Walpole's Strawberry Hill*, Victoria and Albert Museum, London, March 6–July 4, 2010.

56 *Carlton House, the Past Glories of Georges IV's Palace*, The Queen's Gallery, Buckingham Palace, London, 1991–2; Roberts 2001.

57 Walpole was not wrong when he declared, with reference to the palace's décor, "though probably borrowed from the Hôtel de Condé, and other palaces, not one that is not rather classic than French" (cited in Wilton-Ely 2011: 12).

Chapter 8

1   *Mercure de France*, chez Guillaume Cavelier, ruë S. Jacques, la veuve Pissot, Quai de Conty, à la descente du Pont-Neuf, Jean de Nully, au Palais, May 1740, Lettre II, pp. 877–82.

2   *Mercure de France*, A Paris, chez Guillaume Cavelier, Au Palais, Guillaume Cavelier, fils, ruë S. Jacques, au Lys d'Or, Noel Pissot, Quai des Augustins, à la descente du Pont-neuf, à la Croix d'Or, May 1726, p. 990.

3   *Mercure de France*, A Paris, chez Guillaume Cavelier, Au Palais, Guillaume Cavelier, fils, ruë S. Jacques, au Lys d'Or, Noel Pissot, Quai des Augustins, à la descente du Pont-neuf, à la Croix d'Or, May 1726, pp. 990–3.

4   *Mercure de France*, A Paris, chez Guillaume Cavelier, ruë S. Jacques, la veuve Pissot, Quai de Conty, à la descente du Pont-Neuf, Jean de Nully, au Palais, December 1734, vol. 1, pp. 2684–6.

5   *Mercure de France*, chez Guillaume Cavelier, ruë S. Jacques, la veuve Pissot, Quai de Conty, à la descente du Pont-Neuf, Jean de Nully, au Palais, July 1736, pp. 1692–4.

6   In these variations on plate XII the third example on the right of the folio, one recognizes one of the models of by of the most famous English cabinetmakers, who was widely reproduced by his contemporaries, as the evidence shows, for example, with a chair preserved in the Victoria and Albert Museum (anonymous, after Thomas Chippendale's model, *Chair*, between 1755 and 1770, mahogany, W.67–1940).

7   For example, twelve plates in the *Livre de Cartouches*, after François Boucher, are indicated in six books, the *Livre d'Animaux* after Jean Baptiste Oudry, called *Cayer de 12 fables d'Oudry*, bound for three livres twelve sols, or two series of *Divers Ornemens* after Alexis Peyrotte, for seven livres four sols. All these plates had been sold by Gabriel Huquier, as the adresses and the catalog of his resources suggest (Paris, Bibliothèque nationale de France, Res V 1456; [Huquier] 1757).

8   The interesting aspect of this volume derives from its very compilation. It is not a case of being a nineteenth-century edition, as often happens, but definitely a collection compiled in the eighteenth century, as the inscriptions in brown ink, which correspond with this period, confirm (Decrossas 2013: 53–8).

9   Thirty-one booklets numbered from 1st to 31st with six plates each, more numbered "1" to "186": plates representing beds, seats, bathtubs, candlestands, screens, chests o' drawers, writing desks, corner cupboards, bureaus, stands, pedestals, tables and brackets, bookcases, work tables, filing cabinets, coffers, fireplaces, glass doors, cupboard doors, room (to differentiate with other doors, I assume) doors, paneling (*Boucher fil. inv. A Paris chés Le Pere et Avaulez M.ds d'Estampes rue S.t Jacques a la Ville de Rouen.* [*c.* 1777]. Paris, Bibl. INHA, coll. J. Doucet, Fol Res 79 (1), ff. 61–246 [recueils factice]).

10   *Mercure de France*, A Paris, chez Guillaume Cavelier, Au Palais, Guillaume Cavelier, fils, ruë S. Jacques, au Lys d'Or, Noel Pissot, Quai des Augustins, à adescente du Pont-neuf, à la Croix d'Or, January 1726, pp. 7–8.

11   For example the *Livre de douze feüilles de Trophées*, published by Huquier, whose notice precisely stated that "Le grand débit qu'il s'en fait, prouve l'excellence de la composition [the large outlay that he made is proof if the excellence of the composition]." *Mercure de France*, chez Guillaume Cavelier, ruë S. Jacques, la veuve Pissot, Quai de Conty, à la descente du Pont-Neuf, Jean de Nully, au Palais, February 1735, p. 341.

12   *Mercure de France*, chez Guillaume Cavelier, ruë S. Jacques, la veuve Pissot, Quai de Conty, à la descente du Pont-Neuf, Jean de Nully, au Palais, April 1736, pp. 757–8.

13   *Mercure de France*, chez Guillaume Cavelier, ruë S. Jacques, la veuve Pissot, Quai de Conty, à la descente du Pont-Neuf, Jean de Nully, au Palais, July 1745, pp. 127–9.

14 *Mercure de France*, A Paris, chez Chaubert, rue du Hurepoix, Jean de Nully, au Palais, Pissot, Quai de Conty, Duchesne, rue Saint Jacques, Cailleau, quai des Augustins, June 1756, pp. 176–7.

15 *Mercure de France*, A Paris, chez Chaubert, rue du Hurepoix, Jean de Nully, au Palais, Pissot, Quai de Conty, Duchesne, rue Saint Jacques, Cailleau, quai des Augustins, April 1756, vol. 1, p. 214.

16 *Gazette de France*, A Paris, De l'imprimerie de la Gazette de France, no. 19, Du Vendredi, March 6, 1789, p. 94.

17 *Mercure de France*, chez Guillaume Cavelier, ruë S. Jacques, la veuve Pissot, Quai de Conty, à la descente du Pont-Neuf, Jean de Nully, au Palais, April 1737, pp. 765–6.

18 On this subject, see Le Bitouzé (1986).

19 Paris, Bibl. INHA, coll. J. Doucet, 4 Est 420 (1) et (2).

20 The title of the magazine changed in the passage of time: firstly *Cabinet des Modes, ou les Modes nouvelles, Décrites d'une manière claire et précise, et représentées par des Planches en Taille-douce, enluminées*, in 1786 it became *Magasin des Modes nouvelles, françaises et anglaises*, then at the beginning of 1789, *Journal de la Mode et du Goût*.

21 Sébastien-Antoine (1695–1754) and Paul-Ambroise (1702–58) Slodtz often worked in partnership for the Menus-Plaisirs du Roi producing designs for decorations for public events such as official celebrations and state funerals. Among the designs are ones for furniture. Their younger brother, René-Michel or Michelange (1705–64) became Dessinateur de la Chambre et du Cabinet du Roi.

Chapter 9

1 A copy of Langlois's Trade Card is in the Heal Collection, Department of Prints and Drawings, British Museum.

2 All mention of Langlois in the correspondence of the Lennox sisters is cited by Thornton and Rieder (1971: 283–6). See also Tillyard (1995).

3 Clive D.Edwards, Eighteenth-century furniture, Manchester University Press, 1996, pp. 180–181

BIBLIOGRAPHY

PRIMARY SOURCES

Delamair, Pierre Alexis (1737), *La pure vérité. Ouvrage d'architecture en forme de requeste au Roy* …. Paris: Bibliothèque nationale de France, Arsenal, MS 3054.
Grosvenor Family Archive, Chester
    9/278: correspondence between Porden and Lord Grosvenor
Kedleston Hall, Derbyshire (National Trust)
    109264: Adam's design for the house's Dining Room sideboard
    109450: Adam's design for the house's Dining Room sideboard
Lewis Walpole Library, Farmington, CT
    49 2615: Walpole's *Books of Materials*
    49 3582: *A Description of the Villa of Horace* Walpole, 1784—Walpole's extra-illustrated copy
    771.11.01.02+: S. Hooper, *A common council man of Candlestick Ward and his wife on a visit to Mr. Deputy at his modern built villa near Clapham*, 1771
    789.00.00.73dr++: *The Tribune at Strawberry Hill by John Carter*, c. 1789
Metropolitan Museum of Art, New York
    20.40.1: Thomas Chippendale's sketches for the *Director*'s plates
    20.40.2: Thomas Chippendale's sketches for the *Director*'s plates
    38.37.24: Gillows' design for a chair for Lord Grosvenor's Dining Room
    38.37.25: Gillows' design for a chair for Lord Grosvenor's Drawing Room
Sir John Soane Museum, London
    Adam Volume 11: Robert Adam's designs for architecture, interiors and furniture
    Adam Volume 12: Robert Adam's designs for architecture, interiors and furniture
    Adam Volume 14: Robert Adam's designs for architecture, interiors and furniture
    Adam Volume 17: Robert Adam's designs for architecture, interiors and furniture
    Adam Volume 20: Robert Adam's designs for architecture, interiors and furniture
    Adam Volume 50: Robert Adam's designs for architecture, interiors and furniture
    Adam Volume 57: Robert Adam's designs for architecture, interiors and furniture
Victoria and Albert Museum, London
    2553: Matthias Lock's design for a girandole

2848:88: Matthias Lock's design for a girandole
2848:98: Matthias Lock's design for a pair of pier tables (Rococo, upper, and
   "Palladian," lower)
E.93-1929: John Linnell's design for an arm chair
E.148-1929: John Linnell's design for a bed
E.165-1929: John Linnell's design for a pier glass
E.168-1929: John Linnell's design for a pier glass
E.187-1929: John Linnell's design for a pier glass
E.202-1929: John Linnell's design for a pier glass and pier table
E.205-1929: John Linnell's design for a pier glass
E.220-1929: John Linnell's design for a pier glass
E.221-1929: John Linnell's design for a pier glass
York Minster Library, York
YM/F1140: William Kent's designs for the Minster's furniture
YM/F239: William Kent's designs for the Minster's furniture

SECONDARY SOURCES

Académie Française (1694), *Le Dictionnaire de l'Académie Françoise, dédié au Roy*.
   Paris: Vve de J.B. Coignard.
Adam, Robert (1764), *Ruins of the Palace of the Emperor Diocletian at Spalatro in
   Dalmatia*. London: Printed for the Author.
Alcorn, Eleanor M. (1993), *English Silver in the Museum of Fine Arts, Boston*, 2 vols.
   Boston: Museum of Fine Arts.
Alcouffe, Daniel, et al. (2015), *Eighteenth Century: The Birth of Design*. Dijon: Faton.
Aldington, Richard, trans. (1927), *Letters of Voltaire and Frederick the Great*.
   New York: Brentano's.
Archenholz, Johann Wilhelm von (1789), *A Picture of England, Containing a
   Description of the Laws, Customs, and Manners of England*, 2 vols. London:
   Edward Jeffery.
Arminjon, Catherine and Béatrice Saule, eds. (1994), *Tables royales et festins de cour
   en Europe 1661–1789*. Paris: École du Louvre.
Atterbury, Paul, ed. (1995), *A.W.N. Pugin: Master of Gothic Revival*. New Haven,
   CT: Published for the Bard Graduate Center for Studies in the Decorative Arts,
   New York, by Yale University Press.
Augarde, Jean-Dominique (1985), "Historique et signification de l' estampille des
   meubles," *L'Estampille*, (June): 52–7.
Augarde, J.D. and J.N. Ronfort (1991), "Le Maître du Bureau de L'Electeur,"
   L'Estampille, (January): 42–75.
Austen, Jane with P. Hughes-Hallett and E. Drury (1990), *My Dear Cassandra, The
   Illustrated Letters of Jane Austen*. London: Pavillion Books.
Ayres, James (2003), *Domestic Interiors: The British Tradition 1500–1850*. New Haven
   and London: Yale University Press.
Baarsen, Reinier (2006), *Nederlandse kunst in het Rijksmuseum 1700–1800*. Zwolle:
   Waanders.
Baarsen, Reinier (2007), "Sculptor and Chairmaker? Throne Chairs from the
   Workshop of Jan Baptist Xavery," *Furniture History*, 43: 101–13.
Baarsen, Reinier (2008), "Rococo in Holland: The Assimilation of a Foreign Style."
   In Sarah D. Coffin, Gail S. Davidson, Ellen Lupton, and Penelope Hunter-Stiebel

(eds.), *Rococo: The Continuing Curve, 1730–2008*, 150–67. New York: Cooper-Hewitt, National Design Museum.

Barnard, Toby (2004), *Making the Grand Figure: Lives and Possessions in Ireland, 1641–1770*. New Haven and London: Yale University Press.

Baulez, Christian (1991), "Deux Sièges de Foliot et de Sené pour Versailles," *La Revue du Louvre et des Musées de France*, 41 (March): 76–81.

Baulez, Christian (2007a), "Life in the Hall of Mirrors from the 18th Century to the Present Day." In *The Hall of Mirrors: History & Restoration*, 74–83. Dijon: Faton.

Baulez, Christian (2007b), "The 'Grande Galerie' and its Furnishings from Louis XIV to the Present Day." In *The Hall of Mirrors: History & Restoration*, 84–95. Dijon: Faton.

Beard, Geoffrey (1997), *Upholsterers and Interior Furnishing in England 1530–1840*. New Haven and London: Yale University Press.

Beard, Geoffrey and Christopher Gilbert (1978), *Dictionary of English Furniture Makers 1660–1840*. Leeds: Maney & Son.

Bedel, Jean (1996), *Le grand guide des styles*. Paris: Hachette.

Ben-Ur, Aviva (2007), "Peripheral Inclusion: Communal Belonging in Suriname's Jewish Community." In Alexandra Cuffel and Brian Britt (eds.), *Religion, Gender, and Culture in the Pre-Modern World*, 185–210. New York: Palgrave Macmillan.

Berg, Maxine (2005), *Luxury and Pleasure in Eighteenth-Century Britain*. Oxford: Oxford University Press.

Bevington, Michael (1995), *Stowe: the Garden and the Park*, 2nd edn. Stowe, UK: Capability.

Blakemore, Robbie G. (2006), *History of Interior Design and Furniture. From Ancient Egypt to Nineteenth-Century Europe*, 2nd edn. Hoboken, NJ: John Wiley & Sons.

Blondel, Jacques-François (1737–8), *De la distribution des maisons de plaisance et de la décoration des édifices en general*. Paris: Charles-Antoine Joubert.

Blondel, Jacques François ([1771] 2002), *Cours d'Architecture*, edited by Jean-Marie Pérouse de Montclos, vol. 1. Paris: Édition du patrimoine-Phénix éditions.

Blondel, Jacques François (1774), *L'Homme du Monde éclairé par les Arts; par M. Blondel, Architectes du Roi, Professeur Royal au Louvre, Membre de l'Académie d'Architecture publié par M. de Bastide, t. II, A Amsterdam; Et se trouve à Paris Chez Monory, Libraire de S.A.S Monseigneur le Prince de Condé, rue & vis-à-vis de la Comédie Française*. Amsterdam: Monory.

Boithias, J.L. and M. Brignon (1985), *Les Scieries et les Anciens Sagards des Vosges*. Creer.

Bond, Francis (1910), *Wood Carvings in English Churches*, vol. 2: I, *Stalls and Tabernacle Work*; II, *Bishops' Thrones and Chancel Chairs*. London: Henry Frowde.

Bouzin, Claude (2000), *Dictionnaire du meuble*. Paris: Éditions Charles Massin.

Bowett, Adam (1999), "The Mahogany Pulpit, Reredos and Altar Table at St George's Bloomsbury," *Georgian Group Journal*, 9: 166–75.

Bowett, Adam (2002), *English Furniture, 1660–1714 from Charles II to Queen Anne*. Woodbridge, UK: Antique Collectors' Club.

Bowett, Adam (2005), "George I's Coronation Throne," *Apollo*, 161 (515) (January): 42–7.

Bowett, Adam (2012), *Woods in British Furniture-Making, 1400–1900: An Illustrated Historical Dictionary*. Kew, UK: Oblong Creative in association with the Royal Botanic Gardens.

Bowron, Edgar Peters and Joseph J. Rishel, eds. (2000), *Art in Rome in the Eighteenth Century*. Philadelphia: Philadelphia Museum of Art.

Boynton, Lindsay and Nicholas Goodison (1969a), "The Furniture of Thomas Chippendale at Nostell Priory—I," *Burlington Magazine*, 111: 281–5.

Boynton, Lindsay and Nicholas Goodison (1969b), "The Furniture of Thomas Chippendale at Nostell Priory—II," *Burlington Magazine*, 111: 351–60.

Brasbridge, Joseph (1824), *The Fruits of Experience; or, Memoir of Joseph Brasbridge, Written in his 80th and 81st Years*, 2nd edn. London: for the author.

Braudel, Fernand (2002), *Civilization and Capitalism 15th–18th Century*, vol. 1, *The Structure of Everyday Life*. London: Weidenfeld & Nicolson.

Bremer-David, Charissa, ed. (2011), *Paris: Life and Luxury in the Eighteenth Century*. Los Angeles: Getty Publications.

Brewer, John (1997), *The Pleasures of the Imagination: English Culture in the Eighteenth Century*. London: HarperCollins Publishers.

Bristol, Kerry (2006), "James Stuart, the Admiralty, and the Royal Hospital for Seamen at Greenwich." In Susan Weber (ed.), *James "Athenian" Stuart, 1713–1788: The Rediscovery of Antiquity*, 354–83. New Haven, CT: Yale University Press for the Bard Graduate Center for Studies in the Decorative Arts Design and Culture.

Brunel, Georges, ed. (1976), *Piranèse et les français*. Rome: Edizioni dell'Elefante.

Burney, Charles (1771), *The Present State of Music in France and Italy*. London: T. Becket and Co.

Buxton, David (1981), *The Wooden Churches of Eastern Europe: An Introductory Survey*. Cambridge: Cambridge University Press.

Campan, Madame (1824), *De l'éducation*, vol. 1. Paris: Baudoin Frères.

Campbell, Thomas P., ed. (2007), *Tapestry in the Baroque: Threads of Splendor*. New York: Metropolitan Museum of Art.

Casey, Christine and Conor Lucey, eds. (2012), *Decorative Plasterwork in Ireland and Europe: Ornament and the Early Modern Interior*. Dublin: Four Courts Press.

Castelluccio, S. (2007), *Les meubles de pierres dures de Louis XIV et l'atelier des Gobelins*. Paris.

Chambers, Sir William (1757), *Designs of Chinese Buildings, Furniture, Dresses, Machines and Utensils*. London: Printed for the Author.

Chambers, Sir William (1791), *A Treatise on the Decorative Part of Civil Architecture*. London: Printed by Joseph Smeeton.

Chartier, Roger, ed. (1989), *A History of Private Life*, vol. 3, *Passions of the Renaissance*. Cambridge, MA: Harvard University Press.

Chastang, Yannick (2007), "Louis Tessier's 'Livre de Principe des Fleurs' and the Eighteenth-Century Marqueteur," *Furniture History*, 43: 115–26.

Chastang, Yannick (2008), *French Marquetry Furniture: Painting in Wood*. London: The Wallace Collection.

Chastang, Yannick (forthcoming), "The Conservation of a Coffer on Stand by A.C. Boulle from the Lewis Walpole Library."

Chippendale, Thomas (1754, 1755, and 1762), *The Gentleman and Cabinet-maker's Director*, 3rd edn. London: For the author.

Chippendale, Thomas (1762), *Le guide du tapissier, de l'ébéniste, et de tous ceux qui travaillent en meubles; comme aussi celui des honnêtes-gens qui en font faire: ouvrage*

qui consiste en un ample recueil de desseins des meubles les plus utiles & les plus
élégans, dans le gout gothique, chinois & moderne [...] Par Thomas Chippendale,
tapissier & ebeniste, dans St. Martin's Lane, rev. 3rd edn. London: T. Becket & P. A.
De Hondt, the Strand.

Chrisman-Campbell, Kimberly (2011), "Dressing to Impress: The Morning Toilette
and the Fabrication of Feminity." In Charissa Bremer-David (ed.), *Paris: Life and
Luxury in the Eighteenth Century*, 53–74. Los Angeles: J. Paul Getty Museum.

Christie's London (2005), The Wildenstein Collection, December 14–15.

Christie's London (2007), *Dumfries House*, July 12–13.

Clark, Peter (2000), *British Clubs and Societies 1580–1800: The Origins of an
Associational World*. Oxford: Clarendon Press.

Clayton, Antony (2003), *London's Coffee Houses: A Stimulating Story*. London:
Historical Publications.

Clifford, Helen (2004), *Silver in London: The Parker and Wakelin Partnership, 1760–1776*.
New Haven, CT: Yale University Press for the Bard Graduate Center.

Collins, Jeffrey (2004), *Papacy and Politics in Eighteenth-Century Rome: Pius VI and
the Arts*. New York: Cambridge University Press.

Collins, Jeffrey (2013), "Europe, 1600–1750." In Pat Kirkham and Susan Weber (eds.),
History of Design: Decorative Arts and Material Culture 1400–2000, 230–67. New
Haven, CT: Yale University Press for Bard Graduate Center.

Collins, Jeffrey (2016), "Pedagogy in Plaster: Ercole Lelli and Benedict XIV's
Gipsoteca at Bologna's Instituto delle Scienze e delle Arti." In Rebecca
Messbarger, Christopher M.S. Johns, and Philip Gavitt (eds.), *Benedict XIV and
the Enlightenment: Art, Science, and Spirituality*, 391–418. Toronto: University of
Toronto Press.

Collins, Jeffrey (2019), "Sites and Sightseers: Rome through Foreign Eyes." In Simon
Ditchfield, Pamela M. Jones, and Barbara Wisch (eds.), *A Companion to Early
Modern Rome, 1492–1692*, 564–81. Leiden and London: Brill.

Colvin, Howard (2009), "Henry Flitcroft, William Kent and Shobdon Church,
Herefordshire." In David Jones and Sam McKinstry (eds.), *Essays in Scots
and English Architectural History: A Festschrift in Honour of John Frew*, 1–8.
Donington: Shaun Tyas.

Conroy, David W. (1995), *In Public Houses: Drink and the Revolution of Authority in
Colonial Massachusetts*. Chapel Hill: University of North Carolina Press, for the
Institute for Early American History and Culture, Williamsburg.

Cornille, F. (*c*. 1740–55), *Liv. 5. [Recueil de plans et élévations], dessiné par F.
Cornille. Monchelet sculp.* Paris: chés François Chereau.

Cornini, Guido, and Claudia Lega (2013), *Preziose antichità: il Museo Profano al
tempo di Pio VI*. Vatican City: Edizioni Musei Vaticani.

Cowan, Brian (2005), *The Social Live of Coffee: The Emergence of the British Coffee
House*. New Haven and London: Yale University Press.

Cox, Oliver (2012), "An Oxford College and the Eighteenth-Century Gothic Revival,"
Oxoniensia, 77: 117–36.

Crawford, Katelyn D. (2018), "Painting New England in the Dutch West Indies: John
Greenwood's 'Sea Captains Carousing in Surinam'," in David T. Gies and Cynthia
Wall (eds.), *The Eighteenth Centuries: Global Networks of Enlightenment*, 178–96.
Charlottesville: University of Virginia Press.

Crill, Rosemary (2008), *Chintz: Indian Textiles for the West*. London: Victoria and
Albert Museum.

Crowley, John E. (2000), *The Invention of Comfort: Sensibilities and Design in Early Modern Britain and Early America*. Baltimore: Johns Hopkins University Press.

Dargan, Pat (2012), *Georgian London: The West End*. London: Amberley Publishing.

Dassas, Frédéric (2012), "Le mobilier néo-Boulle du XVIIIe siècle: faux, pastiche ou invention?" In *Vrai-Ment Faux, Actes du colloque de la Compagnie d'Expertise en Antiquités et objets d'art, Paris, Drouot-Montaigne, 20 septembre 2011*, 129–46. Paris: CEA.

de Bellaigue, Geoffrey and Anthony Blunt (1974), *Furniture Clocks and Gilt Bronzes: The James A de Rothschild Collection at Waddesdon Manor*. Fribourg: Office du Livre.

de La Live de Jully, Ange-Laurent (1764), *Catalogue historique du cabinet de peintre et sculpture Françoise de M. de Lalive*. Paris.

de la Tour du Pin, Madame (1999), *Memoirs: Laughing and Dancing Our Way to the Precipice*, trans. Felice Harcourt. London: The Harvill Press.

de Lespinasse, René and François Bonnardot (1879), *Les métiers et corporations de la Ville de Paris: XIIIe siècle, Le Livre des Métiers d'Etienne Boileau*. Paris: Imprimerie Nationale.

Decrossas, Michaël (2013), "La constitution d'un 'recueil' d'estampes d'ornements au XVIIIᵉ siècle: le *Livre d'Echantillons* Fol Est 489 de la collection Jacques Doucet de la bibliothèque de l'INHA," *Documents d'Histoire parisienne*, 15: 53–8.

Decrossas, Michaël (2018), "Du modèle à l'objet: le rôle de l'estampe à la période rocaille," in Aziza Gril-Mariotte (ed.), *Artistes & dessinateurs. La création dans les arts décoratifs (XVIIIe–XXe siècle)*, collection Art & Société. Rennes: Presses Universitaires de Rennes.

Decrossas, Michaël and Marianne Grivel (2014), "De l'atelier de l'artisan au cabinet de l'amateur." In Michaël Decrossas and Lucie Fléjou (eds.), *Ornements. XVe–XIXe siècles. Chefs-d'œuvre de la Bibliothèque de l'INHA, collections Jacques Doucet*, 262–76. Paris: éd. Mare & Martin / INHA.

Deflassieux, Françoise (2005), *Guide des meubles et des styles*. Paris: Solar.

Dejean, Joan (2009), *The Age of Comfort. When Paris Discovered Casual—and the Modern Home Began*. London: Bloomsbury.

Delaforce, Angela (2002), *Art and Patronage in Eighteenth-Century Portugal*. Cambridge: Cambridge University Press.

Demetrescu, Calin (2014), "Le cabinet Boulle du duc de Buccleuch. Une énigme résolue," *Dossier de l'art*, 224 (December): 30–59.

Dézalier d'Argenville, Antoine-Joseph (1727), "Lettre sur le choix & l'arrangement d'un Cabinet de curieux, écrite par M. Des-Allier d'Argenville, Secretaire du Roy en la Grande Chancellerie, à M. de Fougeroux, Tresorier-Payeur des Rentes de l'Hôtel de Ville," *Mercure de France* (June): 1295–330.

Díaz Cayeros, Patricia (2012), *Ornamentación y ceremonia: cuerpo, jardín y misterio en el Coro de la Catedral de Puebla*. México, DF: Universidad Autónoma de México.

Dickinson, H.W. (1937), *Matthew Boulton*. Cambridge: Cambridge University Press.

Diderot, Denis and Jean Le Rond d'Alembert (1751–72), *Encyclopédie ou Dictionnaire Raisonné des Sciences, des Art et des Métiers*, Paris: André le Breton, Michel-Antoine David, Laurent Durand, and Claude Briasson.

Dinkin, Robert J. (1988), "Seating the Meetinghouse in Early Massachusetts." In Robert Blair St. George (ed.), *Material Life in America 1600–1800*, 407–18. Boston: Northeastern University Press.

Divers dessins de menuiserie pour la decoration des apartments presentement à la mode
  (*c.* 1750). Paris: chez Charpentier rue St Jacques au Coq.
Dobie, Madeleine (2006), "Orientalism, Colonialism & Furniture in Eighteenth-
  Century France." In Dena Goodman and Kathryn Norberg (eds.), *Furnishing the
  Eighteenth Century*, 13–37. New York: Routledge.
du Monceau, Duhamel (1757), *Descriptions des Arts et Métiers*. Paris.
Dugdale, William (1716), *The History of St Paul's Cathedral in London from Its
  Foundation*. London: D.D. Edward Maynard.
Durand, Jannic (2014), *Decorative Furnishings and Objets d'Art in the Louvre*. Paris:
  Louvre Editions.
Edwards, Clive (2000), *Encyclopedia of Furniture Materials, Trades and Techniques*.
  Farnham, UK: Ashgate.
Edwards, Ralph (1954), *Dictionary of English Furniture*, 3 vols. London: Country Life.
Eikelmann, Renate (2011), *Magnificent Furniture at the Munich Court—A Close
  Look at Baroque Décor* (2011), exhibition from April 8–July 31, 2011, Munich:
  Prünkmobel am Münchner hof: barocker dekor unter, Renate Eikelmann,
  exhibition catalog.
Ekirch, A. Roger (2005), *At Day's Close: A History of Nighttime*. London: Weidenfeld
  & Nicolson.
Ekroll, Øystein (2012), "State Church and Church State: Churches and their Interiors
  in Post-Reformation Norway." In Andrew Spicer (ed.), *Lutheran Churches in Early
  Modern Europe*, 277–309. Farnham, UK: Ashgate.
Eriksen, Svend (1974), *Early Neo-Classicism in France*. London: Faber and Faber.
Fawcett, Jane, ed. (1998), *Historic Floors: Their History and Conservation*. London:
  Routledge.
Fiennes, Celia (1982), *The Illustrated Journeys of Celia Fiennes 1685–c.1712*, edited by
  Christopher Morris. Exeter: Webb & Bower.
Fierens, Paul (1943), *Chaires et confessionaux baroques*. Brussels: Éditions du Cercle
  d'Art.
Fioratti, Helen Constantino (2004), *Il mobile Italiano dall'antichità allo Stile Impero*.
  Florence: Giunti.
Forray-Carlier, Anne (2010), *Le Mobilier du Château de Chantilly*. Dijon: Faton.
Freeman, Sarah (2012), "An Englishwoman's Home is Her Castle: Lady Pomfret's
  House at 18 Arlington Street." *Georgian Group Journal*, 20: 87–102.
Friedman, Terry (1995), "The Transformation of York Minster, 1726–42,"
  Architectural History, 38: 69–90.
Friedman, Terry (2011), *The Eighteenth-Century Church in Britain*. New Haven and
  London: Yale University Press.
Fryman, O. (2015), "Renewing and Refashioning, Recycling Furniture at the Late
  Stuart Court (1689–1714)." In A. Fennetaux, S. Vasset, and A. Junqua (eds.),
  The Afterlife of Used Things: Recycling in the Long Eighteenth Century, 89–106.
  New York: Routledge.
Fuchs, Barbara (2011), *Exotic Nation: Maurophilia and the Construction of Early
  Modern Spain*. Philadelphia: University of Pennsylvania Press.
Gady, Alexandre (2011), *Les hôtels particuliers de Paris du moyen âge à la belle époque*.
  Paris: Éditions Parigramme.
Garric, Jean-Philippe, ed. (2016), *Charles Percier: Architecture and Design in an Age of
  Revolutions*. New York: Bard Graduate Center.
Gerard, Alexander (1759), *An Essay on Taste*. London: A. Miller.

Germain, Pierre (1751), *Livre d'Ornemens Composés Par Pre. Germain Md. Orfevre Joayllier a Paris Prix 2 l.* Paris: chés l'Auteur.

Gilbert, Christopher (1978), *The Life and Work of Thomas Chippendale*, 2 vols. London: Studio Vista and Christie's.

Gilbert, Christopher (1996), *Pictorial Dictionary of Marked London Furniture, 1700–1840*. Leeds, UK: W.S. Maney & Son.

Gilbert, Christopher (1997a), "Chippendale and Adam Triumphant," *Christie's International Magazine*, July–August: 22–4.

Gilbert, Christopher (1997b), "Seddon, Sons & Shackleton," *Furniture History*, 33: 1–29.

Gilbert, Christopher and Tessa Murdoch (1993), *John Channon and Brass-Inlaid Furniture, 1730–1760*. New Haven and London: Yale University Press.

Gilbert, Christopher and Tessa Murdoch (1994), "Channon Revisited," *Furniture History*, 30: 65–85.

Girouard, Mark (1966a), "Coffee at Slaughter's: English Art and the Rococo—I," *Country Life*, 13 (January): 58–61.

Girouard, Mark (1966b), "The Two Worlds of St Martin's Lane: English Art and the Rococo—III," *Country Life,* 3 (February): 224–7.

Girouard, Mark (1978), *Life in the English Country House*, New Haven and London: Yale University Press.

Girouard, Mark (2000), *Life in the French Country House*. London: Cassell & Co.

Glanville, Philippa and Hilary Young, eds. (2002), *Elegant Eating: Four Hundred Years of Dining in Style*. London: Victoria and Albert Museum.

Gomme, Andor (1984), "Badminton Revisited," *Architectural History*, 27: 163–82.

Gondoin, Jacques (1780), *Déscription des Écoles de Chirurgie*. Paris: Ph.-D. Pierres.

González-Palacios, Alvar (2003), "Due coppie di tavoli da Palazzo Borghese: 1773," *Antologia di Belle Arti*: 89–99.

González-Palacios, Alvar (2004), *Arredi e ornamenti alla corte di Roma*. Milan.

González-Palacios, Alvar (2010), "Concerning Furniture: Roman Documents and Inventories, Part 1, *c.* 1600–1720," *Furniture History*, 46: 1–135.

González-Palacios, Alvar (2018), *Luigi Valadier*, New York: Frick Collection, in association with D. Giles Ltd.

Goodison, Nicholas (1990), "William Chambers's Furniture Designs," *Furniture History*, 26: 67–89.

Goodman, Dena (2009), *Becoming a Woman in the Age of Letters*. Ithaca, NY: Cornell University Press.

Goodman, Dena (2011), "The *Secrétaire* and the Integration of the Eighteenth-Century Self." In Dena Goodman and Kathryn Norberg (eds.), *Furnishing the Eighteenth Century: What Furniture Can Tell Us about the European and American Past*, 183–204. New York: Routledge.

Graham, Clare (1994), *Ceremonial and Commemorative Chairs in Great Britain*. London: Victoria and Albert Museum.

Grant, Sarah (2010), *Toiles de Jouy*. London: Victoria and Albert Museum.

Gray, Emily Fisher (2012), "Lutheran Churches and Confessional Competition in Augsburg." In Andrew Spicer (ed.), *Lutheran Churches in Early Modern Europe*, 39–62. Farnham, UK: Ashgate.

Gray, Thomas (1935), *Correspondence of Thomas Gray, 1734–1755*. Oxford: Clarendon Press.

Grieg, Hannah (2013), *The Beau Monde: Fashionable Society in Georgian London*. Oxford: Oxford University Press.

Habermas, Jürgen ([1962] 1991), *The Structural Transformation of the Public Sphere: An Inquiry into a Category of Bourgeois Society*. Cambridge, MA: MIT Press.

Harasimowicz, Jan (2012), "Lutheran Churches in Poland." In Andrew Spicer (ed.), *Lutheran Churches in Early Modern Europe*, 403–44. Farnham, UK: Ashgate.

Harris, Eileen (2001), *The Genius of Robert Adam: His Interiors*. New Haven and London: Yale University Press for the Paul Mellon Centre for Studies in British Art.

Harris, John (1985), "John Talman's Design for his Wunderkammern," *Furniture History*, 21: 211–16.

Harris, John (1989), "William Kent and Esher Place," *Studies in the History of Art*, 25 (Symposium Papers X: The Fashioning and Functioning of the British Country House): 13–26.

Harris, John (1991), "Lady Pomfret's House: the Case for Richard Biggs," *Georgian Group Journal*, 1: 45–9.

Harris, John (2007), *Moving Rooms: The Trade in Architectural Salvages*. New Haven and London: Yale University Press.

Harris, Leslie (1987), *Robert Adam and Kedleston: The Making of a Neo-Classical Masterpiece*. London: National Trust.

Hart, Vaughan (2011), *Inigo Jones: The Architect of Kings*. London: Yale University Press for the Paul Mellon Centre for Studies in British Art.

Hart, Vaughan and Peter Hicks, eds. (1998), *Paper Palaces: The Rise of the Renaissance Architectural Treatise*. New Haven and London: Yale University Press.

Hawkes, Will (2013), "Walpole Right or Wrong? More on No. 18 Arlington Street," *Georgian Group Journal*, 21: 204–11.

Hayward, Helena, ed. (1965), *World Furniture*. London: Hamlyn.

Hayward, Helena (1969), "Chinoiserie at Badminton: The Furniture of John and William Linnell," *Apollo*: 134–9.

Hayward, Helena and Pat Kirkham (1980), *William and John Linnell: Eighteenth Century London Furniture Makers*. London: Studio Vista in association with Christie's.

Hayward, J.F. (1977), "A Further Note on Christopher Fuhrlohg," *Burlington Magazine*, 119 (892) (July): 486–93.

Heal, Ambrose (1953), *London Furniture Makers 1660–1840*. London: Batsford.

Hébert (1766), *Dictionnaire pittoresque et historique de Paris, Versailles, Marly, Triano*, 2 vols.

Heckscher, Morrison H. (2005), *John Townsend: Newport Cabinetmaker*. New York: Metropolitan Museum of Art; New Haven and London: Yale University Press.

Hellman, Mimi (1999), "Furniture, Sociability, and the Work of Leisure in Eighteenth-Century France," *Eighteenth-Century Studies*, 32 (4): 415–45.

Hellman, Mimi (2011), "The Joy of Sets: The Uses of Seriality in the French Interior." In Dena Goodman and Kathryn Norberg (eds.), *Furnishing the Eighteenth Century. What Furniture Can Tell Us about the European and American Past*, 129–54. New York: Routledge.

Hepplewhite & Co. ([1788] 1794), *The Cabinet-Maker and Upholsterer's Guide*. London: I. & J. Taylor.

Herda-Mousseaux, Rose-Marie, Patrick Rambourg, and Guillaume Séret (2015), *Thé, café ou chocolat? L'essor des boissons exotiques à Paris au XVIIIe siècle*. Paris: Musée Cognacq-Jay.

Hill, Rosemary (2007), *God's Architect: Pugin and the Building of Romantic Britain*. London: Allen Lane.

Holtzapffel, C. (1846), *Turning and Mechanical Manipulation*, London.

Hoskins, Lesley, ed. (2005), *The Papered Wall: The History, Patterns and Techniques of Wallpaper*. London: Thames & Hudson.

Howard, John (2004), "Upton Church." In *Five Parishes: Their People and Places. A History of the Villages of Castor, Ailsworth, Marholm with Milton, Upton and Sutton*, 151–6. Peterborough, UK: The Camus Project.

Howlett, F. Carey (1996), "Admitted into the Mysteries: The Benjamin Bucktrout Masonic Master's Chair," *American Furniture*: 195–232.

Hubka, Thomas C. (2003), *Resplendent Synagogue: Architecture and Worship in an Eighteenth-Century Polish Community*. Lebanon, NH: University Press of New England.

Hughes, Peter (1996), *Catalogue of Furniture*, 3 vols. London: Wallace Collection.

Hughes, Peter (2007), "The Grand Trianon Commodes by André-Charles Boulle and Their Influence," *Journal of the Furniture History Society*, 43: 195–203.

Huquier, Gabriel (1757), *Catalogue des estampes provenantes du fond des Planches appartenant à G. Huquier, Graveur, rue des Mathurins, au coin de celle de Sorbonne*. Paris: De l'imprimerie d'Augustin Martin Lottin.

Hurst, Ronald L. and Jonathan Prown (1997), *Southern Furniture 1680–1830: The Colonial Williamsburg Collection*. Williamsburg: The Colonial Williamsburg Foundation.

Impey, Oliver and Johanna Marschner (1998), "'China Mania': A Reconstruction of Queen Mary II's Display of East Asian Artefacts in Kensington Palace in 1693," *Orientations*, (November): 61.

Ince, William and John Mayhew (1762), *The Universal System of Household Furniture: Consisting of above 300 Designs in the most Elegant* Taste, *both Useful & Ornamental*. London: Robert Sayer.

Jackson, Amelia (2017), "André-Charles Boulle as a Collector of Prints and Drawings," Ph.D. diss., Queen Mary, University of London.

Jackson-Stops, Gervase, ed. (1985), *Treasure Houses of Britain: Five Hundred Years of Private Patronage and Art Collecting*. Washington, DC: National Gallery of Art.

Jacobsen, Helen (2017), *Gilded Interiors: Parisian Luxury and the Antique*. London: Philip Wilson Publishers.

Jervis, Simon Swynfern and Dudley Dodd (2015), *Roman Splendour, English Arcadia*, London.

John, Eleanor (2013), "Drawing Rooms, Dining Rooms and Parlours in the Homes of London's Middling Sorts 1740–1810," *Regional Furniture*, 27: 141–55.

Johnson, Thomas (1793), *The Life of the Author*. London: Printed for the Author.

Jones, Yvonne (2012), *Japanned Papier-Mâché and Tinware c. 1740–1940*. Woodbridge, UK: Antique Collectors' Club.

Journal des Luxus und der Moden (1787–1812). Available online: http://zs.thulb.uni-jena.de/receive/jportal_jpjournal_00000029 (accessed August 28, 2016).

Kavanagh, Thomas M. (1993), *Enlightenment and the Shadows of Chance: The Novel and the Culture of Gambling in Eighteenth-Century France*. Baltimore: Johns Hopkins University Press.

Kelly, Alison (1965), *Decorative Wedgwood in Architecture and Furniture*. London: Country Life.

Kelly, Jason M. (2009), *The Society of Dilettanti: Archaeology and Identity in the British Enlightenment*. New Haven and London: Yale University Press.

Kennedy, Máire (2010), "Dublin's Coffee Houses of the Eighteenth Century," *Dublin Historical Record*, 63 (1): 29–38.

Kent, William and Inigo Jones (1744), *Some Designs of Mr. Inigo Jones and Mr. Wm. Kent*. London: John Vardy.

Kenworthy-Browne, John (2009), "The Duke of Richmond's Gallery in Whitehall," *British Art Journal*, 10 (1) (Spring–Summer): 40–9.

Kerber, Peter Björn (2011), "Perfectibility and Its Foreign Causes: Reading for Self-Improvement in Eighteenth-Century Paris." In Charissa Bremer-David (ed.), *Paris: Life and Luxury in the Eighteenth Century*, 75–90. Los Angeles: J. Paul Getty Museum.

Kimball, Fiske (1949), *Le style Louis XV, origine et évolution du Rococo*. Paris: A. et J. Picard.

Kirkham, Pat and Susan Weber, eds. (2013), *History of Design: Decorative Arts and Material Culture, 1400–2000*. New York: Bard Graduate Center; New Haven: Yale University Press.

Kisluk-Grosheide, Daniëlle and Bertrand Rondot (2018), "The Incomparable Versailles." In Daniëlle Kisluk-Grosheide and Bertrand Rondot (eds.), *Visitors to Versailles: From Louis XIV to the French Revolution*, 2–29. New York: Metropolitan Museum of Art.

Kisluk-Grosheide, Daniëlle and Jeffrey H. Munger (2010), *The Wrightsman Galleries for French Decorative Arts, The Metropolitan Museum*. New York: Metropolitan Museum of Art.

Kisluk-Grosheide, Daniëlle O., Wolfram Koeppe, and William Rieder; photography by Joseph Coscia Jr. (2006), *European Furniture in the Metropolitan Museum of Art: Highlights of the Collection*. New York: Metropolitan Museum of Art.

Knight of Glin and James Peill (2007), *Irish Furniture*. New Haven and London: Yale University Press.

Kodres, Krista (2012), "'Das "Geistliche Gebäwde" der Kirche': The Lutheran Church in Early Modern Estonia." In Andrew Spicer (ed.), *Lutheran Churches in Early Modern Europe*, 333–75. Farnham, UK: Ashgate.

Koeppe, Wolfram, ed. (2012), *Extravagant Inventions, The Princely Furniture of the Roentgens*, exhibition at the Metropolitan Museum of Art, New York, October 30, 2012–January 27, 2013, New York: Wolfram Koeppe, exhibition catalog.

Krinsky, Carol Herselle ([1985] 1996), *Synagogues of Europe: Architecture, History, Meaning*, Reprint. Mineola, NY: Dover Publications.

Kulturstiftung Dessau-Wörlitz (2015), *Cranach im Gotischen Haus in Wörlitz*. Munich: Hirmer Verlag.

Langer, Brigitte (1995), *Die Möbel der Residenz München*, vol. 1, *Die französischen Möbel des 18. Jahrhunderts*, Munich.

Langley, Batty (1740), *The City and Country Builder's, and Workman's Treasury of Designs: Or, The Art of Drawing and Working The Ornamental Parts of Architecture*. London: Printed by J. Ilive.

Lanöe, Catherine, Mathieu Da Vinha, and Bruno Laurioux, eds. (2011), *Cultures de cour, cultures du corps: XIVᵉ–XVIIᵉ siècle*, Paris: Presses de l'université Paris-Sorbonne.

Le Bitouzé, Corinne (1986), "Le commerce de l'estampe à Paris dans la première moitié du XVIIIe siècle," thesis for obtaining the diploma of archivist-paleographer, Paris.

Leben, U. (2004), *L'Ecole royale gratuite de dessin*. Saint Remy-en-l'Eau: Editions Monelle Hayot.

Leben, Ulrich (2007), "An Armchair and Folding Screen for the Comte d'Artois at Bagatelle," *Furniture History*, 43: 127–41.

Ledoux-Lebard, Denise (1984), *Les ébénistes du XIXe siècle, 1795–1870: leurs oeuvres et leurs marques*. Paris: Éditions de l'Amateur.

Lefuel, Hector (1923), *Georges Jacob, ébéniste du XVIIIe siècle*. Paris: Éditions Albert Morancé.

Legate, Kim (2016), "More on Chippendale at Hestercombe House," *Burlington Magazine*, November: 904.

Lekhovich, Tatiana (2009), "Copies After Philippe de Lasalle's Silks by the Lazarev Manufactory near Moscow: Problems of Attribution," *Abegg-Stiftung Riggisberger Berichte*, 17: 91–102.

Lemire, Beverly and Giorgio Riello (2008), "East &West: Textiles and Fashion in Early Modern Europe," *Journal of Social History*, 41 (4) (Summer): 887.

Lessard, Michel (1999), *Meubles anciens du Québec*. Montréal: Éditions de l'Homme.

Lever, Jill (1982), *Architects' Designs for Furniture*. London: Trefoil Books.

Lindfield, Peter N. (2012), "The Furnishing of a Gothic Fantasy 1803–1825: Eaton Hall, Cheshire," *Furniture History*, 48: 155–80.

Lindfield, Peter N. (2013), "Porden's Eaton: William Porden's Role in the Development of Eaton Hall, Cheshire, 1802–1825," *Georgian Group Journal*, 21: 137–51.

Lindfield, Peter N. (2014a), "The Countess of Pomfret's Gothic Revival Furniture," *Georgian Group Journal*, 22: 77–94.

Lindfield, Peter N. (2014b), "Serious Gothic and 'Doing the Ancient Buildings': Batty Langley's *Ancient Architecture* and *Principal Geometric Elevations*," *Architectural History*, 57: 141–73.

Lindfield, Peter N. (2015a), "National Identity Through Design: the Anglicisation of the Rococo in Mid Eighteenth-Century Britain." In Peter N. Lindfield and Christie Margrave (eds.), *Rule Britannia? Britain and Britishness 1707–1901*, 1–42. Newcastle-upon-Tyne, UK: Cambridge Scholars.

Lindfield, Peter N. (2015b), "New Light on Chippendale at Hestercombe House," *Burlington Magazine*, 157 (July): 452–6.

Lindfield, Peter N. (2016), *Georgian Gothic: Medievalist Architecture, Furniture and Interiors, 1730–1840*. Woodbridge, UK: Boydell & Brewer.

Lindfield, Peter N. (2017a), "A 'Classical Goth': Robert Adam's Engagement with Medieval Architecture." In Colin Thom (ed.), *Robert Adam*, 161–82. London: English Heritage.

Lindfield, Peter N. (2017b), "William Porden's State Bed for Eaton Hall, Cheshire," *Regional Furniture*, 31: 1–10.

Lock, Matthias (1740), *A New Drawing Book of Ornaments, Shields, Compartments, Masks &c*. London: Robert Sayer.

Lock, Matthias (1770), *The Principles of Ornament, or the Youth's Guide to Drawing of Foliage*. London: Robert Sayer.

Louw, Hentie (1991), "Window-Glass Making in Britain c.1660–c.1860 and its Architectural Impact," *Construction History*, 7: 47–68.

Lowengard, Sarah (2006), *The Creation of Colour in Eighteenth-Century Europe*. New York: Gutenburg-e.

Lunsingh-Scheurleer, Theodoor Herman (1936), "Parmigianino and Boulle," *Burlington Magazine*, 68 (June): 286–8.

Lunsingh-Scheurleer, Theodoor Herman (2005), *Pierre Gole*. Dijon: Faton.

Maës, Antoine (2013), "L'ameublement du salon d'Apollon, XVIIe–XVIIIe siècle," *Bulletin du Centre de recherche du château de Versailles*, Articles et études, published online March 26, 2013. https://doi.org/10.4000/crcv.12144.

Mannlich, Johann Christian von (1989–93), *Histoire de ma vie*, edited by Karl-Heinz Bender and Hermann Kleber, 2 vols. Trier: Spee-Verlag.

Markham, Sarah (n.d.), *The Tours of John Loveday of Caversham*. Available online: http://www.johnlovedayofcaversham.co.uk (accessed May 23, 2021).

McClellan, Andrew (1994), *Inventing the Louvre: Art, Politics, and the Origin of the Modern Museum in Eighteenth-Century Paris*. Cambridge: Cambridge University Press.

Mead, William Edward (1914), *The Grand Tour in the Eighteenth Century*. Boston: Houghton Mifflin.

Meissonnier, Juste-Aurèle (*c.* 1735), *Œuvre de Juste Aurele Meissonnier Peintre Sculpteur Architecte & Dessinateur de la chambre et Cabinet du Roy. Premiere partie executé sous la conduitte de l'auteur*. Paris: chés Huquier.

Melchoir-Bonnet, Sabine (2001), *The Mirror: A History*. London: Routledge.

Melton, James van Horn (2001), *The Rise of the Public in Enlightenment Europe*. Cambridge: Cambridge University Press.

Messbarger, Rebecca (2010), *The Lady Anatomist: The Life and Work of Anna Morandi Manzolini*. Chicago: University of Chicago Press.

Meyer, Daniel (2002), *Versailles: Furniture of the Royal Palace, 17th and 18th Centuries*, 2 vols. Dijon: Faton.

Michel, Christian (2015), "Le système d'ameublement des élites françaises au XVIIIe siècle." In Anne Perrin Khelissa (ed.), *Corrélations: Les objets du décor au siècle des Lumières*, Coll. "Études sur le XVIIIe siècle," vol. 43, 35–46, Brussels: Éd. de l'Université de Bruxelles.

Michel, M. Roland (1982), "L'ornement rocaille: quelques questions," *Revue de l'art*, 55: 66–75.

Michel, M. Roland (1984), *Lajoüe et l'Art Rocaille*. Neuilly-sur-Seine: Arthena.

Middleton, R. (1986), "The Sculpture Gallery at Newby Hall," *A.A. Files*, 13 (Autumn): 48–60.

Miller, Elizabeth and Hilary Young (2015), *The Arts of Living. Europe 1600–1815*. London: Victoria and Albert Museum.

Miller, Lesley Ellis (2009), "Departing from the Pheasant and the Peacock: The Role of Furnishing Textiles in the Career of Philippe de Lasalle (1723–1804)," *Abegg-Stiftung Riggisberger Berichte*, 17: 79–90.

Murdoch, Tessa (1993), "Channon's Rivals and the London Market for Brass-Inlaid Furniture." In Christopher Gilbert and Tessa Murdoch (eds.), *John Channon and Brass-Inlaid Furniture, 1730–1760*, 13–23. New Haven and London: Yale University Press.

Murdoch, Tessa (1997), "A Brass-Inlaid Jewel Chest on Stand Made for Rebecca, Viscountess Harcourt, c. 1735," *Furniture History*, 33: 104–8.

Murdoch, Tessa (1998), "Jean, René and Thomas Pelletier, a Huguenot family of Carvers and Gilders in England 1682–1726; Part II," *Burlington Magazine*, 140: 363–74.

Murdoch, Tessa (2001), "Pierre Langlois: Cabinet-Maker to the World of Fashion," *Proceedings of the Huguenot Society*, 27 (4): 497–508.

Murdoch, Tessa (2002), "Fit for a King, The State Bed from Melville House, Fife," *Apollo*, 155 (479) (January): 3–9.

Murdoch, Tessa (2006a), "A French Carver at Norfolk House—The Mysterious Mr Cuenot," *Apollo*, 163 (532) (June): 54–63.

Murdoch, Tessa, ed. (2006b), *Noble Households: Eighteenth-Century Inventories of Great English Houses. A Tribute to John Cornforth*. Cambridge: John Adamson.

A New Book of Vases Designed by Boucher (1771), London: Printed for R. Brookshaw, October 22.

Nouveau Livre de Vases par F. Bo … (c. 1755–68), Paris: chés la V.e de F. Chereau.

OED Online (n.d.), Oxford University Press. Available online: https://www.oed.com (accessed May 23, 2021).

Oppenord, Gille Marie (*c.* 1749–61), *Œuvres de Gille Marie Oppenord ecuier directeur general des batiments et jardins de son altesse royale monseigneur le duc d'Orleans regent du royaume contenant differents fragments d'architecture, et d'ornements, à l'usage des batiments sacrées, publics, et particuliers, gravés mis au jour*. Paris: chés Huquier.

Orlin, Lena Cowen (2007), *Locating Privacy in Tudor London*. Oxford: Oxford University Press.

Palladio, Andrea (1570), *I Quattro Libri dell' Architectura*. Venice: Dominico de' Franceschi.

Pallot, G.B. (1987), *L'art du Siege au XVIIIe siècle en France*. Paris: A.C.R. Gismondi.

Pardailhé-Galabrun, Annik (1991), *The Birth of Intimacy: Privacy and Domestic Life in Early Modern Paris*, trans. Jocelyn Phelps. Philadelphia: University of Pennsylvania Press.

Parker, Rozsika (1984), *The Subversive Stitch. Embroidery and the Making of the Feminine*. London: Women's Press.

Payne, C. (2003), *Francois Linke, 1855–1946, The Belle Epoque of French Furniture*. Woodbridge, UK: Antique Collectors' Club.

Pellegrin, Nicole (1999), "Les vertus de l'ouvrage: Recherches sur la féminisation des travaux d'aiguille (VXIᵉ–XVIIIᵉ siècles)," *Revue d'histoire moderne et contemporaine*, 46 (4): 747–69.

Perrot, Chloé (2017), "La Nouvelle Iconologie Historique de Jean-Charles Delafosse, faire parler l'ornement," *Actes du Premier Colloque des Etudiants de Master SHAP*, Université Lille 3.

Petroski, Henry (1999), *The Book on the Bookshelf*. New York: Alfred A. Knopf.

Pinkard, Susan (2009), *A Revolution in Taste: The Rise of French Cuisine 1650–1800*. Cambridge: Cambridge University Press.

Pisani, Emiliabianca, trans. (2015), *The Buildings and Designs of Andrea Palladio*. New York: Princeton Architectural Press.

Plommer, Hugh (1979), "Vitruvius and the Origin of Caryatids," *Journal of Hellenic Studies*, 99: 97–102.

Porter, David (2010), *The Chinese Taste in Eighteenth-Century England*. Cambridge: Cambridge University Press.

Prache, Denys and Veronique de Bruignac-La Hougue (2016), *Joseph Dufour: Genie des Papiers Peints*. Paris: Editions Mare & Martin.

Pradère, Alexandre (1989), *Les Ébénistes Français de Louis XIV à la Révolution*. Paris: Editions du Chêne.

Pradère, Alexandre (1990), *French Furniture Makers: the Art of the Ébéniste from Louis XIV to the Revolution*, trans. Perran Wood, London: Sotheby's.

Pradère, Alexandre (2003), *Charles Cressent sculpteur, ébéniste du Régent*, Dijon: Faton.

Pradère, Alexandre (2005), *"Curieux des Indes" Julliot and the fashion for Boulle furniture 1750–1800*, December 14. London: Christie's, sale catalog.

Pradère, Alexandre (2014), "Lerouge, Le Brun, Bonnemaison: le rôle des marchands de tableaux dans le commerce du mobilier Boulle, de la Révolution à la Restauration," *Revue de l'Art*, (184).

Praz, Mario ([1964] 2008), *An Illustrated History of Interior Decoration from Pompei to Art Nouveau*. New York: Thames & Hudson.

Pugin, A.W.N. (1841), *The true principles of pointed or Christian architecture: set forth in two lectures delivered at St. Marie's, Oscott*. London: John Weale.

Purefoy Letters (1931), edited by G. Eland, 2 vols. London: Sidgwick and Jackson.

Randall, Gerald (1980), *Church Furnishing and Decoration in England & Wales*. New York: Holme & Meier.

Range, Matthias (2012), "The Material Presence of Music in Church: The Hanseatic City of Lübeck." In Andrew Spicer (ed.), *Lutheran Churches in Early Modern Europe*, 197–220. Farnham, UK: Ashgate.

Redford, Bruce (2008), *Dilettanti: The Antic and the Antique in Eighteenth-Century England*. Los Angeles: J. Paul Getty Museum.

Rice, Charles B., Rev. (1867), "Historical Address." In *Celebration of the Hundredth Anniversary of the Incorporation of Conway, Massachusetts*, 11–73. Northampton: Bridgman & Childs.

Richardson, Jonathan, Sr. and Jonathan Richardson, Jr. (1722), *An Account of Some of the Statues, Bas-reliefs, Drawings and Pictures in Italy, &c.* London: J. Knapton.

Richardson, Samuel ([1748] 1926), *Clarissa*. New York: Everyman.

Rijksmuseum (n.d.), "Pair of Firebuds, Philippe Caffieri (le Jeune) (possibly), c. 1770." Available online: http://hdl.handle.net/10934/RM0001.COLLECT.295531 (accessed May 8, 2021).

Roberts, Hugh (1989), "Royal Thrones, 1760–1840," *Furniture History*, 25: 61–85.

Roberts, Hugh (2001), *For the King's Pleasure, the Furnishing and Decoration of Georges IV's appartements at Windsor Castle*, London: Royal Collection Trust.

Roberts, Jane (1976–7), "Henry Emlyn's Restoration of St George's Chapel," *Report of the Society of the Friends of St George's and the Descendants of the Knights of the Garter*, 5: 331–8.

Robinson, Eric (1986), "Matthew Boulton and Josiah Wedgwood, Apostles of Fashion," *Business History*, 28 (3): 98–114.

Robinson, John Martin (2012), *James Wyatt (1746–1813): Architect to George III*. London: Published for the Paul Mellon Centre for Studies in British Art by Yale University Press.

Roche, Daniel (1994), *The Culture of Clothing: Dress and Fashion in the "Ancien Régime."* Cambridge: Cambridge University Press.

Roche, Daniel (1997), *Histoire des choses banales. Naissance de la consommation dans les sociétés traditionnelles (XVIIᵉ–XIXᵉ siècle)*. Paris: Fayard.

Roche, Daniel (1998), *France in the Enlightenment*. Cambridge, MA: Harvard University Press.

Ronfort, Jean Nérée (2009), *André-Charles Boulle: un nouveau style pour l'Europe*. Paris: Editions Somogy.

Rosoman, T.-S. (1985), "The Decoration and Use of the Principal Appartments of Chiswick House, 1727–70," *Burlington Magazine*, 127 (991) (October): 663–77.

Roubo, André Jacob (1772), *L'art du menuisier en meubles. Seconde section de la troisième partie de l'Art du Menuisier*. Paris: Saillant et Nyon.

Rozier, M. l'Abbé (1774), *Observations sur la physique, sur l'histoire naturelle et sur les arts*. Paris: Ruault.

Russell, Francis (1989), "The Hanging and Display of Pictures, 1700–1850," *Studies in the History of Art*, 25: 143–53.

Rybczynski, W. (2001), *One Good Turn: a Natural History of the Screwdriver and the Screw*. Simon & Schuster.

Salmon, Frank (2013), "Public Commissions." In Susan Weber (ed.), *William Kent: Designing Georgian Britain*, 314–63. New Haven, CT: Yale University Press for the Bard Graduate Center.

Samoyault, Jean-Pierre (1972), "Un collezionista parigano della fine del Settecento, Lenoir du Breuil," *Arte illustrata*, 50 (September): 326–33.

Samoyault, Jean-Pierre (2009), *Mobilier français: Consulat et Empire*. Paris: Gourcoff Gradenigo.

Sánchez-Jágurgui, Maria Dolores and Scott Wilcox, eds. (2012), *The English Prize: The Capture of the Westmorland, an Episode of the Grand Tour*. New Haven and London: Yale University Press.

Sargentson, Carolyn (1996), *Merchants and Luxury Markets: The Marchands Merciers of Eighteenth-Century Paris*. London: Victoria and Albert Museum.

Sargentson, Carolyn (2008), "Working at Home in Eighteenth-Century France: Writing Desks in the Interiors of the Hôtel Choiseul." In Shelley M. Bennett and Carolyn Sargentson (eds.), *French Art of the Eighteenth Century at the Huntington*. San Marino, CA: The Huntington Library, Art Collections and Botanical Gardens; New Haven and London: Yale University Press.

Sargentson, Carolyn (2011), "Looking at Furniture Inside Out: Strategies of Secrecy and Security in Eighteenth-Century French Furniture." In Dena Goodman and Kathryn Norberg (eds.), *Furnishing the Eighteenth Century: What Furniture Can Tell Us about the European and American Past*, 205–36. New York: Routledge.

Sassoon, Adrian and Gillian Wilson (1986), *Decorative Arts: A Handbook of the Collection of the J. Paul Getty Museum*. Los Angeles: J. Paul Getty Museum.

Saule, Béatrix (2007), 'The Hall of Mirrors during Louis XIV's Reign: From the Ordinary to the Extraordinary." In *The Hall of Mirrors*, 54–73. Dijon: Faton.

Saxton, Eveline B. (1948), "Early Records of the Mock Corporation of Sefton," *Transactions of the Historic Society of Lancashire and Cheshire*, 100: 73–89.

Schott, Howard (1985), *Catalogue of Musical Instruments in the Victoria and Albert Museum, Part I: Keyboard Instruments*. London: Victoria and Albert Museum.

Scott, Katie (1995), *The Rococo Interior: Decoration and Social Spaces in Early Eighteenth-Century Paris*. New Haven and London: Yale University Press.

Scott, Katie and Deborah Cherry, eds. (2005), *Between Luxury and the Everyday: Decorative Arts in Eighteenth-Century France*. Malden, MA: Blackwell.

Shammas, Carol (1994), "The Decline of Textile Prices in England and British America Prior to Industrialization," *Economic History Review*, 47 (3): 483–507.

Sharp, Samuel (1766), *Letters from Italy, Describing the Customs and Manners of that Country, in the Years 1765, and 1766*. London: R. Cave.

Shenton, Caroline (2016), *Mr Barry's War: Rebuilding the Houses of Parliament After the Great Fire of 1834*. Oxford: Oxford University Press.

Sherrill, Sarah B. (1996), *Carpets and Rugs of Europe and America*. New York: Abbeville Press.

Simon, Jacob (2003), "Thomas Johnson's *The Life of the Author*," *Furniture History*, 39: 1–64.

Sloboda, Stacey (2010), "Fashioning Bluestocking Conversation: Elizabeth Montagu's Chinese Room." In Denise Amy Baxter and Meredith Martin (eds.), *Architectural Space in Eighteenth-Century Europe: Constructing Identities and Interiors*, 129–48. Farnham, UK: Ashgate.

Smart Martin, Anna (2011), "Tea Tables Overturned: Rituals of Power and Place in Colonial America." In Dena Goodman and Kathryn Norberg (eds.), *Furnishing the Eighteenth Century. What Furniture Can Tell Us about the European and American Past*, 169–84. New York: Routledge.

Smith, Adam (1759), *The Theory of Moral Sentiments*. London: A. Miller, A. Kincard, and J. Bell.

Snodin, Michael (1984), "English Rococo and its Continental Origins." In *Rococo: Art and Design in Hogarth's England*, 27–73. London: Trefoil Books and the Victoria and Albert Museum.

Snodin, Michael (2009), *Horace Walpole's Strawberry Hill*. New Haven and London: Yale University Press.

Snodin, Michael and Nigel Llewellyn, eds. (2009), *Baroque, 1620–1800: Style in the Age of Magnificence*. London: Victoria and Albert Museum, exhibition catalog.

Society of Upholsterers and Cabinet-Makers (1763), *Household Furniture in the Genteel Taste for the year 1763*. London: Robert Sayer.

Sotheby's (2002), *The Croft Castle Sale*. London: Sotheby's.

Souchal, Geneviève (1962), *Le mobilier français au xviiie siècle*. Paris: Hachette.

Spang, Rebecca (2000), *The Invention of the Restaurant: Paris and Modern Gastronomic Culture*. Cambridge, MA: Harvard University Press.

Spicer, Andrew (2012a), "'Hic Coeli Porta Est, Hic Domus Ecce Dei': Lutheran Churches in the Dutch World, c. 1566–1719." In Andrew Spicer (ed.), *Lutheran Churches in Early Modern Europe*, 445–82. Farnham, UK: Ashgate.

Spicer, Andrew (2012b), *Lutheran Churches in Early Modern Europe*. Farnham, UK: Ashgate.

Stevens, Sacheverell (1756), *Miscellaneous Remarks Made on the Spot, in a Late Seven Years Tour through France, Italy, Germany and Holland*. London: S. Hooper and J. Swan.

Stewart, Rachel (2009), *The Town House in Georgian London*. New Haven and London: Yale University Press.

Stichting Ebenist (2014), "Furniture Finishes, Past Present and Future of Transparent Wood Coatings", *Proceedings of the 12th International Symposium on Wood and Furniture Conservation*, Stichting Ebenist, Amsterdam, November 14–15, 2014.

Stratman Döhler, Rosemarie (2002), *Jean François Oeben*. Paris: Les éditions de l'amateur.

Stuart, Susan E. (2008), *Gillows of Lancaster and London 1730–1840*. Woodbridge, UK: Antique Collectors' Club.

Sweet, Rosemary (2012), *Cities and the Grand Tour: The British in Italy, 1690–c. 1820*. Cambridge: Cambridge University Press.

Tessin, Nicodemus the Younger (1926), "Relation de la visite de Nicodème Tessin à Marly, Versailles, Clagny, Rueil et Saint-Cloud en 1687," *Revue de l'histoire de Versailles e de Seine-et-Oise*, 28: 150–67, 274–300.

The Hall of Mirrors: History & Restoration (2007), Dijon: Faton.

Thicknesse, Philip (1777), *A Year's Journey Through France, and Part of Spain*, vol. 2. Bath: R. Cruttwell.

Thiéry, Luc-Vincent (1787), *Guide des amateurs et des étrangers voyageurs à Paris*, 2 vols., Paris.

Thillay, Alain (2002), *Le Faubourg Saint-Antoine et ses "faux ouvriers": Liberté du travail à Paris aux XVIIe et XVIIIe siècles*. Paris: Champ Vallon.

Thornton, Peter and William Rieder (1971), "Pierre Langlois, Ébéniste, Part I," *Connoisseur*, 178 (December): 283–8.

Tillerot, Isabelle (2011), *Jean de Jullienne et les collectionneurs de son temps*. Paris: Editions Maison des Sciences de L'homme.

Tillyard, Stella (1995), *Aristocrats: Caroline, Emily, Louisa and Sarah Lennox, 1740–1832*. London: Vintage.

Tinniswood, Adrian (1998), *The Polite Tourist: A History of Country House Visiting*. London: National Trust Enterprises.

Tolbecque, Auguste (1903), *L'Art du Luthier*, published by the author.

Van Dijk, Suzanne, "n° 0188—Cabinet des Modes (1785–1786)," in *Dictionnaire des Journaux (1600–1789)*, édition électronique revue, corrigée et augmentée. Available online: http://dictionnaire-journaux.gazettes18e.fr/journal/0188-cabinet-des-modes (accessed August 28, 2016).

van Eck, Xander (2012), "Rhetorics of the Pulpit." In Lieke Stelling, Harald Hendrix, and Todd M. Richardson (eds.), *The Turn of the Soul. Representations of Religious Conversion in Early Modern Art and Literature*, 373–91. Brill: Leiden.

Verlet, Pierre ([1955] 1992), *Le Mobilier royal français*, 4 vols. Paris: Picard.

Verlet, Pierre (1958), "Le commerce des objets d'art et les marchands-merciers a Paris au XVIIIe siècle," *Annales* (January–March): 10–29.

Verlet, Pierre (1966), *La maison du XVIIIᵉ siècle en France, Société, décoration, mobilier*. Fribourg, Switzerland: Office du livre.

Verlet, Pierre (1968), *L'Art du Meuble a Paris au XVIIIeme siècles*, editions "que sais je?" Presse Universitaires de France.

Verlet, Pierre (1982), *Les meubles français du XVIIIᵉ siècle*. Paris: Presses Universitaires de France.

Verlet, Pierre (1987), *Les bronzes dorés Français du XVIIIe siècle*. Paris: Picard.

Verlet, Pierre, ed. (1972), *Styles, meubles, décors du Moyen âge à nos jours*, 2 vols. Paris: Larousse.

Vertue, George (1934), "George Vertue's Notebooks", *The Walpole Society*, 22: 61.

Vernova, N.V., ed. (1996), *The Tsars at Paleis Het Loo: Treasures from the Peterhof Palace from Peter the Great to Nicholas II*. Zwolle: Uigeverij Waanders.

Vickery, Amanda (1998), *The Gentleman's Daughter: Women's Lives in Georgian England*. New Haven and London: Yale University Press.

Vickery, Amanda (2006), "'Neat and Not Too Showey': Words and Wallpaper in Regency England." In John Styles and Amanda Vickery (eds.), *Gender, Taste and Material Culture in Britain and North America, 1700–1830*, 201–22. New Haven, CT: Yale Centre for British Art; London: Paul Mellon Centre for Studies in British Art.

Vitruvius (1914), *The Ten Books of Architecture*, trans. M.H. Morgan. Cambridge, MA: Harvard University Press.

Völker, Angela (2009), "Oriental Carpets in Eighteenth-Century Interiors," *Abegg-Stiftung Riggisberger Berichte*, 17: 153–66.

Voskuhl, Adelheid (2013), *Androids in the Enlightenment: Mechanics, Artisans, and Cultures of the Self*. Chicago: University of Chicago Press.

Wainwright, Clive (1985), "Only the True Black Blood," *Furniture History*, 21: 250–7.

Wainwright, Clive (1989), *The Romantic Interior: The British Collector at Home, 1750–1850*. London: Published for the Paul Mellon Centre for Studies in British Art by Yale University Press.

Walker, Stefanie and Frederick Hammond, eds. (1999), *Life and the Arts in the Baroque Palaces of Rome: Ambiente Barocco*. New Haven, CT: Yale University Press for the Bard Graduate Center.

Walpole, Horace ([1770] 2010), *On Modern Gardening*. London: Pallas Athene.

Walpole, Horace (1765), *The Castle of Otranto*, 2nd edn. London: William Bathoe and Thomas Lownds.

Walpole, Horace (1784), *A description of the villa of Mr. Horace Walpole, the Youngest Son of Sir Robert Walpole Earl of Orford, at Strawberry-hill, near Twickenham. With an inventory of the furniture, pictures, curiosities, &c*. Strawberry Hill: Thomas Kirgate.

Walpole, Horace (1941), "Horace Walpole's Correspondence with George Montagu 2." In W.S. Lewis (ed.) *The Yale Edition of Horace Walpole's Correspondence*. London: Oxford University Press.

Walpole, Horace (1973), "Horace Walpole's Correspondence with John Chute, Richard Bentley, the Earl of Strafford, Sir William Hamilton, the Earl and Countess Harcourt and George Hardinge." In W.S. Lewis, A.D. Wallace, R.A. Smith, and Edwine M. Martz (eds.), *The Yale Edition of Horace Walpole's Correspondence*. London: Oxford University Press.

Walsh, Claire (2006), "Shops, Shopping and the Art of Decision-Making in Eighteenth-Century England." In John Styles and Amanda Vickery (eds.), *Gender, Taste and Material Culture in Britain and North America, 1700–1830*, 151–77. New Haven, CT: Yale Centre for British Art; London: Paul Mellon Centre for Studies in British Art.

Ward-Jackson, Peter (1958), *English Furniture Designs of the Eighteenth Century*. London: Her Majesty's Stationery Office and Victoria and Albert Museum.

Ware, Isaac (1756), *A Complete Body of Architecture: Adorned with Plans and Elevations, from Original Designs*. London: T. Osborne and J. Shipton.

Watin, Jean-Felix (1772), *L'art du Peintre, Doreur, vernisseur*, Paris.

Watson, F.J.B. (1963), "The Choiseul Box," *Charlton Lectures on Art*. Oxford: Oxford University Press.

Watson, F.J.B. (1966), *The Wrightsman Collection. Furniture, Gilt Bronze and Mounted Porcelain, Carpets*, 2 vols. New York: Metropolitan Museum of Art.

Weber, Susan (2006a), "James 'Athenian' Stuart and Furniture Design." In Susan Weber (ed.), *James "Athenian" Stuart, 1713–1788: The Rediscovery of Antiquity*, 412–65. New Haven, CT: Yale University Press for the Bard Graduate Center.

Weber, Susan, ed. (2006b), *James "Athenian" Stuart, 1713–1788: The Rediscovery of Antiquity*. New Haven, CT: Yale University Press for the Bard Graduate Center for Studies in the Decorative Arts Design and Culture.

Weber, Susan (2013), 'The Well of Inspiration: Sources for Kent's Furniture Designs." In Susan Weber (ed.), *William Kent: Designing Georgian Britain*, 448–67. New Haven, CT: Yale University Press for the Bard Graduate Center.

Wharton, Edith and Ogden Codman (1898), *The Decoration of Houses*. New York: Charles Scribner.

White, Lisa (1990), *Pictorial Dictionary of 18th Century English Furniture Design*. Woodbridge, UK: Antique Collectors' Club.

White, R. (1986), "Isaac Ware and Chesterfield House." In Charles Hind (ed.), *The Rococo in England: A Symposium*. London: Victoria and Albert Museum.

Williams, Hannah (2019), "Drifting through the Louvre: A Local Guide to the French Academy." In Stacey Sloboda and Michael Yonan (eds.), *Eighteenth-Century Art Worlds: Global and Local Geographies of Art*, 171–89. New York: Bloomsbury Visual Arts.

Wilson, G., C. Bremer-David, and J. Weaver (2008), *French Furniture and Gilt Bronzes: Baroque and Régence, Catalogue of the J. Paul Getty Museum Collection*. Los Angeles: Getty Publications.

Wilton, Andrew and Ilaria Bignamini, eds. (1996), *Grand Tour: The Lure of Italy in the Eighteenth Century*. London: Tate Gallery, exhibition catalog.

Wilton-Ely, John (2011), "Style and Serenpidity: Adam, Walpole and Strawberry Hill," *British Art Journal*, 11 (3) (Spring): 3–14.

Wood, Lucy (2005), "William Hallett's Lantern Stand for Chevening," *Furniture History*, 41: 21–4.

Wood, Lucy (2014), "Georg Haupt and his Compatriots in London," *Furniture History*, 50: 238–75.

Woodforde, James (1979), *The Diary of a Country Parson 1758–1802*, edited by John Beresford. Oxford: Oxford University Press.

Wright, Edward (1730), *Some Observations Made in Travelling Through* France, *Italy, etc., in the Years 1720, 1721, and 1722*, 2 vols. London: Thomas Ward and E. Wicksteed.

INDEX